# Stars, Studios, and the Musical Theatre Screen Adaptation

*An Oxford Handbook of Musical Theatre Screen Adaptations, Volume 3*

**EDITED BY**
**DOMINIC BROOMFIELD-MCHUGH**

**OXFORD**
UNIVERSITY PRESS

# OXFORD
### UNIVERSITY PRESS

Oxford University Press is a department of the University of Oxford. It furthers
the University's objective of excellence in research, scholarship, and education
by publishing worldwide. Oxford is a registered trade mark of Oxford University
Press in the UK and certain other countries.

Published in the United States of America by Oxford University Press
198 Madison Avenue, New York, NY 10016, United States of America.

Library of Congress Control Number: 2022042575

ISBN 978-0-19-766325-7

1 3 5 7 9 8 6 4 2

Printed by Marquis, Canada

# STARS, STUDIOS, AND THE MUSICAL THEATRE SCREEN ADAPTATION

*In loving memory of my aunt,*
*Linda Riley (1951–2015),*
*who shared my passion for film musicals*

# CONTENTS

# ACKNOWLEDGEMENTS

The initial inspiration for this volume came from a conference I convened at the University of Sheffield in May 2014. Titled *Restaging the Song: Adapting Broadway for the Silver Screen*, it brought together scholars from a range of disciplines to discuss stage-to-screen adaptations across the decades and ran alongside an exhibition and film festival at the Workstation and Showroom at Sheffield. I am grateful to all the presenters at the conference for their support, to Hannah Robbins and Danielle Birkett (then PhD students of mine) for their help in organising the conference, to Amy Ryall for her support in organising funding for the festival and exhibition through the University's Arts Enterprise scheme, and in particular to my fellow conference committee members, Stephen Banfield (who also acted as respondent to the conference), Geoffrey Block (keynote), and Jeffrey Magee, for their unswerving help and enthusiasm. The conference was especially important to me as it initiated a particularly close and important friendship between Geoffrey and me, and he has been incredibly helpful in reading and commenting on drafts of my material in this book.

I am also grateful to all the contributors to this volume, which was several years in the making. I am delighted that the original material is now available in paper form as three slimmer volumes. As always, I cannot begin to thank Norm Hirschy at Oxford University Press nearly enough for his incredible patience and support: it is difficult to imagine scholarship on musicals existing without his energy and enthusiasm in the background, and I am thrilled he was willing to make this new version of the *Handbook* available. Thanks also to Lauralee Yeary at Oxford, to the copyeditor, and to the team at SPi for seeing the volume through to completion. Special thanks are due to Cliff Eisen, who has been a wonderful mentor throughout my career and is now a very special friend.

As ever, my family and numerous friends are almost the only reason I managed to bring this volume to fruition, especially my partner Lawrence Broomfield, my mother Gilly and my late father Larry McHugh, and my friend Richard Tay. This volume is dedicated to the memory of my aunt Linda Riley, who died suddenly and unexpectedly in May 2015, leaving a gap in our family that will never be filled. She was a great fan of film musicals and I'm proud to leave behind this memorial to her.

Dominic Broomfield-McHugh
*Sheffield, 2018 and 2022*

# CONTRIBUTORS

**Dean Adams**, Associate Dean and Professor, University of North Carolina at Charlotte

**Richard J. Allen**, Professor, Film, Television and Digital Media, Texas Christian University

**Tim Carter**, David G. Frey Distinguished Professor of Music Emeritus, University of North Carolina at Chapel Hill

**Todd Decker**, Professor and Chair, Music, Washington University in St. Louis

**Dominic Broomfield-McHugh**, Professor in Musicology, University of Sheffield

**Amanda McQueen**, Lecturer in Media Studies/Auburn Global, Auburn University

**Allison Robbins**, Associate Professor of Music, University of Central Missouri

**Susan Smith**, Associate Professor of Film Studies, Sunderland University

**Robynn J. Stilwell**, Associate Professor of Music, Georgetown University

# ABOUT THE COMPANION WEBSITE

www.oup.com/us/oxomtsa

Oxford has created a website to accompany *The Oxford Handbook of Musical Theatre Screen Adaptations*. Readers are encouraged to consult this resource in conjunction with each chapter of the book. Examples available online are indicated in the text with Oxford's symbol ⏵.

# Introduction

DOMINIC BROOMFIELD-MCHUGH

■ □ ■

FROM *SHOW BOAT* (1936) TO *The Sound of Music* (1965) and from *Grease* (1978) to *Chicago* (2002), many of the most beloved film musicals in Hollywood history originated as Broadway shows. And in the three years since the original publication of the chapters in this volume (as *The Oxford Handbook of Musical Theatre Screen Adaptations*, 2019) the phenomenon has persisted, with new adaptations such as *Cats, In the Heights, Tick, Tick . . . Boom!, Dear Evan Hansen*, and Spielberg's remake of *West Side Story*. Yet in general, the number of screen adaptations of Broadway musicals and operettas is far greater than the number that have met with success, especially both critical and commercial success (i.e., good reviews and a profit at the box office). This is all the more surprising since Hollywood tended almost (if not quite) exclusively to buy the rights to musicals that had been successful on the stage as a means of guaranteeing a profitable outcome. After all, musicals that had already enjoyed long runs and nationwide productions on the stage ought to have a readymade audience. One might also think that because the authors had puzzled over the individual challenges posed by such properties in their stage incarnations, it ought to be easier to turn them into strong film musicals. But for every *West Side Story* there were several *Finian's Rainbows*, *Man of La Manchas*, and *Carousels*: movies that simply did not do justice to the 'enchanted evenings'[1] these works provided in their stage incarnations.

This phenomenon is at the heart of this volume and explains why the book deals with as many unpopular films as it does popular ones. Rather than turning the wheel with a series of chapters on what makes the movies *My Fair Lady*, *West Side Story*, and *The Sound of Music* successful, I have invited a group of scholars on musicals to contribute articles on some of the deeper issues that are at the heart of Hollywood's troubled love affair with Broadway, as well as some of the more overlooked stage-to-screen adaptations that have appeared over the last ninety years or so. Movies such as *Brigadoon*, *Evita*, and *Half a Sixpence*, which may not easily fit into some of the more obvious trends in the Hollywood musical, reveal new insights into the ways in which we might think about the nature of adaptation. A chapter on how *The Carol Burnett Show* might be read through the lens of adaptation expands our understanding of the concept, while other chapters examine how stars (e.g. Barbra Streisand, Madonna, and Gene Kelly) and technology have had an impact on the ways in which musical theatre works have been transferred to the silver screen. The book's aim, then, is not to provide an encyclopaedia of Broadway-to-Hollywood adaptations (such volumes already exist) but rather to sharpen the critical discourse on the subject and to share some of the latest scholarship on the topic from a range of disciplinary backgrounds.

Most film musicals feature a bankable star name and the first half of the volume examines how stars act as an additional consideration when adapting musicals for the screen. Todd Decker opens with a chapter on the series of operettas made by MGM for Jeanette MacDonald and Nelson Eddy in the 1930s and early 1940s. Describing the series as 'a sustained exercise in nostalgia' and 'prestige product,' Decker examines the films' legacy as 'nostalgic romantic film operettas, richly realized in visual and musical terms and shaped entirely around the two stars' distinct voices and personas.' The movies are marked by lavish production values and 'the recurrent grafting onto these musical films of narrative tropes from more prestige-oriented genres, such as historical epics and period-setting melodramas.' Regular plot devices, the use of a legitimate singing style, similar character types, approaches to key and tonality in the arrangement of the songs, the preservation of racial whiteness: the films featured consistent elements, a formula that was facilitated by a liberal approach to the source material in all but *Bitter Sweet*.

Susan Smith offers a complementary analysis of Gene Kelly and Cyd Charisse in her chapter on the MGM adaptation of *Brigadoon*. On the stage, this musical was designed for singers, but the film version cast Kelly and Charisse, the latter replacing soprano Kathryn Grayson, who was the original choice for the character of Fiona. This necessitated enormous changes to the Broadway material, including the deletion of some of the most vocally demanding songs ('There but for You Go I' and 'From This Day On') and the reworking of 'The Heather on the Hill' and 'Almost Like Being in Love' into solos for Tommy (Kelly) rather than duets for Tommy and Fiona. Kelly's presence also meant that he served, naturally, as the film's choreographer, replacing Agnes de Mille, whose choreography had been one of the cornerstones of the Broadway production. Because the leads were now dancers, with additional opportunities for them to dance added to the piece, the role of Harry Beaton, which had revolved around the famous Sword Dance on the stage, was reduced and his number cut. Yet Smith also identifies benefits from the casting changes and argues that it is 'one of MGM's most underrated musicals, gaining tension and complexity from some of its perceived flaws.'

Coming many decades later, Alan Parker's film version of Lloyd Webber and Rice's *Evita* (1996) provides a different case study of how a star's agency can affect a film musical's narrative. Richard J. Allen's chapter on the movie reveals how changes made to the piece for its movie incarnation result in a change of presentation of the title character, played by Madonna. Whereas the stage show depicts Eva as a figure of 'moral ambiguity,' the film turns her into 'a probably well-meaning, mostly sympathetic, inherently romantic heroine' with a series of 'newly created flashbacks, scenes, lyrics, and entire songs crafted for the purpose of gaining insight into and empathy for Eva.' For example, Eva, rather than Peron's mistress, now sings 'Another Suitcase in Another Hall,' one of the hit songs from the score, and the 'Waltz for Evita and Che' is staged as a romantic duet, without conveying the cynicism of the lyrics. The addition of 'You Must Love Me' adds a new insight into 'her realization that if Peron can still show her such attention and affection when she is dying and no longer of any use to him, then he must love her after all.' In these and many other ways, Eva is humanized in a way that is not the case in the Broadway original.

My chapter on Barbra Streisand's first three film musicals considers how her star text affects the adaptation of the three Broadway musicals on which they are based. Although Streisand starred in *Funny Girl* on the stage, the screen version made significant changes to the musical so that it could be telescoped through her perspective. Most of the other characters' songs were cut, a ploy that was also used in *On a Clear Day You Can See Forever* to emphasize Streisand as the star. In both films, as well as in *Hello, Dolly!*, Streisand was cast opposite men with weak singing voices, empowering her performance musically in each case: a good example of how this works is in the title song of *On a Clear Day*, where Yves Montand performs the number complete with a simple orchestration and staging, followed by Streisand's much grander performance. Meanwhile, in *Dolly!* it was necessary to make changes to the title character in order to draw attention away from the fact that Streisand was much too young for the role; thus she is depicted as a general busybody in 'Just Leave Everything To Me,' which replaced 'I Put My Hand In,' a song that focuses on Dolly as a matchmaker.

The other half of the book deals with aspects of production, commerce, and technology. Tim Carter's opening chapter deals with the problematic movie adaptation of Rodgers and Hammerstein's *Carousel* from a number of perspectives, including the team's reluctance to allow their musicals to be adapted into movies too quickly and particularly the use of the new CinemaScope 55 widescreen process for making the movie; 'The R&H brand clearly had a role to play in the emergence of new, competing technologies,' Carter explains. The mid-1950s saw a war of technologies between the major studios, not only because of rivalry within the industry but also because of the decline in cinema audiences caused by the rise of television. Rodgers and Hammerstein were happy to jump on the bandwagon offered by CinemaScope 55 because it also meant a roadshow release to a limited number of theatres in major cities, with longer playing time, souvenir programmes, higher admission rates, and the more proscenium-like screen proportions. Although the film was not a success, Carter's chapter explains how technology became a huge player in the development of the screen musical in the 1950s.

By contrast, Robynn Stilwell's chapter examines Hollywood's great rival, television, in a study of how television adapted the Broadway musical. Rather than looking at conventional stage-to-small-screen adaptations, however, Stilwell focuses on how Carol Burnett's TV show provided adaptations of another kind, that is, parodies of famous musicals. For example, Stilwell explains how 'Hold Me, Hamlet' can be read as a parody/adaptation of Cole Porter's *Kiss Me, Kate*, even retaining the doubling of the onstage/backstage musical format of the latter. Meanwhile, *The Wiz* is 'the clearest referent' for

'Cinderella Gets It On.' In Stilwell's opinion, these Burnett shows 'approach poesis' because they 'take the form of the musical, and they often do comment upon it, but they are also genuine expressions of the form and the creators' deep love and understanding of it.'

Contemporaneous with the launch of *The Carol Burnett Show* was the roadshow release of the movie adaptation of *Half a Sixpence*. Amanda McQueen's chapter reads it as 'a product of its immediate industrial context': it was one of a number of Broadway-Hollywood adaptations that were intended as part of 'a risk-reduction strategy'; it was spectacular and relatively faithful to its stage version; and it had 'an unusual and markedly contemporary visual style, akin to that found in the low-budget, youth oriented films of the Hollywood Renaissance.' Thus, although the movie was no hit, it was not 'a completely misguided production': McQueen explains that instead it was intended to address the musical genre's need to adapt to 'a new industrial climate in order to prolong its marketability into the 1970s.'

Marketability is also the focus of Dean Adams's chapter on *The Producers* and *Hairspray*, movies based on stage musicals that were originally based on low-budget, largely nonmusical movies. Adams compares the two movie adaptations, noting that in *The Producers* Susan Stroman 'restaged her original work for film, and many of the original creative team (including costume designer William Ivey Long) reprised their Broadway visual contributions for film,' while the producers of *Hairspray* 'select[ed] Hollywood professionals instead of the original Broadway creative team to supervise the making of the film.' In another contrast, the 2005 film of *The Producers* is 134 minutes long to *Hairspray*'s 116, and *The Producers* used its Broadway stars rather than using the latest Hollywood names;[2] *Hairspray* chose movie stars. With these contrasting strategies and their relationship to the audience demographics for cinema today, it is unsurprising that *Hairspray* was a hit on the screen and that *The Producers* was a flop.

Allison Robbins's chapter concludes the volume with a study of 'Hollywood's commercial approach to making musicals.' Focusing on the 1936 movie adaptation of *Anything Goes*, Robbins looks at its production environment, one in which 'interpolations were common, song sales mattered more than wit, and risqué content was frowned upon, a combination that proved deadly for Porter's score.' Although some of the latter's songs were retained, the studio's music department head Nathaniel Finston 'assigned Leo Robin, Richard Whiting,' and several others to write some new numbers for the film. In the context of a Hollywood in which studios capitalized on purchasing publishing companies and then copyrighting new songs by (usually, staff) Hollywood songwriters to in-house publishing firms, it is unsurprising that Robbins concludes that faithful film adaptations are 'unlikely.' Hollywood was 'devoted' to commercial music while Broadway was 'divorced from it'; and fidelity to 'Broadway's canonized songwriters' ran contrary to 'the commercial goals of Hollywood's tunesmiths.' Such tensions run throughout this book and help to explain the culture behind the unsettling but fascinating phenomenon of the stage-to-screen musical adaptation.

## NOTES

1. Here, I invoke the title of Geoffrey Block's seminal survey of the Broadway musical. Geoffrey Block, *Enchanted Evenings*, 2nd ed. (New York: Oxford University Press, 2009).
2. Matthew Broderick had appeared in a number of Hollywood films but his stage profile was bigger than his movie profile at this point.

# 1

# Loud, Pretty, Strong, White [Repeat]

## The Jeanette MacDonald and Nelson Eddy Operettas at MGM (1935–1942)

TODD DECKER

■ □ ■

SOPRANO JEANETTE MACDONALD AND BARITONE Nelson Eddy shared top billing in eight musical films for Metro Goldwyn Mayer (MGM) between 1935 and 1942. All eight bear the titles of Broadway shows. In all but one case, the film versions radically alter their stage originals. These very free adaptations are best understood as acts of opportunistic scavenging of Broadway show titles and songs by a Hollywood studio producing a well-made line of lucrative prestige products: nostalgic romantic film operettas, richly realized in visual and musical terms and shaped entirely around the two stars' distinct voices and personas.

MacDonald and Eddy's six signature films—*Naughty Marietta* (1935), *Rose Marie* (1936), *Maytime* (1937), *Sweethearts* (1938), *New Moon* (1940), and *Bitter Sweet* (1940)—are ostensibly derived from operettas staged on Broadway between 1910 and 1929, halcyon years for the singing- and spectacle-centred musical theatre genre on the commercial New York stage.[1] The cycle draws in equal measure on the pre–World War I and the 1920s Broadway operetta, with the genre's signature composers, mostly European expatriates, well represented. Prewar stage sources include Victor Herbert's *Naughty Marietta* (1910, 136 performances) and *Sweethearts* (1913, 136 performances), as well as Sigmund Romberg's *Maytime* (1917, 492 performances). Long-running hits of the 1920s adapted for MacDonald and Eddy include Romberg's *The New Moon* (1928, 509 performances) and Rudolf Friml and Herbert Stothart's *Rose-Marie* (1924, 557 performances). *Bitter Sweet*, a late entry in the operetta repertory by the English composer, lyricist, and playwright Noel Coward—a multiyear hit in London that lasted 159 performances in New York in 1929—found a place as well at MGM. The chronological gap between the respective stage and screen versions for each of these titles is telling: just over a decade for *Rose Marie*, *New Moon*, and *Bitter Sweet*; two decades for *Maytime*; a quarter century for *Naughty Marietta* and *Sweethearts*. None of these operettas had seen commercially successful Broadway revivals before MGM acquired and adapted them for the synchronized sound screen. Indeed, lavish, large-cast, long-running operettas—abundant on the New York stage for the quarter century before the stock market crashed—were mostly a thing of the past during Broadway's lean, musical-comedy-centred 1930s. MGM's costly investment in operetta proved extraordinarily successful at the box office, finding a depression-era movie audience who longed for a sweeping sort of musical narrative that was, elsewhere in popular culture, going out of style.

The inherently conservative, indeed old-fashioned theatrical sources MGM acquired for MacDonald and Eddy mark this star-centred operetta cycle as a sustained exercise in nostalgia. MacDonald and Eddy virtually never nod towards contemporary popular music or culture—even in *Sweethearts*, their only film set in the American urban present day.[2] Use of operetta sources from prior decades also speaks to a studio strategy of prestige. Herbert, Romberg, and Friml were names to conjure with—icons of an elevated but in its day popular musical style untouched by the constant advance, since about 1910, of syncopated popular musics such as ragtime, jazz, and swing that were derived from African American sources. (Herbert is singled out with his name above the title in *Naughty Marietta* and *Sweethearts*, as is Coward in *Bitter Sweet*—a distinction only songwriter Irving Berlin otherwise enjoyed in Hollywood at the time.) Further marks of MGM's treatment of the cycle as prestige products includes consistently lavish investment in production and costume designs and the recurrent grafting onto these musical films of narrative tropes from more prestige-oriented genres, such as historical epics and period-setting melodramas. For example, Eddy as the hero tragically dies in *Maytime* and *Bitter Sweet* and threatened or actual violence treated seriously, as in a dramatic film, is a regular plot device.

The at-once nostalgic and elevated register of the MacDonald/Eddy films comes into focus when compared to two contemporary couple-based musical cycles: Fred Astaire and Ginger Rogers' nine films for RKO made between 1932 and 1939 and four films pairing Mickey Rooney and Judy Garland made by MGM between 1939 and 1943. All but two of Astaire and Rogers' films bear original titles and plots and feature new songs by the top Broadway musical comedy talents of the day, songwriters such as Berlin, Cole Porter, Jerome Kern, and George and Ira Gershwin, known nationally for writing popular music hits.[3] These films celebrated cutting-edge Art Deco design, swanky and sexy fashion trends (especially in Rogers' gowns), and, most importantly, contemporary popular music and dance, in particular jazz as heard in nightclubs.[4] The Rooney/Garland films are similarly immersed in popular music, specifically the youth culture surrounding swing music and dance, with an added orientation towards the New York commercial musical comedy stage facilitating elaborate production numbers and a 'let's put on a show' energy. Following studio strategy used with MacDonald and Eddy, three of the four Rooney/Garland films borrow their titles from Broadway shows—jazzy musical comedies from the late 1920s and 1930s—and generally rewrite the stage originals' plots and mix up the song list.[5] Put beside Astaire/Rogers and Rooney/Garland, the MacDonald/Eddy cycle comes into focus as adult-oriented, backward-looking, and aligned more with historical and melodramatic film genres than with current popular culture.

The MacDonald and Eddy films were successful from the start. *Naughty Marietta* turned a $407,000 profit and *Film Daily*'s Critics of America Poll ranked it the fourth best feature of the year and the best musical (ahead of Astaire and Rogers' *Top Hat*). *Rose Marie* more than tripled *Marietta*'s profits ($1,488,000) and was MGM's second-highest grossing film of 1936 (exceeded only by MacDonald's *San Francisco*). *Maytime*, despite being very expensive to produce, made money as well, as did all the pair's successive films except for their last. *Sweethearts*, MacDonald and Eddy's first Technicolor film (made and released just before MGM's *The Wizard of Oz* [1939]), was voted Best Picture of 1938 by the readers of *Photoplay*.[6]

At the core of MacDonald and Eddy's distinctiveness lies the matter of musical and vocal style. MacDonald and Eddy alike sing in a full-voice, supported, classically trained, operatic style—also known as legitimate or legit singing—taken from the European bel canto tradition and historically associated with the opera stage. The characters they play and the plots of their films carve out an innovative narrative space where classically trained singing could find a home in the commercial film industry and in the genre of the film musical, which was otherwise oriented towards popular music and singing styles. This insertion of operatic voices into commercial musical film marks the cycle's primary aesthetic achievement in its time and since.[7]

Among the six adapted operettas in the MGM cycle, only the film *Bitter Sweet* follows the plot of its stage original with any faithfulness. *Naughty Marietta, New Moon,* and *Rose Marie* retain their respective original stage settings but run substantial variations on their characters and plots, tailoring the film versions tightly to MacDonald's persona as a beautiful and independent-minded woman with a powerful voice and personality. (MacDonald was an established star when the cycle began and she made successful films with other leading men during her years with Eddy. Eddy's fame was entirely tied to his films with MacDonald.) *Maytime,* a melodramatic tale of late nineteenth-century American opera singers, and *Sweethearts,* an anachronistic satire of contemporary Broadway operetta stars, depart entirely from their sources as to plot and (mostly) music. MGM's attraction to the Broadway originals was a matter of the name recognition of the titles and the opportunity to mine each show's musical resources.

Still, these films feature rather few songs from the original shows: *New Moon* and *Bitter Sweet* include six songs from their respective stage scores; *Naughty Marietta* and *Sweethearts,* five; and *Rose Marie,* just four. *Maytime* includes only one song from its purported Broadway source. Musical films generally include fewer songs and less music than musical shows. But given the musical richness and the generous extent of operetta scores on the stage, the constrained song lists for the MacDonald/Eddy films marks a radical reduction of the genre on the screen. In the case of these six adaptations, a stage musical subgenre known for large and varied casts and opulent choral singing is reduced almost entirely to two singers singing mostly solos and, to a surprisingly limited extent, duets. Indeed, on only four occasions in the cycle does an individual performer other MacDonald or Eddy perform a complete musical number lacking either of the two stars.[8]

Two of the pair's eight films stand out in terms of their sources. *The Girl of the Golden West* (1938) borrows the title and the plot (just barely) of writer, director, and producer David Belasco's 1905 play, which had 224 performances in its original Broadway run. Audiences for the film might have also known the Italian opera composer Giacomo Puccini's 1910 operatic version *La fanciulla del West*, but the film makes no musical nods towards it. Romberg was engaged to compose original music—six songs in all—for the film.[9] MacDonald and Eddy's final film, *I Married an Angel* (1942), adapted Richard Rodgers and Lorenz Hart's musical comedy, which enjoyed a 338-performance run on Broadway in 1938. This film is not considered here for several reasons. *I Married an Angel* falls chronologically outside the pair's most intense period of filmmaking and fame: 1935–1940. The plot centres on Eddy— rather than MacDonald, as the others mostly do—and both stars are cast against type: Eddy as a sophisticated man about town; MacDonald as a simple bank clerk. The plot offers a satirical and sardonic view of love and romance that jars against the earnest and sincere tone of the pair's combined persona. Musically, *I Married an Angel* draws on musical comedy and even features MacDonald in a swing number (dancing with another woman). The film failed commercially: it was the only entry in the cycle not to earn a profit. Markedly different from all their other films, *I Married an Angel* offers little insight by way of contrast into the MacDonald and Eddy partnership which, across their first seven collaborations, is remarkably consistent.

On the opera and operetta stage, sopranos and baritones do not normally fall in love. Indeed, all but one of the source operettas for the MacDonald and Eddy cycle feature soprano and tenor romantic leads, by far the norm across the opera and the pre–World War II operetta repertory.[10] The primary musical innovation of the MacDonald and Eddy cycle is the romantic pairing of a soprano and a baritone.

The musical changes to the stage sources required by the pairing of MacDonald and Eddy can be tracked by comparing the keys of the love duets in the films and in the original stage versions. At issue, of course, is the comfortable range of a given song for both singers and the crucial matter of where the climactic high notes for each singer lie. For Eddy, music composed for tenors had to be lowered. For MacDonald, retaining the original soprano range was crucial, especially to preserve sufficiently high top notes to show off her voice.

*Naughty Marietta* set the pattern for the refashioning of soprano-tenor duets into soprano-baritone duets. In show's climactic love duet, 'Ah, Sweet Mystery of Life,' Marietta and Dick share the same key (D major), sing the melody in unison, and hit the same high note (A) (⊙ audio example 16.1). In the film, MacDonald and Eddy require three keys—hers, his, and theirs—each, of course, yielding different top notes. MacDonald introduces the tune, ostensibly performed to entertain her party guests but aimed squarely at Eddy, in its original stage key (D major) which provides a range-topping high A. After she completes her chorus, the score falls briefly silent and five seconds of applause from the party guests further muddle any continuity of tonal centre. Eddy, ready to declare his love in return, launches without instrumental introduction into his solo chorus, sung a major third lower (B-flat major) with a baritone-friendly top note of F. An efficient modulation to a shareable key (D-flat major) follows, setting up a final duet chorus. In this key, MacDonald sings the melody in a high enough register to display her soprano voice. For Eddy, however, the new key is simply too high to sing the melody in unison with MacDonald— as a stage operetta tenor would do. And so, he is relegated to a secondary harmony part in his baritone range (likely composed by music director Herbert Stothart), the first of many musically uninteresting supporting parts Eddy sings in the cycle while MacDonald takes the tune (⏵ audio example 16.2).[11] 'Ah, Sweet Mystery of Life' as remade for *Naughty Marietta* the film employs three strategies to negotiate the sharing of a love song by a soprano and a baritone: each singer gets his or her own key for solo choruses; breaks in musical continuity (silence in the score) or quick modulations mask the changing tonal centre between choruses; and on the requisite duet choruses, MacDonald's range on the melody is favoured in the choice of key, relegating Eddy to singing harmony.

The above strategies were employed again and again in the cycle. For example, 'Indian Love Call' in *Rose Marie* is similarly sung in three keys: his (D-flat major), hers (F major), and theirs (E-flat major). In the stage version, the song is introduced by Rose-Marie in a solo chorus in F major. Then, Rose-Marie and Jim Kenyon, by operetta standards a not-very-high tenor role, share a chorus, still in F major but with Jim singing in harmony a third below Rose-Marie most of the time (in tenor range). In the film, Eddy introduces 'Indian Love Call' in a comfortably lower key, a major third below the stage original. Then, after a lengthy stretch of dialogue and underscoring has clouded any continuing sense of tonal centre, the couple shares a chorus in a key more comfortable for MacDonald, the same as the stage original. Eddy proves able to sing the original harmony part from the show. At the close of the film, the couple again share a chorus, only this time a compromise key is required to meet the narrative imperative that Eddy alone sing the soaring melodic phrase that begins 'that means I offer my love to you.' The previous shared key of F major must have been too high for him to manage the melody in this passage and Eddy's solo key of D-flat major not amenable to MacDonald, who had to offer a thrilling high note to end the film. And so, they share the final reprise of 'Indian Love Call' in E-flat major, a 'theirs' key at the exact midpoint between 'his' and 'hers.'

'Wanting You,' the love duet in *New Moon*, reveals a further strategy informing the making of soprano-baritone love duets: the strategic assignment of individual phrases within a tune to either singer based on range. In the published vocal score for the stage version, Marianne and Robert (a rather high baritone role), share the tune in unison and in F major. The 'B' section in this AABA tune, marked *molto espressivo, appassionato*, rises to a sustained high G, a top note that exceeds the comfortable limit for most baritones. Operatic baritone Rodney Gilfry, singing Robert in the 2004 Encores! concert production of *The New Moon*, delivered the passage as written (▶ audio example 16.3). Howett Worster, the 1929 London Robert, avoided the song's very high phrase entirely and sang an uninspired alternate melody on his contemporary recording (▶ audio example 16.4). The song and the moment demand that any convincing romantic male lead sing Romberg's *molto espressivo* phrase as written: an outburst of unbounded passion, the passage captures the essence of operetta's defining asset—vocally centric lovemaking of an especially yearning, lyrical, light classical kind. In the film, Eddy begins 'Wanting You' in E-flat major as a solo declaration of love. In this key, the *molto espressivo* phrase is simply too high for him to sing, and so MacDonald takes over just for the first half of the B phrase—the high part. Eddy reenters for the second half of the B phrase—which repeats the same yearning upper-neighbour note motion a third lower—and finishes his solo chorus (▶ audio example 16.5). There is no dramatically compelling reason for MacDonald to take over vocally for eight bars during Eddy's solo chorus and the decision for her to do so seems dictated by matters of range and anticipation of what comes next musically. At the end of Eddy's chorus, an efficient, longingly expressive, perhaps slightly overwrought modulation upwards by whole step moves the tonal centre to (the original key of) F major for MacDonald's solo (▶ audio example 16.6). From the *molto espressivo* phrase on, Eddy joins her on a lower harmony part as per usual. Eddy's final high note on his solo chorus—higher than it would have been were he in a key that allowed him to sing the *molto esppressivo* passage—and the overheated modulation into MacDonald's chorus come at a key moment in the film's narrative. What had been a kind of musical play-acting between Eddy's house servant and MacDonald's plantation-owning princess—a classic example of what Oscar Hammerstein II called a conditional love duet—turns serious on the final 'A' phrase of Eddy's solo chorus, mostly by way of Eddy's vocal and physical intensity and the in context transgressive act of a servant grasping his mistress's hands. The swooning modulation between the two choruses expresses the lovers bursting through a (perceived) barrier of love across social class. (In fact, Eddy is a nobleman pretending to be a bondservant.) On a more practical level, ending the duet in F major favours MacDonald's vocal comfort and provides her with the chance to sing a high C at the close.

In one case—the opening duet scene 'I'll See You Again' in *Bitter Sweet*—favouring MacDonald and the nature of the stage original worked against finding a compromise key that Eddy could negotiate. And so, Eddy speaks instead. In the show, the character of Carl, a tenor role, sings a lovely rising line when he invites Sarah, as her music teacher, to begin her voice lesson (▶ audio example 16.7). In the film, Eddy speaks Carl's too-high phrases (▶ audio example 16.8). The extent to which the MacDonald/Eddy cycle favours the soprano is audibly evident here. And there are further consequences for how the lovers' voices interact. In the stage version, the intense waltz-time strain features an intimate intertwining of the soprano and tenor voices (▶ audio example 16.9). Such reciprocity and tight interchange are not possible for MacDonald and Eddy's conventionally mismatched soprano and baritone ( ⊙ audio example 16.10). (A similar effect can be heard in 'Will You Remember?' as composed for the stage version of *Maytime* and as revised for the film [⊙ audio examples 16.11 and 16.12]).

'I'll See You Again' occurs unusually early in the film: this love duet, full of suppressed longing and ardent looks, starts some three minutes into *Bitter Sweet* and, pointedly, does not end in a passionate kiss, the cycle's characteristic post-singing action that signals shared acknowledgement of requited love.[12] The love duets discussed above occur much later in their respective films: 'Wanting You' comes forty-three minutes into *New Moon*; 'Will You Remember?' some eighty minutes into *Maytime*; the duet to 'Indian Love Call' is held off for ninety minutes into *Rose Marie*; and 'Ah, Sweet Mystery of Life' is finally sung a full ninety-five minutes into *Naughty Marietta*, just before the picture concludes. Love duets in the cycle mark serious character transformations, specifically the willingness to admit—or inability to any longer deny—feelings of love for the romantic other. Passionate kisses immediately after the final sung notes in 'Indian Love Call,' 'Will You Remember?,' and 'Wanting You' seal—as the cliché goes—the just-sung bond between MacDonald and Eddy's characters (Figures 1.1a–1.3b). All three duets are set in isolation in the beauties of nature: 'Indian Love Call' on the top of a mountain (shot on location in California's Sierra Nevadas); 'Will You Remember?' in an idealized glade with blossoming trees around a still pool of water; 'Wanting You' in a mossy, overgrown southern forest. The mechanics of the plot prevent MacDonald and Eddy from falling into a kiss at the end of 'Ah, Sweet Mystery of Life.' Singing to each other during a party, the crowd of guests understand their song as a performance, even though the pair only has eyes for each other, singing in full voice when physically very close (Figure 1.4a). This social context for shared song postpones the post-duet kiss to the next scene in a private room (Figure 1.4b).

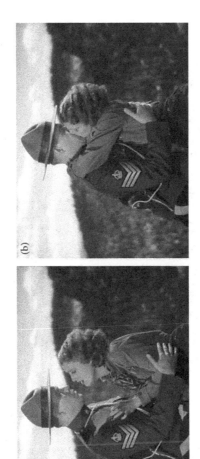

FIGURE 1.1A,B 'Indian Love Call' (*Rose Marie*).

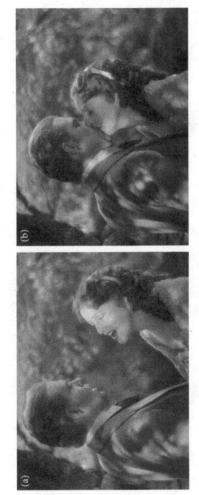

FIGURE 1.2A,B 'Will You Remember?' (*Maytime*).

FIGURE 1.3A,B 'Wanting You' (*New Moon*).

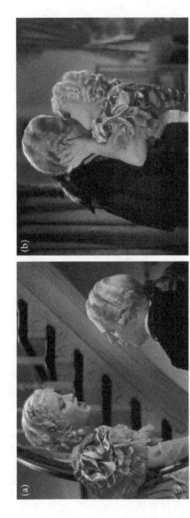

FIGURE 1.4A,B Singing on the stair at the party, kissing in private in the next room in 'Ah, Sweet Mystery of Life' (*Naughty Marietta*).

Grand outdoor settings can only be suggested by painted backdrops on the stage. At the movies, lovers can raise their (powerful) voices while in visibly realistic nature (usually done with back projections) and rest assured their audience can hear them with clarity and at a high volume in the still somewhat novel sonic space of the sound cinema.[13] The setting in nature isolates the lovers and permits their expressions of love to be both loud and private, at once specific to each plot (as expressed in costuming and hair) and mythic (in the sense that evidence for human society and culture goes unseen; the lovers abstractly representing a man and a woman sublimating, just barely, their erotic attraction in song). In nature, lovers torn apart by custom or circumstance can imagine and dwell within—crucially by singing together—a world where their love might live. Love duets in nature also suggest, without the tension of an adjacent couch or bed, more intimate acts the Production Code would never allow to be shown but which passionate melodies and climactic high notes might stand in for sonically. Operetta love duets set in nature serve another purpose: naturalizing the film operetta's presentation of full-voice singers and singing in the medium of motion pictures. Film operetta in the sound era offers an aesthetic experience that cannot be had on the operetta stage: amplified love duets framed in close-up.[14] Setting such singing in the wilds of nature proved a recurring visual solution to the potential mismatch between the scale of the image and the volume of the voice.

Electronic microphones were introduced in 1925. Within a few years, popular singing fundamentally changed with the advent of crooners—male singers, such as Rudy Vallee, Russ Columbo, and Bing Crosby—who sang at the level of a whisper but could be easily heard by way of speakers. Electronic microphones and speakers, still relatively new technology when MacDonald and Eddy's career began, were essential to the development and commercial success of the synchronized sound cinema. Related technological developments such as optical recording for film soundtracks and the mixing desk (both in place by 1934) had made film sound an especially flexible technological medium. Fred Astaire, emerging as a film musical star in 1934, brought the low-volume, nontechnical, microphone singing of popular music into the film musical, where it comfortably matched Hollywood's default privileging of dialogue in the soundtrack mix. Operatic singing, however, posed a different test: effectively and transparently recording and mixing a kind of singing that provided its own projecting power and that, in the pre-microphone era, was experienced live and at a distance. The challenge of simply recording and mixing the classically trained voice was a recognized achievement of *Naughty Marietta*, which received the Academy Award for Best Sound Recording.

MacDonald and Eddy put the still-new sound recording and amplification technologies of the day to a less than timely but challenging technical test capturing and reproducing a vocal style that evolved in the absence of microphones and speakers. On the musical stage, full-voiced singing was necessary to reach the audience and defined the larger-than-life romantic stories operetta typically told. On screen, this same vocal style worked differently. No longer needed to project to the back of the hall, the recorded operetta voice—thrillingly loud in the wired-for-sound cinema—could be experienced as sometimes at odds with the colossal yet also intimate scale of human bodies and faces on the silver screen. As mentioned, one recurring solution to the sound and image challenge posed by the operetta love duet was to locate the lovers in the great outdoors, where they could be simultaneously loud and alone and close enough to kiss. MacDonald and Eddy's combination of loud, legitimate singing in tightly framed two shots and close-ups, often climaxing in a kiss, pushes to its realistic limit the fundamentally synthetic and antinaturalistic nature of film musical sound.

MacDonald and Eddy's films are somewhat stingy with love duets. Indeed, each film typically includes only one passionate duet (sometimes with a film-ending reprise) that serves as both narrative crux—the shared admission they are in love—and musical high point.[15] Often the song they share is sung several times, as solo and duet, and fairly dominates the score: 'Indian Love Call' is sung on four occasions in *Rose Marie*; 'Will You Remember?,' three times in *Maytime*.

To fill out the score with more singing, MacDonald and Eddy delivered multiple solo numbers in each of their films. These solos define their individual personas in consistent fashion across the cycle. Eddy's solos present him as a manly man who naturally leads other men and as an ardent lover eager to declare himself in a serenade (often, like the love duets, in an outdoor setting). MacDonald's solos virtually all present her as a woman of artistic and technical accomplishment who sings for eager audiences that delight in her voice. Only once does she sing in a private moment to express her inner self.

Eddy's solos assemble a composite cinematic operetta masculinity that draws selectively on tenor and baritone parts in the source operettas.[16] In *Rose Marie*, Eddy leads 'The Mounties,' (sung by the minor character Malone in the show) and also sings 'Rose Marie' and 'Indian Love Call' (numbers assigned to the show's tenor romantic lead, Jim). In *Bitter Sweet*, Eddy sings the tenor Carl's songs but also the baritone Captain Lutte's rousing drinking song 'Tokay.' In show and film, the Captain, a lecherous and presumptuous military man, easily kills Carl in a duel over Sarah's honor. In taking 'Tokay' for himself, Eddy pulls star rank, renders the Captain a minor speaking role, and gives the cinematic Carl the chance to lead some robust, wine-driven bonhomie. *New Moon* combines songs taken from the tenor role Philippe ('Softly, as in a Morning Sunrise') and the high baritone role Robert ('Stouthearted Men,' 'Wanting You'). In the show, Robert introduces 'Stouthearted Men' and sings its top note—a high G—to get the musical scene going. On the choral repeat, a prime example of the mighty male chorus aesthetic characteristic of 1920s operetta, Philippe sings a new topmost line and all subsequent high notes whilst Robert's part folds into the vocal mass. In the film, Eddy introduces 'Stouthearted Men' in F major—a whole-step lower than the stage version—in a manner that invites straightforward singing along rather than vocal display (for him or the company as a whole). Eddy's solos display solid, resolutely unflashy baritone singing: he is not a show-off but instead a man with a great voice singing material the listener might imagine singing as well—in short, a classically trained version of popular baritone Bing Crosby.

Staging, framing, camera movement, and editing combine to forge a visually dynamic masculine persona for Eddy's singing in his three most memorable solos. Each number places Eddy at the head of a moving group of men who join him in song. He enters *Naughty Marietta* and the cycle leading an orderly group of scouts through the forests of Louisiana singing 'Tramp! Tramp! Tramp!' The group's conventional good looks stand in sharp contrast to the leering pirates who have taken MacDonald and a group of vulnerable young women hostage nearby. The sound alone of the scouts' singing sends the pirates, who have already killed an old woman at point blank range, scurrying in a panic that allows MacDonald to grab a torch and cry for help. But before this can happen, *Naughty Marietta* lingers on Eddy as a leader of men, marching forward with rows of men following behind. In a treadmill effect, Eddy and company march forward as the camera tracks smoothly backwards (Figure 1.5a). Their relentless and resolved physical forward motion powerfully interacts with the march they sing. The effect is both startlingly realistic—the men's movement

FIGURE 1.5A 'Tramp! Tramp! Tramp!' (*Naughty Marietta*).

through space is palpable, with the lighting suggesting the sequence was shot outside in natural light—and solidly cinematic—only the medium of motion pictures could put the viewer into motion with the men in this way. The viewer moves through space with the men but never adopts their point of view. Their resolve, rather than any specific place they are headed, is the topic of the sequence.

*Rose Marie* recycles to lesser effect the stunning visual realization of 'Tramp! Tramp! Tramp!' Eddy enters the film leading a group of Royal Canadian Mounted Police. But before the song 'The Mounties' begins, a montage of real Mounties riding and training in Canada treats the film audience to a mini travelogue—a genre of film short that escaped the otherwise studio-bound classical Hollywood style. But while Eddy and MacDonald did travel to Lake Tahoe to shoot exterior sequences and 'Indian Love Call' on location, Eddy did not go to Canada to shoot with the Mounties. And so, when 'The Mounties' begins he appears alone on a horse walking a treadmill (on a soundstage at MGM's lot in Culver City) with

FIGURE 1.5B 'The Mounties' (*Rose Marie*).

a poorly matched back projection of real Mounties behind (Figure 1.5b). The effect has none of the dynamism or physical texture of 'Tramp! Tramp! Tramp!' and reveals a rare technical compromise undermining the development of a defining trope of the cycle.

Eddy's third marching song, 'Stouthearted Men' from *New Moon*, returns to the capturing of real motion through space, this time enhanced with multiple quick cuts of men running to catch up with a huge singing crowd. The men move through a vast soundstage forest which, through crane shots and dynamic cutting, seems to go on and on (Figure 1.5c). At the climax, Eddy leads the large, torch-bearing crowd across a small lake. The visual grandeur of the cycle lies in just such moments. Eddy initiates 'Stouthearted Men' with a speech calling on the men to join together and seize their freedom. He starts the song proper by speaking the lyrics rather than singing. This thoroughly integrated number can, if the viewer wishes, be understood not as actual song—the men aren't really

FIGURE 1.5C 'Stouthearted Men' (*New Moon*).

singing—but instead as song being used to express, more force-fully than mere dialogue, the characters' ideas and intentions in a heightened form that is naturalized by the dramaturgical allowances of operetta.

This distinction is supported by Eddy's position vocally within the groups of men he leads. He does not sing any of these solos in a manner that makes his voice the primary in-terest. Instead, he sings to rouse other men to action or to express their shared identity as men of action. Bursting into song is a leadership tactic and not a performance per se. And—crucially—in all three cases the men sing for themselves and not for an audience. A fourth Eddy marching solo reveals how *not* performing forms a crucial part of his masculine persona. In *Sweethearts*, Eddy's only solo is contextualized as a re-cording session of the Victor Herbert tune 'On Parade.' Eddy is accompanied by a large uniformed military band arrayed on risers and playing without music. Various sections of the band rise from their chairs during the number—similar to how swing bands were shot in this period—and by the end the entire band is standing. The camera pans smoothly across the scene, eventually passing into the control room where a sound engineer adjust the dials on the recording console and a spinning disc cutting machine transforms an ephemeral performance into a permanent artefact—literally, a record. Crucially, no audience witnesses the recording, which ends without applause. (In the scene just prior, MacDonald sings for a studio audience at a live radio show.) The entirely male 'On Parade,' lacking physical motion except for the band members standing up or sitting down and the disc cutter spinning, is—like the three marching solos described above—all about men of action doing things in the world. In each of these masculine solos, Eddy sings not for show or attention but to express, in song, his fundamental character as a man of action.

By contrast, MacDonald's solos are virtually all public performances where her skill as a singer and beauty as a woman is attended to by an enthusiastic in-film audience. She exists in these often quite extended, plot-arresting numbers to be listened to, looked at, and applauded. Such moments are facilitated by MacDonald's characters being either professional singers (*Rose Marie, Maytime, Sweethearts*) or young women with natural singing ability that has been cultivated due to her high social status (*Naughty Marietta, New Moon, Bitter Sweet*) or her good luck and interest in the finer things (*The Girl of the Golden West*). MacDonald playing women who sing forms a natural extension of MacDonald herself as a singer.[17]

The necessarily social contexts for MacDonald's solos for in-film audiences include fully realized opera house performances (*Rose Marie, Maytime, Bitter Sweet*), more commercial popular music settings (a New York theatre and radio show in *Sweethearts*; a Viennese café in *Bitter Sweet*), religious rituals (*Naughty Marietta, The Girl of the Golden West*), elaborate occasions with royalty in attendance (*Maytime, New*

*Moon*), fancy parties (*Naughty Marietta, New Moon*), and informal musical moments in daily life (with street musicians in *Naughty Marietta* and *Maytime*, with social others both elite and common in *Rose Marie, The Girl of the Golden West*, and *Bitter Sweet*). This considerable range of contexts makes a tacit argument that MacDonald's kind of singing is welcome just about everywhere—at least in the overwhelmingly pre-twentieth-century historical settings where the cycle mostly journeys.

Opera enters the cycle at the start of *Rose Marie* and continues strongly in the next film, *Maytime*. These two films—among the pair's best-performing at the box office—use opera as a prestige element and assume movie audiences who either know a bit about opera or who are willing to sit through extended stretches of opera as part of a movie narrative. Minimal nods are made towards the latter, less informed group.

*Rose Marie*'s image track opens on the marquee of the Royal Theatre announcing '*Romeo & Juliet*' starring 'Canada's own Marie de Flor.' A crowd stands outside the theatre evidently listening to an opera chorus, the sound of which fades in on the soundtrack during the conclusion of the opening titles. An usher hushes a shouting paperboy walking past the theatre, telling him 'there's a show going on.' The paperboy pauses, turns towards the open doors of the lobby, and joins the rapt sidewalk listeners. The populist appeal of opera is reinforced several times over here: the performance is in a theatre (not an opera house), everyday people passing by—like the folks who go to movies—are shown listening (even though it's doubtful they could hear much in the real world), and even lowly paperboys find themselves lending an ear to what's described colloquially as a 'show.' *Rose Marie*'s opening makes an invitation to all to listen and enjoy.

After the sidewalk set-up, *Rose Marie* ushers the viewer into the theatre where the Capulet's ball is in progress. So begins a five-minute tab show-cum-montage of Charles Gounod's 1867 opera *Romeo et Juliette*, sung in French (without English subtitles). The more extended excerpts include Romeo (played by tenor Allan Jones) catching sight of Juliet, MacDonald as Juliet in a complete performance of Juliette's waltz song (a staple of the soprano repertory), and the very end of the love duet concluding the opera. One cut to the audience during the waltz song instructs the viewer on how to assess MacDonald's musicianship: an excited older man in the gallery (cheap seats taken by the most devoted fans) whispers something about 'the high C' and the opera lovers around him show great appreciation. The cycle's second film insists not only that MacDonald plays an opera singer but that she is, in fact, capable of singing opera.

A second opera scene concludes *Rose Marie*. It's MacDonald and Jones together again, this time as Tosca and Cavaradossi in the final five minutes of act 3 of Giacomo Puccini's 1900 opera *Tosca*, misidentified as '*La Tosca*' on the Royal Theatre marquee. Sung in Italian, the film audience is assumed to be instantly familiar with the events unfolding in the opera: Cavaradossi's fake, in fact real, execution by firing squad; Tosca's horrified discovery that he's dead, followed by her leaping to her death off the parapet of the Castel Sant'Angelo.[18] With the dramatic events of the opera unfolding according to Puccini's musical-dramatic pacing, MacDonald's character, unstable after the arrest of her brother for murder, begins to hear Eddy's voice singing 'Indian Love Call.' Some knowledge of *Tosca* is required to understand immediately that the sound of Eddy's voice—which could be a voice from offstage within the opera—is only audible to MacDonald. (Prominent cries from offstage during *Tosca* act 2 might even briefly confuse a viewer who knows the opera.) Indeed, Eddy's second intrusion fits tonally into Puccini's score. *Tosca* continues to move towards its climax and MacDonald continues singing but she also keeps on hearing Eddy's voice, giving ample evidence on her distressed face that she has lost the thread of the part. Cuts to audience members give clues pitched to the knowing that she has gone off script: 'She ought to be upstage,' says one gentleman to his companion, signalling rather subtly, and only to the filmgoer who knows *Tosca*, that scant time remains in the score for MacDonald to get to the parapet for Tosca's dramatic exit. Indeed, MacDonald's Tosca never jumps: she sings to the end of the role but faints downstage to the consternation of all onstage, backstage, and in the audience. While the fact that something has gone wrong is evident, an opera-literate viewer enjoys a much more nuanced film narrative, with *Rose Marie* and *Tosca* in a sustained and intense interplay. MGM bets heavily on a prestige audience here: reaching out to opera fans; assuming all others—surely in the majority—will go along for the ride, gleaning what they can (like, perhaps, most audiences for musical theatre in another language are wont to do).

*Maytime* follows up on *Rose Marie*'s assumption of audience knowledge of opera, with MacDonald again playing a diva and with extended opera scenes that go unexplained to the film audience. In a production of Giacomo Meyerbeer's *Les Huguenots* in Paris, MacDonald performs the aria 'Nobles seigneur, salut' in the trouser role Urbain. Dressed as a man, MacDonald wears a seventeenth-century style (and figure- and legs-revealing) costume (Figure 1.6). Opera audiences accept such gender-bending displays as a matter of course—although *Les Huguenots* was far from standard repertory in the 1930s. Most film audiences would lack the cultural knowledge to understand exactly what was going on. *Maytime* tacitly assumes they will accept the conventions and high cultural status of opera, with little more prompting than the enthusiastic in-film audiences presented here and in *Rose Marie*.

Indeed, the plot of *Maytime* rests on the filmgoer's ability to read through representations of the operatic stage to revel in and weep over MacDonald and Eddy's forbidden love,

FIGURE 1.6  MacDonald in pants on the opera stage in Paris (*Maytime*).

which—as the story goes—can only be expressed under cover
of their playing lovers on stage. The opera they perform together, especially composed for MacDonald's diva character by
a fictitious Italian composer named Trentini, is called *Czaritza*.
Stothart concocted this work using melodies taken from Pyotr
Illyich Tchaikovsky's Fifth Symphony to meet the unique
needs of MacDonald and Eddy, who—of course—required a
romantic stage work that paired a soprano and a baritone, of
which there are none in the standard repertory. The *Czaritza*
sequence takes a full twelve minutes—sung in Russian and
French with a plot no one in the film audience knows since
it's not a real opera. Some events seem clear: MacDonald, who
has some personal connection to Eddy, is declared empress
(or, presumably, 'Czaritza'). Eddy, a rebel of sorts, comes before her under guard and sings defiantly of 'liberté,' after which
MacDonald reluctantly signs what is likely his death warrant.
She then clears the room to speak with Eddy alone and they
share a love duet that begins 'Mon amour.' The broad aesthetic

strokes of love on the romantic operatic stage—passionate but for some reason impossible—are here expressed with utmost seriousness using instrumental melodies from the symphonic repertory and within a film plot that has the singers acting out real love for each other within dramatic roles. The duet ends in a kiss—like all MacDonald and Eddy love duets—that lasts twelve seconds (in 1937 to the consternation of the Production Code Administration), followed by a whispered exchange where MacDonald and Eddy's characters declare their intention to finally be together.[19] But *Czaritza*'s not over yet—to still more singing, the lovers are parted and the curtain falls.

The operatic sequences in *Rose Marie* and *Maytime* are extraordinary for their length and the assumptions they make about film audience knowledge of and tolerance for opera. With no snootiness or satire, these films assume MacDonald and Eddy's audience will enjoy long stretches of opera performed in a foreign language, will absorb the genre's stranger practices without feeling alienated from the film's stars, and can interpret basic operatic tropes even when the opera being performed is, in fact, made up. (All of this from a studio that made the Marx Brothers' *A Night at the Opera* just two years earlier. Stothart served as music director on that film, too.) While not typical of the cycle, *Rose Marie* and *Maytime* invest heavily in presenting MacDonald as a legitimate opera singer who could succeed on the stage. (After her film career, MacDonald made a largely unsuccessful attempt to do so.)[20]

Most of MacDonald's solos offer light classical favourites in picturesque surroundings: song-like arias, often with an exotic flavour, that endear her to the crowds that clamour to listen and sometimes join in. Such solos happen early on in most of the films, as if answering a presumed desire among MacDonald's movie audience to hear her sing soon after the opening titles. Indeed, *Naughty Marietta* begins with a bit of coloratura from MacDonald (about which more below) and continues with the number 'Chansonette,' which has MacDonald's down-to-earth French princess leading a group of commoners in song. Positioned just after the *Romeo and Juliette* sequence in *Rose Marie*, 'The Walking Game' similarly imagines a crowd of various classes wanting to hear and singing along a bit with MacDonald. At Emperor Louis Napoleon's elaborate ball early in *Maytime*, MacDonald as a young American opera singer enchants the court with 'Les filles de Cadix' by Leo Delibes, then offers a rousing patriotic rendition of 'Le Régiment de Sambre et Meuse' by Robert Planquette: again, the crowd joins in. In *New Moon*, she offers the interpolated song 'Paree' at the very start of the picture: the bondsmen on the deck below, led by Eddy, answer with a parody version. In *Naughty Marietta* and *The Girl of the Golden West*, MacDonald performs prayerful solos as part of religious moments or solemn occasions, offering in the latter film bits of Liszt's 'Liebestraum' and the Bach/Gounod 'Ave Maria.' All these performances employ MacDonald's legitimate singing voice in repertoire that is crowd-pleasing and either rhythmic or reverent. Her selections would be comfortable on a mid-century pops concert program. These important, persona-defining moments frame MacDonald as a diva in touch with her popular and mass audience. She *can*, of course, sing opera—*Rose Marie* and *Maytime* insist—but mostly she offers lighter fare designed to please: pretty songs prettily sung by a pretty lady in a pretty dress.

All of MacDonald and Eddy's films end with the couple together and singing. The tragic *Maytime* and *Bitter Sweet* conclude with the lovers in a mystical union: in the latter, Eddy, having died, appears to the still-living MacDonald in the clouds. In the former, the years-dead Eddy is there to greet the spirit of MacDonald as she rises, young again, from her old body (Figure 1.7). The other six films end with the lovers together and very much alive: back on Broadway still singing 'Sweethearts' in *Sweethearts*; reunited in bourgeois comfort by

FIGURE 1.7  United in death at the close of *Maytime*.

a fireside in *Rose Marie*; together at last for real rather than in Eddy's dream in *I Married an Angel*.

Three films explicitly connect MacDonald and Eddy's union in the final reel with larger political tales of the land: democratic soil in the New World. In *Naughty Marietta*, MacDonald and Eddy ride into the wilderness, escaping soul-destroying aristocratic and military obligations to a rotten French monarchy (Figure 1.8a). In *New Moon*, they enter their humble new home in a French colony that has just received word of a victory for the republic over the monarchy back home (Figure 1.8b). And in *The Girl of the Golden West*, the pair rides a covered wagon into a shared life in California, leaving behind Eddy's upbringing by Mexicano bandits (Figure 1.8c). All three of these films present the New World as the dominion of whites. *Naughty Marietta* and *New Moon* similarly imagine Louisiana and the Caribbean as a space defined by Old World issues of class rather than New World racial encounters or mixing. *The Girl of the Golden West* tackles racial mixing in Old California

FIGURE 1.8A *Naughty Marietta.*

FIGURE 1.8B *New Moon.*

FIGURE 1.8C *The Girl of the Golden West.*

and promises that the influence of 'Mexicanos' can be overcome by pure love.

*Naughty Marietta* and *New Moon* alike centre on French
aristocrats or military men who embrace Revolutionary values,
choosing New World democratic norms over Old World
strictures. MacDonald's good-humoured French princess in
*Naughty Marietta* walks freely among the common people in
the opening scene, declaring to her black-clad, status-conscious
duenna, 'I have my native dignity.' She escapes a forced
marriage to a Spaniard by disguising herself as a commoner
and journeying to America, sharing the goals of her maid, who
goes along and says of the New World, 'Maybe I can become a
new person there.' MacDonald's character shares this desire.
Eddy, introduced as a hearty backwoodsman, turns out to be a
military officer—he's thus a natural leader of both casual and
formal groups of men. The pair exits the film fleeing society's
expectations—in MacDonald's case, her wealth; in Eddy's, his
military commission in an unjust context—as a pair of pioneers

journeying into the wilderness, destined to be what the plot of the film has made them: Americans who rule the land by natural right. In *New Moon*'s reciprocal tale, Eddy plays a nobleman fleeing the French king and disguised as a bondsman sent to Louisiana (an exact male corollary to MacDonald's character in *Naughty Marietta*). MacDonald's bejewelled French aristocrat takes to the democratic milieu of a community of escaped bondsmen with easy grace: she casts aside the finery of her life as a plantation mistress in favour of hard work on the land. At the end of *New Moon*, the pair's love story is resolved in political joy as the island learns of the triumph of democracy back home in France. (In a similarly class-conscious narrative, MacDonald's Sarah in *Bitter Sweet* rejects the proper path for an upper-middle-class English girl and elopes with her one true love, Eddy's Carl, a penniless Viennese composer. Together they defy the masculine sexual presumptions of the Old World, Eddy sacrificing his life for MacDonald's honor in the process.) All these plots and characters present the viewer with European-born, white characters who choose their own life paths—in short, who act like white Americans free to set their own course for the future.

Racial contrasts regularly define the couple when their characters are American-born or their plots encounter distinctly American racial others. In *Maytime*, playing opera singers born in the American South but living in Paris, they linger together around a piano singing a tender version of James Bland's minstrel tune 'Carry Me Back to Old Virginny.' In this duet, MacDonald and Eddy (and MGM) offer, with characteristic sincerity and aesthetic craft, a hymn to a racist Old South vision of enslaved African Americans content in their labor for 'dear old massa.' In the afterglow, MacDonald says wistfully, 'Makes you kind of homesick doesn't it.'

Scenes of distant observation of racial others in performance occur in three of the pair's films. Each speaks to the privileges of whiteness. In *Rose Marie*, they watch an ill-imagined Hollywood-style indigenous festival. The massive production number 'Totem Tom Tom,' from the stage version of the show, nonsensically combines totem poles (an aspect of indigenous culture in the forested northern reaches of North America) with the feathered bonnets of the Plains Indians in a dance described as a 'corn festival.' The scene, watched from a distance by the couple, climaxes with the appearance of a gigantic drum straight out of MGM studio aesthetics. However syncretistic its content, 'Totem Tom Tom' presents the indigenous peoples of *Rose Marie* as a coherent culture, against which the leads' whiteness finds a contrast. MacDonald, with her character's eye for beauty, responds when the dance concludes, 'Oh, that was thrilling.' Eddy, a Mountie, declares 'We have to police these things.'

In an analogous moment of shared and distant observation of the ritual actions of racial others, MacDonald and Eddy watch and listen to the black slaves on MacDonald's plantation perform the so-called trouble tree ceremony in *New Moon*. The entire sequence begins with black voices singing a faux Negro spiritual that begins 'no more weepin' and wailin'.' 'It's a strange ritual,' Eddy comments. MacDonald describes it as an 'old jungle superstition.' The ceremony is more heard than seen for the film audience: MacDonald and Eddy look on the sight and describe it. At one point, the black women begin singing a wordless, haunting, minor-mode tune. MacDonald leans back and listens, saying, 'My nurse used to hum that strain. I've often tried to find words of my own to go with it.' She hazards a few lines but lapses into humming. Indeed, later in the film, MacDonald finds the words and turns the tune into 'Lover, Come Back to Me'—her only solo-as-private-reflection in the entire cycle. Eddy, in turn, speaks of a song from back home in France about 'a humble shepherd who loved a lady of high rank.' The shepherd sang his song and she answered (just like the lovers in 'Indian Love Call' any fan of the cycle would know). The song Eddy's story refers to is, of course, 'Wanting You,' into which the trouble tree ceremony seamlessly segues. Both of the sophisticated and romantic songs by Romberg featured in this scene are described in the dialogue as originating among socially low others, whether country folk in the Old World or racial others in the New. *New Moon* executes these turns without irony, absorbing the musical style of operetta and legit voices—both associated with elite European culture—into a vision of the New World peopled almost solely by whites.

Indeed, *New Moon*—like *Naughty Marietta*—offers a strange twisting of the historical facts of race in the Americas. The film opens on a French ship bound for the French colony of Louisiana, its hold filled with white bondservants. On arrival, MacDonald, an aristocrat arriving to take her place as the mistress of a plantation, buys Eddy. All of her house servants, Eddy among them, are white. Black children are seen around her house—Eddy sings his 'Shoes' solo to one cute boy—but the black field slaves only appear in the distance dancing around the trouble tree. In the later reels, MacDonald and Eddy and an all-white group of French men and women are shipwrecked on an uninhabited Caribbean island. An egalitarian culture develops where 'the one to command is a mere matter of circumstances.' Eddy and MacDonald emerge as natural leaders of this island society, which resembles nothing so much as a group of maroons—escaped African slaves who set up hidden free societies beyond the reach of the law in the remote reaches of the Americas—including, until the 1760s, parts of colonial Louisiana.

*The Girl of the Golden West* also includes an elaborate exotic production number titled 'Mariache,' a display of elite Mexicano otherness that chimes with 'Totem Tom Tom' and the trouble tree ceremony. At the number's height, Eddy, in disguise as an Anglo military officer, lassos MacDonald about the waist: this romantic display of Latin exoticism welcomes white participation. But before Eddy can claim MacDonald's orphan girl from Kentucky, he must slough off his Mexicano self. Eddy's character is a white boy, evidently the sole survivor of a westward-bound family killed by Indians en route to California. Raised by Mexican bandits under the moniker 'Gringo,' he speaks both Spanish and a native language and grows to be a bandit leader who speaks with a 'Mexicano accent' when in disguise. The film's romance plot involves Eddy being sold out to the authorities by his 'half-breed' lover. MacDonald, wishing for a pure love, learns of Eddy's other 'girl' and says to him, 'You made me feel all cheap inside.' To be together, Eddy must return to the boy he was when he first travelled west with his white family.

As noted, Eddy and MacDonald exit *The Girl of the Golden West* in a covered wagon, committing to a shared life of respectable whiteness. As they ride, they sing together Romberg's exotically tinged serenading song, 'Senorita.' All that remains of Eddy's Mexicano identity at the close is a popular tune by an expatriate European composer with English words on a Mexican theme that Eddy effectively deployed earlier in the film—attired in his dashing Anglo officer disguise—to romance MacDonald by a seashore in the moonlight. A white viewer of *The Girl of the Golden West*—or any of the other fantasies of a white New World offered by MGM's MacDonald and Eddy cycle—is, of course, welcome to sing along.

## NOTES

1. For a summary of American operetta on the New York stage as drawn upon by MGM, see Richard Traubner, *Operetta: A Theatrical History*, rev. ed. (New York: Routledge, 2003), 366–392.

2. MacDonald briefly sings in a quasi-scat style during the number 'Pretty as a Picture' in *Sweethearts* during the only scene in the cycle set in a nightclub. In *Rose Marie*, MacDonald tries to sing 'hot' at a low-down saloon in the Canadian wilderness. Gilda Grey, a minor star of 1920s Broadway musical revue, takes over when MacDonald fails to deliver. The songs in the scene are old pop favourites: 'Dinah' (1925) and 'Some of These Days' (1910). MacDonald's opera singer character behaves as if she has never heard them.

3. Astaire and Rogers's Broadway adaptations come early in their output: *The Gay Divorcee* (1933) and *Roberta* (1934), their second and third films together. Only one Astaire/Rogers film is set before World War I: the pair's final RKO film, *The Story of Vernon and Irene Castle* (1939), uses mostly older songs but also features a new tune, 'Only When You're in My Arms' (music by Con Conrad, lyrics by Burt Kalmar and Harry Ruby), in a bid for pop relevance.

4. Todd Decker, *Music Makes Me: Fred Astaire and Jazz* (Berkeley: University of California Press, 2011), 101–103.

5. *Babes in Arms* (MGM, 1939; Broadway, 1937, 289 performances), *Strike Up the Band* (MGM, 1940; Broadway, 1930, 191 performances), *Girl Crazy* (MGM, 1943; Broadway, 1930, 272 performances).

6. Edward Baron Turk, *Hollywood Diva* (Berkeley: University of California Press, 1998), 159, 172, 230.

7. The other Hollywood stars known for singing in a trained style are Deanna Durbin (a contract star at Universal in the late 1930s and 1940s) and Kathryn Grayson and Jane Powell (both at MGM in the years after MacDonald's career ended). Durbin's persona, emphasizing her youth, contrasted strongly with MacDonald's. See Gaylyn Studlar, *Precocious Charms: Stars Performing Girlhood in Classical Hollywood Cinema* (Berkeley: University of California Press, 2013), chap. 3.

8. Buddy Ebsen, 'The West Ain't Wild Anymo,' in *Girl of the Golden West*; Ray Bolger's clog dance near the start of *Sweethearts*; Edward Everett Horton's 'To Count Palaff (There Comes a Time),' and the women's small group number 'Tira Lira La' in *I Married an Angel*.

9. See William A. Everett, *Sigmund Romberg* (New Haven, CT: Yale University Press, 2007), 250–255.

10. To the end of the 1920s, tenors served as leading men in almost all stage operettas. From the early 1940s, beginning with Richard Rodgers and Oscar Hammerstein II's *Oklahoma!* (a work some have categorized as an operetta), leading males in Broadway musical plays have tended to be baritones, with the tenor relegated to a character or supporting part or absent entirely. A general historical drift away from trained singing towards belting from the chest and other vocal styles, facilitated by the advent of wireless microphones, accompanied this shift in Broadway masculinity.

11. Herbert Stothart worked on every MacDonald and Eddy film except *I Married an Angel*. He was most often credited with a special title card for 'musical adaptation,' signalling his important role solving basic musical challenges inherent in adapting stage operettas for MacDonald's and Eddy's star personas and unusual soprano-baritone pairing. For a detailed discussion of Stothart's musical work on *Maytime*, see Ronald Rodman, 'Tonal Design and the Aesthetic of Pastiche in Herbert Stothart's *Maytime*,' in *Music and Cinema*, ed. James Buhler, Caryl Flinn, and David Neumeyer (Middletown, CT: Wesleyan University Press, 2000), 187–206.

12. *Bitter Sweet* originally began with a prologue set in the present, casting the main narrative as a flashback (as in the stage version). 'On the basis of a few responses from a preview audience, [MGM] decided this frame-and flashback device would strike moviegoers as too reminiscent of *Maytime* (whose 1937 story was probably inspired by *Bitter Sweet*).' Turk, *Hollywood Diva*, 244.

13. For a later analogy, consider the contrast between the title song for *The Sound of Music* as sung in the enclosed space of a Broadway theatre and as realized on location in the Austrian Alps in the 1965 film.

14. While present-day musical theatre singers wear wireless microphones, which amplify their voices through speakers as in a movie theatre, their bodies and faces remain at a distance from the audience.

15. *Rose Marie*, *Maytime*, and *Bitter Sweet* reprise their respective love duets at the close. *Maytime*, exceptionally, has two duets that end in a kiss: one with the couple alone together in nature; the other with the couple playing lovers on the opera stage.

16. In *Naughty Marietta*, Eddy sings "Neath a Southern Moon,' assigned on stage to the female character 'Adah, a Quadroon.'

17. This emphasis on MacDonald's natural talent and cultivated skill is entirely absent in her Paramount films made between 1929 and 1932. Only at MGM did her identity as a classically trained singer form an essential part of her star persona.

18. The *Tosca* sequence originally included Jones singing Cavaradossi's act 3 aria, 'E lucevan le stelle.' After seeing the film at a public preview, Eddy threatened studio head L. B. Mayer that he would 'go on strike; you'll have trouble with me' if the aria remained in the film. Turk, *Hollywood Diva*, 173.

19. Turk, *Hollywood Diva*, 199.

20. See Turk, *Hollywood Diva*, chap. 14.

# 2

# 'Is This the Right Material, Girl?'

## How Madonna Makes Us Like Eva, but Not Necessarily Evita

### RICHARD J. ALLEN

■ □ ■

ALTHOUGH MUSICALS HAVE BEEN A staple of international cinema since the movies began to talk—with Warner Bros.' 1927 *The Jazz Singer*, generally considered the first *feature* film to utilize synchronized sound—the film industry has constantly struggled with the process of successfully adapting stage musicals to the screen. The studio musicals of the 1930s, 1940s, and early 1950s, starring the likes of Gene Kelly, Fred Astaire, and Judy Garland, often centred on original but threadbare stories that were merely 'excuses' to thematically incorporate high-concept musical numbers, such as *Top Hat* (1935), *Meet Me in St Louis* (1942), and *Singin' in the Rain* (1952). But when Broadway and West End stages found success in the 1940s and 1950s with plot-based, dramatically structured 'book musicals' such as Rodgers and Hammerstein's *Oklahoma!* and Frank Loesser's *Guys and Dolls*, converting these more realistic, dramatic vehicles from stage to screen became a trickier—and riskier—proposition.[1]

Besides the inherent artistic challenges in adapting work from the fantastical setting of the stage to the increasingly realistic medium of mid-twentieth century film, the story-centred stage musicals of 1940s–1950s—which were major commercial successes on Broadway and the West End—rarely turned a profit in their cinematic incarnations. And considering the enormous expense of producing these lavish spectacles on film, these box office disappointments cost several Hollywood studios many millions of dollars over a relatively short period of time.

The particular story of the attempt to adapt the international hit stage musical *Evita* to the medium of film is one of the most extraordinary and revealing examples of this artistically and commercially treacherous process, incorporating legends of stage, screen, and the recording industry with distinguished careers off- and onstage, behind and in front of the camera.

Before beginning a comprehensive comparison of the 1978 original stage version of *Evita* to its 1996 cinematic counterpart, it would be prudent to examine the genesis of the project, which famously chronicles the brief but eventful life of the infamous Eva Peron, wife of Argentinean president Juan Peron. As so often is the case with stage musicals, the first spark of inspiration comes from the writers, composer Andrew Lloyd Webber and lyricist/librettist Tim Rice. Lloyd Webber and Rice began their long-running collaboration working on *The Likes of Us* in 1965.[2] Although that show wasn't professionally produced until some forty years later (at Lloyd Webber's own Sydmonton Festival in 2005), the duo's next two collaborations—*Jesus Christ Superstar* and *Joseph and the Amazing Technicolor Dreamcoat*—opened to critical acclaim and box office success on Broadway in 1971 and London's West End in 1973.

As young writers seeking a fast track to production, Lloyd Webber and Rice took an unorthodox route with both *Superstar* and *Joseph*, producing them as 'concept albums' before imagining a scripted or stage version. The commercial success of those albums attracted sufficient financial backing to spawn the aforementioned stage productions of both shows. Thus, it was not surprising when the team decided to employ a similar process with *Evita* in 1976.

The initial idea for *Evita* came to Tim Rice in 1973, when he happened to catch the last part of a radio program about Eva Peron, the actress turned politically influential wife of one-time Argentinian president, Juan Peron. Having known little about the details of her life but intrigued by what he had heard, Rice began to research Mrs Peron's past to the point of what one might term 'obsession.' He claims to have watched *Queen of Hearts*—a 1972 British made-for-television documentary about Eva Peron—'at least twenty times,' then travelled to Buenos Aires to research original documents and interview contacts about the details of her life.[3] As further evidence of his obsession, in 1976, Rice named his newborn daughter Eva. Based on this research, Rice pitched the idea for an Eva Peron–inspired musical to Lloyd Webber. At this juncture the concept hinged at least in part on a score that would incorporate a variety of Latin musical forms and styles including tangos, *passos doble*, and others. Although tempted, Lloyd Webber ultimately rejected the project in favour of collaborating with iconic British playwright Alan Ayckbourn on a more traditional musical entitled *Jeeves*, based on the popular P. G. Wodehouse character. Ironically, the initial idea for a musical about the unflappable butler Jeeves was suggested to Lloyd Webber by Rice himself, but Rice eventually lost interest in the project, leaving Lloyd Webber to proceed with Ayckbourn.

When *Jeeves*'s West End production 'flopped magnificently,'[4] closing in May of 1975 after garnering almost universally negative reviews and accumulating only 38 performances, Lloyd Webber reconsidered Rice's offer and began working with his former partner on the songs for an *Evita* concept album. Interestingly, though *Jeeves* was considered a failure, two pieces of music from the show were used for *Evita*, becoming 'Another Suitcase in Another Hall' and 'Goodnight and Thank You.' Years later, other sections of *Jeeves'* extensive score were repurposed by Lloyd Webber in shows he wrote with lyricists other than Rice: 'Unexpected Song' in *Song and Dance* (1982) and *Sunset Boulevard*'s 'As if We Never Said Goodbye' (1993), two of the composer's most often-recorded songs.[5]

Although Rice was clearly determined to dramatize Eva Peron's brief but very eventful and impactful life, there is some question about the specific inspiration for the style and substance of the musical itself. Besides the aforementioned 1972 television film *Queen of Hearts*, by 1975 there had been a number of published biographies on the one-time First Lady of Argentina. It has been suggested, however, that the majority of Rice's depiction is based on 1952's *The Woman with the Whip*, written by Mary Main under the pseudonym 'Maria Flores' (apparently for fear of repercussions from the Peron regime). Main was of British descent but grew up in Argentina, and while her mostly negative account of Eva Peron's life is more consistent with the Evita of Rice's libretto, Rice insists that—although he was influenced by Main's book—the musical is based on a wider spectrum of source material. It is interesting to note, however, that some of the facts about Peron's life that were challenged for accuracy in *Evita*, are similar to events described by Main.[6]

Considering that Rice and Lloyd Webber's project was intended to eventually lead to a full production, it is not surprising that their artistic choices in crafting the album would be influenced more by theatricality than authenticity. To support that assertion, one need only look at the manner in which Rice and Lloyd Webber choose to tell Eva's story: through the sardonic and often scathingly critical narration of a character known only as 'Che.' In the original concept album phase of *Evita*, Che was meant to represent a sort of Argentine 'everyman,' providing reflection, insight and criticism to explain, analyze, and assess Eva Duarte Peron's rise to power and her subsequent demise. There is nothing in the original lyrics to suggest any connection between the narrator and the real-life South American Marxist revolutionary figure Che Guevara, after whom the character was fairly explicitly modelled in Hal Prince's original West End and Broadway versions of *Evita*. Instead, the completely fictionalized, original conception of the Che character was meant to represent 'an 'everyman' of the lower/working class, serving as the voice of the people; not the revolutionary, Che Guevara.'[7] The reasons for Prince's interpretation of Che's role in the staged version are discussed in more detail below. But for the concept album, the name Che was likely inspired by the traditional Argentinian usage, which— according to website gringoinbuenosaires.com—'is ubiquitous in Argentina' and is often 'used as the equivalent of mate, dude or buddy.'[8] This artistic choice effectively renders the *facts* of Eva Peron's life as secondary in priority to the 'people's' *perception* of her actions in her personal life and public career.

Upon completion of the score, Lloyd Webber and Rice decided to produce the original *Evita* recording themselves, using MCA Records—the company that had successfully marketed the original album of *Jesus Christ Superstar*—to release the record. They cast actress Julie Covington, a veteran of the hit West End production of Steven Schwartz's *Godspell*, in the role of Eva. Che was sung by Colm Wilkinson, who had played Judas in the London production of *Jesus Christ Superstar* (and later originated the role of Jean Valjean in Cameron Mackintosh's record-breaking West End and Broadway productions of *Les Misérables*). Others included Paul Jones as Juan Peron, Barbara Dickson as Peron's teenage mistress, and Tony Christie as

Magaldi, the lounge singer whose affair with Eva provides her with a route to Buenos Aires. Released as a two-disc set in 1976, the album outsold the very successful *Jesus Christ Superstar* in Great Britain, Australia, South America, and a number of European markets. Although it was not quite as big a commercial hit in the United States, the song 'Don't Cry for Me, Argentina' was covered by various artists in America, including Olivia Newton-John and Karen Carpenter. Released separately as a single in the United Kingdom (under the title 'It's Only Your Lover Returning') Julie Covington's version of the song became a number one hit on the U.K. Singles Chart in the fall of 1976, boosting the popularity and awareness of the concept album worldwide and providing impetus for Producer Robert Stigwood to undertake a West End production with Hal Prince—who had been sent a copy of the recording by Lloyd Webber himself—agreeing to direct.[9] Prince's 1978 London production was a huge commercial success (it ran for eight years) encouraging Stigwood and Prince to proceed with a Broadway incarnation featuring Patti LuPone, Mandy Patinkin, and Bob Gunton as Eva, Che, and Peron, respectively.

Although those first London and New York productions of *Evita* are now remembered for their success at the box office and their domination of the Olivier and Tony Awards, our collective memory seems to have misplaced the fact that the initial reviews of both productions were mixed. The mostly familiar score (Rice and Lloyd Webber had revised, cut, and added songs since the release of the concept album) generally received high praise, as did the star-making performances of LuPone and Patinkin in New York, but many critics took issue with the show's inability to engage the audience in caring for its self-serving heroine. Reviewing the 1979 New York opening, venerated *New York Times* critic Walter Kerr called the character of Eva 'dubious and remote,' comparing the experience of watching *Evita* to the 'emotional limbo we inhabit when we're just back from the dentist but the Novocain hasn't worn off yet.'[10]

Another point of view held that the musical was intended as a critical take on its cold-blooded protagonist. In fact, when the show was revived on Broadway in 2012, David Sheward of *Backstage* bemoaned director Michael Grandage's attempt to engage the audience by creating a more sympathetic portrayal of Eva Peron, claiming that 'Harold Prince's Brechtian staging [had] infused the otherwise flimsy material with a frightening political edge. *Evita*'s slick stagecraft in presenting herself as a saintly benefactor to the downtrodden while accumulating wealth and power was starkly presented in imaginatively surrealistic terms.'[11] As Sheward and others saw it, Prince envisioned *Evita* as a cautionary tale about a woman so obsessed with power and popularity that the pretence of 'helping the people' was merely a means to a selfish end. And given the success of Prince's Brechtian *Cabaret* in the 1960s, Bob Fosse's *Cabaret*-like staging of *Chicago* in the 1970s, and an acclaimed revival of Brecht's own *Threepenny Opera* in 1976, Prince certainly had precedent for fashioning a musical around an unsympathetic character and took pains to underscore that interpretation at every turn.

The timing of the New York opening might also have influenced the foreboding tone of Prince's production and its negative view of Eva Peron's moral and political intentions. Opening in September 1979, the show arrived during a period of major change in the cultural and political climate of the United States. With the economy floundering under the leadership of liberal Democratic president Jimmy Carter, conservatives like Republican Ronald Reagan were on the verge of winning the support—and votes—of a generation that had been strongly influenced by the idealistic liberalism of the 1960s. With the focus of younger Americans seeming to move towards an 'individualistic, competitive, and materialistic ethos that shared

much in common with Reagan's own worldview,'[12] it is likely
that Prince saw Eva's ascension to power and wealth as the dangerous result of a culture that values materialism over idealism.
When one considers that like Eva Peron, Ronald Reagan began
his career as a modestly successful entertainment figure, the
potential for comparison is undeniable. And while Prince's intention of making this comparison, or purposely channelling
any particular political point of view, is subject to debate, it is
a fact that his production about the materialistic Argentinian
icon ran for nearly four years, booming on Broadway during
Reagan's transformative first term as president.

Subsequent theatrical productions of the musical, especially those mounted long after the 'Reagan Era,' have taken
issue with Prince's interpretation. Scott Miller, the artistic director of St Louis's New Line Theatre, believed that Tim Rice
was originally more concerned with the duality of Eva Peron as
a character. On the New Line Theatre's website, in anticipation
of its 2010 revival of the show, Miller quotes Lloyd Webber:

> *Evita* was Tim Rice's idea. He was very intrigued by the fact that
> she [Eva Peron] was mentioned in the context of a whole load
> of fifties figures who were very successful, including people
> like James Dean, and I think he was curious to find out why she
> became this kind of cult figure, this huge figure in Argentina.
> The biggest problem for me as the composer of it is that of
> course I could have let the whole thing go as a high romance.
> I could make everybody cry their eyes out at the end of all this,
> but that was not the point of the piece. In a way, the piece had to
> keep this slightly Brechtian approach to the whole thing, where
> you have the Che character able to comment on the quite grisly
> things that she did.[13]

From such comments, Miller gleaned that while the writing
team saw Eva as a complex, multidimensional character, it was

Prince's choice to present Eva as basically heartless and opportunistic. But in Miller's mind, Eva Peron 'was certainly complicated. It's that conflicting legacy—and our inability to know for sure one way or the other which is more true—that makes her story so fascinating. But as a character she's not the cold-hearted bitch that Patti LuPone portrayed on Broadway. That's just not what Tim Rice wrote.'[14]

In fact, Walter Kerr was only one of many critics who were not fans of Prince's interpretation. Comparing the 1979 Broadway production to the West End original, Clive Barnes wrote in the *New York Post*, 'They have upped the Brechtian atmosphere—but unfortunately, Brecht himself was not around. The fault of the whole construction is that it is hollow. We are expected to deplore *Evita*'s morals but adore her circuses. We are asked to accept a serious person onstage, and yet the treatment of that person is essentially superficial, almost trivial. The gloss of the surface is meant to be impenetrable—and it is.'[15] Given this ambivalent reaction to the character of Eva Peron, it is not surprising that—despite its international success on stage—Hollywood was reluctant to produce a film version. To be fair, although there were legitimate artistic concerns about translating *Evita* to the screen, the biggest stumbling block was probably the litany of commercial disasters that resulted from the screen adaptations of hit stage musicals in the decades leading up to *Evita*.

Ironically, the end of Hollywood's proclivity for bringing stage musicals to the screen via lavish, star-studded adaptations, was propelled by one of the most phenomenal success stories in film history, Twentieth Century-Fox's *The Sound of Music* (1965). In order to appreciate that irony, however, one must refer back to the 1950s, when cinematic realism became more fashionable than fantasy and America's appetite for film musicals had severely waned. Evidence of that transition can be found in the fact that MGM's Gene Kelly-Stanley Donen–directed musical, the aforementioned *Singin' in the Rain*, raked in a $7.7-million profit on its initial release in 1951, while four years later, *It's Always Fair Weather*—directed by the same duo and receiving mostly positive reviews—resulted in a loss of $1,675,000 for the studio.[16] *Brigadoon*, an MGM musical adapted from the Lerner and Loewe Broadway hit, starring Kelly and directed by the legendary Vincente Minnelli, lost a similar sum the previous year.

Thus, with even its biggest stars, writers, and directors unable to garner much response at the box office, MGM began turning its attention away from musicals. But with Broadway conversely experiencing a 'Golden Age' of musicals in the 1950s,[17] Twentieth Century-Fox, Warner Bros., and others took up the business of bringing hit stage musicals to the screen. Such star-laden adaptations as *The King and I*, *Guys and Dolls*, *Carousel*, and *Oklahoma!* met with varying degrees of commercial success. Ultimately in 1961, United Artists achieved a box office bonanza with the grittier, youth-focused *West Side Story* becoming one of the most successful film musicals to that date.

Spurred by the success of *West Side Story*, Jack L. Warner invested record-breaking amounts of money to bring *My Fair Lady*—at the time, the longest-running Broadway musical ever—to the screen. His investment paid off, and *My Fair Lady* bypassed *West Side Story* at the box office. With musicals seemingly back on track—especially those spawned in Broadway's Golden Age—Richard Zanuck (son of pioneering studio executive Daryl Zanuck, who had been the driving force behind the Warner Bros. 1933 classic, *42nd Street*) set Twentieth Century-Fox into motion producing a screen version of Richard Rodgers and Oscar Hammerstein's last Broadway collaboration, *The Sound of Music*.

Without having the theatrical box office pedigree of *My Fair Lady* (*The Sound of Music*'s Broadway run was about half as long) or the raw dynamism of *West Side Story*, there was no assurance that Zanuck's vision for *The Sound of Music* would result in profits anywhere near those garnered by the aforementioned smash hits. But working primarily with key members of the team that had so deftly adapted *West Side Story* to the screen, notably director Robert Wise, screenwriter Ernest Lehman, and associate producer Saul Chaplin (a major contributor to MGM's biggest musicals under producer Arthur Freed), Zanuck shocked the cynics and produced a film that was to surpass *Gone with the Wind* as the most successful of all time.

But as Matthew Kennedy convincingly asserts in his 2014 book, *Roadshow! The Fall of Film Musicals in the 1960s*, the unprecedented success of *The Sound of Music* (coming on the heels of the hugely profitable big-budget *My Fair Lady*) ended up doing far more harm than good for the future of its studio (Fox), its genre (musicals), or the film industry in general. Two separate quotes by Richard Zanuck highlight this phenomenon. When it was clear that the *Sound of Music*'s profits would effectively save Twentieth Century-Fox from the near-bankruptcy it faced due the catastrophic losses incurred by 1963's colossal failure, *Cleopatra*, Zanuck effusively stated that *The Sound of Music* 'unquestionably marked the dramatic turnaround of Twentieth Century-Fox. Everything about this picture has a happy ending.' Years later, when Fox was losing money with every over-produced, multimillion-dollar musical it produced, Zanuck changed his tune, admitting '*The Sound of Music* did more damage to the industry than any other picture. Everyone tried to copy it. We were the biggest offenders.'[18]

The long-lasting extent of the damage stemmed from the intrinsic production realities of the film industry. Once a film opens, calculating its ultimate profitability can take years. And if the profits of one or more films are so stupefying that they tempt others to use those films as templates for future projects, the resulting movies will need to be written, cast, designed, directed, edited, and distributed before they are projected on a single screen or earn their first dollar. As such, in the late 1960s the pages of *Variety* were overrun with news about one box office disaster after another, among them *Camelot* and *Doctor Dolittle* (1967); *Finian's Rainbow, Chitty Chitty Bang Bang,* and *Star!* (1968); *Paint Your Wagon, Sweet Charity, Goodbye, Mr Chips,* and *Hello Dolly!* (1969). In fact, the millions upon millions of dollars lost on *Doctor Dolittle, Star!,* and *Hello Dolly!* ended up costing Richard Zanuck his job at Fox (he was fired by his own father) and left the studio forced to auction off a large portion of their property and assets to avoid folding completely.[19] It should be noted here that while some of the aforementioned flops were not film adaptations of Broadway musicals, films like *Doctor Dolittle* and *Chitty, Chitty Bang, Bang*—among others—had the narrative structure and cinematic style of Broadway adaptations, were created by and cast with Broadway talent, and were clearly meant to evoke the tone and spirit of *The Sound of Music.*

The very early 1970s saw some success in film musicals like *Fiddler on the Roof* (1971) and *Cabaret* (1972), both of which deviated in significant ways from the original stage versions. The highly stylized stage *Fiddler* adopted a more realistic, serious cinematic tone. For the film version of *Cabaret,* entire storylines and characters were added, others removed, while director Bob Fosse and screenwriter Jay Allen eliminated any instance in which a character (who is not actually performing on a stage within the story) 'bursts' into song. As such, the film version of *Cabaret* was able to portray the reality of the Nazi influence on Berliners in the 1930s without having to accommodate the temporary suspension of disbelief that a traditional 'book musical' would inherently require.

Thus, with only a few such exceptions, the vast majority of traditional 1970s film musicals, particularly those adapted from the stage, were significant failures, including *Song of Norway* and *On a Clear Day You Can See Forever* (1970); *The*

*Boyfriend* (1971); *Man of La Mancha* and *1776* (1972); *Godspell* and *Jesus Christ Superstar (1973); Mame* (1974); *A Little Night Music* (1977); *The Wiz* (1978), and *Hair* (1979). *Darling Lili* (1970); *Lost Horizon* (1973); *The Little Prince* (1974); *At Long Last Love, Tommy,* and *Funny Lady* (1975) are among the other large-scale 1970s 'Broadway-style' musical failures, though they were not stage adaptations per se.

Arguably one of the most famous examples of 1970s stage-to-film musical adaptations was notably *unsuccessful* in both its Broadway run and as a newly released feature film. Richard O'Brien's *The Rocky Horror Show* was a huge commercial hit from its opening in London through its seven-year run in the West End. The New York version closed in less than two months and the 1975 film version—*The Rocky Horror Picture Show*—did so poorly in its original release that it was quickly pulled from theatres by an understandably skittish Twentieth Century-Fox (clearly, the raunchy science fiction parody was the polar opposite of *The Sound of Music* in virtually every way, from its edgy content to its counterculture demographic). It was only in subsequent years, due to weekend midnight screenings—rife with a then-unique element of audience participation—that the film became a cult classic. Ironically, *The Sound of Music* has had a revival in the twenty-first century with family-friendly audience-participation sing-alongs selling to sold-out audiences in theatres throughout the world.[20]

As previously implied, the plethora of movie musicals (especially adaptations of stage hits) was more prominent in the *early* 1970s, as many of those film rights were purchased and productions set in motion when *My Fair Lady* and *The Sound of Music* still represented a sort of 'holy grail' for film studios trying to repeat—or at least build on—the success of those films. Hollywood's musical output (and income) drops off towards the end of that decade, with the notable exception of *Grease*, which grossed $150 million in its initial 1978 release.

A quick examination of its history shows that *Grease* generated staggering results at every stage of its existence. First presented as a low-budget show at a small Chicago theatre, its novice creators, Jim Jacobs and Warren Casey, received enough positive response during an eight-month run to prompt producers Ken Waissman and Maxine Fox to bring the show to New York, where it moved from off-Broadway to Broadway and was on the way to a then record-breaking 3,388 performances when the movie was released in 1978. Much of the credit for the success of the film version of *Grease* was given to its capitalizing on the 1950s nostalgia craze of the period. The very simple, nearly bare set of the Broadway production (the proscenium was decorated with black and white 1950s-style high school yearbook photographs) was replaced by a colorful, almost cartoon-like design. In fact, the opening number 'Grease Is the Word'—written specifically for the movie and performed by the then chart-topping Bee Gees—was sung over an extended cartoon sequence, introducing the major characters and the actors (led by 1970s stars John Travolta and Olivia Newton-John), portraying them in comic book fashion. Thus, although *Grease* the film was released one year before the Broadway opening of *Evita*, its success would not have much bearing on the decision of whether to turn the politically fraught *Evita* into a film.

Nonetheless, even if Stigwood and Paramount (the movie studio that originally held the rights to *Evita*) had been encouraged by the success of *Grease*, two colossal Hollywood failures of the early 1980s invariably dampened Hollywood's enthusiasm towards bringing Broadway musicals to the screen. *A Chorus Line* opened on Broadway in 1975 and proceeded to run for 6,137 performances, passing *Grease* as the longest-running Broadway musical to that point (and held the record until surpassed by Lloyd Webber's *Cats* in 1997). *Annie* (based on the iconic comic strip, *Little Orphan Annie*) opened one year later than *A Chorus Line* and had similar financial success, lasting six years on Broadway while spawning an astounding four simultaneous North American touring companies and a long-running West End production.

Yet despite the phenomenal commercial success of both shows, the film versions of *Annie* (1982) and *A Chorus Line* (1985) were failures of similar scope to *Hello Dolly* and its ilk. Touted as the most expensive movie musical ever made, the 1982 *Annie*'s total revenue did not come close to recouping its expenses. *Chorus Line*, the even bigger Broadway hit, grossed only $14 million at the box office, not close to its $25 million budget.[21]

Perhaps the many negative reviews garnered by both of these 1980s stage-to-screen adaptations were the major reason for their commercial failures. Both films could deservedly be accused of extracting well-crafted—if simplistic—plotlines and replacing them with pointless spectacle, in the case of *Annie*, and soap opera convolution for *A Chorus Line*. But even had Stigwood promised to deliver the highest quality cinematic product with the best available creative team, he would have been hard-pressed to convince the 1980s' Paramount brass to gamble on an expensive film version of *Evita* or to claim that it would revive the popularity of the film musical. For if *Annie* and *A Chorus Line*, with their likeable, sympathetic characters, could not attract an audience, why would anyone expect a purposefully alienating musical about an egotistical woman who pretends to be a champion for the masses while lining her own pockets and heightening her dubious legacy to appeal to a mass audience?

Nonetheless, soon after the show's 1978 West End opening, Stigwood hired director Ken Russell to begin conceiving a screen version of *Evita*. As the next decade went by and the project foundered in the 'development' stages, many actresses were considered for the lead role, including Barbra Streisand, whose work in both the stage (1964) and film (1968) versions of *Funny Girl* had turned her instantaneously into a bona fide superstar. But Streisand eventually rejected the role of Evita, perhaps reticent to play a heartless manipulator, given her own reputation as a demanding offscreen diva. It is equally conceivable that Stigwood and his potential business partners were reticent to build a film around Streisand, considering the devastating losses of *Hello, Dolly!* Concurrently, Tim Rice pressed hard for the original West End Eva, Elaine Paige, who also happened to be romantically linked to Rice at the time. But with no Hollywood box office track record, Paige was never given serious consideration.

As for Ken Russell, the presumptive director had set his sights on Liza Minnelli in the role. Minnelli, who had won an Oscar playing narcissistic Sally Bowles in Fosse's 1972 *Cabaret*, was a reasonable choice, especially given her ease in handling the Brechtian tone of *Cabaret*. But by the 1980s, Minnelli's box office appeal was waning and Russell—who had already screen-tested the brunette Minnelli in a blonde wig—found himself alone on the Liza bandwagon. In the end, it was Russell's refusal to work with anyone but Minnelli as Evita that cost him his contract as director of the film.[22]

By 1987, the in-fighting and indecision over casting, script, and other major elements of production seemed poised to extinguish any possibility that the film would ever get made. But the road to production took a positive turn that year when the Weintraub Entertainment Group (WEG), led by producer Jerry Weintraub, purchased the film rights from Paramount. Soon after, Weintraub was contacted by writer-director Oliver Stone, whose success with controversial dramas such as *Wall Street* and *Platoon* would seem to have prepared him to tackle the political and personal affairs of Eva and Juan Peron. Stone was not only eager to write and direct the project but also willing to meet with and consider casting the internationally known rock superstar, Madonna, in the title role.

In fact, Madonna's determination to portray the onscreen Evita had been made evident a year before Stone's involvement with the project even began. In 1986 (a full ten years before the film version of *Evita* was shot and released) the singer/actress arranged a meeting with Weintraub to express her desire to play Eva Peron. She even went as far as to dress the part, adorned in extravagant period attire and wearing her hair in chic 1940s style. Apparently, Stigwood was duly impressed and it is possible to trace the eventual casting of Madonna as Eva back to this 1986 encounter.[23]

As stated, however, there was still a decade of turmoil ahead before a deal would be sealed and production begun. This includes another meeting in 1988 in which Stone and Lloyd Webber met with Madonna to discuss the artistic approach that would be taken with the film version. The meeting left both the film's would-be writer/director and the show's composer dumbfounded as Madonna demanded final script approval and massive changes to the musical score. Stone found these demands both audacious and insulting. By 1990, Stone had not only ended the negotiations with Madonna but backed out of the project completely.

Over the next few years, the project ping-ponged between a host of studios (including Disney in the early 1990s), producers, directors, writers, and stars, while Stone and Madonna took turns being in and out of the picture. It was not until 1994 that the eventual creative team was set. With Stone turning his attention to *Nixon*, Stigwood found new producing partners in Andrew G. Vajna's independent film company, Cinergi Pictures, and investor Arnon Milchan of Regency Enterprises. The newly formed team put the screenwriting and directing chores in the hands of Alan Parker, who had directed the edgy and successful musicals *Fame*, *Pink Floyd: The Wall*, and *The Commitments*, as well as the taut historical dramas, *Midnight Express* and *Mississippi Burning*. Like Stone, Parker had proven that he was up to the challenge of translating explosive material to the screen. The fact that he could direct musicals was an added factor in his favour.

In coming to the project, Parker was focused on two aspects of production: the script and the star. For the script, Parker opted to discard both Stone's version and the original stage version, choosing instead, in his words, to 'write a balanced story, as thoroughly researched as possible, inspired always by the heart of the original piece, which was Andrew's score and Tim's lyrics.'[24] Although it was Parker who penned the final version, the Writers' Guild of America awarded Stone shared credit as screenwriter. Casting the lead actress would be even more complicated than crafting the script. At the time Parker came on board as writer-producer-director, the previous regime had finally settled on Michelle Pfeiffer, then a big box office name who had starred in film musicals and dramas, including *The Fabulous Baker Boys* and *Grease 2*. But just as Parker took over the artistic reins of *Evita*, Pfeiffer announced that she was pregnant with her second child and would not be available. When renewed negotiations with Meryl Streep could not bring about an agreement, Parker considered Glenn Close for the role. It was during this period of indecision, at the end of 1994, that Madonna made the crowning gesture that finally won over the support of Parker: a personal letter designed to persuade Parker that she was destined to play Eva Peron. As Parker later explained, 'her handwritten, four-page letter was extraordinarily passionate and sincere. As far as she was concerned, no one could play Evita as well as she could, and she said that she would sing, dance and act her heart out, and put everything else on hold to devote all her time to it should I decide to go with her.'[25]

With Madonna having won over Parker and eventually Rice, Lloyd Webber remained the sceptic among the creative team. For although Madonna was well known for her string of pop hits, the composer was still concerned about her ability to sing the more legitimate, opera-like aspects of his score. Proving her respect for the magnitude of the role and its vocal demands, Madonna embarked on intensive vocal coaching sessions and extensive research of Eva Peron's place in Argentinian history, including a 1996 trip to Buenos Aires where she personally interviewed aging contemporaries of the Perons.[26]

Madonna's enthusiasm and passion for the project was evident in the diary she wrote during the film shoot, published in the November 1996 issue of *Vanity Fair*. 'This is the role I was born to play,' she wrote. 'I put everything of me into this because it was much more than a role in a movie. It was exhilarating and intimidating at the same time. . . . And I am prouder of *Evita* than anything else I have done.'[27] The long road that ironically began and ended with Madonna as Eva is arguably the defining aspect of how *Evita* got made, how the character was reinvented for the film, and how the film itself was received by the public. For Parker, knowing the glamourous pop star would be at the centre of the film clearly affected his more romantic approach to the script. 'While *Evita* is a story of people whose lives were in politics, it is not a political story,' he explained later. 'It is a Cinderella story about the astonishing life of a girl from the most mundane of backgrounds, who became the most powerful woman her country (and indeed Latin America) had ever seen, a woman never content to be a mere ornament at the side of her husband, the president.'[28]

Parker's reference to 'Cinderella' may have been more prescient than he intended, as it bespeaks a major shift in the source, focus, and style of film musicals in the waning years of the twentieth century. During the fifteen-plus years (1978–1995) when the *Evita* movie project was floundering—and, as discussed, traditional film musicals were not getting made—the Disney Company found a new way to package and present its signature animated musicals. Beginning with 1989's *Little Mermaid*, Disney found huge financial and critical success by rebranding a genre that was formerly geared almost exclusively to children. Hiring Alan Mencken and Howard Ashman, the composing team that was responsible for the off-Broadway hit *Little Shop of Horrors*, Disney encouraged them to approach story and character on *The Little Mermaid* with the depth and complexity that had been a staple of Broadway's 'book' musicals since 1943's *Oklahoma!* In return, *The Little Mermaid* set a box office record for an animated film and won two Academy Awards in 1989. Its success spurred the making of *Beauty and the Beast*, which was not only a box office hit but was the first animated film ever to be nominated for a Best Picture Oscar. With *Aladdin* in 1992 and *The Lion King* in 1994, each Disney musical continued to earn record profits, both films having the highest worldwide grosses of their respective release years. Not so coincidentally, Tim Rice was the lyricist for both of these films (taking over on *Aladdin* when Ashman passed away during production). As Kantor and Maslon describe it, 'Disney ingeniously adapted the formula of the Golden Age of Broadway for a contemporary audience' and not only revived a faltering studio but saved a dying genre in the process.[29]

With these Disney successes signalling the possibility that 1990s audiences might be more open to a heroine bursting into song, taking a chance on *Evita* suddenly seemed less of an artistic or commercial stretch. And with Madonna now guaranteed to play Evita, the film was likely to attract an audience that might not otherwise have been interested in a Broadway-generated musical film. On the other hand, having Madonna on board did not guarantee a financial 'slam dunk.' Whereas the 1980s began with Madonna exploding onto the pop scene and ended with her being named 'Artist of the Decade' by MTV, *Billboard* and *Musician* magazine, the 1990s started out less auspiciously for Madonna. With the release of a controversial sexually explicit book, aptly entitled *Sex*, as well as playing lead roles in graphic films (such as 1993's *Body of Evidence* and *Dangerous Game*) that were received negatively by fans and critics alike, the once high-flying superstar was facing an identity crisis: would she be known for her creative influence on popular music and her well-received performances in quality films like *Desperately Seeking Susan* (1985) and *A League of Their Own* (1992)? Or would she be viewed as an overrated narcissist, whose career took a fatal turn emphasizing shock over art. By 1996 it seemed very likely that the answer would come by way of her performance in *Evita*, which was now in the seemingly able and experienced hands of Alan Parker. Given Parker's hard-nosed, edgy style as a director, one might have suspected him to follow some aspects of Hal Prince's ambivalent interpretation, shining a harsh light on the sort of scheming, ambitious, sexually charged vixen usually played by Madonna. Instead, the writing and direction of the film version of *Evita* takes basically the *opposite* approach. 'I ignored the stage play completely,' said Parker, 'as the theatrical decisions that Hal Prince made bore little relevance to a cinematic interpretation.'[30]

As suggested, Parker did view *Evita* as a Cinderella story, which could explain his gentler approach. But in casting a celebrity who daringly evoked a much darker persona, one would imagine Parker would invoke *some* of the moral ambiguity that made the stage Eva so fascinating. Yet Parker, Madonna, and Stigwood seemed bent on evoking the audience's sympathy for its tragic heroine.

There could be a variety of possible explanations for Parker's more 'heroic' Evita. He simply might have seen the way the superstar's own fans had turned on her when she began producing and performing more salacious material or 'behaved badly' in public, as when she swore inappropriately throughout a TV interview with David Letterman in 1994. Or perhaps the film's more sympathetic Eva was designed to combat the increasingly shallow, egotistical reputation of its star, fearing that the moviegoing masses would not be as tolerant of an unsympathetic heroine as their theatregoing counterparts. Or perhaps Parker (a fan of the original album version of Evita) shared Scott Miller's view that Tim Rice's material (and Eva's story) was inherently sympathetic. Whatever the reason, the Eva Peron presented in the film is indeed sympathetic, with newly created flashbacks, scenes, lyrics, and entire songs crafted for the purpose of gaining insight into and empathy for Eva. Although these changes may have succeeded in giving superstar Madonna a more compassionate role to play, did they serve to make *Evita* a better film? Before attempting to answer that question, it is advisable to look at the most significant changes and adjustments made to story and character in adapting *Evita* from stage to screen.

Interestingly, the first—and one of the most significant—changes involves a character other than Eva. In the original conception of *Evita*, both as a concept album and theatrical production, Rice and Webber envisioned Che as a sort of Argentinian Everyman, narrating and commenting on the positive and negative aspects of *Evita*, presenting a fairly objective point of view. As mentioned earlier, Prince *chose* to portray the character as the embodiment of the iconic South American Marxist revolutionary figure Che Guevera. Although historical facts reveal that Guevera and Eva almost certainly never crossed paths, and that Guevera's years as the militant rebel portrayed by David Essex and Mandy Patinkin, respectively, in the original London and New York productions, did not coincide with Eva Peron's rise to power and fame, Prince felt it would be effective to position Che as a combination narrator/judge. The real Che Guevera would not have been a fan of Eva Peron, and the character of Che as played in these initial productions represents her harshest critic.

But for the film version, Parker and company abandon the Guevera model, and opt for the 'everyman' figure as envisioned by Lloyd Webber and Rice. Casting heartthrob Antonio

Banderas in the role, Che is first seen seated among the stricken audience members in a Buenos Aires movie theatre, reacting to the news of the death of Eva Peron. It is obvious by his wardrobe and bruised face that Banderas is playing a commoner, not Che Guevera. And while there is something of an ambivalence about Banderas's reaction to the news of her death, he is clearly neither cynical nor unmoved, which is the attitude portrayed in the original production, as the words 'Oh what a circus, oh what a show' emanate from Che's lips as he takes in the spectacle of the mourning masses. This shot of a grieving Che transitions to a flashback sequence, added for the film version, which is positioned as perhaps the defining moment of Eva's life. Captioned 'Chivilcoy—1926' we are transported to the scene of Eva's father's funeral, where we find a seven-year-old Eva with her mother and siblings being barred from attending the funeral. Eva's mother, clearly of the lower classes, pleads with the man's wife—of a higher class—to let his children into the funeral. But the wife calls the children bastards, propelling Eva to run past the blockade into the elaborate church, to the shock of the well-dressed mourners. After Eva places flowers on her father's embalmed corpse, she is dragged away, literally kicking and screaming. This incident—alluded to only by a single sentence in the stage version—seems to motivate and even justify much of Eva's animosity towards the 'middle classes' for the rest of the film's narrative.

The subsequent transition back to Eva's own extravagant, lavish state funeral is interrupted by Che, now seated alone at a bar, singing the same 'Oh What a Circus,' but here, in civilian clothes, he seems more like a jilted lover drowning his sorrows than a rebel with a political axe to grind. As he walks through the crowd of mourners, though the words he sings are critical of Eva, Banderas exudes more bitterness than hatred. It is interesting to note that twenty-first-century theatrical director Michael Grandage must have had a positive reaction to the choice of Che as 'everyman,' as he chose the non-Guevera approach in his 2012 revival.

What follows immediately is the story of Eva's rise to fame, from her seduction of small-time tango singer Magaldi to her eventual bedding of the highly decorated Colonel Juan Peron. On stage, as indicated by the cynical lyrics of such songs as 'Buenos Aires,' Eva's ascension is calculated, fuelled by a lust for power, devoid of sympathy or feeling for those she encounters along the way. Magaldi is presented as a pathetic, if not sympathetic, character who genuinely warns Eva to 'Beware of the City.' But Eva uses blackmail and sex to get her way, blithely tossing Magaldi aside for more 'useful' paramours. As a disgusted Che sings the cynical 'Goodnight and Thank You,' we watch Eva seduce then toss aside a string of other men, once they have served her purpose in advancing her career as an actress in Buenos Aires.

Via sometimes subtle but always significant changes, Eva's rise to fame is portrayed quite differently in the movie. The major change involves her relationship with the small-time singer Magaldi. Although the lyrics still indicate that she is guided by ambition and she flirts heavily with other men, the audience is apparently meant to believe that she is indeed in love with, or at least cares for, Magaldi—so much so that when Magaldi ends their fling by returning to his wife and children, Eva looks on heartbroken.

At this point, a major change occurs in the storytelling. In response to the rejection by Magaldi, Madonna launches into 'Another Suitcase in Another Hall.' The most logical reason for this change is that the song is generally considered one of the Lloyd Webber-Rice team's best and surely a pop legend like Madonna would want to sing all the best songs in the show. The difficulty with this choice, however, is that the lyrics indicate that the singer is the kind of person who repeatedly trusts in people then finds herself tossed back onto the streets, asking plaintively, 'So what happens now? Where am I going to?' When this song is sung as originally intended—by Peron's teenage mistress—it is meant to convey a character who is completely the opposite of Evita. In fact, it is when Evita coldly displaces the mistress and throws her out of Peron's house that she sings the song. The implication is that unlike this lost soul, Eva Peron never has to ask what happens now or where she is going. She knows what happens next because she decides where she is going, who she is going with, and what she will do when she gets there. (Tellingly, Eva does sing these words later in the play—when she knows she is dying, the one obstacle she cannot conquer.) But the film leaves us with a very different Eva at this point. After being rejected by Magaldi, the song continues as Eva suffers humiliations at auditions and other rejections. She is thus presented as a naïve, jilted young woman looking for love and success and Che's newly softened, borderline romantic reactions to her do nothing to dissuade us from that view.

The second act of the film, beginning when Eva and Peron meet at a major charity event, sticks a bit closer to the original stage musical. One might attribute this in part to the fact that once she marries Peron, Eva's actions are a matter of public record, so there is less room for blatant reinterpretation. But the portrayal of Eva's relationship with Peron and her subsequent tenure as the First Lady of Argentina do lean towards the sympathetic. One clear example is when Eva addresses the masses in *Evita*'s signature number, 'Don't Cry for Me, Argentina.' Parker makes use of the close up here to draw us inside Eva's mind and see this musical monologue from her point of view. So, whereas on stage, the theatre audience is left to watch Eva from afar—much like the Argentinians watching from beneath the balcony of the Casa Rosada—and can only speculate about her sincerity, the film brings us up-close and personal, where Madonna betrays nothing but sincerity and even genuine humility behind the now-familiar words. The accompanying close-ups of the adoring crowd, the shots of Peron—played by an intensely focused Jonathan Pryce—bathed in light as he looks at her lovingly, and especially the flashbacks of her rise to the top, beginning with the crying little girl banished from her Daddy's funeral, all combine to present a woman who is both loving and beloved. Che is only given two brief reaction shots during the number, and though he shakes his head with slight scepticism when she sings of her disinterest in 'fortune and fame,' he is compelled to look at her more as an object of desire than scorn.

On both stage and screen, when the song is done, a stuffy politician rains on Eva's parade singing, 'Statesmanship is more than entertaining peasants.' On stage, Eva sharply replies, 'We will see, little man!' The implication of course is that she agrees that they are peasants but she knows how to handle them. In the film, Eva does not seem to hear his remark, and the snide retort is given by her mother, thus preserving the sincerity of Eva's address to her people. The sequences involving Eva's jaunt through Europe, the so-called Rainbow Tour, invariably evoke some sympathy even in the stage version of *Evita*, in part because she is portrayed as a victim of prejudice by arrogant aristocrats. Additionally, this is the sequence where Eva's health begins to fail, and vulnerability is inevitable, no matter what the directorial interpretation.

Upon Eva's return home, she starts her charitable foundation, leading to the cleverly double-edged 'And the Money Kept Rolling In (and Out).' Onstage, the song is sung by Che with vitriolic disdain. In the film, Che sings the song, but it is accompanied by images of Eva Peron doing a series of wonderful things for a grateful nation. When the lyrics suggest that funds are being misappropriated, we see other government officials doing the dirty deeds, possibly without Eva's knowledge.

Two songs that are performed during the film's final act potentially solidify the film's point of view of Eva Peron as a probably well-meaning, mostly sympathetic, inherently romantic heroine. In his extended synopsis of the original 1979 Broadway production of *Evita* for his 1995 volume, *Gänzl's Book of the Broadway Musical*, Kurt Gänzl describes the 'Waltz for Eva and Che' as the point in the show when 'Che faces up to Evita to belittle both her work and her image.'³¹ But even though the lyrics indicate a hostile encounter between adversaries, the movie stages the number romantically, with soft lighting and sweeping choreography that evoke memories of the waltz in *Beauty and the Beast* and 'Shall We Dance?' of *The King and I*. It is probably not a coincidence that both those numbers represent a revelation of romantic interest for the participants—and one gets the feeling that the same is happening in the film version of *Evita*. As if to underscore the point, the stage version of the dance ends with Che physically pushing Eva away. In the film, the dance ends when Eva passes out, too weak to go on.

The original stage version of *Evita* proceeds quickly from this point to Eva's ultimate death. Peron sings of Eva's value, albeit a declining one, in 'She Is a Diamond' while Eva tries to ignore the inevitable and voices her desire to be Argentina's next vice president. But Peron insists she is too ill and 'a jeering Che,' in Gänzl's words, 'is only too happy to remind her [that] this time she has lost,' Eva then takes to the airwaves with a farewell radio broadcast reprising her mantra of 'Don't Cry for Me, Argentina,' and then she dies, her final words indicating that she leaves no regrets behind. As such, the play's final focus is on the passing of a dubious political figure and the still-unanswered questions about her value to her country and the sincerity of her stated plight.

Although the template for the story remains the same for the film, following the documented history of Eva Peron's final days, the film uses music and cinematic techniques to shift the focus of the ending to Eva as a romantic figure, not just in the eyes of the people, but specifically in her relationship with her husband. It is customary for film adaptations of stage musicals to add at least one totally new number, with the goal, at least in part, to garner an Academy Award nomination for Best Original Song. But the addition of 'You Must Love Me' has far greater impact and resonance on the story, theme, and tone of *Evita*.

To demonstrate the public's perspective on both Madonna and Eva prior to the film's release, when word came out that a number had been added with the title 'You Must Love Me,' some assumed that the song would be about the character of Eva angrily insisting—even ordering—those around her that they *must* love her, because she is insisting they do and that is reason enough. It was therefore very surprising to see the film and discover that the song is meant as an epiphany on Eva's part, her realization that if Peron can still show her such attention and affection when she is dying and no longer of any use to him, then he must love her after all. When she sings 'Deep in my heart I'm concealing/Things that I'm longing to say/Scared to confess what I'm feeling/Frightened you'll slip away'[32] it is really the first time since their courtship that Eva realizes that she does love Peron, the man, and is afraid of losing him, not just the love of the people or the power it brings.

When Ernest Lehmann's 1965 screenplay of *The Sound of Music* proved so much more effective—and commercially successful—than the Lindsay/Crouse book for the 1959 stage version, subsequent stage productions began incorporating its changes into the script. The same is true for other musicals, most notably revivals of *Cabaret* produced after the hit Bob Fosse film. Given this trend, it is interesting that 'You Must Love Me' is the most prominent newly created aspect of the film that made its way into Michael Grandage's recent revival.

The author attended a performance of that production on the US tour, and it was clear that Grandage's choice went beyond the desire to include an Oscar-winning song in his version. Because even though the new stage version still presents a mostly unsympathetic portrait of Eva, the addition of the poignant song—and its admission of legitimate emotional feelings—urges the audience to look at Eva Peron's impending death as tragic, the passing of a character who, late in her short life, discovers that she could be needed or loved for something beyond power, fame, or money. Without the revelatory 'You Must Love Me,' *Evita* ends as basically an 'I told you so' for our narrator Che Guevera or otherwise. With it, the element of romance shares the stage with politics.

Of course, Parker's film version, which has shown us Eva's vulnerability, sensitivity, and sincerity for over two hours by this point, serves up an ending filled with extended close-ups of Eva on her deathbed, her emotional confessions unquestionably heartfelt, followed by the reactions of those around her, most notably her devoted mother and loving husband. And finally, at her funeral, Peron and Che stand over Eva's coffin, like two lovers vying for a claim on the beautiful glass-encased corpse before them. Though the words he sings still invoke questions about Eva's true motivations and impact, the tenderness in Bandera's voice is unmistakable. And when he leans down and kisses her coffin, Peron, played by the older, less gorgeous Pryce, glares at Che as though Eva's lover has been revealed. In metaphoric terms this could mean that Peron is jealous that the people—symbolized by Che—were Eva's true love. But in the well-established language of Hollywood, the kiss, the very last action of the film, proves what was hinted at all along, that Banderas's Che was always in love with Madonna's Eva.

The success or failure of any big-budget Hollywood-produced motion picture is inevitably going to be judged by its success at the box office, and *Evita*, taking in over $100,000,000 worldwide definitely qualifies as a success, as well as probably encouraging investment in subsequent musicals like *Moulin Rouge* and *Chicago*. But the critical reception to *Evita* was lukewarm at best, with Madonna receiving some particularly scathing reviews and being ignored by the Motion Picture Academy for an Oscar nomination. (The Foreign Press did award her a Golden Globe for the performance.) In any event, the film certainly did not evoke the extreme reactions that emanated from the Harold Prince stage version. And after careful examination of the differences between the versions, these alternate results make perfect sense. For onstage, Prince's production was straightforward and critical, as if to say 'You think this show is shallow and simplistic? Look who it's about!' Whereas for a movie counting on the box office appeal of its mega-star, the filmmakers seemed well aware that whether we're referring to Madonna or Eva, you 'must love her' or you're not going to pay to see the film.

## NOTES

1. Ted Sennet, *Hollywood Musicals* (New York: Harry N. Abrams, 1981), 283.
2. Stephen Citron, *Sondheim and Lloyd-Webber: The New Musical* (New York: Oxford University Press, 2001), 111.
3. Citron, *Sondheim and Lloyd-Webber*, 192–193.
4. Citron, *Sondheim and Lloyd-Webber*, 191.
5. Scott Miller, 'Inside Evita,' 2010, https://www.newlinetheatre.com/evitachapter.html. accessed 4 January 2019.
6. Miller, 'Inside Evita.'
7. Andrew Ganz, 'In Upcoming Revival of *Evita*, Che Will Be the "Everyman" Not Che Guevara,' February 2012, Playbill.com, accessed March 2017.

8. https://www.gringoinbuenosaires.com/five-argentine-spanish-words/, accessed 4 January 2019.
9. Citron, *Sondheim and Lloyd-Webber*, 230.
10. Ben Brantley, *Broadway Musicals* (New York: Abrams, 2012), 264.
11. David Sheward, NY Review: Evita, 5 April 2012, https://www.backstage.com/magazine/article/ny-review-evita-52397/, accessed 4 January 2019.
12. Shmoop Editorial Team, 'Culture in the Reagan Era,' November 2008, http://www.shmoop.com/reagan-era/culture.html, accessed 4 January 2019.
13. Miller, 'Inside Evita.'
14. Miller, 'Inside Evita.'
15. Miller, 'Inside Evita.'
16. The Eddie Mannix Ledger, Margaret Herrick Library, Center for Motion Picture Study, Los Angeles.
17. Michael Kantor and Lawrence Maslon, *Broadway: The American Musical* (New York: Bulfinch Press, 2004), 190.
18. Matthew Kennedy, *Roadshow: The Fall of Film Musicals in the 1960s* (New York: Oxford University Press, 2014), 23–24.
19. Kennedy, *Roadshow*, 23–24.
20. Kennedy, *Roadshow*, 249.
21. https://www.boxofficemojo.com/movies/?id=chorusline.htm, accessed 4 January 2019.
22. James Greenberg, 'Is It Now Time to Cry for Evita?' *New York Times*, 19 November 1989.
23. David Ansen, 'Madonna Tangos with Evita,' *Newsweek*, 15 December 1996.
24. Alan Parker, 'EVITA – Alan Parker – Director, Writer, Producer,' http://alanparker.com/film/evita/making/, accessed 4 January 2019.
25. Parker, 'EVITA.'
26. Lucy O'Brien, *Madonna: Like an Icon* (London: Bantam Press, 2008), 305–306.
27. Madonna Ciccone, 'The Madonna Diaries,' *Vanity Fair*, November 1996.
28. Gonthier, David F. Jr, and Timothy L. O'Brien, *The Films of Alan Parker, 1976–2003* (Jefferson, NC: McFarland, 2015).

29. Kantor and Maslon, *Broadway*, 420.
30. Parker, *Evita*.
31. Kurt Gänzl, *Gänzl's Book of the Broadway Musical* (New York: Schirmer Books, 1995).
32. Tim Rice, 'You Must Love Me,' *Evita* (1996).

# 3

# *Brigadoon* and Its Transition to MGM Dance Musical

## *Adapting a Stage Show for Star Dancers*

### SUSAN SMITH

■ □ ■

REFLECTING ON THE SECOND OF three MGM film musicals in which she appeared with Gene Kelly,[1] Cyd Charisse once mused:

> *Brigadoon* was a beautiful film, but somehow it missed. I've never really understood why that happened but it did. Motion pictures are funny that way; they can seemingly have all the ingredients, as *Brigadoon* had, and yet when they are all put together, the whole is less than the sum of its parts. Whatever the reason, *Brigadoon* never lived up to our expectations. It made money—I'm proud of the fact that I was never in a financial flop—but it wasn't quite the picture it should have been, despite Lerner's great talents.[2]

In the memoirs from which the above quote is taken, Charisse alludes to some of the problems encountered during the filming of *Brigadoon*—the studio's original intention, reportedly, to shoot the picture on location in Scotland along with the lesser known tension between director Vincente Minnelli and actor Van Johnson[3] and her own one-and-only spat with Kelly.[4] Overall, though, she presents *Brigadoon* as something of an enigma in failing to realize its full potential, despite referring to it as 'one of my favorite films.'[5] If Charisse is noncommittal as to why *Brigadoon* supposedly fell short of expectations, Alan Jay Lerner—the film's screenwriter and lyricist (and librettist for the stage show)—is more forthright: 'It was a picture that should have been made on location in Scotland and was done in the studio. It was a singing show that tried to become a dancing show, and it had an all-American cast which should have been all-Scottish.'[6]

In his autobiography, Vincente Minnelli mirrors Lerner's comments, invoking Gene Kelly's views in support.[7] Of these, two factors—the decision to shoot the picture entirely on MGM's sound stage at Culver City instead of on location, as originally planned, and to turn *Brigadoon* from a show that had been designed for singers on the stage into one suited for dancers on the movie screen—are most frequently cited as proof that the film transpired into a disappointing adaptation of a highly successful Broadway musical. In relation to the first reason, Clive Hirschhorn, one of Kelly's biographers, attributes the film's perceived failure, above all, to the lack of location work. His view that '[Dore] Schary's decision to confine *Brigadoon* to a sound stage was, unfortunately, a bad one, and the film never recovered from it'[8] would become enshrined in the dominant narrative regarding *Brigadoon*'s critical reception. The decision to film in CinemaScope is also described by Alvin Yudkoff (another Kelly biographer) as 'the nail in the coffin for the movie' and something about which 'Gene was to complain bitterly in interviews throughout the years.'[9]

Criticisms of the film on account of its studio-bound artifice have sometimes become entwined, as well, with indictments of its portrayal of Scotland according to an ersatz view that has no correspondence in reality. Producer Arthur Freed's much-quoted statement (on returning to Hollywood from a scouting trip to the Highlands) that 'Scotland did not look Scottish enough,'[10] has occasionally been enlisted in support, with the film criticized for eschewing the greater naturalism that cinema (compared to theatre) affords through (among other things) location shooting. Yet although this line of thought has become strongly entrenched in *Brigadoon* scholarship, it has been challenged in recent years, most notably by Colin McArthur and Murray Pomerance. Despite their very different approaches, both scholars take issue with some of the recurring criticisms of the film on account of its studio artifice. Hence, McArthur maintains that 'there is no intrinsic reason why shooting outdoors should be more artistically valuable than shooting on a built set' and indeed, for him, the latter's 'unreality' actually gels far more with the film's 'overall theme' 'than the stubborn authenticity of actual landscapes.'[11] Noting critics' failure to recognize Kelly and Freed's need—as makers of cinematic musicals—'to create a space more mythical than historical,'[12] Pomerance also reconstrues the extreme artifice of *Brigadoon*'s setting not as 'a flaw . . . as so many critics scathingly thought at the time' but, rather, as a strength that enables 'viewers of *Brigadoon* [to] have a deliriously mixed sensation of reality and illusion.'[13]

If this counterargument regarding the imaginative effects arising from *Brigadoon*'s studio-bound set suggest there may be more to our experience of this movie than previously cited criticisms have tended to allow, then what of the claim that the film also suffered from being reworked into a musical for dancers (rather than singers)? This other crucial dimension to the show's transfer to the movie screen has received much less critical scrutiny so, with that in mind, the purpose of my chapter is to redress such neglect. Basing my analysis on two songs which each played a prominent role in the original

Broadway production but which met starkly different fates in the film adaptation, I hope to demonstrate, above all, both the benefits and losses arising from MGM's transformation of the stage show along these lines.

To describe the original Broadway production as a musical for singers requires some qualification, however, since it overlooks the significant contribution made to that show by dance, the responsibility for which lay with the show's choreographer Agnes de Mille, who had already received acclaim for her work on Rogers and Hammerstein's landmark Broadway production of *Oklahoma!*[14] In her study of de Mille, Kara Anne Gardner traces this important female choreographer's role in shaping the Broadway production of *Brigadoon*.[15] Gardner notes how de Mille worked harmoniously with director Robert Lewis to create seamless transitions between the drama and musical numbers, and she also examines how de Mille built up the character of Harry Ritchie, the dissatisfied figure (renamed Harry Beaton in the film) who (as developed by her) tries to leave Brigadoon, making him central to her staging of the dances.[16]

Nonetheless, as originally written for the stage, *Brigadoon* was primarily conceived for singers. The libretto for the 1947 Broadway show lists twelve songs (fourteen including the 'Prologue' and 'Vendors' Calls') while both male and female leads are specified as singers: Tommy is described as 'Light Baritone' (Low B–High G) and Fiona as 'Lyric Soprano' (Low B–High A [optional B flat]).[17] Under de Mille's expert guidance, the dance component of the stage show evolved alongside the singing although, according to Stephen Harvey, these two elements coexisted fairly independently of each other:

> As with many of the ambitious stage musicals written in the shadow of Rodgers and Hammerstein, *Brigadoon*'s principals were singers who couldn't move, complemented by a dance

troupe barely required to speak. As pop arias alternated with Agnes de Mille ballets, they rarely shared the stage, brushing kilts in the wings and then again at the final curtain call.[18]

In interview, Gene Kelly himself comments that 'when the studio bought [*Brigadoon*] from the stage play it was certainly done for singers' and that 'the only big dancing in it were the Scottish dances and sword dances.'[19] *Brigadoon*'s status as predominantly a stage show for singers can be linked to the post-*Oklahoma!* phase of the Broadway musical which, as Jerome Delamater points out, was characterized by a 'trend in stage musicals towards a kind of folk opera, [in which] dance became less significant, even though it did have persistent manifestations.'[20] Indeed, according to Delamater, 'By the late fifties film makers were rationalizing not using dance in films,'[21] and he quotes Vincente Minnelli as saying that 'Alan Lerner started the kind of school of musicals that had very little dancing, and the lyrics are like dialogue.'[22] As Delamater notes, the 1950s was also a time when the American film musical— weakened by economic pressures within Hollywood and the advent of rock music in popular culture—became increasingly reliant on producing respectful adaptations of successful Broadway shows (a growing feature of which was their song-driven nature).[23] Harvey concurs, observing that Hollywood's deference towards 'the security of pre-sold hits from the stage' was largely at the expense of the original film musical, despite (as he maintains with regard to MGM) the latter's continuing box office popularity.[24]

'One result of [all] this,' Delamater argues, 'was a general feeling of obeisance to the property—an attitude that what had worked once should work again, and many of the films were transferred to the screen without consideration of their potential as film.'[25] Delamater contrasts MGM musical director George Sidney, as an exponent of ultra-fidelity to the stage original, with 'composer and music director Dimitri Tiomkin,' who expressed concern that such an approach 'hardly strikes me as right, healthy or forward looking.'[26] He also quotes Freda June Lockhart as saying in 1957 that the trend towards slavish adherence to the original was 'combining to bring dancing musicals once more to a standstill, to take us to another age of stationary singing spectacle.'[27]

It's fascinating to consider the MGM version of *Brigadoon*, released on 8 September 1954, in the context of all this since it suggests that the film's more specific difficulties may be symptomatic of broader pressures and trends facing the movie musical at this time. MGM's decision to shoot the picture entirely on a sound stage rather than on location in Scotland highlights the financial pressures affecting Hollywood generally, not to mention the studio's waning confidence in the movie musical's profitability. For some critics, this decision also rendered *Brigadoon* vulnerable to the charge that it sought to play safe by subscribing to a form of artifice more reminiscent of a work of musical theatre.[28] That *Brigadoon* was an adaptation of a Broadway show couched in the folk opera tradition can only have compounded its struggle to establish an independent identity. Yet while the casting of dancers in the lead roles may have been partly influenced by financial considerations concerning who was already under contract, the studio's decision to reorient *Brigadoon* in this way and to hire not Agnes de Mille but Gene Kelly as choreographer suggests a less than faithful adherence to the stage play, countering that tendency towards 'obeisance' that Delamater detects in movie musical adaptations during the mid- to late fifties.

Thus, when *Brigadoon* was adapted into an MGM musical, the lead roles that had been performed by singers David Brooks and Marion Bell on Broadway were assigned to Gene Kelly and Cyd Charisse, two of Hollywood's most famous dancers, with Kelly doubling up as choreographer. As Dominic McHugh notes, there had been initial interest from J. Arthur Rank, who 'for many months . . . pursued the rights to make the film in England, with Bing Crosby as the lead.'[29] Once MGM bought *Brigadoon*, however, it seems that Gene Kelly was always the first choice for the male lead although Kathryn Grayson was initially envisaged for the role of Fiona before being replaced by Charisse when Grayson's contract expired. Harvey and Yudkoff both suggest that Scottish-born ballet dancer Moira Shearer was considered for the part before Charisse, but McArthur casts doubt on this idea.[30]

That singing star Grayson was initially earmarked to play Fiona suggests MGM had initially contemplated closer adherence to the stage original. Irrespective of whether Shearer was then considered, though, the decision to cast a dancer as Kelly's female costar appears to have been taken fairly easily despite the deviation this posed from the Broadway show. On the mismatch created by MGM's casting of two of its foremost star dancers in a show originally designed for singers, the film's musical director, Johnny Green, refers to this as tantamount to having 'two dancers in a vocal operetta,' describing Kelly as someone 'who sings with a kind of appealing, husky, Irish high baritone to low tenor' while the 'monotone' Charisse 'cannot carry a tune.'[31]

To accommodate the casting of 'two dancers in a vocal operetta,' significant changes were made to the songs. Most obviously, Charisse's singing had to be dubbed, as it was in all of her pictures, in this case by Carol Richards.[32] Possessed with a more proficient singing voice, Kelly sings his own songs in *Brigadoon*—whether joining in with Van Johnson (who plays his character's best friend, Jeff) in the all-male ensemble number 'I'll Go Home with Bonnie Jean' or serenading Fiona in the lyrical lead-in to 'The Heather on the Hill' or celebrating 'Almost Like Being in Love' in front of a bemused Jeff. But two of his character's songs that had been such a prominent part of the stage show—Tommy Albright's solo ballad 'There But for You Go I' and his duet 'From This Day On' with Fiona—were cut at various points during production.

Of the songs that survived, several (e.g., 'Go Home with Bonnie Jean,' 'Waitin' for My Dearie') were reworked either entirely or in part around the dancing talents of the film's stars. Two of the show's major songs—'The Heather on the Hill' and 'Almost Like Being in Love'—were originally designed as romantic duets sung by Tommy and Fiona to each other. In the MGM production, though, the first is reworked so that only Tommy sings the opening verses to Fiona as a prelude to a balletic dance they perform together instead (accompanied by an orchestral version of the song) while the second is recast as Kelly's big solo number which he now sings and dances to entirely in the presence of his best friend Jeff, Fiona being absent throughout.

Not all of the song deletions arose from the film's casting of star dancers in the lead roles. Two of the Broadway production's most successful songs—Meg Brockie's 'The Love of My Life' and 'My Mother's Wedding Day'—were censored by the Breen Office on account of their salacious lyrics, so much so that these numbers were never part of the screenplay and hence never shot. Another key song, 'Come to Me, Bend to Me'—sung by Charlie Dalrymple (Jimmy Thompson, dubbed by John Gustafsen) to his bride-to-be Jean (Virginia Bosler) outside her father's home on their wedding day—was cut during production, a decision perhaps also partly motivated by a desire to trim the romantic subplot so it didn't distract from the main romance between Tommy and Fiona. The more minor tune, 'Jeannie's Packin' Up' (performed on stage as part of an ensemble piece involving Jean's female friends) was removed as well. One other song by Fiona—'Dinna You Know Tommy'—sung by her to Tommy just before he leaves Brigadoon and originally as a prelude to 'From This Day On'—was dropped too. In total, then, seven of the twelve Lerner and Loewe songs present in the original stage show didn't make it into the film (two due to censorship, five as a result of decisions made during production). In their feedback on the two audience preview screenings of MGM's *Brigadoon* on 4 and 15 June 1954, viewers protested repeatedly about the omission of these songs[33] as well as the 'Sword Dance' (performed during the Wedding scene), commenting on the contribution they had made to the stage show and questioning why New York Ballet dancer Hugh Laing's role as Harry Beaton in the film had been reduced to a mainly acting part only. 'I'll never understand why people buy a lot of good material and throw out much of it to make room for some inferior added material' carped one audience member, before adding, 'but, in this case, there is plenty left.'[34] Others complained testily about Kelly's performance and MGM's adapting of the stage show to suit him: 'I loved play, but with picture M-G-M took a vehicle for voices and made it into a Gene Kelly show case, cutting good show tunes and Pamela Britton [Meg Brockie] part especially. Kelly's dances getting to look all alike.'[35] Although frequent comments about the painted sets and scenery are generally very positive, with some even suggesting the film is more successful than the stage show, the recurring complaints about the cutting of certain songs tend to endorse the idea that *Brigadoon* was a musical for singers that had to be adapted into one for dancers. As if to bear this out, the award-winning telecast in 1966 goes some way towards re-turning the show to its original format, casting baritone Robert Goulet in Gene Kelly's role and soprano Sally Anne Howes[36] as Fiona, restaging the MGM film's dance-oriented numbers as songs, and reinstating several (albeit not all) of the omitted numbers.

It wasn't just certain songs that were cut from the film version of *Brigadoon*. Many of the dance elements were also dropped or altered when the Broadway show was transferred to the big screen (most notably the 'Sword Dance,' which had been performed adeptly on Broadway by James Mitchell in the role of Harry Ritchie/Beaton). This can be explained partly in terms of the adjustments necessitated by the CinemaScope format but it also owes much to MGM's decision to replace De Mille with Gene Kelly as choreographer. According to Yudkoff, although de Mille's choreographic approach chimed artistically with Kelly's, 'he had no intention of collaborating with her' since 'at this point it would do his fading career no good merely to serve as a conduit for De Mille, ushering her well-received dance concepts into the film version.'[37]

In the case of the chief choreographic casualty arising from *Brigadoon*'s transition from stage to screen, it's possible to concur with McArthur: 'Measured against the stage version, the film may have lost dramatic force by dropping the Sword Dance in which symbolically violent activity Harry was the main actor.'[38] Yet perhaps it isn't altogether surprising that a number centred around a dancer (Hugh Laing), highly regarded in the world of ballet[39] but relatively unknown cinematically, was eliminated from a film driven largely by the star talents of its two main dancers.[40] According to Delamater, however, the notion of the musical as a star vehicle was itself under threat in the 1950s. Drawing on John Cutts, he argues that whereas 'formerly the star—not the property itself—drew the audience . . . later the property became the attraction, thus reflecting a change in the audience's attitude.'[41] If this is the case, then perhaps part of *Brigadoon*'s difficulty as a movie musical is that its appeal lay somewhere confusingly on the border between still being perceived as a star vehicle (for Kelly and Charisse), on the one hand, but now also being considered as a 'property,' on the other (namely, a screen transfer of a Broadway show with all of the 'adaptation baggage' this entails).

In moving on to consider how MGM's reworking of *Brigadoon* into a dance musical for its two main stars affects the finished film, my aim is to remain sensitive to the possibilities and rewards—not just difficulties and problems—resulting from this crucial aspect of the show's adaptation. Rather than concentrating exclusively on the depletions arising from, say, the dropping or reframing of certain songs, we need to ask what does it mean to have the lead characters now engaging in dance instead of or as well as song, and how does this enhance, rather than merely detract from, the show? Conversely, what are the implications of having Kelly sing and what issues arise from the cutting of some of his songs?

In addressing these questions in the next two sections, our main focus is on the reconceptualized 'The Heather on the Hill' number and the deleted 'There But for You Go I' ballad, respectively. By scrutinizing, in turn, the contrasting destinies of these two songs, the chapter considers how the cinematic restaging of 'The Heather on the Hill' number demonstrates what can be gained when a stage musical composed primarily for singers is altered to suit the dancing talents of its film counterpart's costars. Having done so, it turns to reflect (in the second and final section) on how the cutting of the ballad 'There But for You Go I' conversely shows what may be squandered, too, in the process.

## DANCING TO 'THE HEATHER ON THE HILL'

On assessing the implications arising from the reconfiguring of 'The Heather on the Hill' number, it's easy to see how the film version threatens to remove the more equal interplay made possible through the singing duet. By having only Kelly sing the opening section and removing Fiona's singing part altogether, it places him in the conventional male role of initiator and serenader of the romance. In terms of the dance itself, moreover,

McArthur finds the choreography suggestive of 'a patriarchal wooing with Kelly quite literally chasing Charisse across the hill and she feigning resistance and then succumbing.'[42] But restaging the second half of the number as a pas de deux also enables Fiona and Tommy to discover their feelings for each other in ways that now entail a physical exploration (and interaction) with the landscape around them. This is very different from the more introspective performance style encouraged by the romantic sung duet, where the would-be lovers—on singing passionately to each other—are liable to become isolated from and oblivious to their surroundings.

The inclusion of a dance segment therefore makes greater sense, arguably, of the song's subject matter, which is after all about Fiona and Tommy searching for the heather on the hill and, in the process, falling in love with each other. In emphasizing the landscape as a brooding physical presence that literally surrounds and envelops the two lovers while their romance is playing out, this reworked number is more in tune with the story's dramatic needs, suggesting that their relationship cannot be forged in isolation of Brigadoon's world but, rather, must be defined in relation to it.

Minnelli and Kelly's staging of 'The Heather on the Hill' creatively exploits this idea in ways that complicate any sense that the hillside setting affords Fiona and Tommy a romantic release from the confines of the village. Moments before their dance begins, for example (with Tommy still singing to Fiona), they walk up the hill and stand facing each other beside a silver birch tree. As they remain in this pose, a wayward branch cuts diagonally between them, reaching upwards from left to right of screen, symbolically separating them in a visual reminder of Brigadoon's ability to intrude on their romance and keep them apart (see ▶ video example 18.1). This detailed use of mise-en-scène invests the couple's burgeoning love for each other with a special fragility, building on the solitary flute/oboe at the start of Conrad Salinger's exquisite orchestration and the song's tentative couching of Tommy's serenade in the form of a question ('Can't we two go walking together . . .?') (Figure 3.1).

The heather of the song's title itself represents not simply a literal goal but an object of yearning that encapsulates and stands in for their romantic desire. As the setting for their dance, the heather-clad hillside is located within the boundaries of the village and, as such, represents a distant yet safe site wherein Fiona and Tommy can begin to explore their feelings for each other, allowing them to test out their viability as a couple. Yet, situated on a hillside away from the village, the heather at the same time carries a frisson of danger. Hinting at the prospect of a world beyond Brigadoon, their search for it threatens to pull them away from the town's physical confines and rules, the breaching of which countenances the possibility that the 'miracle' that's brought them together will be destroyed. Indeed, it's shortly after this number—following a comic interlude involving Jeff being pursued by Meg Brockie (Dodie Heath)— that a frightened Fiona calls out to Tommy on seeing him at risk of breaching the invisible boundary of their world.

Kelly's choreography beautifully capitalizes on this ambivalence to the hillside setting, investing the initially coy but increasingly enraptured movements of the two dancers with a heightened charge. With their outstretched limbs, lifts, spins, turns, and arching lines counterpointed by inwardly enfolding movements, Tommy and Fiona's dance seems shaped by the landscape within which it's performed, making their acting out of their desire for each other a response also to the spaciousness *and* enclosure afforded by the heather-clad hillside. This idea is encouraged by Kelly's staging of the dance to suit the CinemaScope frame,[43] the greater breadth and shorter height of which (compared to the standard square format or even widescreen ratio) help evoke the tension between freedom and constraint in their emerging relationship.

FIGURE 3.1 The visual composition of this shot complicates the romance of 'The Heather on the Hill' as Tommy (Kelly) sings to Fiona (Charisse) prior to their dance together.

Kelly's choreography also combines with the painted sets and the director's characteristically imaginative use of colour. His organization of the dance 'so that Charisse frequently leans back or bends over with a leg out, in a classical ballet pose that seems inadvertently to mimic the lines of the hills that Gibson has painted'[44] articulates Fiona's affinity with the fantasy world of Brigadoon, suggesting how much her fate is bound up with its landscape. But her balletic movements also suggest a young woman attempting to unfurl herself physically and emotionally in the relatively more open space of this heather-clad hillside, exploring newly awakened feelings for Tommy and finding at least some relief from the social pressures that had previously motivated her to perform 'Waitin' for My Dearie.'

Although the title of that earlier song alludes to the passivity inscribed in her gender destiny, the musical number itself is triggered by one of the young women asking Fiona whether it doesn't worry her that she might not marry by the time she's twenty-five. During the course of 'Waitin' for My Dearie,' Fiona explicitly voices her disagreement with this expectation. 'One day he'll come walkin' o'er the horizon/But should he not then an old maid I'll be' she sings early on. Then, later, in a mock playing out of the courtship ritual, one of the other women appears dressed as a potential suitor and sings, 'But when lassies sit an' have no men/Oh, how long becomes the night,' only for Fiona to respond, 'But I fear the night is longer/When the lad's no' right.' At the time of the film's release, one critic ridiculed the idea that Charisse should play a young woman born in the eighteenth century, arguing that the urban modernity of this dancer's screen image simply wasn't suited to such a role.[45] Yet this quality that Charisse brings to her performance seems to chime with the sentiments expressed by Fiona during 'Waitin' for My Dearie.' It tends to strengthen Fiona's compatibility with Tommy, as well, not to mention her underlying affinity with Harry Beaton (significantly, it's Fiona who empathizes with Harry's sense of entrapment: 'I'm truly sorry' she tells him, on hearing him explain how he feels).

Charisse had, of course, created a stir as the vampish siren who seduces Kelly's character during the 'Broadway Ballet' dream in *Singin' in the Rain* (1952) and one wonders whether this association influenced Minnelli's creative use of editing so as to suggest a more predatory side to Fiona in the sequence leading up to 'The Heather on the Hill' number. Sitting at home, visibly affected by her first encounter with Tommy earlier, Fiona affects outrage on hearing her sister (intrigued by reports that two men have turned up in the village and wondering what they're like) indicate her intention to go and find out whether they're still around. Scolding Jean for even thinking about venturing outside and risk being seen on her wedding day, Fiona is shown hurrying away from the house, basket in hand.

Technically, this scene ends with her turning away from camera and exiting round a tree (doubling back to left of screen). But, in splicing together this shot with the next one showing Meg Brockie emerging (right of screen) from around the corner of another tree (carrying a lamb) and eyeing Jeff as a potential suitor, Minnelli deftly edits them together in a way that presents the unrestrained lust of this comic female figure as an extension or physical embodiment of Fiona's active desires (see ⏵ video example 3.2).

It's a moment of cinematic subterfuge that opens up another dimension to Charisse's character, complicating her outward acceptance of her fate (unlike Harry Beaton) and challenging the film's more explicit assertion of Tommy as romantic predator moments later: 'I thought we were going hunting?' asks Jeff on being plied with another jar of ale to keep him happy, only for Tommy to respond, with a knowing Kelly smile: 'I am,' just before hurrying off in pursuit of Fiona. Charisse's expressive dancing during 'The Heather on the Hill' number consequently

FIGURE 3.2  Fiona leaves the family home, intent on finding Tommy again.

FIGURE 3.3  She exits this scene by hurrying round a nearby tree . . . .

FIGURE 3.4 ... Only for the lustful Meg Brockie to appear from another tree (in a continuation of Fiona's movement) in the next shot.

develops this more complex sense of Fiona, extending those earlier suggestions of her resistance to the cramping social, not just physical, restrictions of life in Brigadoon and providing space for the gradual release of her pent-up desire.

The very different opportunities arising from the decision to stage the second part of 'The Heather on the Hill' as a dance rather than a sung duet culminate as the number draws to a close. As McArthur points out, 'In the stage version, the love duet of 'The Heather on the Hill' ends quietly with Tommy and Fiona looking at each other,' whereas in the film 'Minnelli uses the freedom the cinema confers by ending on a grander note with the camera pulling back rapidly into a long shot to reveal the highland panorama with Tommy and Fiona, just like the audience, turning to admire its "picturesqueness."'[46] McArthur attributes the sweeping camera movement involved to Minnelli, the film's director, but the staging of the two dancers within this shot also seems informed and complicated by Kelly's outlook as choreographer and performer. Hence, as the couple turns to look out towards the distant landscape, Charisse assumes a seated position on a nearby rock while Kelly remains standing, his body appearing more tense and strained than hers as he stares out longingly at the loch and mountains (▶ video example 18.3).

To understand the significance of Kelly's taut physical posture at the end of this number, it's helpful to consider it in the context of his overall approach to dance on film. In a detailed study of this, Delamater writes of Kelly's experimentation 'with the camera in ways specifically aimed at capturing some cinematic equivalent to the sense of kinetic energy inherent in live dance.'[47] In particular, he cites Kelly's awareness of the role of the camera and how the latter's position can affect the viewer's impression of dance in film, noting that 'Kelly felt, therefore, that the camera's movements and/or the dancer's movements must provide some of that same kinetic force which the viewer

FIGURE 3.5 Fiona and Tommy look out towards the loch and mountains at the end of 'The Heather on the Hill' number.

would appreciate seeing dance on a stage.'[48] For Kelly, then, 'the more [the dancer] can go into the camera the more force you'll get . . . [while, on the contrary] as he goes away from the camera, he decreases that force.'[49] Observing that 'this greater involvement with the pro-filmic space required both a choreographing *of* the camera and a conscious choreographing *for* the camera,'[50] Delamater finds examples of dancers moving towards the camera in *It's Always Fair Weather*, another mid-fifties MGM musical released just a year after *Brigadoon* and which Kelly both starred in and codirected with Stanley Donen. Delamater goes on to point out that

Kelly's dictum about movement away from the camera is manifest in the films, too; for when he wants a number to end more or less unobtrusively, to have the dancer or dancers move easily back into the narrative of the film, he ends with movement away from the camera or with the camera pulling back from the action. [Hence] . . . Withholding that kinetic force could serve as advantageously as emphasizing it.[51]

Minnelli's adroit pulling back of the camera to take in a panoramic view of the 'Highlands' at the conclusion of 'The Heather on the Hill' number is at odds with Kelly's theory of the kinetic energy that can be generated through the dancer moving *towards* the camera, offering conditions more suited to an unobtrusive ending. Yet Kelly's taut figure, as he looks out yearningly at the Scottish vista before him, seems to run counter to any sense of unobtrusiveness encouraged by the camera's movement away from the performer, conveying a feeling of tension that isn't entirely dispelled by the number's other-wise uplifting finale. Tommy doesn't yet know about the spell cast over the village (although he suspects something strange about the place) so Kelly's pose doesn't entirely make sense at this point, except perhaps to suggest an instinct in his char-acter to move beyond Brigadoon's invisible boundaries into the world outside (all of which bodes ill for Tommy's relationship with Fiona once he commits to staying in the village with her). Kelly's strained stance gains an altogether profounder resonance, however, when viewed in light of the studio's decision not to shoot the film on location and this actor/choreographer's creative frustrations with the studio-bound set. Considered in relation to that, his longing posture as he stands looking out towards the mountains—towards a painting of a landscape that doesn't really exist but represents (for Kelly) the actual location of Scotland he strove for but could not have—acquires a deeper logic.

The decision to shoot entirely on the studio sound stage rather than on location has often been cited as evidence of the film's flaws, with any shortcomings in Kelly's choreography and performance commonly explained as a consequence of his disappointment with that decision. The complexity of this moment at the end of 'The Heather on The Hill,' however, arguably offers an instance where his creative frustrations (indicative of a broader interest in expanding dance *into* cinematic space) actually seem to enrich and inform the detailed texture of a number. That Kelly should play a character who is ultimately faced with the dilemma of whether to give up the outside world in favour of the physically constrained but emotionally fulfilling Brigadoon is ironic, certainly. Retrospectively, though, this dancer's final pose at the end of 'The Heather on the Hill' enacts in microcosm a tension that's integral to the overall structure of *Brigadoon*'s filmic universe, articulating, as it does, his character's dilemma, ultimately, of being drawn to Fiona yet yearning for a space that lies beyond 'the heather on the hill.' Tommy's final decision to renounce his life in the outside world in favour of Fiona therefore appears all the more momentous and precarious given the containment it signifies for the actor concerned.

In a sense, then, the person with whom Kelly has the greatest affinity within the narrative is Harry Beaton, the discontented villager who in seeking to escape can be read as an embodiment of a darker, potentially more frustrated side to this male star that needs to be killed off so as to enable him/ Tommy to accept the containment posed by Brigadoon. To read Harry as Kelly's shadow self goes against the story's more likely paralleling of Tommy Albright with Charlie, who is about to marry Fiona's younger sister, and the pairing of the cynical Jeff with Brigadoon's outcast instead (in the bar in New York later in the film, Jeff alludes to his kinship with Harry when referring to Brigadoon as 'his kid brother who ran away'). But the Harry Beaton/Gene Kelly parallel endows the confrontation between these two dark-haired figures on the bridge during the chase sequence (⊙ video example 18.4) with a stronger psychological force. This seems especially the case since that encounter between them occurs at the very boundary point that Kelly's character inadvertently almost transgressed when gathering heather with Fiona. His kinship with Harry Beaton is inscribed, above all, in Kelly's tense stance at the end of 'The Heather on the Hill,' encapsulating an impulse to break free from *Brigadoon*'s circumscribed world that seems expressive of both the star and the character he plays.

## 'THERE BUT FOR YOU GO I': RECLAIMING GENE KELLY'S SINGING SELF IN *BRIGADOON*

In the previous section, we explored MGM's reworking of *Brigadoon* as a musical for dancers, with emphasis on the creatively enriching effects arising from the incorporation of dance into this movie adaptation. Using 'The Heather on the Hill' rather than, say, 'Almost Like Being in Love' to demonstrate this might be deemed an easier task, given that the first is by far the most critically lauded number in the film. My objective, though, was to counter some of the unfavourable criticisms levelled at the film for adapting a singers' show into one for dancers. Having done that, I now want to adopt a different tack, using the rest of this chapter to consider some of the challenges and difficulties stemming from MGM's screen adaptation of *Brigadoon*. Indeed, if the previous section addressed what is gained by the introduction of dance into song-based numbers like 'The Heather on the Hill,' then this one contemplates what may have been lost, conversely, by the removal of tracks such as 'There But for You Go I' from the production.

Aside from the Breen Office's censoring of Meg Brockie's songs, MGM's cutting of others like 'There But for You Go I' and 'From This Day On' has usually been explained in terms of pacing and the limitations of Kelly's singing voice. In an interview, the dancer-choreographer recalls how 'the music in *Brigadoon* generally was on the slow side, and the solo numbers were excised,' with one number involving himself and Charisse (presumably 'From This Day On') being 'cut from the film because of length, just slowness.'[52] In his liner notes to the 1996 soundtrack album's release on CD, Will Friedwald concurs, maintaining that 'most of the excised material consisted of ballads, which Freed and Minnelli felt slowed down the picture's pacing.'[53] Friedwald also cites Arthur Freed as stipulating a film running time of 108 minutes, and this concern with economy by MGM's prestigious producer seems to have been borne out by some of the recurring comments on the audience preview cards about the film dragging in places. On Kelly's vocal limitations, the film's director cites the star as modestly admitting, 'My voice wasn't good enough to do the Lerner and Loewe numbers.'[54] And elsewhere Kelly concedes that

Fred Astaire has a better voice than I, but we both have tiny voices. . . . We sing, usually, to set up the scene, to set up the dance. Neither Fred nor myself . . . pretend that we can put ourselves in league with the good, popular singers, and we don't try. But, like every song and dance man, we tell the lyrics, we speak them as they were written and give them whatever nuance the lyricist intended.[55]

Both of the reasons cited above for cutting certain songs—their slowness, Kelly's vocal limitations—are closely bound up with MGM's overall decision to turn *Brigadoon* into a dance musical. This is perhaps most acutely evident in the case of 'There But for You Go I,' a slow, pensive, solo ballad that fulfills a vital role on stage, enabling Tommy to confess his love to Fiona. Displaying an almost conversational style of delivery ('This is hard to say/But as I wandered through the lea') and possessing lyrics that demand to be listened to, it's easy to understand how this song proved resistant to being reworked as a dance number. In the audio outtake version that's available (the first verse of which can be heard in ▶ video example 18.5), Kelly's rendition is followed by an orchestral only passage, raising the possibility that some form of follow-up dance may have been considered. Even so, Kelly sings all five verses of the song in the outtake before the instrumental section begins. Taking into account his well-documented insecurities about his singing voice, having him stand and perform this entire ballad to Fiona (whatever else might have ensued) may simply have made the number feel too prolonged and liable to expose any vocal weaknesses.

The decision to cut a song like this perhaps suggests, then, that the circumscribed nature of the studio set may not have been the biggest or only problem facing the creators of the film spatially. Rather, it was the slower, serious ballads (associated in all but one case in the stage show with the lead roles) that risked reducing the film version of *Brigadoon* to what Lockhart (quoted earlier) refers to as a 'static singing spectacle'—the nature of which seems so at odds with Kelly's own investment in the kinetic energy of film dance.

That 'There But for You Go I' pushed Kelly to his vocal limits is hinted at by archival material relating to the film's production. A schedule of prerecordings by MGM's Music Department reveals that Kelly attended two studio sessions, with full orchestra present, for this song—one on 30 November 1953, the second on 18 February 1954—and that four takes of the song were recorded in total. This isn't particularly unusual since some of *Brigadoon*'s other songs also entailed a similar number of sessions and takes. But in an inter-office communication (dated 21 June 1954) about preparations for a record album of *Brigadoon*, Lela Simone, a member of the Arthur Freed unit who had worked on other album soundtracks, makes a telling comment in relation to 'There But for You Go I': 'We must be sure that we use the Kelly Vocal Re-Do ['Re-Do' is underlined in the memo] and not his original vocal track,'[56] she cautions, gesturing towards possible difficulties with the star's first recording of that song.

That the song appears not to have reached the shooting stage and was cut from the picture before it was shown at the audience preview screenings in June 1954 suggests there was some consensus among Freed, Minnelli, and Kelly about dropping it. A memo dated 1 March 1954 indicates that 'There But for You Go I' was the last part of the film to be rehearsed and shot, after the Wedding sequence on 2 March, with preparations and final rehearsals diarized for early that same month and the number due to be filmed on 12 March. Significantly, the author of the memo, Bill Ryan, stresses that 'Mr Freed feels he should see the Wedding Sequence cut [and run it with Minnelli] before he okays the final rehearsal of the Kelly-Charisse number.'[57] This seems to tie in with McArthur's speculation that the song was probably dropped not just for its perceived slowness but because 'Minnelli very likely (and Kelly possibly) found the song too low-key emotionally after the frenzy (both musically and in terms of *mise-en-scène*) of the chase'[58] (which follows directly from the drama of the Wedding sequence).

The fact that the song has disappeared from a draft script dated March 1954 (having been included in earlier versions of the screenplay) indicates that the decision to eliminate it from the film took place around this time. In all likelihood, this was probably after Freed had watched the Wedding-Chase sequence in consultation with Minnelli (presumably on or just after 8 March that year, when, as that same memo outlines, the Wedding sequence was expected to be cut and ready to run). A studio schedule (dated 25 October 1954) outlining all of the footage that was shot but eliminated from the final film (and the approximate costs) confirms by the song's absence that it was never filmed (while in contrast, there *are* entries for 'Come to Me, Bend to Me,' the 'Sword Dance,' and 'From This Day On').[59] And when the remastered film was released on DVD in 2005, Kelly's rendition of 'There But for You Go I' (presumably the 'Re-Do' version) is only made available as an audio outtake (unlike those other three musical sequences, the deleted footage of which appears in all cases).[60]

In the finished film, 'There But for You Go I' is replaced by Kelly and Charisse dancing to an orchestral reprise of 'The Heather on the Hill.' This statement masks a much more complicated adaptation process, however, since 'The Heather on the Hill' reprise was only included following a late change that took place at some point after the audience preview screenings in June 1954 and before the film's final release two months later on 8 September. Prior to that, the intention seems to have been to replace 'There But for You Go I' with 'From This Day On,' another major song from the stage show, meant to be performed in the film (as on Broadway) as a duet between Fiona and Tommy but now occurring slightly earlier in the narrative and segueing into a sensual dance (accompanied by an orchestral only version of this song) between the two lovers.

As a result of its narrative relocation (to replace the dropped 'There But for You Go I'), 'From This Day On' would no longer serve (as in the stage version) as the lovers' parting duet (following Tommy's realization that he can't stay in Brigadoon after all). Instead, it was construed as the number that prompts him to announce that he loves Fiona so much that he can't leave her. At some point after the preview screenings, though, 'From This Day On,' the song designed to replace 'There But for You Go I,' was itself dropped, hence its inclusion in MGM's listing of footage eliminated from the final film. Although Kelly's vocals with Carol Richards (Charisse's singing stand-in) were deleted, his dance with Charisse directly afterwards was retained—only now it's accompanied by a new orchestral reprise of 'The Heather on the Hill' (rather than 'From This Day On').

Bearing in mind this taxing sequence of changes involving 'There But for You Go I' and 'From This Day On,' it's tempting to read the demands placed on Kelly's voice, as he strove to do justice to these and his other songs in *Brigadoon*, as a metaphor for the strains placed on the Hollywood musical as it sought to adapt hit Broadway shows intended for singers. That several songs were cut during production at least suggests some form of resistance on MGM's part to any slavish adherence (or 'obeisance,' to use Delamater's term) to the stage original. But it's also indicative of a pressure to adapt in ways that are geared around showcasing the main talents of the film's star dancers. The risk arising from this, however, is that it may result in a closing down of the opportunities such a production affords, especially if the studio only panders to what it assumes audiences expect of a star like Kelly. Already insecure about his vocal limitations, it's possible that Kelly himself may have felt constrained and unable to take his skills in new directions and this may have contributed to the downsizing of his singing role in the film.

It may be that MGM had no choice except to dub Charisse's singing, but in Kelly's case it's worth considering what may have been lost as a result of the decision to excise his rendition of a song like 'There But for You Go I.' Quite how we respond to the paring down of his singing role may depend largely on whether one evaluates this part of his performance repertoire strictly according to standards of tonal range, timbre, pitch, and so on or, rather, in terms of how it relates to his character, the narrative, and indeed Kelly's own star persona. His singing voice isn't comparable technically with that of David Brooks or Robert Goulet (who played Tommy Albright on Broadway and television, respectively) and, while Kelly was defined as a song-and-dance man (like Astaire), this first part of his performing identity was always an unequal adjunct to the second.

Clive Hirschhorn recounts how this star's singing was even 'once described as "gargling with pebbles," '[61] although, for him, Kelly's vocal work in *Cover Girl* (Charles Vidor, 1944) marks a significant turning point in his career as a singer. Citing none other than composer Jerome Kern's appreciation of Kelly's rendition of 'Long Ago and Far Away,' 'a difficult song which needed more than the simple ability to remain in the right key,' Hirschhorn contends that in this film, 'Gene not only found his feet but his voice as well. These light, high, slightly grainy notes are heard to marvelous effect as they caress Kern's tender melodies and joke with the rousing, more sprightly ones.'[62]

Notwithstanding Hirschhorn's comments, Kelly's singing— both generally and specifically in relation to *Brigadoon*—has suffered from critical disparagement and neglect. For some, it seems to be all too easy to conflate it with other supposedly less favourable aspects of this star's screen persona. During his discussion of Kelly's performance of *Brigadoon*'s 'Almost Like Being in Love,' for example, McArthur notes that he 'had a colleague to whom Kelly's singing and dancing was anathema, the reason being that "he always looks so damned pleased with himself." '63 Citing Stephen Harvey, moreover, he describes that critic as 'merciless in traducing what he describes as "Kelly's throbbing falsetto" and his "patented irresistible grin." '64 At times, even fans of Kelly have taken issue with his singing. Jennifer Welsh, for example, acknowledges that 'he does have some shining moments, "Love Is Here to Stay" from *An American in Paris* (1951) chief among them' but claims 'he was often forced to stretch his voice beyond its powers,' arguing, 'The songs from 1954's *Brigadoon* (particularly the outtakes) reveal his voice at its weakest.'65

In the case of the ballad 'There But for You Go I,' McArthur ventures that the fault may not lie entirely with Kelly. Describing it as 'one of the least memorable of the show's songs,'66 he suggests that it 'is, indeed, often dropped for that reason.'67 The numerous complaints by audience members at the preview screenings regarding the song's omission don't appear to bear out McArthur's dismissal of it, however. And from among Gene Kelly's online fan community, Canadian jazz singer Mary-Catherine McNinch-Pazzano ventures that there's an emotional honesty to this star's rendition of 'There But for You Go I' that's very particular to him.68

This affecting aspect to Kelly's rendition of Lerner and Loewe's lovely ballad seems far removed from the sort of traits that some critics have detected in the star's screen persona. In the words of John Russell Taylor:

> Kelly is the open, confident, brash . . . straight-forward American male, with a smile on his face for the whole human race, as one of his songs puts it. The personality is not altogether appealing. There is sometimes the feeling that the charm is laid on a little too thickly, that the smile is a trifle synthetic, that, to

quote another of his songs, he may like himself just a fraction too much.[69]

Arguing for a greater complexity in Kelly's screen persona, Delamater maintains that 'Taylor's comments . . . do not recognize the great variety of Kelly's roles, nor do they relate the ways in which he presents his personality through dance, for it is precisely through his dance roles that the persona is revealed.'[70] Yet, for Michael Wood, it is precisely in Kelly's dancing that a complex mixture of 'brash confidence' laced with uncertainty reveals itself: 'Gene Kelly has plenty of skill,' Wood asserts, 'but ease is the last thing we associate with him.'[71] Describing this mood projected on screen by Kelly as 'an odd confidence,' Wood considers it premonitory of 1950s America, arguing that 'Kelly was always trying too hard. . . . He suggests fantastic skill edged with uncertainty. He's got things together but his achievement seems too precarious for him to be happy. He can't rest.'[72] Indeed, according to Wood, 'part of his appeal is a touch of strain and even faint fear, an air of scenting locusts on the wind.'[73]

Considering this star's films in relation to the MGM musical's attempt in the 1950s to offer a show of confidence at a time when it was 'ebbing fast'—in fact 'because it was ebbing fast'[74]—Wood juxtaposes earlier Kelly musicals like *Singin' in the Rain* (1952) and *An American in Paris* (1951) plus the Astaire vehicle *The Band Wagon* (1953) with a new breed of melodramas (populated by troubled protagonists) such as *On the Waterfront* (1954), *East of Eden* (1955), and *Rebel Without a Cause* (1955). Rather tellingly, *Brigadoon* isn't included in his list. Yet, if the doubt that lay underneath America's confidence in the 1950s is, as Wood contends, 'contained in Kelly's style,'[75] then *Brigadoon* offers a fascinating vehicle through which to consider this. In terms of the character Kelly is playing, Tommy Albright is someone who at the start of the film has lost his way literally and metaphorically and, on confessing that he doesn't feel 'satisfied,' engages in the following exchange with his friend Jeff:

JEFF:     Oh, that's the silliest thing I ever heard. You've got a fine job, and you're engaged to a fine girl, and you're lost in a fine forest. What more do you want?
TOMMY:  I don't know. Something seems wrong, especially about Jane and me. And that makes everything seem wrong. Look how I postpone getting married. I just can't get myself to that altar.
JEFF:     Well you love her, don't you? At least you did three days ago when you left New York.
TOMMY:  Sometimes I think I'm really not capable of loving. [Then, on seeing Jeff's dismayed response.] Sometimes I think nobody is anymore.
JEFF:     Oh, that's nonsense. Now don't start talking yourself into an inferiority complex. You don't deserve it.
TOMMY:  What do you mean?
JEFF:     Well, most of my friends who have inferiority complexes are right. They're not as good as everybody else. [Tommy laughs] But you! Young. Dashing. Loaded.

The very name of Kelly's protagonist—Tommy *Albright*—implies the kind of effervescent optimism that Wood finds in this star's screen personality. Yet, considering the anxieties to which Tommy admits early on, it's as if everything that had previously given Kelly grounds for confidence has now been eroded (significantly, it's directly after this disclosure by Tommy that Brigadoon appears, as if in response to the male protagonist's emotional needs). It's an admission that suggests a puncturing of the self-assurance inherent in Kelly's star persona, exposing cracks in the confidence that Wood argues the MGM musical sought to project by way of masking the reality of its disintegration.

Moving beyond Kelly's role in the film to his performance style, it's possible to regard his singing voice as another element that punctures (or at least complicates) his confident screen persona, articulating the very sense of doubt and strain that Wood identifies. His light, 'high baritone to low tenor' voice[76] certainly offers a softer counterbalance to some of the brasher masculine excesses that Taylor and Wood detect in Kelly's persona. The insecurity his singing evokes (will Kelly manage to reach the required note or not?) also seems entirely relevant to his portrayal in *Brigadoon* of a young man in crisis, investing Wood's contention that Kelly 'suggests fantastic skill edged with uncertainty'[77] with another dimension.

Considered dramatically and in light of the above, therefore, Kelly's solo ballad 'There But for You Go I' marks a major breakthrough in Tommy's emotional development, enabling this character to overcome his earlier anxiety about being incapable of loving. The song 'Almost Like Being in Love' had marked a movement forward in this regard but, as suggested by the qualified nature of its main refrain ('It's *Almost* Like . . .), Tommy hasn't fully comprehended his feelings for Fiona at that point. In his 1954 review of the film, critic Edward Jablonski argues that Kelly 'spoils the beautiful ballad "Almost Like Being in Love" by ignoring the caesura after the word "it's" in the chorus,'[78] his failure to do so presumably suggesting insufficient grasp of the song's irony. This criticism seems a bit unfair since (as ▶ video example 18.6 demonstrates) Kelly does inject a noticeable pause before the relevant word on the first two out of three occasions when it appears in the lyrics (as does Brooks in the relevant track on the original Broadway album and Goulet in the 1966 telecast). Salinger's orchestration encourages this vocal hiatus by providing a brief accompanying halt in the music each time and, as Kelly starts to dance, the 'almost like being in love' section of the title refrain becomes purely instrumental (as apparent in ⊙ video example 18.7). Although, on resuming his singing, Kelly's introduction of a pause before 'almost' tends to become less consistent (and increasingly played for comedy), the fact that he dances as well as sings is a mitigating factor and this particular aspect to his performance of the song isn't all that much different from Brooks's or Goulet's renditions anyhow.

In other respects, there is a sense in which Kelly's ebullient performance risks overpowering the more ironic qualities of 'Almost Like Being in Love.' Indeed, whereas that song toys with the possibility that Tommy is in love with Fiona but doesn't yet know it, Kelly performs (and stages) it as if it were a rerun of *Singin' in the Rain*'s title number, the mood he projects through his dancing and singing conveying the sense of a man who has fallen in love and surely knows it. As a grinning Kelly launches into the song, seizing Jeff's hat and placing it jauntily on his head before going on to sing cheekily to the highland animals nearby, then tap dancing along the stone wall and throwing off his hat and jacket in a rousing finale, one can't help but feel that a little less polished routine and greater hesitancy might have gelled more convincingly with the song's lyrics and what we know of Tommy at this point. There is, in other words, a trifle too much self-confidence imparted by Kelly's performance, here, and (perhaps encouraged by lines like 'I could swear I was falling') this tends to work against the more qualified romantic assertion inherent in the song's title.

One could invert this argument, of course, and say that Kelly's performance during 'Almost Like Being in Love' purposefully conveys a sense of Tommy as someone not yet fully in touch with his deeper emotional self. That is to say, it presents a character who at this stage in the narrative is too overtaken by his incipient feelings for Fiona and, not really knowing whether

FIGURE 3.6 In celebration of Tommy's newfound feelings for Fiona, Kelly launches into his rendition of 'Almost Like Being in Love' while Van Johnson's Jeff looks on.

he's capable of loving (or presumably what love is like), can only admit that what he's feeling is 'almost like being in love.' That Tommy performs this number so enthusiastically in front of Jeff also suggests someone as yet too surprised by his feelings to reflect more seriously on what they mean and the fact he doesn't yet know about the 'miracle' of Brigadoon may be another extenuating factor in his (and Kelly's) defence. At the very least, though, 'There But for You Go I' would have offered an important counterpoint to this song, providing a necessary moment of stasis wherein Kelly can no longer hide behind the kind of habitual tricks-of-the-trade that were formerly on display in his dancing routine. His tender vocals would also have evoked a humility and vulnerability quite different from his singing in that earlier number, potentially revealing a charm in Kelly's screen persona that's often obscured by claims regarding his overconfidence and self-satisfied demeanour.

In gesturing towards a realm of sorrow, loneliness, and unfulfilled longing that the male protagonist realizes would have been his destiny had it not been for his newfound love for Fiona, 'There But for You Go I' is profoundly suited to the less buoyant side of Kelly's screen persona. The song's lyrics (particularly those lines italicized below) are strikingly resonant of Delamater's claim that 'there is a somewhat melancholy aspect to almost all the Kelly roles, for it is the character's nature to brood about his loneliness'.[79]

This is hard to say, but as I wandered through the lea,
*I felt for just a fleeting moment that*
*I suddenly was free of being lonely.*
*Then I closed my eyes and saw the very reason why. . . .*
*I saw a man with his head bowed low.*
*His heart had no place to go.*
*I looked and I thought to myself with a sigh:*
*There but for you go I.*

*I saw a man walking by the sea,*
*Alone with the tide was he.*
*I looked and I thought as I watched him go by:*
*There but for you go I.*
*Lonely men around me, trying not to cry,*
*Till the day you found me, there among them was I.*
*I saw a man who had never known a love that was all his own.*
*I thought as I thanked all the stars in the sky:*
There but for you go I.

Kelly's tremulous delivery of the word 'Alone' on the tenth line (as can be heard in ⊙ video example 18.8) captures the vulnerability and sincerity of his singing—qualities that soften his muscular dancing style and complicate his rugged masculine image. Indeed if, as Delamater argues, 'in spite of his aligning himself with buddies or companions, Kelly's characters are also frequently alone, and significant dances are soliloquies—almost meditations on the essential loneliness of his role at that point,'[80] then this finds its most poignant expression, arguably, not in his dancing but in his singing of this excised song.

It's only on the penultimate word of the last line that Kelly (unlike David Brooks or Robert Goulet)[81] injects a small embellishment into his delivery (captured in ⊙ video example 18.9). His final iteration of 'go' in the song's title refrain is uttered with a little trill which could easily have been overdone to the point of sounding amateurishly out of place. But Kelly executes this rhetorical flourish with such delicate restraint, emerging as it does out of an otherwise unadorned vocal performance, that it appears far from vainglorious or attention seeking. Indeed, there's something entirely fitting about how, through this tiny piece of vocal decoration, he allows himself to express just the right modicum of delight, release, even relief at the end of a challenging ballad so preoccupied with the loneliness of others.

Following on from the gently ascending scale he adopts with the previous line ('I thought as I thanked all the stars in the sky') this moving undulation in his voice (which mirrors and extends his lilting delivery of the word 'sky') subtly confirms Tommy's gratitude at the fate he's been dealt, implying that some form of emotional transcendence (also inherent in his rising pitch throughout the last line) has been quietly reached. It's a moment of subdued vocal ornamentation that exemplifies how Kelly's tender, humble rendition of a ballad so mindful of the fate of others could not be further removed from those overly confident, egotistical traits that some have ascribed to his screen personality. Delivered without a hint of self-congratulation, Kelly's rendition of 'There But for You Go I' is the antithesis of all that.

Perhaps, then, what makes 'There But for You Go I'—and Kelly's interpretation of it—so poignantly memorable is that it isn't simply a self-preoccupied love song (nor, hence, a simple love song). Instead, the joy of Tommy's discovery of his love for Fiona is countered by a sorrowful realization (couched almost like a lament) that not all men are so fortunate; in other words, he sings of a fate—of never finding great love and leading an emotionally unsatisfied life—that might have been his destiny had he not met Fiona. That Tommy should declare his love for Fiona in this way—acknowledging who he has become and what he might have been—suggests a much greater emotional maturity, humility, and self-awareness than anything conveyed earlier by his ebullient performance of 'Almost Like Being In Love.' Indeed, if the film as a whole can be read as an attempt to restore Tommy's emotional self-belief, then his discovery of this is to be found not in the grandstanding 'Almost Like Being in Love' but in his tender grieving for men like his former self in 'There But for You Go I.'

As such, this song promises the opposite of what I argued regarding the film's incorporation of dance into 'The Heather on the Hill.' Whereas that earlier number had exploited dance in ways that suggest the couple's interaction with their environment (eschewing the more introspective tendencies encouraged by a sung duet), in the reprise (available in ⓥ video example 18.10), Kelly and Charisse's balletic dance is, by contrast, clingingly self-absorbed, suggesting the two lovers' infatuation with each other and their inability to be apart (Figure 3.7).

In contrast, the romantic impulse and physical stasis of 'There But for You Go I' are offset by a wider, more mobile viewpoint that's conveyed through this song's lyrics (rooted as these are in a comparison between Tommy's former and reborn selves). The song begins with Tommy describing himself wandering 'through the lea' only to then close his eyes and imagine other men who have not been fortunate enough to find a love like he has with Fiona. Although still a love song that expresses Tommy's joy of discovery, in contrast to his earlier tendency merely to project his happiness onto the world around him ('There's a smile on my face for the whole human race,' he sang in 'Almost Like Being in Love'), the lyrics now suggest a more melancholic regard for the lovelorn other. Inherent in the song's words, therefore, is an imaginative capacity, the power of which implies an outward-looking perspective that isn't dependent on location shooting for its impact ('I saw a man who had never known a love that was all his own').

It would be naïve in the extreme to suggest that all criticisms of the film version would evaporate, Brigadoon-style, with the inclusion of 'There But for You Go I.' But if this song had been retained, it would have amounted to a bold, significant piece of decision making by the filmmakers. Its presence would have prevented the stage show from simply being recast into (and typecast as) a film musical for dancers, signalling MGM's ability to see beyond the dominant attributes of its stars' screen personae and to understand that fidelity to the source play may not necessarily be a barrier to creativity.

FIGURE 3.7 Fiona and Tommy dance passionately to a reprise of 'The Heather on the Hill'.

Kelly's virtuosity as a dancer was such that there may have been little agonizing by the film's creators about the decision to relegate 'There But for You Go I' to the cutting room floor despite its fundamental relevance to his character and its logical place in Tommy's emotional development. Far from slowing down the narrative too much, his sincere admission through song of the extent of his love for Fiona seems wholly suited to the dramatic needs of the moment, its contemplative pace potentially affording viewers a welcome pause in the action after the drama of the chase and allowing Tommy to reflect on the intensity of his feelings for Fiona at this crucial point. The song's more measured approach is deeply in tune with his emotional needs and the awakening of his love that it expresses could have provided the motivation for any ensuing dance between the couple.

Of course, the wonderfully sensuous dance between Kelly and Charisse in the finished film only came about through a series of changes triggered by the cutting of 'There But for You Go I.' But on playing the audio outtake of Kelly's rendition of that song over a freeze frame of Tommy and Fiona facing each other while they stand at the archway of the old kirk and then watching them dance to an orchestral reprise of 'The Heather on the Hill' directly after this, I'm struck by how effective this combination could have been. Lovely as the cut version of 'From This Day On' is (the closing duet section of which can be found in ⏵ video example 18.11), I can accept that song's excision as a necessary casualty of the adaptation process.

Kelly's rendition of 'There But for You Go I,' on the other hand (at least the version publicly available), would have brought something else dramatically to the show. While this star's singing voice plays an important role in softening his screen persona elsewhere in his musical films, arguably it's in his heartfelt delivery of this excised song that it reveals its greatest emotional depth, yielding a dimension that, if anything, intensifies the vulnerability beneath the self-confidence and the sense of strain that comes from trying too hard. In cutting this song from the film, MGM displayed a lack of conviction in the dramatic possibilities afforded by Kelly's singing, committing an error that would anticipate academic neglect of this part of his performing identity. Given that some of the criticisms of Kelly's performance in *Brigadoon* at the audience preview screenings were that it was too derivative of his earlier work ('It's too bad Gene Kelly has to always be the same—I mean dancing style mostly'[82] complained one viewer), one can't help but think that this gentle ballad by him might have offered something substantively different, revealing a tender sincerity often obscured by the brasher elements of his star persona and reclaiming a song otherwise cut from the stage show that might have appeased any countervailing criticism that the film dragged in places.

As I hope to have demonstrated through my earlier analysis of the creative restaging of 'The Heather on the Hill' number along with this reflection on the cutting of the ballad 'There But for You Go I,' *Brigadoon* is a musical for singers that both benefits and suffers from MGM's efforts to turn it into a vehicle for its star dancers. It did indeed 'have all the ingredients,' as Charisse observed, and arguably qualifies as one of MGM's most underrated musicals, gaining tension and complexity from some of its perceived flaws. But the studio's faltering confidence in the cinematic potential of the show's tunes and in Kelly's talents as a *song-and*-dance man may well account for any sense of the film being 'less than the sum of its parts.'

## NOTES

1. The other two films in which Charisse appeared with Gene Kelly are *Singin' in the Rain* (1952) and *It's Always Fair Weather* (1955). Kelly codirected both with Stanley Donen. *Brigadoon* is the first film in which Charisse plays the female lead. For more

on Charisse's career, see, for example, her obituary by Robert Berkvist, 'Cyd Charisse, 86, Silken Dancer of Movies, Dies,' *New York Times*, 18 June 2008, https://www.nytimes.com/2008/ 06/18/arts/dance/18charisse.html.

2. Cyd Charisse in Tony Martin and Cyd Charisse, as told to Dick Kleiner, *The Two of Us* (New York: Mason/Charter, 1976), 207–208.
3. Apparently, Van Johnson would leave work promptly at 6:00 PM, thwarting Minnelli's attempt to shoot a sequence he'd been preparing all day. Charisse in Martin and Charisse, *The Two of Us*, 206.
4. Charisse in Martin and Charisse, *The Two of Us*, 206–207.
5. Charisse in Martin and Charisse, *The Two of Us*, 206. In *That's Entertainment! III* (1994), Charisse admits that *Brigadoon* was her favourite collaboration with Gene Kelly, highlighting their 'Heather on the Hill' dance routine together. *That's Entertainment! III*, DVD, directed by Bud Friedgen and Michael J. Sheridan (Burbank, CA: Warner Home Video, 1994).
6. Alan Jay Lerner, *The Street Where I Live: The Story of My Fair Lady, Gigi and Camelot* (London: Hodder and Stoughton, 1978), 127.
7. Vincente Minnelli, with H. Arce. Foreword by A. J. Lerner. *Vincente Minnelli: I Remember It Well* (Hollywood, CA: Samuel French, 1990 [1974]), 279.
8. Clive Hirschhorn, *Gene Kelly: A Biography* (London: W. H. Allen, 1974), 239.
9. Alan Yudkoff, *Gene Kelly: A Life of Dance and Dreams* (New York: Back Stage Books, 1999), 231.
10. Arthur Freed, quoted in Colin McArthur, *Brigadoon, Braveheart and the Scots: Distortions of Scotland in Hollywood Cinema* (London: I. B. Tauris, 2003), 70.
11. McArthur, *Brigadoon, Braveheart and the Scots*, 89.
12. Murray Pomerance, *The Eyes Have It: Cinema and the Reality Effect* (New Brunswick, NJ: Rutgers University Press, 2013), 200.
13. Pomerance, *The Eyes Have It*, 218–219.
14. Robert Emmet Long, *Broadway, The Golden Years: Jerome Robbins and the Great Choreographer-Directors, 1940 to the Present* (New York: Continuum, 2001), 37–40.

15. Kara Anne Gardner, *Agnes De Mille: Telling Stories in Broadway Dance* (New York: Oxford University Press, 2016), 117–140.
16. Gardner, *Agnes De Mille*, 124–131.
17. Alan Jay Lerner and Frederick Loewe, *Brigadoon (Libretto): A Musical Play* (London: Faber Music, 2007), v–vii.
18. Stephen Harvey, *Directed by Vincente Minnelli* (New York: Museum of Modern Art/Harper & Row, 1989), 128.
19. Gene Kelly in Jerome Delamater, *Dance in the Hollywood Musical* (Ann Arbor: UMI Research Press, 1981), 217.
20. Kelly in Delamater, *Dance in the Hollywood Musical*, 176.
21. Kelly in Delamater, *Dance in the Hollywood Musical*, 175.
22. Vincente Minnelli quoted in Delamater, *Dance in the Hollywood Musical*, 176.
23. Minnelli in Delamater, *Dance in the Hollywood Musical*, 170–171.
24. Harvey, *Directed by Vincente Minnelli*, 126.
25. Delamater, *Dance in the Hollywood Musical*, 170.
26. Dimitri Tiomkin quoted in Delamater, *Dance in the Hollywood Musical*, 171.
27. Freda June Lockhart quoted in Delamater, *Dance in the Hollywood Musical*, 171.
28. On the stagey nature of *Brigadoon*'s Cinemascope, see Harvey, *Directed by Vincente Minnelli*, 130–131.
29. Dominic McHugh, ed., *Alan Jay Lerner: A Lyricist's Letters* (New York: Oxford University Press, 2014), 16.
30. According to McArthur, 'The story of MGM's interest in Shearer seems to be a myth since she herself denies that any such discussions took place.' McArthur, *Brigadoon, Braveheart and the Scots*, 89.
31. Johnny Green quoted in Pomerance, *The Eyes Have It*, 195–196.
32. Carol Richards also dubbed Charisse's singing in *Deep in My Heart* (1954), *It's Always Fair Weather* (1955), and *Silk Stockings* (1957); in *The Band Wagon* (Minnelli, 1953), India Adams performs this role. For further information regarding who dubbed Charisse in other films, see Ray Hagen, Laura Wagner, Steve Tompkins, et al., *Movie Dubbers*, http://www.janettedavis.net/Dubbers/dubberslist.php.
33. Audience feedback from preview screenings of *Brigadoon* (Arthur Freed Collection, USC, Cinematic Arts Library), First

Preview: First Report, 4 June 1954, 1–14 and Second Preview: First Report 15 June 1954, 1–15.

34. Audience feedback from preview screenings of *Brigadoon* (Arthur Freed Collection, USC, Cinematic Arts Library), First Preview: First Report, 4 June 1954, 14.

35. Audience feedback from preview screenings of *Brigadoon*, Second Preview: First Report, Arthur Freed Collection, USC, Cinematic Arts Library), 15 June 1954, 5.

36. *Brigadoon*, directed by Fielder Cook, 1966. Broadcast on CBS as a television special on 15 October 1966.

37. Yudkoff, *Gene Kelly: A Life of Dance and Dreams*, 230.

38. McArthur, *Brigadoon, Braveheart and the Scots*, 90.

39. For more on Hugh Laing's career, see his obituary by Jack Anderson, 'Hugh Laing, Specialist in Ballets by Antony Tudor, Is Dead at 77,' *New York Times*, 11 May 1988, https://www.nytimes.com/1988/05/11/obituaries/hugh-laing-specialist-in-ballets-by-antony-tudor-is-dead-at-77.html.

40. According to Kelly, the Sword Dance may have been cut simply because the excitement it garnered on stage didn't translate well onto the screen (Kelly in Delamater, *Dance in the Hollywood Musical*, 217). At the time of the film's release, though, one disgruntled critic speculated that perhaps it was deleted because the dancing 'badly outclassed Kelly's own numbers' (Dick Williams, 'Assets of "Brigadoon" Are Color, Music, Sets,' *Los Angeles Mirror*, 9 September 1954). The force of such conjecture is blunted by this critic's mistake in incorrectly naming the chief sword dancer as Matt Mattox (who would perform the role in the 1957 Broadway stage revival). On the cutting of Hugh Laing's role to 'primarily an acting part,' however, Stephen Harvey similarly observes that 'as a choreographer, Kelly was not generous to other male dancers unless they were cast as his clownish lower-case pal.' See Harvey, *Directed by Vincente Minnelli*, 128.

41. Jerome Delamater, *Dance in the Hollywood Musical*, 170.

42. McArthur, *Brigadoon, Braveheart and the Scots*, 85.

43. On the use of CinemaScope, see Pomerance, *The Eyes Have It*, 208–209.

44. Pomerance, *The Eyes Have It*, 209.

45. 'Whoever cast Cyd Charisse, the most contemporary and empty of danseuses, as Fiona must be as fey as the person who should have had the part.' Clayton Cole, 'Brigadoon,' *Films and Filming* 10, no. 54.

46. McArthur, *Brigadoon, Braveheart and the Scots*, 86.

47. Delamater, *Dance in the Hollywood Musical*, 135–136.

48. Delamater, *Dance in the Hollywood Musical*, 136.

49. Delamater, *Dance in the Hollywood Musical*, 136.

50. Delamater, *Dance in the Hollywood Musical*, 140.

51. Delamater, *Dance in the Hollywood Musical*, 140–141.

52. Gene Kelly in Delamater, *Dance in the Hollywood Musical*, 217.

53. Will Friedwald, Compact Disc (CD) liner notes, *M-G-M's Brigadoon: Music from the Original Motion Picture* (1996), 16.

54. Kelly quoted in Minnelli, *Vincente Minnelli*, 279.

55. Kelly in Delamater, *Dance in the Hollywood Musical*, 151.

56. Lela Simone, M-G-M Inter-office Communication, Roger Edens (M-G-M Music Department) Collection, USC Cinematic Arts Library, 21 June 1954.

57. Bill Ryan, M-G-M Inter-office Communication, Arthur Freed Collection, USC Cinematic Arts Library, 1 March 1954.

58. McArthur, *Brigadoon, Braveheart and the Scots*, 91.

59. 'Eliminations' (MGM Collection, University of Southern California, 25 October 1954) lists all footage recorded but removed from *Brigadoon* (along with the estimated time taken to shoot and the approximate cost of the material deleted). This four-page schedule is accompanied by an inter-office communication from Joe Finn to J. J. Cohn, 26 October 1954.

60. The remastered version of *Brigadoon* was released on DVD by Warner Home Video on 15 March 2005, with all four outtakes included in the 'Special Features' section. *Brigadoon*, DVD, directed by Vincente Minnelli (Burbank, CA: Warner Home Video, 2005).

61. Hirschhorn, *Gene Kelly*, 133.

62. Hirschhorn, *Gene Kelly*, 133.

63. McArthur, *Brigadoon, Braveheart and the Scots*, 87.

64. McArthur, *Brigadoon, Braveheart and the Scots*, 87.

65. Jennifer Welsh (2015), 'Fred Astaire vs. Gene Kelly: A Fan of the Song-and-Dance Men Weighs In,' *The Outtake*, 5 June 2015, https://theouttake.net/fred-astaire-vs-gene-kelly-736f795c3b39.

66. McArthur, *Brigadoon, Braveheart and the Scots*, 61.

67. McArthur, *Brigadoon, Braveheart and the Scots*, 62.

68. Claiming that Kelly is an underrated singer, Mary-Catherine McNinch-Pazzano argues,'Fans, scholars, and critics alike talk all the time about Gene Kelly the dancer, Gene Kelly the director, Gene Kelly the choreographer, and Gene Kelly the actor. But rarely do they discuss Gene Kelly the singer. As a singer who is completely enchanted by Kelly's light, clear, and pure tenor voice, I often wonder why it doesn't get the appreciation it should. . . . While Kelly is constantly heralded as one of Hollywood's favourite song-and dance men, the "song" aspect of this phrase is too often silenced or dismissed in discussions of Kelly's work and talents.' McNinch-Pazzano also recounts Kern's complimentary response (briefly alluded to via a reference to Hirschhorn's biography of Kelly earlier in this chapter) on hearing the star's rendition of 'Long Ago and Far Away' during rehearsal one day on the set of *Cover Girl* (see note 61). Mary-Catherine McNinch-Pazzano, 'Gene Kelly: The Underrated Singer,' 12 July 2012, https://classicmoviemome nts.blogspot.co.uk/2012/01/.

69. John Russell Taylor quoted in Delamater, *Dance in the Hollywood Musical*, 144.

70. Delamater, *Dance in the Hollywood Musical*, 144.

71. Michael Wood, *America in the Movies: Or, 'Santa Maria, It Had Slipped My Mind'* (New York: Columbia University Press, 1989): 149.

72. Wood, *America in the Movies*, 164.

73. Wood, *America in the Movies*, 164.

74. Wood, *America in the Movies*, 155.

75. Wood, *America in the Movies*, 163.

76. Johnny Green quoted in Pomerance, *The Eyes Have It*, 195–196.

77. Wood, *America in the Movies*, 164.

78. In a generally negative review of the film, Jablonski is highly critical of Kelly's overall performance. Arguing that his 'choreography and dancing seem repetitive and tired, and the gestures, patterns, and facial expressions of *An American in Paris* and *Singin' in the Rain* appear in *Brigadoon* as clichés,' he maintains that 'Kelly's singing voice is hollow and strained.' 'As

for Cyd Charisse, she neither looks nor dances like a Highland lass.' '*Brigadoon*' by Edward Jablonski, *Films in Review* 5, no. 8 (October 1954): 429–430.

79. Delamater, *Dance in the Hollywood Musical*, 146.
80. Delamater, *Dance in the Hollywood Musical*, 146.
81. Robert Goulet, for example, in his rendition of this song in the 1966 telecast, maintains a steady, deep baritone hold over his notes in the last line.
82. Audience feedback from preview screening of *Brigadoon* (Arthur Freed Collection, USC, Cinematic Arts Library), First Preview: First Report, 4 June 1954, 15.

# 4

# 'I'm Once Again the Previous Me'

## Performance and Stardom in the Barbra Streisand Stage-to-Screen Adaptations

DOMINIC BROOMFIELD-MCHUGH

■ □ ■

AFTER THE GRADUAL DEMISE OF the studio system in the 1950s, the film musical became a less regular fixture. With a handful of exceptions, Hollywood looked to Broadway hits as the basis of screen musicals and many fewer examples of the genre were produced in the 1960s. At the same time, more money was spent on each project and each film became more of an event. Matthew Kennedy has explored at length the phenomenon of the theatrical 'roadshow' presentation that became an important marketing tool in the 1960s: 'To generate something akin to the crackling energy of a Broadway opening, roadshow musicals often came with an overture, intermission, entr'acte, and exit music, in addition to a souvenir program and bookings in the most lavish single-screen theatres in large cities.'[1] Following the release of *The Sound of Music* in 1965, Kennedy notes, 'it became de rigueur for any film musical to be released in the roadshow format if it wanted to rightfully be labelled "major," "important," or "lavish." [2]

As well as importing Broadway hits, Hollywood also brought over two of musical theatre's most promising young stars in an attempt to guarantee quality: Julie Andrews and Barbra Streisand. On the screen, each enjoyed enormous success (*Mary Poppins*, *The Sound of Music*, *Funny Girl*), a hint of the average (*Thoroughly Modern Millie*, *On a Clear Day You Can See Forever*), and a major disappointment (*Star!* and *Hello, Dolly!*). The two actresses could not have been more different. The very English Andrews was primarily a stage animal, but in addition to her film musicals she also appeared in a few nonsinging movie roles in the 1960s, including in Hitchcock's *Torn Curtain* (1966). Streisand, on the other hand, was American, had made her name through her recording career, and also had made a series of successful television specials starting with *My Name Is Barbra* (1965; unusually, for a newcomer, she was the main performer on the specials and did not rely on other big names to boost the shows' appeal).

Although being an English star in a series of hit Hollywood musicals was uncommon, Andrews otherwise conformed to an old-school stereotype of the squeaky-clean, charming soprano, a little like a British Jane Powell but with unusual vocal purity and clarity. Streisand, on the other hand, was (and is) sui generis: a one-off talent and persona that left her mark on any material she performed. Although both stars are worthy of being the focus of a case study in stardom, in this chapter I focus on Streisand's first three screen musicals, all of which are adaptations of successful Broadway productions from the same decade: *Funny Girl* (Broadway: 1964; Hollywood, 1968), *Hello, Dolly!* (Broadway: 1964; Hollywood: 1969), and *On a Clear Day You Can See Forever* (Broadway: 1965; Hollywood: 1970). In each case, I examine how the nature of Streisand's star persona affects decisions made in the adaptation of each musical and also how her performance of the text reframes the original material (e.g., through vocal inflection). What emerges is a sense of how a combination of performance, personality, and the presence of the performer's body acts as an agent of adaptation as potently as the writing of the screenplay and score.

## CASTING STREISAND IN HOLLYWOOD ADAPTATIONS

Of her three stage-to-screen projects, *Funny Girl* was by far the most obvious fit for Streisand because she starred in the original Broadway production. Although the musical had a difficult pre-Broadway tryout period, with various songs being added and dropped, the producer Ray Stark noted that Streisand had gradually absorbed the character of Fanny Brice, the beloved comedienne who was the subject of the musical, to create a compelling performance: 'Somehow the two personalities have come together. . . . I don't know what is Barbra and what is Fanny. Barbra plays Fanny as an extension of herself—which is something that Fanny could never have done. Fanny wasn't an actress but a satirist.'[3] Stark's observation about the differences between the two figures is also reflected in Norman Nadel's Broadway review of Streisand's performance in which he declares: 'Hail to thee, Barbra Streisand; Fanny Brice thou never wert! But there you have the whole paradox of this show—one spectacular talent in the role of another spectacular talent, but never becoming, or perhaps even trying to become, the woman this play is about. Streisand prefers to create a 1918 Barbra Streisand, and the justification is that she does it superbly.'[4]

Other reviews of the show on Broadway were undeniably mixed—the *Times* called it 'hokum and schmaltz' and the *Post* labelled it 'a disappointing entertainment'—but it went on to run an impressive 1,348 performances, following its premiere on 26 March 1964. Composer Jule Styne's opening night telegram to the actress noted that 'it takes a star to play a star'[5] and Streisand's recordings of his songs 'People' and 'Don't Rain on My Parade' quickly turned them into standards. She also went on to recreate her portrayal of Brice in the London production of *Funny Girl* in 1966 and this time met with greater critical success. The *Daily Express* noted: 'Barbra Streisand opened in "Funny Girl" in London last night and performed the daunting feat of living up to her legend. The girl and the myth are indivisible. A gawky, loping, long-limbed lass with the ant-eater profile of a long-ago Egyptian queen, Miss Streisand is a compendium of uncommon talents.'[6] The show ran only four months in London because Streisand became pregnant, but she had already been contracted by Columbia Pictures to appear in the film version,[7] thus guaranteeing her indelible link with the musical.

Work on the screenplay began in 1966 and continued through 1967, with rehearsals beginning in July of that year. Army Archerd reported in Variety: 'A song and a (film) star born? Yesterday, in the nostalgia-filled recording Stage 7 at Goldwyn studios, newcomer Barbra Streisand pre-recorded "Funny Girl" [*sic*] title tune to the Columbia epic she starts filming Monday. It is one of four new Jule Styne-Bob Merrill numbers for the pic version. The orch, [*sic*] made up of the town's top musicians under the baton of Walter Scharf, and accustomed to the best, applauded her after the dramatic playbacks.'[8] Filming continued throughout the remainder of 1967, with locations including New Jersey and California, and concluded in December 1967. After a long delay, the movie received its premiere on 18 September 1968 in New York, with international premieres occurring throughout the ensuing months, leading up to Streisand's triumph at the Academy Awards (as Best Actress) on 14 April 1969.[9]

Even before this landmark event in Streisand's career, she had already signed up to her next two film musical roles. It is extraordinary that the young actress was fast-tracked to a series of such large and important movie projects, given her lack of experience and in particular the fact that her clout at the box office had not yet been proven. Her casting as the matchmaker Dolly Levi in Jerry Herman's *Hello, Dolly!* was especially controversial and unexpected, since the musical was the biggest Broadway hit of the decade and was a vehicle for a well-established, mature star: actresses such as Mary Martin, Ginger Rogers, Martha Raye, Betty Grable, Pearl Bailey, and Ethel Merman followed the original star, Carol Channing, in the role on the stage. When Streisand began shooting the film in 1967, she was just twenty-five years old versus the forty-three-year-old Channing. Since the character of Dolly is a widow who has stayed away from society for some time after the death of her first husband, Streisand was an implausible choice on paper. Her casting was announced on 8 May 1967 and the outrage in the press was unusually scathing. For example, Richard Coe in the *Washington Post* declared: 'Would you believe Barbra Streisand for the screen's "Hello, Dolly!"? Well, that's the knuckle headed fact. . . . With all due respect to young Miss Streisand, the mournful Nefertiti is clearly not the outgoing, zestful Irishwoman whose vitality brightens Thornton Wilder's mature, life-loving Dolly Gallagher-Levi. The perversity of not choosing to get Carol Channing's musical-comedy classic on film is hard to fathom.'[10] (Channing had won the Tony Award for her performance on Broadway.)

Yet, as the *New York Times* review of the movie would much later go on to observe, the objections to Streisand's casting were arguably irrelevant. Vincent Canby openly declared:

> The screen adaptation of 'Hello, Dolly!,' which began a reserved-seat engagement last night at the Rivoli Theater (after

a private, somewhat violent, invitational premiere Tuesday night), is not invulnerable to criticism, but I suspect that Barbra Streisand is. At the age of 27, and for the very good reason that she is one of the few, mysteriously natural, unique performing talents of our time, she has become a National Treasure. Casting her as Dolly Levi (the 'née Gallagher' has been dropped from the film), is rather like trying to display Yellowstone National Park in a one-geyser forest preserve. It doesn't really work, but most people probably couldn't care less. Miss Streisand is at that point of her career where her public personality invests everything in which she happens to appear with an importance and a resonance that have no relation to the vehicle itself.[11]

Filming of the movie began on 15 April 1968 and took ninety days, following several months of rehearsal earlier in the year.[12] It was a stellar affair: the legendary Gene Kelly was hired as director, with Michael Kidd (of the Broadway *Finian's Rainbow* and *Guys and Dolls*, as well as MGM's *Seven Brides for Seven Brothers*) providing the choreography; Walter Matthau was cast opposite Streisand as Horace Vandergelder and Michael Crawford played Cornelius, Vandergelder's young clerk. With the rights alone costing a reported $2 million, Twentieth Century–Fox meant business.[13] Yet the film was surrounded by stories of tension between the figures involved. For example, composer-lyricist Jerry Herman reported that Kelly refused to collaborate with him: 'Gene Kelly, who directed, did not want to have anything to do with me. It wasn't that he hated me personally, he just didn't want his movie to be contaminated by anyone from Broadway. Gene Kelly wasn't the only one who had that old anti-Broadway bias. So many of these movie people are like that. I am not the kind of person who generally gets a cold reception, because the smart ones know that I can be very helpful. But these Hollywood types

didn't like any theatre people. They considered us the enemy—
and that's the God's truth.'[14]

There was also at least one major disagreement between
Streisand and Matthau and there was little chemistry between
the two, with the actress supposedly confiding to her stand-in,
Marie Rhodes: 'What I needed was Rhett Butler to sweep me
back up again. What I got was Walter Matthau.'[15] Streisand is
also reported to have become open in her awareness that she
was unusual casting for the role, ringing screenwriter Ernest
Lehman in the middle of the night and asking: 'What the hell am
I doing in this picture? . . . There is no way I can play Dolly Levi
in a way that makes sense of the woman.'[16] She even discussed
the issue frankly in an interview with *Look* magazine: 'I did feel
that *Dolly* was a story of older people and that they should hire
Elizabeth Taylor to play her. I thought that would be a great role
for her first musical. But when everybody seemed to be against
me as Dolly, I took up the challenge. I've never been an underdog
in Hollywood, and people get spiteful about me. They tell lies
that make good journalistic copy. I have very little in common
with a character like Dolly, who fixes people up and lives other
people's lives. I do share the fun she gets in bargaining and buys,
and can understand her experience as a woman who has loved
and lost. A woman can be any age for that. But I really didn't
respond to the Broadway show—a piece of fluff. It's not the kind
of thing I'm interested in. I'm interested in real life, real people,
and in playing Medea. *Dolly* takes place in an age before people
realized they hated their mothers—the whole Freudian thing. So
it wasn't something I could delve psychologically into too deeply,
but I could have fun with Dolly and get days off because I didn't
have to be in every single scene for once. I call *Hello, Dolly!* my
last big voice picture.'[17]

Streisand's equivocation about the role is palpable in
this statement, but this was a movie at which everything
was thrown—names, energy, and over $20 million—and

the studio was determined to have a hit. Release of the film was delayed until 16 December 1969 because the original Broadway production was still running and Fox had to pay David Merrick (the Broadway producer of *Dolly*) a fee of $1.85 million to allow them to bring forward the release date.[18] But with mixed reviews and a drop off in box office, the deficit was great: within thirty-four weeks it had made a gross of less than $8 million, and according to the *Los Angeles Times* in December 1972, the film had lost around $16 million up to that date (though it would continue to make money from television and home video).[19] It became known as a landmark flop that contributed to the downfall of the studio and was a disappointment after the critical success of *Funny Girl*.

Yet even before the latter had been released, Streisand was cast in a third screen adaptation of a Broadway musical, and for a third studio, too. On 1 September 1968, Paramount announced that they had hired the actress to play Daisy in the Hollywood version of Alan Jay Lerner and Burton Lane's modestly successful *On a Clear Day You Can See Forever*, which had opened on Broadway in 1965 and run a little under a year.[20] Like *Funny Girl*, it had received mixed reviews on Broadway, and the screen adaptation would be liberal in every way. The original Broadway production was to have starred Louis Jourdan and Barbara Harris, but Jourdan was fired out of town and replaced by John Cullum, Richard Burton's understudy in Lerner's *Camelot* (1960). For the film, Vincente Minnelli was hired as director, following his previous collaborations at MGM with Lerner on *An American in Paris* (1951), *Brigadoon* (1954), and *Gigi* (1958). Paramount approached a number of stars—including Frank Sinatra and Richard Harris—to play opposite Streisand before French actor Yves Montand signed to the role.[21] Cecil Beaton and Arnold Scaasi shared the costume designs, with a diverse supporting cast that included the young Jack Nicholson as Streisand's former stepbrother and a number of British veterans for the Regency scenes. Filming began at Paramount on 6 January 1969 and moved in April to England, where some of the regression scenes were shot at the Brighton Pavillion. In May, the production moved to New York for location shooting (mainly for the 'Come Back to Me' sequence) and completed back in California in early June.[22]

Before the movie's release, it was condensed in length by at least fourteen minutes—an uncut version was accidentally played for a preview audience and reported on in *Variety*—leaving gaps where 'She Isn't You,' 'Wait Till We're Sixty-Five,' and 'Who Is There among Us Who Knows' should have appeared.[23] The reviews of the film were varied, but they also recognized the film's merits. For example, the *New York Times* reviewer said it was a movie of fits and starts, but because the fits are occasionally so lovely, and the starts somewhat more frequent than Fifth Avenue buses, I was eventually hypnotized into a state of benign though not-quite-abject permissiveness. The reasons have to do with nostalgia, and with expectation. 'On a Clear Day' is the first conventional musical film to open this year, the first Minnelli musical since 'The Bells Are Ringing' in 1960, and the first Barbra Streisand movie to suggest—even briefly—that she is capable of playing someone other than Fannie [*sic*] Brice in the seven stages of woman. The film . . . is solidly grounded in a casting coincidence: Barbra Streisand, a performer who sometimes seems too big for movies as well as for life, portrays a girl who is so full of life that she leads a succession of lives.[24]

Generally, the film's pace and the peculiarity of the material were criticized, but Streisand's performance was widely praised and, critically at least, she came out of the project much better than was the case with *Dolly*.

## ADAPTING AND STAGING THE FILMS FOR STREISAND

Putting Broadway musicals on the screen always requires some element of change, even when the adaptation is relatively faithful. But in the case of the three films under investigation here, both the medium and the star motivated far-reaching changes. On top of that, all three films were helmed by major directors—William Wyler, Gene Kelly, and Vincente Minnelli—who inevitably left their authorial stamp on the material in distinctive ways, thus adding an additional significant creative force to that of Streisand as the star. Of the three films, by far the most imaginative and cinematic adaptation is *Funny Girl*, which is perhaps surprising given that Streisand had also appeared in the stage version. Arguably, Wyler's *Funny Girl* even hints at what was to come a few years later in Bob Fosse's *Cabaret* (1972) in its mixture of the psychological and the visual: like Fosse, Wyler does not hesitate in making changes to the material in order to accommodate the screen (and in particular the screen Streisand). Of course, screenwriter Isobel Lennart—who also wrote the book for the Broadway version—deserves credit for the reconception of the musical too: the combination of writer and director seems to have provided an effective team around Streisand.

Two interconnected elements of the movie particularly deal with the medium in ways that serve Streisand's needs: the flashback device and the framing device. First, the story's delivery as a flashback is considerably expanded, returning to an idea that Lennart originally had in an early draft of the Broadway script dated 16 October 1962 (preserved in the David Merrick Collection at the Library of Congress).[25] In the stage version, this consists of a few lines of brief dialogue between Fanny and her dresser Emma, and the flashback begins rapidly.

For the film, Lennart expands and extends the framing device that promotes the notion that the story is all in Fanny's memory; Lennart adds an opening tableau in which Fanny is seen entering the New Amsterdam Theatre. The camera follows her from behind—we do not see her face for some time—and her name lights up on the marquee as she passes the facade. She continues through the doors to the backstage area until eventually she stands in front of a mirror. She pulls back her lapel and we finally see her face in the mirror. With a slight tear in her eye, Streisand speaks her first words on camera: 'Hello, gorgeous!' Although much has been made of this moment, what follows is arguably more striking. She moves to the empty theatre, where she plays a few notes of the melody of 'People' on the piano. The sound of applause is heard, and she mimes 'shooting' the audience. She then goes to sit in the audience and her maid, Emma, comes to see her. Fanny comments, 'Maybe things look different from here'; she puts her head back, closes her eyes, and the flashback begins with a fade to Mrs Brice's saloon.

Both the direction and acting of this scene, especially in the mock-gunfire section, are so compellingly disjointed as to almost render it a mad scene. Certainly there is such a remarkable blurring of the watcher and the watched, the spectator and spectacle, that the movie immediately becomes telescoped through Fanny's eyes (a device that Rob Marshall would later exploit in the movie version of *Chicago*, in which the story is viewed through Roxie's eyes). The lack of underscoring and the focus on Streisand's body, with very few words spoken, accentuates her presence and helps to frame her as the star. The combination of diegetic and nondiegetic sounds is also sophisticated and poignant. The sound of applause is in Fanny's head but the mock gunshot noises are made by Fanny herself; the piano's notes are heard in 'reality' but since the song 'People' is a 'book' number, it is illogical that Fanny knows the melody. Most of the rest of the film is told in chronological order, without any reiteration of the flashback device, until 'Funny Girl,' the penultimate number of the movie.

Here, Fanny and Nick have just said goodbye while he sets off for prison, and Fanny sings part of the song in the flashback/past. Halfway through the number, the acoustic changes and we are back in the empty theatre from the beginning of the film, with Fanny still sitting in the audience. The editing of the soundtrack gives the impression that the song is now an echo of a memory bouncing around the theatre; Streisand is shown sitting in the theatre but her mouth does not move until the last couple of lines of the song ('Funny how it ain't so funny, / Funny girl'), when the vocal becomes 'present' again. The rest of the story, with Nick's return and final farewell, continues chronologically. All of this gives the plot a new subjectivity that it did not have in the Broadway show: Lennart's framing device turns Fanny into the limited narrator of *Funny Girl*, telling the story from her point of view. The film becomes personal rather than a simple biopic, and by setting up Fanny's psyche so compellingly at the opening, Wyler and Lennart establish the film as truly belonging to Streisand.

The opening sequence also sets up a leitmotif that will return throughout, whereby Streisand confronts herself in the mirror. The rapid juxtaposition of the 'Hey, gorgeous!' line and the film's first song, 'If a Girl Isn't Pretty,' which starts at the very beginning of the flashback, help to make sense of this gesture: Brice/Streisand is not a traditional Hollywood beauty, yet the film's recurring debate about her physical appearance explores her image in such detail that the camera's objectification of her ultimately emphasizes her sui generis beauty. Yet this is also a personal process because she constantly examines her image, and identity, through the mirror, and therefore comes to terms with her own appearance (and self). Examples include a moment where she sees herself, pre-Ziegfeld, in the mirror during 'If a Girl Isn't Pretty,' when her mother and her friends are discussing her limited chances of success, based on the way she looks; a comedic moment in the Ziegfeld production number 'His Love Makes Me Beautiful' when she recoils in shock at seeing the reflection of her pregnant figure (the line 'I ask my looking glass, "What is it / Makes me so exquisite?"' underlines the idea); a brief moment in the 'You Are Woman' scene when she is shown in the mirror during Nick's seduction of her; another in 'Sadie, Sadie' when she looks at herself in the mirror when sitting in the bath, at last a 'married lady'; and most memorable of all, the final dialogue scene of the film, when Fanny/Streisand sits putting on her makeup, using the three panels of her dressing room mirror, when Nick returns. The act of grooming herself with a triple reflection of herself here implies a greater level of self-acceptance about her appearance, even as Nick enters to say farewell.

Wyler extends the device of framing Streisand's image and performance in other scenes too. For example, in the 'Second Hand Rose' number, the Follies ensemble sit or stand around onstage behind her, watching and reacting to her performance; Ziegfeld is also seen at several points, watching from the audience. Earlier, Fanny's star quality emerges in 'I'd Rather Be Blue' when she relaxes (after an initially tentative performance) on the line 'For you I'm strong.' The audience at Keeney's slowly warms to Brice's performance and by the end there is rapturous applause. (In this sense, the number is designed rather like Louise's 'Let Me Entertain You' in *Gypsy*, an earlier Jule Styne musical.) Wyler also subtly creates a dynamic of spectacle versus spectator in the filming of the 'People' number. Initially, Brice delivers the number to Nicky as if in conversation, but the latter part of the song is staged so that it is no longer addressed to him as a character: instead, he stands in the background, watching passively, while Streisand performs and emotes to nobody in particular. Her next appearance in the film also has an element of framing: Fanny is asked to pose for photographs while disembarking the train. During the second half of the film, she is also framed by the doorway when she arrives at Nick's cabin on board ship.

In addition to 'People,' various scenes that are ostensibly about Nick are filmed to emphasize Fanny/Streisand instead, most notably the card game at which Nick wins enough money for the pair to get married. Wyler focuses on Fanny's anxiety (played as a comic tour de force by Streisand) rather than Nick's gambling manoeuvres. Similarly, in the argument scene after 'The Swan,' the camera looks at Nick (who is standing) from behind Fanny's head on the sofa, channelling the viewer's attention towards her emotional reaction to his words rather than the words themselves. This kind of technique is also used in their conversation after the trial. When Nick asks for a divorce ('We're just no good for each other') the camera lens on him is blurred when he is speaking and instead focuses on her; Wyler constantly underlines her reactions to his lines rather than what he is saying. Then in the final scene of the movie (before 'My Man'), when Nick leaves the dressing room we only see the door close in the mirror, with Fanny's reaction, rather than Nick's physical departure. In short, the movie is entirely about Fanny and therefore about Streisand (or at least her performance): even Nick/Sharif is a surprisingly incidental presence. She is, as Fanny declares in her first big number, 'the greatest star' of this movie, and the entire picture articulates Streisand's star persona.

*Hello, Dolly!* is a somewhat different matter because, as noted above, Streisand's age was inappropriate for the character of Dolly Levi. She was in her mid-twenties when filming the role, but Dolly is supposed to be a widow (at least forty or fifty) who has spent years hiding away from life, finding matches for other couples. By the time the film was made, and particularly by the time it was released, the stage show had been firmly established as a vehicle for a veteran actress: Carol

Channing, Ginger Rogers, Mary Martin, and so on. Part of the musical's appeal was the presence of a familiar figure of a certain seniority that the audience already knew well. For Streisand, then, the role was particularly difficult to make sense of. Therefore, screenwriter Ernest Lehman and director Gene Kelly went about reconceiving the story as much as possible, as well as emphasizing Dolly's humorous and vulnerable qualities (which suited Streisand's star persona) and changing numerous aspects of her songs to show off her vocal prowess (this is discussed at length in the next section).

In particular, Kelly embraces Streisand's youthful energy rather than hiding it. Although her costumes, hair, and makeup have hints of a slightly older character, there is no obvious attempt to make Streisand look or, more importantly, behave as a middle-aged woman. From her first appearance in the movie, she skips and runs around with limitless reserves of energy and is rarely out of breath. In this telling of the story, Dolly apparently displaces her feelings of bereavement by being everywhere and doing everything, so that she never has free time to fill. This is in contrast to the stage Dolly, who seems more of a maternal figure who is motivated by passing on her warmth and wisdom to help others to reach the kind of happiness she once felt. Streisand's Dolly implausibly gets the train to Yonkers simply to inform Horace that she has set him up on a date, and while she is there she also encourages Cornelius and Barnaby (Horace's clerks) to play truant for the evening; the physical presence of the train in the film draws attention to how much effort this relatively brief errand has required, arguably pointing to how Dolly's work expands to fill the time available.

The flip side of this characteristic is that in two scenes where Dolly is absolutely alone, there is a strong feeling of poignancy, stasis, and isolation. As 'Dancing' comes to an end at the climax of the first half of the film, Dolly is shown on her own on a park bench and Streisand's delivery of her speech about 'rejoining the human race' is intimate and sorrowful. The camera is in close-up and Streisand's performance is beautifully understated, as if to reveal the true sadness that underlies the humour that she portrays in her fast-paced comic dialogue scenes when interacting with other characters. The same is also true of the 'Love Is Only Love' scene. This number, which was added for the movie adaptation, takes place in the private/personal space of Dolly's apartment, where she is shut off from the rest of the world; Kelly and Lehman contrast the claustrophobia of this scene with the 'Elegance' number that precedes it, in which Irene (Horace's intended, and a shop owner), Minnie (her assistant), Cornelius, and Barnaby wander freely around the town (the outdoors) without a care.

One of the most complex implications of having a younger Dolly is that she suddenly becomes close in age to the six junior characters: Cornelius, Irene, Barnaby, Minnie, Ermengarde, and Ambrose. Lehman's solution is to make the difference between her and them in the movie that she is smart and they are passive: Michael Crawford's Cornelius is excessively buffoonish and has little chemistry with Marianne McAndrew's Irene, while the others tend to turn to Dolly for guidance on their every move rather than showing spirit or agency of their own. One of the major changes for the movie is the removal of the courtroom scene, in which Cornelius saves himself and his friends from being convicted by singing 'It Only Takes a Moment'; the number is performed as a simple romantic ballad (nothing more than a declaration of love) in the park instead. In other words, the song is recontextualized into a less pivotal scene and the secondary characters become less substantial, thus providing less competition for Streisand's Dolly, who appears at the start of the next scene and breaks into her arresting performance of 'So Long, Dearie.' Lehman and Kelly constantly make Streisand's Dolly energetic and resourceful, but in the process the other characters and plot elements often seem generic or watered-down. Since the film is also unquestionably overblown—the external dance section of 'Dancing,' for example, has no purpose other than display of the opulent sets, costumes, and athletic choreography—the film's framing of Streisand as the star does not make the movie as a whole coherent (unlike with *Funny Girl*).

Despite being the most uneven of the three movies, *On a Clear Day You Can See Forever* is perhaps the most interesting example of how a stage musical was adapted into a film musical for Streisand's talents. Alan Jay Lerner's screenplay diverges significantly from his book for the stage version, from opening scene to last (the score is also extensively changed, as shown in the next section). For example, the first scene of the Broadway show takes place in Dr Mark Bruckner's office, where he meets Daisy Gamble for the first time and discovers that she has extra-sensory perception through her own admission. The movie, however, provides an opportunity to introduce Daisy as an outsider: she attends Dr Marc Chabot's (as he becomes in the movie) lecture on hypnosis and is accidentally hypnotized herself. By planting her in the audience but having her behave unconventionally, Lerner establishes her as an unusual character, an outsider, a star. The added scene also gives her the opportunity to show off her comic talents, when she starts taking off her stocking on post-hypnotic suggestion. The scene cleverly makes Daisy into a layered character: it's amusing that she cannot control herself but it is also the cause of discomfort on Daisy's part, and therefore a reason to feel compassion for her.

Lerner and Minnelli try to give the film a sense of mystery by presenting the story of Melinda—Daisy's former incarnation, that is, in another life—in reverse chronological order during a series of flashbacks under hypnosis.[26] As with *Funny Girl*, the device of the flashback helps to frame the film through Streisand's eyes, and even though Chabot puts her under hypnosis, it is Daisy's story: Chabot/Montand is passive through most of the film, as are Sharif/Nick and Matthau/Horace in the previous movies. Chabot sits around discovering the story of Melinda (and even falls in love with her) but he never really psychoanalyzes Daisy, who is much more insightful. The first regression scene shows Melinda's trial, followed by a further flashback to a scene where Melinda meets her beloved, Robert Tentrees (a lavish sequence filmed at the Royal Pavilion, Brighton). Subsequent regressions show Melinda's escape from school—a grotesque scene in which the character accidentally lassos a woman around the neck from the other side of a wall—as well as a scene at a gambling table in which Melinda helps Robert to win through extra-sensory perception.

This narrative device—of telling the story-within-the-story in reverse order—contributes to the mystery and fragmentation associated with Streisand's character. In the film, she alternately plays a kooky New York girl (Daisy), a cockney British teenager (Melinda as a girl), and a British (fake) aristocrat (Melinda as a woman). In addition, Daisy's personality has different facets: she claims to be 'normal' and have 'no neuroses' but she alternates between faux dumb and feistily wise, the latter brought about because she remembers several previous lives and also knows what happens in the future. This combination of character traits allows Streisand to play the full range of her acting abilities (her lamentable English accent notwithstanding), including comedy, romance, and drama. And while Chabot is convinced by Daisy's stories in the end, everything other than the scenes in the present day is a fantasy, which means that the different incarnations of Melinda (and the 'other' Daisy in the duet 'Go to Sleep') is a fragment of Streisand's personality, unified only by her body on the screen. Therefore, while the main narrative of the film makes very little sense at all, as a film it reaches coherence as a showcase of Streisand's acting talent and diverse star persona.

## ADAPTING THE SCORES

Yet it is through the scores of the three films that Streisand makes her biggest mark. By the time of the films' releases, she was already a major recording artist and it was inevitable that all three films would find every opportunity to showcase her voice. Changes were made to the score of each film to accommodate both the shift in medium and the change in star (in the case of *Dolly* and *Clear Day*). **Tables 4.1–3** outline the Broadway and movie incarnations of the three scores, with some striking differences in the song list in each case. With *Funny Girl*, Streisand appears in all the vocal numbers in the movie version, accentuating the feeling that the film is in her psyche, and hardly anyone else sings. According to Matt Howe, several songs involving other characters were filmed but cut, most importantly Nick's 'Temporary Arrangement,' 'Locked in a Pink Velvet Jail,' and reprise of 'Don't Rain on My Parade,' as well as Eddie and Mrs Brice's 'Who Taught Her Everything She Knows.'[27] The silencing of Nick is especially noticeable in the final film, where his vocal contributions are confined to 'You Are Woman, I Am Man' and a brief part of 'Sadie, Sadie.' Styne reportedly hoped to cast Frank Sinatra in the movie rather than Sharif and was disappointed in the latter's vocal abilities; either that or the decision to focus on Fanny's story led to the cuts in his songs.[28]

The musical style of the score also features several shifts of style and emphasis in comparison to the Broadway version. Overall, the movie score is much more symphonic in sound (much to Styne's chagrin),[29] especially in the book numbers (e.g., 'People'). The movie makes a much stronger distinction between the vaudeville sound of the diegetic Follies numbers and the book songs, whereas on the stage Styne gives most of the score a vaudevillian feel (e.g., by being highly rhythmic and quirky) to provide coherence. In fact, the Broadway songs that

### Table 4.1

## A COMPARISON OF THE PRINCIPAL NUMBERS OF THE SCORE OF *FUNNY GIRL* ON THE STAGE (LEFT) AND SCREEN (RIGHT)

| Broadway | Movie |
| --- | --- |
| **Act 1** | |
| Overture | Overture |
| Poker Change No. 1/If A Girl Isn't Pretty [Mrs Strakosh, Mrs Brice, Eddie and Ensemble] | If A Girl Isn't Pretty [Fanny, Mrs Brice, Mrs Strakosh] |
| I'm The Greatest Star [Fanny] | I'm The Greatest Star [Fanny] |
| Eddie's Fifth Encore [Eddie] | Rollerskate Rag [Fanny and Female Ensemble] |
| Cornet Man [Fanny and Dancing Chorus] | I'd Rather Be Blue [Fanny] |
| Nicky Arnstein No. 1 [Fanny] | Nicky Arnstein [Fanny] |
| Who Taught Her Everything? [Mrs Brice and Eddie] | Second Hand Rose [Fanny] |
| His Love Makes Me Beautiful [Fanny and Ziegfeld Ensemble] | His Love Makes Me Beautiful [Fanny and Ziegfeld Ensemble] |
| I Want To Be Seen With You Tonight [Nicky and Fanny] | |
| Nicky Arnstein No. 2 [Fanny] | |
| Henry Street [Ensemble] | |
| People [Fanny] | People [Fanny] |
| Poker Chant No. 2 [Mrs Brice and Mrs Strakosh] | |
| You Are Woman, I Am Man [Nicky and Fanny] | You Are Woman [Nicky and Fanny] |
| Don't Rain On My Parade [Fanny] | Don't Rain On My Parade [Fanny] |

(*continued*)

## Table 4.1

## CONTINUED

| Broadway | Movie |
|---|---|
| **Act 2** | |
| Entr'acte | Entr'acte |
| Sadie, Sadie [Fanny and Friends] | Sadie, Sadie [Fanny and Nick] |
| Find Yourself a Man [Mrs Strakosh, Mrs Brice, Eddie] | The Swan [Fanny] |
| Rat-Tat-Tat-Tat [Eddie, Fanny and Ziegfeld Ensemble] | Funny Girl [Fanny] |
| Who Are You Now? [Fanny] | My Man [Fanny] |
| Don't Rain on My Parade – Nick's Version [Nick] | |
| The Music That Makes Me Dance [Fanny] | |
| Don't Rain On My Parade - Reprise [Fanny] | |

were left out of the film nearly all (apart from 'Who Are You Now?' and 'The Music That Makes Me Dance') contain a sense of the theatre, which is curious in light of the decision to insert 'Second Hand Rose' and 'I'd Rather Be Blue,' two period vaudeville songs by composers other than Styne. This creates a sharp division between true vaudeville songs, which are diegetic and totally generic, and the book numbers, which are mostly expressive and personal. Also added to the score is 'My Man,' one of Fanny Brice's signature songs, which replaced the finale reprise of 'Don't Rain on My Parade,' against Styne's protestations.[30] Although the lyric to 'My Man' suggests a downbeat ending for Fanny, Streisand's performance—the tearful first part of which was recorded live on set—is so powerful as to portray a sense

## Table 4.2

## · A COMPARISON THE PRINCIPAL NUMBERS OF THE SCORE OF *HELLO, DOLLY!* ON THE STAGE (LEFT) AND SCREEN (RIGHT)

| Broadway | Movie |
| --- | --- |
| **Act 1** | |
| Overture | Call On Dolly [Ensemble] |
| Opening: Call On Dolly [Ensemble] | Just Leave Everything To Me [Dolly] |
| I Put My Hand In [Dolly] | Main Titles |
| It Takes a Woman [Horace, Cornelius, Barnaby and Ensemble] | It Takes a Woman [Horace, Cornelius, Barnaby and Ensemble] |
| It Takes a Woman - reprise [Horace and Dolly] | It Takes a Woman - reprise |
| Put On Your Sunday Clothes [Cornelius, Barnaby, Dolly, Ambrose, Ermengarde and Ensemble] | Put On Your Sunday Clothes [Cornelius, Barnaby, Dolly, Ambrose, Ermengarde and Ensemble] |
| Ribbons Down My Back [Irene] | Ribbons Down My Back [Irene] |
| Ribbons Down My Back - reprise [Irene] | Dancing [Dolly, Cornelius, Barnaby, Irene, Minnie and Ensemble] |
| Motherhood [Dolly, Irene, Minnie and Horace] | Before The Parade Passes By [Dolly and Ensemble] |
| Dancing [Dolly, Cornelius, Barnaby, Irene, Minnie and Ensemble] | |
| Before The Parade Passes By [Dolly and Ensemble] | |
| Finale Act 1: Before The Parade Passes By [Dolly] | |

(*continued*)

## Table 4.2

### CONTINUED

| Broadway | Movie |
| --- | --- |
| **Act 2** | |
| Entr'acte | Entr'acte |
| Elegance [Cornelius, Barnaby, Irene and Minnie] | Elegance [Cornelius, Barnaby, Irene and Minnie] |
| The Waiters' Galop [Waters' Ensemble] | Love Is Only Love [Dolly] |
| Hello, Dolly! [Dolly and Waiters] | The Waiters' Galop [Waters' Ensemble] |
| The Waiters' Galop - reprise [Waters' Ensemble] | Hello, Dolly! [Dolly and Waiters] |
| The Polka Contest [Ensemble] | The Polka Contest [Ensemble] |
| It Only Takes a Moment [Cornelius, Irene and Ensemble] | It Only Takes a Moment [Cornelius, Irene and Ensemble] |
| So Long, Dearie [Dolly] | So Long, Dearie [Dolly] |
| Hello, Dolly! [Dolly and Horace] | Hello, Dolly! [Dolly and Horace] |
| Finale [Ensemble] | Finale [Ensemble] |

of defiance, especially in her aggressive delivery of the words 'what's the difference.' The chiaroscuro design of the number augments the potency of the vocals: Streisand wears a black dress against a black backdrop, so the white appearance of her face, neckline, and hands is stark and bold.

Streisand's vocal performances of several songs are quite different in the Broadway cast album and movie soundtrack. On the Broadway album Streisand adheres much more strictly to the pulse, perhaps most especially in 'Don't Rain on My Parade,' 'His Love Makes Me Beautiful' and 'I'm the Greatest

Table 4.3

## A COMPARISON OF THE PRINCIPAL NUMBERS OF THE SCORE OF *ON A CLEAR DAY YOU CAN SEE FOREVER* ON THE STAGE (LEFT) AND SCREEN (RIGHT)

| Broadway | Movie |
|---|---|
| **Act 1** | |
| Overture | Hurry, It's Lovely Up Here |
| Hurry, It's Lovely Up Here | [Daisy] |
| [Daisy] | On a Clear Day: Main Titles |
| Ring Out the Bells [Samuel, | [Ensemble] |
| Mrs Welles, Sir Hubert and | Love With All the Trimmings |
| Ensemble] | [Daisy] |
| Tosy and Cosh [Daisy] | Melinda [Marc] |
| On a Clear Day [Mark] | Go To Sleep [Daisy] |
| On the S.S. Bernard Cohn [Daisy, | He Isn't You [Daisy] |
| Muriel, Preston and Millard] | What Did I Have That I Don't |
| At the Hellrakers [Ballet] | Have [Daisy] |
| Don't Tamper with My Sister | Come Back to Me [Marc] |
| [Edward, Sir Hubert and | On a Clear Day [Marc] |
| Ensemble] | On a Clear Day - reprise |
| She Wasn't You [Edward] | [Daisy] |
| Melinda [Mark] | |
| **Act 2** | |
| Entr'acte | |
| When I'm Being Born Again | |
| [Kriakos] | |
| What Did I Have at I Don't Have | |
| [Daisy] | |
| Wait Till We're Sixty - Five | |
| [Warren and Daisy] | |
| Come Back to Me [Mark]] | |
| On a Clear Day [Ensemble] | |

Star.' One can almost hear the conductor, Milton Rosenstock, beating time in these numbers, and it is striking that Streisand observes most of the syncopated rhythms in 'Parade' compared to the much freer rendition in the movie. Her part in 'You Are Woman' is also much straighter and less colourful on the Broadway album, and 'Sadie, Sadie' is delivered like a vaudeville song, with a strong, deliberate sense of the metre, whereas the montage version in the film is much smoother and seems more personal. Interestingly, a few documents from the Broadway production in Bob Merrill's papers at the Library of Congress indicate that Streisand was inclined to take a liberal, spontaneous approach to the score even on the stage and that—assuming Merrill's notes were communicated—she was encouraged to observe the score more closely. For example, a copy of the sheet music of 'Who Are You Now' is annotated: 'Please don't let Barbra improvise so!' Another document says: 'Please have Barbra make up mind before orchestrating.' A lyric sheet for 'People' is annotated: 'Barbra—must not do her second version improvising too much.'[31] Perhaps the writers exerted more authorial control against her creativity during preparations for the Broadway version, when their songs would be heard for the first time, but when it came to making the film, Streisand the star was able to follow her own artistic path.

By the time of *Hello, Dolly!*, there was no doubt that Streisand was going to give the songs her own spin—and her youth meant that her delivery of the score was the freshest on record. There were fewer changes to the song set than with *Funny Girl*: Table 4.2 shows two new songs, 'Just Leave Everything to Me' in place of 'I Put My Hand In' and 'Love Is Only Love' (originally written for but dropped from Jerry Herman's *Mame*) to give Streisand another solo in the second half of the movie. Streisand was also given an extended reprise of 'It Takes a Woman' that was mainly sung by Horace in the Broadway version. (The maternalistic 'Motherhood' was deleted.) These three extra numbers support the strategies to emphasize specific elements of the character as discussed above, namely, Dolly's feelings of bereavement (the intimate 'It Takes a Woman' reprise and particularly 'Love Is Only Love' showcase the elegiac, poignant facet of Streisand's performance, making her more believable as the widow) and energy ('Just Leave Everything' is a comic patter song that established the youthfulness of Streisand's version of the role, recalling 'Come to the Supermarket' and 'Down with Love' from her first two studio albums). Importantly, 'Just Leave Everything' outlines a range of roles (including importing cheese and tweezing eyebrows) for Dolly, whereas 'I Put My Hand In' (the song it replaces from the Broadway version) is focused on matchmaking; in the movie, she is a general busybody. Also, the opening of 'Love Is Only Love' recycles the aural technique of the second half of the title song from *Funny Girl*: Streisand's voice is muffled, like an echo in the memory, and only becomes 'present' when she reaches the refrain. This adds to the nostalgia of her characterization, versus the general energy of 'Just Leave Everything.' These are the two main modes of Streisand's performance, and the contrast between the two helps to establish the framework for her unusual assumption of the role.

Yet the more arresting aspect of her performance in *Dolly* is how she delivers the familiar songs carried over from the Broadway show. Engineered into the arrangements of the songs is a new approach to Dolly's music, especially in relation to tempo and vocal writing; on top of this, Streisand frequently pulls the melodic line, rhythm, and pulse around, as a means of taking ownership of the material. In 'Put On Your Sunday Clothes,' she is (quite illogically) assigned the male chorus's line 'To town we'll trot to a smoky spot / Where the girls are hot as a fuse'—Kelly has her walk through the middle of the railway carriage to frame her gutsy and musically liberal performance—and she sings a kind of chesty descant part on the final lines of the song too, supported by the chorus. Then in 'Before the Parade Passes By,' Herman expands Dolly's opening solo, giving her a complete refrain sung ad lib with some new lyrics ('Before it all moves on / And only I'm left' and 'Life without life / Has no reason or rhyme left'). This section homes in on the intimacy of Streisand's portrayal of Dolly's lifelessness because of her widowhood, and in the spoken monologue that follows she resolves to 'rejoin the human race,' leading to a grand accelerando during the next refrain. To end the first half of the film, Dolly/Streisand is given the climax of the song, holding the final note for over half a dozen bars while the parade moves on around her and the camera pans out: another spectacular assertion of her star status.

For the title song, the production team came up with an additional device to make the number more exciting: near the end of the sequence, Louis Armstrong, who had made a hit record of the number, appears and sings a refrain as a duet with Streisand. In order to make that moment a highlight, the earlier parts of the number create a slow build. The opening refrain is sung freely by Streisand, with only an intermittent sense of pulse. The waiters take over, then Streisand sings the verse, whose recitative-like quality is turned into an intimate moment thanks to close-up camera work and total freedom in the vocal delivery by Streisand. In particular, the words 'good old days' are stretched out to emphasize the feeling of nostalgia. After another sung refrain and a dance break, Dolly/Streisand encounters Armstrong and the pair improvise their vocal lines, both with interaction and (at the end) in harmony. Here, Streisand has met her musical equal and her own star power is augmented by being able to hold her own in such distinguished and experienced company. It is also a true 'Streisand moment' because she appears to have total freedom in her interjected responses to Armstrong's singing of the written lines of the refrain. Indeed, the number as a whole is different in the screen version because it becomes a vehicle for Streisand's vocal talents, which are considerably fresher, more flexible, and bigger than those of most of the actresses who played the part on the stage. Yet an even more salient shift is seen in the adaptation of 'So Long, Dearie,' Dolly's mock farewell to Vandergelder after the chaos at the Harmonia Gardens. For Streisand, the song was rearranged from a steady 'in 4' feel to a swift 'in 2' delivery. It is considerably faster, which transforms it into a rhythm song: the orchestra provides a fast-moving foundation over which Streisand delivers the vocal line with, again, considerable freedom and flexibility. As is the case with most of her recordings, she places little importance on observing written note lengths and frequently elides or elongates notes and phrases like a jazz performer. In fact, in places where she delivers a phrase straight, such as 'Don't you come a-knockin' at my door' in this song, this accurate rendition of the notes becomes an expressive gesture. This is at the heart of her expressivity as a singer.

In all three films, Streisand is cast opposite a male actor without vocal prowess. Even Yves Montand (the best of the three—a competent crooner and a recording artist) is often silenced or outsung in *On a Clear Day*. For example, Daisy/ Streisand's 'He Isn't You' was originally supposed to be immediately followed by a complementary version for Marc/Montand, 'She Wasn't You.'[32] It was cut, leaving Montand without a song for a long stretch. Then in the final scene of the film, Montand sings the title song complete, in his intimate crooner style, but Streisand is allowed to reprise the entire refrain again to close the movie. Her version is much more spectacular, both vocally and in staging. Montand's is sung in his study but Streisand's is set outdoors, as she wanders back through the university gardens she walked through in the opening scene of the film; at the end, she is suspended in space against a superimposed backdrop of clouds, illustrating the 'you can see forever' line in the lyric. Furthermore, Montand's version has a light scoring, with most of the refrain performed against an easy rhythm section accompaniment with light fills between the phrases; Streisand's is scored for full strings and has a considerably more complex texture and much more contrapuntal edge. Few would come away from the film remembering Montand's rendition over Streisand's, not only because her performance is vocally stronger but also because her version is set up to magnify her presence, for example, through the kinetic energy of walking through the gardens.

Also cut from the film is 'Wait Till We're Sixty-Five,' a duet for Daisy and her fiancé Warren; it was to be his only song in the film so its excision is significant. The role of Tad, Daisy's step-brother, played by Jack Nicholson, was also trimmed generally and his only song, 'Who Is There among Us Who Knows,' in which Streisand hummed along, was filmed but then cut.[33] It is striking, in fact, that all musical interaction between Streisand and other characters is completely excised from the movie. But in an ingenious move, Lerner and Lane add a duet for Streisand with her alter ego, a song called 'Go to Sleep' that was written specially for the film. Lerner conceives the number as an inter-action between Daisy, who is attracted to Marc despite being engaged to Warren, and her conscience, who encourages her not to follow her erotic impulse. It is the most playful scene in the movie, partly because the design of Streisand's costume, bedclothes, and wallpaper all match one another, as if Daisy's psychological fracturing has spread to her surroundings. More importantly, the scene affirms Streisand's stardom by implying that the only performer she can duet with in the film is herself.

Her allure, and that of Melinda, is also accentuated in the performance of 'He Isn't You.' Here, in another regression se-quence, Melinda is seen at the harp. Streisand's voice can be heard delivering the song, but her mouth does not move—the return of a device used in both *Funny Girl* and *Dolly*. The vocal performance is intimate and because there is no physical effort shown in the onscreen visuals, the audience focuses on the nuances of Streisand's vocals. The set-up also serves the dramatic situation well: Marc is now thoroughly obsessed with Melinda and believes she is interacting with him, in the past. Later in the song, Marc and Melinda are shown dancing together in a fantasy sequence that transcends the limitations of time and realism. As the impossible object of male desire, Melinda/Streisand is once again framed as the star.

Streisand's other important musical moment in the movie is 'What Did I Have That I Don't Have.' In the Broadway version, the song is a straightforward blues song in which Daisy laments the fact that Mark does not love her. It was a highlight of the show for the Broadway actress, Barbara Harris, but it explored one expressive idea throughout (the lament of the jilted lover). In the film, however, it becomes a much more extensive dramatic scene for Streisand. Daisy has just discovered the tapes on which Chabot has recorded her sessions of hypnosis, as well as his reactions to them, and she is devastated. The delivery of the verse is relatively free and the vocal performance is saturated with the sound of sobbing, but the treatment of the first section of the first refrain is particularly interesting. The arrangement engineers a long, slow growth in momentum and speed. Initially, the orchestra plays just one chord per bar, accompanying *colla voce* to allow Streisand to deliver the vocal part almost like a spoken monologue: the presence of pitch perhaps distracts from the fact that all sense of metre is absent at first, in contrast to the tighter rhythmic pattern of the Broadway version heard on the cast album. In Streisand's version, the rhythm kicks in after a few lines but is still fairly lazy and light. The performance becomes more emphatic leading into 'I'm just a victim of time,' where a harp glissando initiates a warmer and more assertive string accompaniment. The final section of the first rendition resumes the easier feel of the first part, then Daisy has a spoken section where she mourns her situation.

She then takes a phone call from Chabot, in which she loses her temper. The underscore changes to a hot drum rhythm to communicate a change of mood from despair to defiance. Streisand then performs another refrain of the song at double tempo and with constant deviation from the pitches of the vocal line and notated rhythms. The blueprint of the routine would appear to be 'My Man' from the *Funny Girl* film. Both songs feature a slower opening that is tearful, spontaneous, emotional, metrically free, and highly 'acted.' In the middle, a change of mood leads to a defiant continuation of both songs that is more up-tempo (though this aspect is exaggerated in 'What Did I Have') and richly scored. The dramatic situation of both songs is similar—a rejected woman reflects on her position—yet although the second half of both songs continues in the torch song vein from a lyrical point of view, Streisand's rendition (and the accompaniment/arrangement) implies a contradiction or rejection of the words. This tension between language and message helps to draw attention to Streisand's presence and power: the message ultimately overwhelms the language, and this enhances the status of the messenger.

## CONCLUSION

In his insightful book on Streisand, Neal Gabler observes: 'Every movie Streisand made, the awful ones as well as the good ones, were unmistakably Streisand movies—movies in which her personality dominated, as is usually the case in star vehicles, but also in which her theme dominated, which is not always the case, even for major stars. . . . [S]he is always the auteur, the major creative force, and in her films, no less than in her music, she provides the governing idea, the overarching continuity.'[34]

We have seen how what Gabler describes as Streisand's 'creative force' functions as an agent of adaptation in *Funny Girl, Hello, Dolly!* and *On a Clear Day You Can See Forever*, both in the revision of material or the framing of her performances. The extension of her musical (vocal) presence and the trimming or deletion of other characters' (especially the male stars') songs in all three films contributes to the feeling that they are Streisand movies; with *Funny Girl* and *On a Clear Day*, her musical domination almost gives the impression that the movies are Streisand albums with dramatic context. Indeed, aspects of musical arrangement that can be found in Streisand's early albums are adopted in these movies too. For instance, she made various records where she reversed the conventional tempo of a song, most famously in her down-tempo version of 'Happy Days Are Here Again,' and this approach individualizes her tempo-reversing rendition of 'So Long, Dearie' in *Dolly*. Similarly, the division of her recording of 'Down with Love' into a very slow, ad-libbed opening refrain and a hyper-fast closing one, was mirrored in the arrangement of 'What Did I Have' in *On a Clear Day*. Adding songs especially for Streisand's screen performances ('Funny Girl,' 'Just Leave Everything to Me,' 'Go to Sleep,' etc.) further individualizes the films as works so that she is not simply required to reperform fixed texts that had been widely performed on the stage: the films are new texts in every sense.

Yet the dramatic element matters too, of course, and each musical has been adopted for the screen in ways that accommodate Streisand. The screen *Funny Girl* adds a framing device to render the story as a flashback in her head, allowing Streisand to act as the lens for the story and removing other characters' perspectives; the screen *Dolly* emphasizes aspects of the character that attempt to deflect the problems of the actress's age; and the screen *Clear Day* taps into her fragmentation as a star by allowing her to play a range of roles from the young Melinda to Daisy's alter ego/conscience (in the 'Go to Sleep' scene). The latter is particularly successful in showing her range, from vulnerable to strong and from comic to serious, though these aspects are also well demonstrated in *Funny Girl* and hinted at in the finer moments of *Dolly*. Pamela Robertson Wojcik observes that Streisand's 'star persona produces a unique variant of the musical genre.'[35] As part of this personal stamping process, certain elements of Streisand's film musicals run throughout her career, such as the 'travel and stride' sequences in 'Don't Rain on My Parade' (*Funny Girl*), 'Before the Parade Passes By' (*Dolly*), 'Come Back to Me' (*Clear Day*), 'Let's Hear It for Me' (*Funny Lady*), and 'A Piece of Sky' (*Yentl*).[36] Streisand's artistic output as a whole—whether it is to one's personal taste or not—has a coherence based on artistic choices, presentation, and aspects of production that are common to multiple examples of her work, regardless of genre or character; but it was potent from the beginning of her screen career with her three Broadway-to-Hollywood musicals, where her stardom was a powerful agent of adaptation.

## NOTES

1. Matthew Kennedy, *Roadshow! The Fall of Film Musicals in the 1960s* (New York: Oxford University Press, 2014), 4.
2. Kennedy, *Roadshow*, 5.
3. Quoted in Kennedy, *Roadshow*, 60. Original source: *New York Times*, 19 September 1968.
4. Quoted in Steven Suskin, *Opening Night on Broadway* (New York: Schirmer, 1990), 236, 238.
5. Telegram reproduced at http://barbra-archives.com/live/60s/fun ny_girl_broadway_1b.html, accessed 14 February 2018.
6. Hebert Kretzmer, 'Super Girl!,' *Daily Express*, 14 April 1966; reproduced on http://barbra-archives.com/live/60s/funny_girl_l ondon_5.html, accessed 14 February 2018.

7. Kennedy, *Roadshow*, 60. According to http://barbra-archives. com/films/funny_girl_streisand_1.html, accessed 14 February 2018, the announcement was made on 25 December 1965.

8. Army Archerd, *Variety*, 7 July 1967; reproduced at http://bar bra-archives.com/films/funny_girl_streisand_1.html#filming, accessed 14 February 2018.

9. Various relevant primary sources appear at http://barbra-archives.com/films/funny_girl_streisand_2.html, accessed 14 February 2018.

10. Quoted in Lorraine LoBianco's TCM blogpost on *Hello, Dolly!*, http://www.tcm.com/this-month/article/188872%7C0/Hello-Dolly-.html, accessed 16 February 2018.

11. Vincent Canby, 'On Screen, Barbra Streisand Displays a Detached Cool,' *New York Times*, 18 December 1969, http://www.nytimes. com/movie/review?res=9807E2D6123CEE34BC4052DFB46 78382679EDE, accessed 16 February 2018.

12. In the absence of other sources, the Barbra Archives website was consulted; it cites an article in *American Cinematographer* from 1970, which gives these facts. See http://barbra-archives.com/ films/hello_dolly_streisand.html, accessed 16 February 2018.

13. Darcie Denkert, *A Fine Romance* (New York: Billboard, 2005) 290.

14. Jerry Herman, *Showtune* (New York: Donald Fine, 2001), 210–211. Herman overlooks the fact, of course, that Kelly began his career as a Broadway performer, his most notable appearance being in Rodgers and Hart's *Pal Joey*.

15. Quoted in Anne Edwards, *Streisand: A Biography* (New York: Taylor Trade, 2016 [reprint]), 199.

16. Quoted in Edwards, *Streisand*, 199.

17. 'Barbra Streisand: On a Clear Day You Can See Dolly,' *Look*, 16 December 1969, http://barbra-archives.com/bjs_library/60s/ look_69_dolly.html, accessed 16 February 2018.

18. Howard Kissel, *The Abominable Showman* (New York: Applause, 1993), 366.

19. See Kennedy, *Roadshow*, 205, for details.

20. The announcement is quoted in Kennedy, *Roadshow*, 147.

21. See Kennedy, *Roadshow*, 174. The casting is also discussed at http://barbra-archives.com/films/clear_day_streisand_1.html, accessed 16 February 2018.

22. Details of the filming are covered comprehensively in Stephen Harvey, *Directed by Vincente Minnelli* (New York: Harper and Row, 1989), 287–289, and at http://barbra-archives.com/films/clear_day_tests_filming.html, accessed 16 February 2018.

23. See Dominic McHugh, *Alan Jay Lerner: A Lyricist's Letters* (New York: Oxford University Press, 2014), 183–184, for an explanation of this issue.

24. Vincent Canby, 'On a Clear Day You Can See Forever Begins Its Run,' 18 June 1970, http://www.nytimes.com/movie/review?res=9C06E4D6103EE034BC4052DFB066838B669EDE, accessed 5 March 2018.

25. Although the dialogue for the scene is quite different, the show was similarly to have started with Fanny 'picking out the notes of "People"' on the rehearsal piano.

26. In his memoir, Minnelli takes the credit for the reverse order of the regression sequences, which he describes as 'not much of a story,' in an attempt to add tension to the film. However, several drafts of the screenplay show reverse chronology in these sequences, so Lerner may also have had this idea. Vincente Minnelli, with H. Arce, *Vincente Minnelli: I Remember It Well* (Hollywood, CA: Samuel French, 1990 [1974]), 364.

27. See http://barbra-archives.com/films/funny_girl_movie_cut1.html, accessed 9 March 2018.

28. See http://barbra-archives.com/films/funny_girl_movie_cut1.html, accessed 9 March 2018.

29. Theodor Taylor, *Jule: The Story of Composer Jule Styne* (New York: Random House, 1979), 247.

30. In fact, Styne started objecting to the idea of interpolating 'My Man'—which Streisand had sung as an encore after the final curtain of her last Broadway performance of *Funny Girl*—as early as July 1965. In a letter in the Bob Merrill Collection at the Library of Congress, producer Ray Stark reassures Styne that 'I have neither the desire nor the intention to use the song "MY MAN" in the motion picture version of "FUNNY GIRL."' Bob Merrill Collection, Library of Congress, box 2.

31. 'Who Are You Now?,' annotated copyist score, Bob Merrill Collection, Library of Congress.

32. A draft of the screenplay with Marc's version can be read in the Alan Jay Lerner collection at the Library of Congress. The song was prerecorded and can be heard at http://barbra-archives.com/films/clear_day_streisand_8.html, accessed 8 March 2018.

33. Matt Howe discusses the filming and cutting of these numbers, with illustrations, at http://barbra-archives.com/films/clear_day_streisand_9.html ('Wait Till We're Sixty-Five') and http://barbra-archives.com/films/clear_day_streisand_8.html ('Who Is There'), accessed 8 March 2018.

34. Neal Gabler, *Barbra Streisand: Redefining Beauty: Femininity, and Power* (New Haven, CT: Yale University Press, 2016), 124–125.

35. Pamela Robertson Wojcik, 'The Streisand Musical,' in *The Sound of Musicals*, ed. Steven Cohan (London: BFI, 2010), 129.

36. Wojcik, 'The Streisand Musical,' 134.

# 5

# Lost in Translation

## *Rodgers and Hammerstein's* Carousel *on the Silver Screen*

TIM CARTER

■ □ ■

IN THE MID-1950S, RICHARD RODGERS and Oscar Hammerstein II did what they had hitherto said would never happen: they sanctioned screen versions of their classic Broadway musicals, *Oklahoma!* (which had opened in 1943), *Carousel* (1945), *South Pacific* (1949), and *The King and I* (1951). The films of *Oklahoma!* (1955; directed by Fred Zinnemann), *The King and I* (1956; Walter Lang), and *South Pacific* (1958; Joshua Logan) were showered with awards. *Carousel* (1956; Henry King), however, was not. Rodgers was particularly fond of the original show:

> Oscar never wrote more meaningful or more moving lyrics, and to me, my score is more satisfying than any I've ever written. But it's not just the songs; it's the whole play. Beautifully written, tender without being mawkish, it affects me deeply every time I see it performed.[1]

But the film of *Carousel* is widely regarded as the least successful of the Rodgers and Hammerstein transfers from stage to screen.

Its stage version was already less wholesome than *Oklahoma!*, less exotic than *The King and I*, and more ambiguous in moral terms than *South Pacific*. It was also the most 'operatic' of all those shows in terms of its extensive and quite complex musical fabric. All that was enough to steer an onscreen *Carousel* into troubled waters. The bigger question, however, is why it hit the rocks. Answering it forces consideration of a range of issues: the fluctuating fortunes of Rodgers and Hammerstein in the 1950s and their consequent move into the film industry; changing cinematic technologies; competition between Hollywood and Broadway; the pressures of shooting on location; and the inherent problems of *Carousel* itself. It is easy enough to conclude that the film fell victim to an unfortunate concatenation of circumstances; more provocative, however, is what this tells us about transfers from stage to screen whether in the 1950s or more broadly conceived.

## THE UPS AND DOWNS OF 'R&H'

On 16 October 1955, Philip K. Scheuer's regular column in the Sunday *Los Angeles Times* ('A Town Called Hollywood') presented a gushing account headlined 'Rodgers, Hammerstein Spin Show Business Carousel':

> Sometimes it seems as if Rodgers and Hammerstein are the whole of show business these days. Last week the film *Oklahoma!* was launched triumphantly in Manhattan; *Pipe Dream*, their new musical play, from John Steinbeck's *Cannery Row* stories, is selling out weeks ahead of its premiere, and both *Carousel* and *The King and I* are in production here at 20th Century Fox.

As with most such stories in the newspapers, it seems likely that this one was less a result of deep investigative journalism than prompted by press releases issued by one or more public relations departments (in the present case, within Rodgers and Hammerstein's own production company and/or Twentieth Century–Fox). The facts are not in dispute: the film version of *Oklahoma!* was indeed launched at the Rivoli Theatre, New York, on 11 October 1955; Rodgers and Hammerstein's new show, *Pipe Dream*, reached the stage of the Shubert Theatre on Broadway on 30 November; and *Carousel* and *The King and I* had their screen premieres on 16 February and 29 June 1956. The spin placed on these facts, however, was a different matter.

There is no doubt that by now, Rodgers and Hammerstein were regarded as a (singular) national institution. Since their first collaboration on *Oklahoma!* in 1943, they had created a major sequence of Broadway musicals on a two-year cycle that would continue until *The Sound of Music* (1959).[2] They also operated a production company to curate at home and abroad their own shows and others under their belt (including Irving Berlin's *Annie Get Your Gun* of 1946), plus a music publishing company (Williamson Music) to market their products more widely. This enabled R&H to licence performances of their shows under uncommonly strict conditions in terms of adhering to the original script, score, and even production values. As the profits rolled in, Rodgers and Hammerstein were regarded as a unique combination: consummate theatrical professionals and outstanding businessmen. Recognition came in other ways as well. On 28 March 1954—in effect marking ten years of the official R&H partnership—all four major US networks broadcast the two-hour television special, *A Salute to Rodgers and Hammerstein* (produced as the *General Foods 25th Anniversary Show*). Here stars of stage and screen gathered to introduce or perform the greatest hits from the R&H canon to date, some by the original cast members; the show reached an estimated seventy million viewers.[3] On 4 April 1956, Columbia College (the main undergraduate college of Columbia University) granted

Rodgers and Hammerstein its highest honor for distinguished alumni, the Alexander Hamilton Award, at a special ceremony attended by the New York glitterati. The accolades kept coming in.

At the same time, one might be forgiven for wondering whether Rodgers and Hammerstein really did represent 'the whole of show business these days.' Of the major players in musical theatre of the 1930s and 1940s, Jerome Kern had died in 1945 and Kurt Weill in 1950, and Irving Berlin seemed to have come to the end of a long stage career with his *Call Me Madam* (1950; 644 performances): only Cole Porter was still producing hit shows, although *Can-Can* (1953; 892 performances) and *Silk Stockings* (1955; 478) were his last. Younger figures were starting to take over the field: Berlin's *Call Me Madam* was roundly beaten by Frank Loesser's *Guys and Dolls* which opened some five weeks later but played for nineteen months longer (1,200 performances); Harold Rome had two surprising hits with *Wish You Were Here* (1952; 598 performances) and *Fanny* (1954; 888), as did Richard Adler and Jerry Ross with *The Pajama Game* (1954; 1,063) and *Damn Yankees* (1955; 1,019); Leonard Bernstein had already made a name for himself with *On the Town* (1944; 462 performances), and his *Wonderful Town* did well enough in 1953–54 (559 performances); and Sandy Wilson's *The Boy Friend* reached Broadway in 1954 (485 performances) fresh from its sell-out success in London's West End. The music-theatrical landscape was also on the verge of shifting in favour of that other double-barrelled songwriting team, Alan Jay Lerner and Frederick Loewe, who had established a reputation with *Brigadoon* (1947; 581 performances) and *Paint Your Wagon* (1951; 289) but would sweep the boards with a show that Rodgers and Hammerstein had themselves contemplated doing, *My Fair Lady* (2,717 performances from 1956 to 1962).[4]

The world of Broadway was fickle at best. But many felt that in creative terms, Rodgers and Hammerstein were on a downward slide: their shows from 1953 and 1955, *Me and Juliet* (358 performances) and *Pipe Dream* (246), would have rated reasonably well for any lesser team, but pundits were accustomed to the much higher figures of *South Pacific* (1,925 performances) and *The King and I* (1,246). Not since their *Allegro* of 1947 (315 performances) had Rodgers and Hammerstein seen such a dip. Some may have noticed one common factor to their three short-running shows: *Me and Juliet* and *Pipe Dream* were each set in modern times and places—as to a large degree also was *Allegro*—with none of the historical distance and local colour of *The King and I* (Siam in the 1860s), *Carousel* (Maine, 1873–88), *Oklahoma!* (around 1900), or even *South Pacific* (World War II). *Allegro* was innovative in concept; *Me and Juliet* should have been a successful 'backstage musical'; and *Pipe Dream* had the prestige of being based on a novel by John Steinbeck. But none of these shows seems to have suited the R&H profile (or perhaps better, what audiences considered it to be): when it came to modern subjects, Rodgers and Hammerstein appeared to lose their Midas Touch.

They themselves put a brave spin on it. On 4 May 1955, *Variety* carried an article headlined 'R&H Paradox: Office Never Busier Despite No B'way Show, Only 1 on Tour.' There was no real 'paradox,' Rodgers and Hammerstein would have claimed: they had plenty to do in terms of handling the numerous other productions of their classic shows.[5] But the apparent drop in their Broadway fortunes certainly offers some explanation for their decision to take a step they had long resisted: to put their most successful musicals on the silver screen. It was a risky business given the precipitous decline in the US film industry in the early 1950s, due not least to the rise of television. But the studios may have seen some advantage as well: musicals suited the medium (at least, up to a point) and seemed a safer bet in the context of the Hollywood Blacklist.[6] For their part, Rodgers and Hammerstein perhaps

LOST IN TRANSLATION | 169

took hope from Irving Berlin: his *Annie Get Your Gun* (which they had produced in 1946) had transferred well enough to film in 1950 once Betty Hutton replaced an ailing Judy Garland, as did his *Call Me Madam* in 1953 (with Ethel Merman, Donald O'Connor, Vera-Ellen, and George Sanders in the star-studded lineup); Berlin also continued his successes with straight-to-screen musicals such as *There's No Business Like Show Business* and *White Christmas* (both 1954). MGM's treatment of Cole Porter's 1948 musical, *Kiss Me, Kate* (1953) had done well at the box office, in part because of the cast (Kathryn Grayson, Howard Keel, and Ann Miller) but also given its use of the latest fad: 3D projection (for those cinemas able to show it). *Guys and Dolls* (Samuel Goldwyn Productions, 1955; with Marlon Brando, Jean Simmons, Frank Sinatra, and Vivian Blaine) was even more successful, reportedly scoring $20 million on a $5.5 million production budget, more than justifying Goldwyn's insistence on filming it in expensive CinemaScope. (I return to the issue of screen formats later in this chapter.)

Rodgers and Hammerstein knew full well that they could not match such high-octane musicals. Nor would they have found much comfort in the film version of Lerner and Loewe's *Brigadoon* (MGM, 1954), even though its plot and music were in a vein closer to the R&H mould. This, too, was filmed in CinemaScope, but because of reductions in its budget, the soundstage sets did not take advantage of the medium. (I return to this issue of sets, too.) Nor was it a success: it failed by a long way to recoup its $3 million cost. Critics blamed the cast— Gene Kelly, Van Johnson (but Donald O'Connor had been in for his role), and Cyd Charisse (replacing Kathryn Grayson)— and also the omission of favourite songs from the stage version: 'Come to Me, Bend to Me,' 'There But for You Go I,' 'From This Day On,' and 'The Sword Dance' were filmed but cut prior to release, while 'The Love of My Life' and 'My Mother's Wedding Day' had already fallen foul of the censors because of their risqué lyrics. Indeed, by most reckonings *Brigadoon* was a model of how not to adapt an effective stage musical to film. But Rodgers and Hammerstein clearly had ambitions to protect and profit from their own shows in more effective ways.

## CONTRACTUAL NEGOTIATIONS

Shortly after the Broadway opening of *Oklahoma!* on 31 March 1943, various Hollywood studios made successive bids to produce a film version of the show. All were roundly rejected by Rodgers and Hammerstein and by the show's producers, the Theatre Guild. As Lawrence Langner, one of the Guild's executive directors, wrote to producer Harry Sherman on 22 June 1944, 'We have ño interest in having a picture made of *Oklahoma!* for many years to come. We are making a net profit of between $750,000 and $1,000,000 a year out of the stage rights and expect to do so for a number of years to come. So why bother with a picture until, let us say, 1950!'[7] An article in *Variety* on 23 February 1949 made a similar point: Rodgers and Hammerstein 'Won't Sell *Okla!* to Pix, at Least in Their Lifetime,' given their huge income from stage royalties. But this was not true. *Oklahoma!* had ended its record-breaking five-year Broadway run on 29 May 1948, and while it was still doing well enough on its national tour, in its production on London's West End, and internationally, Rodgers and Hammerstein had already started thinking about the silver screen. Indeed, by 1950 (so Joshua Logan said) they had decided to form a company to produce film versions of all their musicals based on the stage productions.[8] However, that decision remained secret for a number of important reasons.

The notion that any film of an R&H musical should be based on its stage version was important, given that the production was part of its identity. Rodgers and Hammerstein preferred to 'freeze' each of their shows once they reached Broadway: cast members might come and go, but the sets, costumes, and staging would stay the same. In the case of *Oklahoma!* the publicity shots of, say, successive Ado Annies remain remarkably consistent; performances were monitored for uniformity by spot-check visits; and when the touring company's costumes and sets were destroyed in a warehouse fire in March 1952, the original scene designer, Lemuel Ayers, was immediately contracted to supervise their exact reconstruction.[9] In part, this was because Rodgers and Hammerstein had an outstanding product to sell (so there was no reason to change it), but more important, it was a case of branding. Any audience attending an R&H musical—whether on Broadway or in the West End, or on national and international tours—was guaranteed to see more or less the same thing. This raised the bar significantly when it came to transferring any such show to film.

But Rodgers and Hammerstein could not go public with their plans until various complex contractual issues had been resolved. In particular, *Oklahoma!*, *Carousel*, and *Allegro* had been done in partnership with the Theatre Guild (R&H broke away with *South Pacific*), which in effect co-owned them subject to various conditions being met by either side. Thus, in March 1952, R&H began a protracted series of negotiations to buy out the Guild and gain exclusive rights to these three shows. The Guild held out, haggling to its advantage precisely because of the film prospects on the horizon. The agreement for *Oklahoma!* was signed on 6 August 1953; four days later (on 10 August), the *New York Times* reported that a film version of the show was in the cards, and on the 17 August it announced that a firm agreement had been made for it between Rodgers and Hammerstein, producer Arthur Hornblow Jr, and director Fred Zinnemann.[10] Hornblow had only limited experience with film musicals—he produced the Esther Williams showcase *Million*

*Dollar Mermaid* (1952)—and Zinnemann had none: his recent films included *High Noon* (1952) and *From Here to Eternity* (1953).[11] However, Zinnemann had a reputation for his realistic shooting on 'authentic' locations, which, we shall see, had a direct bearing on the film of *Oklahoma!*

Again, the newspapers were being manipulated by press releases. Rodgers and Hammerstein had already joined (in March 1953) the board of directors of the newly formed Magna Theatre Corporation, created by Joseph M. Schenk of Twentieth Century–Fox and Michael Todd, who were promising to begin the output of films in the new Todd-AO widescreen process: Schenk none too convincingly denied rumours that the first such film would be *Oklahoma!* though in fact the screenplay—by Sonya Levien and William Ludwig—was already in development (they hid the project behind the title 'Operation Wow!'). At the same time, the Theatre Guild presented its own conflicting information about whether the show was set for Hollywood. This may just have been part of the Guild's bargaining strategy over the rights, however, given that any film of *Oklahoma!* was clearly going to rest in the hands of a new company: Rodgers and Hammerstein Pictures, Inc.[12]

## THE 'BATTLE OF SCOPES'

Rodgers and Hammerstein knew enough of the film industry from their various, and variously mixed, experiences with it in the 1930s. They had also collaborated on their own straight-to-screen musical in the case of *State Fair* (Twentieth Century–Fox, 1945). But writing six songs to meet the typical studio contract was a very different matter from filming a Broadway musical play, and so far as Rodgers and Hammerstein were concerned, forming their own company was the only way to retain what they considered to be the necessary degree of creative control over film versions of their shows. There were still other contractual issues to be resolved, however. Back in 1943, the Theatre Guild had made the smart move of buying from MGM the rights that playwright Lynn Riggs had sold to his *Green Grow the Lilacs*, the source-play for *Oklahoma!* With the Guild now out of the reckoning, this left Rodgers and Hammerstein without restriction in terms of pursuing the film. Likewise, R&H managed the screen version of *South Pacific* without interference from the main Hollywood studios by forming the company 'South Pacific Enterprises,' co-owned with Magna Theatre Corporation, Leyland Hayward (who coproduced the Broadway production), and Joshua Logan (who directed the stage and film versions).[13] *Carousel* and *The King and I* were more problematic, however, because screen rights to their sources—Ferenc Molnár's play *Liliom* (1909) and Margaret Landon's novel *Anna and the King of Siam* (1944)— were owned by Twentieth Century–Fox: Fox Studios produced a film of *Liliom* in 1930 (and Fox Europa another one in French in 1935), and the company in its later incarnation released the film *Anna and the King of Siam* (with Irene Dunne and Rex Harrison) in 1946. Darryl F. Zanuck, head of production at Twentieth Century–Fox, took advantage of those rights so as to have *Carousel* and *The King and I* done by his studio instead, if still paying R&H handsomely for the privilege. This is why *Oklahoma!* and *South Pacific* are truer to their originals than *Carousel* and *The King and I*, which were subject to greater studio interference. It also explains why the first four screen versions of Rodgers and Hammerstein's musicals were in two different formats: Todd-AO (*Oklahoma!* and *South Pacific*) and CinemaScope 55.[14]

The 27 June 1954 issue of the *Los Angeles Times* included Philip K. Scheuer's article 'New Wide-Screen Process Enters Battle of Scopes.' He was reporting on Michael Todd's demonstration 'last Tuesday' (22 June) of his new Todd-AO system, 'a wide-film, wide-screen process':

> Todd-AO offers potential competition only to Cinerama whose mammoth proportions it most nearly approaches. Where Cinerama uses three strips of standard 35-mm film, three projectors and a three-sided screen, Todd-AO employs one strip of 65-mm film, one projector and a curved 'unbroken' screen. Its angle of vision is, I gather, 128 degrees compared to Cinerama's 146, in a ratio of 2 (wide) to 1 (high).

This proportion, Scheuer wrote,

> is, like VistaVision's, more nearly that of the congenial screen shape we are accustomed to, and so different from 20th Century Fox CinemaScope's 2.55-to-1 'ribbon.' In simpler words, it's higher. But like Cinerama, it will require far more special equipment and so is likely to be limited to single theaters in key spots.

Scheuer was impressed by Todd's demonstration reel, though he thought the experience slightly inferior to Cinerama's. But

> Todd-AO's real gimmick, its ace in the hole, is something known as R & H—the rights to Rodgers and Hammerstein's *Oklahoma!* and *South Pacific*. With these and other fabulous R & H properties, Todd-AO can support its own exclusive circuit for years.

The final point was also clear:

> One thing is plain in this War of the Shapes and Scopes: the motion picture is undergoing profound changes. All these systems are spectacular in themselves. We have spawned a new

race of giants as an 'answer' to the dwarfs of TV: now we shall need stories and themes of commensurable stature and breadth. Bigger facades and bigger faces alone will not suffice.

In fact, Todd-AO was not linked exclusively to Rodgers and Hammerstein (through the Magna Theatre Corporation): another film planned for it was the spectacular *Around the World in 80 Days* (1956), which Michael Todd produced on his own. But the R&H brand clearly had a role to play in the emergence of new, competing technologies. As Scheuer reported in that same article, Twentieth Century–Fox had held its own press conference also on 22 June, bringing another musical into the fray:

> Same day, Darryl Zanuck—who owns one R & H treasure, *The King and I*—starred himself as principal actor in a demonstration of the latest in CinemaScope. It was all to the good. Excerpts from forthcoming productions, filmed with improved Bausch & Lomb lenses, revealed almost stereopticon depth and contained shots so magnificent that the trade audience burst frequently into applause. Those ranged from a full-scale South African native uprising to Newcomer Sheree North's leggy legs.[15]

Zanuck was probably engaging in a spoiling operation against Todd (although to be fair, Zanuck's lenses were new). Twentieth Century–Fox's CinemaScope had already made its impact with the release of the biblical epic, *The Robe*, on 16 September 1953 and the romantic comedy *How to Marry a Millionaire* (with Marilyn Monroe, Betty Grable, and Lauren Bacall) on 5 November. The next significant improvement in the Twentieth Century–Fox system was still to come: the development of CinemaScope 55 in 1955, introduced, we shall see, by way of the film of *Carousel*.

But Michael Todd was out to upstage the competition as well. His choice of images to demonstrate Todd-AO on 22 June 1954 was no coincidence: the full-length documentary *This Is Cinerama*, released on 30 September 1952 to show off another new technology, began (after the opening narration) with a spectacular roller-coaster ride, and its subsequent vignettes included a tour through Venice. Cinerama, however, remained little more than a gimmick given that it required specially designed theatres. Another attempt on the part of the film industry to improve the visual experience was the reintroduction of 3D film—with *Bwana Devil* released on 30 November 1952 ('A LION in your lap! A LOVER in your arms!') and Warner Brothers' *House of Wax* (10 April 1953)—but it had similar issues in terms of needing a special screen and coordinated equipment (two projectors running simultaneously); furthermore, audiences had to wear special glasses, and the sightlines were problematic in larger theatres. This left two main competitors in the field of widescreen formats: Twentieth Century–Fox's CinemaScope ('The Modern Miracle You See without Glasses!'—so the advertising for *The Robe* proclaimed) and its competitor created by Paramount, VistaVision.

Todd-AO was to be the third, and according to the newspapers, it was making the biggest splash. On 24 April 1955, Louis Berg puffed the technology in the Baltimore *Sun* ('Biggest Movie News of the Year') with seven photographs from the film and set of *Oklahoma!* (including one demonstrating the span of the widescreen image compared with the normal projection ratio), most taken during the location shooting the previous summer:

> The film version of the Rodgers and Hammerstein musical (greatest hit in the history of show business) and the startling wide screen (nearest thing to Cinerama) have been the talk of the movie industry for two years. It is predicted that when they hit

the public, there will be another Hollywood revolution, similar to the one started by Cinerama and CinemaScope. New screens, new sound, new projectors, new methods of photography and a fresh wailing on the part of movie exhibitors, who will have to adapt their theaters to the changed medium.

Berg went on to note that as a result, Paramount was producing an 'improved' VistaVision, and Twentieth Century–Fox was 'tinkering' with CinemaScope: 'The battle of the big screens rages afresh and a war of words rages with it.'

This 'battle' was an inevitable result of inter-studio competition, although Twentieth Century–Fox was willing to licence CinemaScope to any rivals who found it cheaper than coming up with a comparable system (such as Superscope, used by RKO). It was also intended to counteract the serious decline in cinema audiences and, as Philip Scheuer noted, to put the 'dwarf' of television back in its place. Film posters made a splash of the new widescreen formats in increasingly extravagant fashion, and audiences noted the difference in terms not just of perspective but also of colour saturation, finer grain, and clearer focus (even if CinemaScope and VistaVision still had problems in that last regard). Moreover, the aim was to provide an immersive experience not just for the eyes but also for the ears by way of new tools for mixing monophonic sound across three channels (in the Perspecta system used with VistaVision) and stereophonic sound on four (CinemaScope), six (Todd-AO, CinemaScope 55), or seven (Cinerama). This explains the attraction of musicals as a way of vaunting the results: Irving Berlin's *Call Me Madam* (1953) looked well enough in Technicolor, but it is no coincidence that Paramount used his *White Christmas* (released on 14 October 1954) to introduce the public to VistaVision (previous displays of the system had been only for the trade), even if Twentieth Century–Fox's *Carmen Jones* (28 October 1954) and *There's No Business*

*Like Show Business* (16 December 1954) looked and sounded even better in CinemaScope—as indeed MGM's *Seven Brides for Seven Brothers* (22 July 1954) in that format had already proved—at least in those houses that had the correct equipment to show them.[16]

Not all did. Cinemas across the country were gradually adapting to the projection and sound systems, and screens, required for VistaVision and CinemaScope, if not always in ideal ways. However, Todd-AO and then CinemaScope 55 went beyond such capabilities and needed still more special facilities (hence the 'fresh wailing' noted by Louis Berg). This, plus changing approaches to studio marketing, led to a new focus on so-called roadshow releases restricted to long-term engagements in a limited number of theatres in major urban centres (New York, Chicago, Los Angeles) remodelled to maximize the benefits of the technology. Films given roadshow releases were longer than the norm, they played as a single feature (sometimes in two 'acts' with an intermission), seats were to be reserved for individual showings (evenings and matinées), admission prices were higher, and audiences were often given souvenir programmes (obviating the need for opening credits, although that was a matter of dispute with the various guilds and unions that governed the film industry).[17] The experience was meant to be akin, but far superior, to live theatre, aided, of course, by the screen proportions looking more like a proscenium stage. This is no doubt another reason why Rodgers and Hammerstein were willing to jump on the bandwagon. The film of *Brigadoon* was cut down to 108 minutes (close to a standard length for general release); the one of *Oklahoma!* ran for a luxurious 145, and *South Pacific*, for 171.[18]

Roadshow versions of films would have to be reworked in some way for general release unless they had already been created in two formats. *Oklahoma!* was filmed in Todd-AO (on 65-mm film) and CinemaScope (35 mm)—with some significant differences—although the latter version was held back for just over a year (released on 1 November 1956). Twentieth Century–Fox used *Carousel* to pioneer its new CinemaScope 55 system (on 55-mm film) but started parallel filming in normal CinemaScope as a security measure. However, the 35 mm filming was dropped midstream after the studio viewed the CinemaScope 55 rushes and also quickly developed the technology to transfer the negatives to normal 35 mm film (and four-track sound) for general release.[19] *The King and I* was filmed just in CinemaScope 55. But 35 mm versions of both *Carousel* and *The King and I* were granted general release much sooner than had been the case with *Oklahoma!* as a result of pressure from cinemas lower down the distribution chain that were severely disadvantaged by the roadshow system.[20] Audiences in the Washington, DC, area were able to see *Carousel* sooner than they had access to *Oklahoma!*[21]

An overview of films released in 1954 suggests that widescreen formats were deemed all well and good for biblical epics (*Demetrius and the Gladiators*, the sequel to *The Robe*) or large-scale adventure films (*20,000 Leagues under the Sea*) and westerns (*River of No Return*, *Vera Cruz*), but not for dramas (*The Caine Mutiny*, *On the Waterfront*, Hitchcock's *Rear Window*) or comedies (*It Should Happen to You*, *Sabrina*, Dean Martin and Jerry Lewis's semi-musical *Living It Up*). Most of the major film musicals issued that year were in widescreen formats (*Brigadoon*, *Carmen Jones*, *Lucky Me*, *New Faces*, *Rose Marie*, *Seven Brides for Seven Brothers*, *A Star Is Born*, *The Student Prince*, *There's No Business Like Show Business*, *White Christmas*), although some were not, including *Athena* (with Jane Powell), *Deep in My Heart* (a biopic of Sigmund Romberg), *Red Garters* (featuring Rosemary Clooney), *Top Banana* (Phil Silvers; filmed in 3D but not released as such), and *Young at Heart* (Frank Sinatra and Doris Day). For the studios, and aside from questions of genre, the choice of one format over the other came down to budget on the one hand, and the intended market on the other. But some of these widescreen musicals suited the new medium better than others. As a classic case in point, *White Christmas* seems distinctly ambivalent over how best to handle VistaVision, even though it should have been encouraged by its settings (Montecassino, Florida, Vermont), and still more, by its stars (Bing Crosby, Danny Kaye, Rosemary Clooney, and Vera-Ellen). Nor were those involved in creating film musicals always enthusiastic over the new format: Gene Kelly and Fred Astaire, for example, had to work hard to adapt their typical dance routines to the wide screen.

In general, however, the race towards new technologies was irresistible. Cole Porter spoofed the trend in his stage musical *Silk Stockings* (1955):

> Today to get the public to attend a picture show,
> *It's not enough to advertise a famous star they know.*
> *If you want to get the crowds to come around*
> *You've got to have glorious Technicolor,*
> *Breathtaking Cinemascope, and*
> Stereophonic sound.[22]

The question for film musicals was what to do with them.

## A CLASH OF STAGE AND SCREEN

In the 14 January 1956 issue of *Billboard*, Lee Zhito noted how 'Hollywood Tunes Up to Send Box Office on a Musical Whirl.' He wrote that all the Hollywood studios were beefing up production of musicals for 1956, with a projected thirty-five or more releases compared with twenty in 1955 (which had, of course, included *Oklahoma!*): his long list of titles includes *Anything Goes* (which came out starring Bing Crosby, Donald

O'Connor, Jeanmaire, and Mitzi Gaynor), *High Society* (Crosby, Grace Kelly, Frank Sinatra), *Kismet* (Howard Keel, Ann Blyth), and *The Vagabond King* (Kathryn Grayson, Oreste Kirkop). Zhito pointed to three issues explaining this new flurry of activity: competition with television (again!); the profits to be made from tie-ins with broadcast radio; and the growth of foreign markets in a flourishing postwar economy.[23]

*The Vagabond King* was a remake of Rudolf Friml's 1925 operetta, but out of the other twenty-nine titles on Zhito's list, only four had direct links to Broadway shows (as *Anything Goes* did not): *Can-Can, Carousel, The King and I,* and *Pal Joey.* Of those four, only two in fact appeared in 1956 (*Pal Joey* came out in 1957, and *Can-Can* in 1960). This was par for the course. Nowadays our perception skews in favour of filmed versions of the classic shows from Broadway's Golden Age: they are often the only way to catch some glimpse of their originals, although that is a dangerous strategy. But they formed a very small proportion of a genre—the American film musical—that operated according to quite different principles. Thus, the vast majority of musicals released by the studios in 1956 fit its parameters. On the one hand stood biopics of prominent real-life musical figures—*The Benny Goodman Story, The Best Things in Life Are Free* (on the songwriters Buddy DeSylva, Lew Brown, and Ray Henderson), *The Eddy Duchin Story*—or imagined ones ('Damon Vincenti' played by Mario Lanza in *Serenade*). On the other we have some version of the 'backstage musical' or, and increasingly, its 'nightclub' variant: *The Girl Can't Help It* (Jayne Mansfield), *Meet Me in Las Vegas* (Dan Dailey, Cyd Charisse), *The Opposite Sex* (June Allyson, Joan Collins, Dolores Gray, Ann Sheridan, Ann Miller). Lower down the list come screwball comedies with occasional songs: *Bundle of Joy* (Eddie Fisher, Debbie Reynolds), *Pardners* (the penultimate film in the Dean Martin and Jerry Lewis franchise), *You Can't Run Away from It* (June Allyson and Jack Lemmon in a remake of *It Happened One Night*). Relatively new to the field were lower-budget black-and-white films building on the new craze for rock 'n' roll: *Don't Knock the Rock* (with Bill Haley & His Comets, Little Richard, etc.), *Rock Around the Clock* (Bill Haley & His Comets again), *Rock, Rock, Rock,* (Tuesday Weld, Chuck Berry), and *Shake, Rattle, and Rock!* (Fats Domino, etc.), to which one might well add *Love Me Tender* (Elvis Presley's first film), although it is more in the 'Western with songs' mould.

Stage musicals were a different matter altogether. Cole Porter's song 'Stereophonic Sound' was witty enough, but it exposed a number of anxieties within a genre that already had a wide-'screen' format, colourful sets and costumes, and high-quality sound. Broadway and Hollywood existed in a complex relationship, both symbiotic and fractured.[24] When the Theatre Guild was casting the stage version of *Oklahoma!* it first considered film stars for the main roles as a way of capturing an audience: Deanna Durbin as Laurey, Shirley Temple as (probably) Ado Annie, Groucho Marx as Ali Hakim, and Anthony Quinn as Jud Fry.[25] None of them worked out—whether for lack of interest or for contractual reasons—which the Guild then claimed was an advantage by allowing them to bring to the stage a group of relatively unknown actors willing to work as a coherent team. In the case of subsequent cast members in *Oklahoma!* the Guild repeatedly complained about their being lured to (or poached by) the Hollywood studios.[26] But it happily did the reverse by recruiting actors who had (often unwisely) signed Hollywood contracts that had yet to gain them exposure: two cases in point were the lead players in the original stage *Carousel*, Jan Clayton (a 'Metro starlet') and John Raitt (who broke his contract with the low-budget Producers Releasing Corporation). In general, however, not many actors were able to cross back and forth between stage and screen given the quite different demands in terms of looks, ability, temperament, and contract status: they may have fit one mould perfectly, but rarely the other. In the case of the R&H musicals, only Yul Brynner (King Mongkut in *The King and I*) and Juanita Hall (Bloody Mary in *South Pacific*) took the same roles in the film versions as they had done in the onstage premieres, and Juanita Hall's songs were dubbed by Muriel Smith (who had played Blood Mary onstage in London).[27]

If the stars of stage and screen largely lived in different worlds, so, too, did the works they performed. Part of Hollywood's resistance to transfers from the stage was no doubt due to the complex contractual problems they created in terms of who had rights to what: it was easier to stick within a single system of production and its legal administration. Far more important, however, was Hollywood's antipathy to musical theatre as it was now developing on the stage. In the 1930s, the studios had posed a serious threat by way of appropriating what Broadway then did best: spectacular revues with their roots in vaudeville, plus their 'backstage musical' derivatives. It was impossible for Broadway to compete with the likes of Busby Berkeley, or of Fred Astaire and Ginger Rogers. The rise of Technicolor film from the mid-1930s was still more dangerous, especially when it was used to such effect as in, say, *The Wizard of Oz* (1939). One might well argue that Broadway's turn to the so-called integrated musical in the early 1940s was a clear response: *Oklahoma!* is usually granted 'landmark' status in that regard, though there were plenty of other, even earlier, examples. But any show that brought drama, dance, and music into some kind of coherent whole—a 'musical play' to use the contemporary term—went very much against the Hollywood grain, and probably deliberately so.

The problem was the perennial one of opera and musical theatre: the plausibility of song. The medium of film retained certain canons of verisimilitude—matters needed to be 'lifelike'—and also depended on audiences imagining themselves in the middle of the action in ways that made singing problematic unless it could somehow be done in realistic (or nearly so) circumstances or otherwise justified by way of convention or fantasy. Even the MGM musicals produced by Arthur Freed—who is generally considered to have done the most to free up the genre—reflected many of the same constraints. This explains Hollywood's continuing preference for musical biopics or 'backstage' scenarios, where songs could largely be presented as diegetic save in certain restricted circumstances. 'Book'-musicals of the 1940s, however, increasingly pushed against those boundaries. True, in the case of Rodgers and Hammerstein's first collaboration a cowboy might feasibly wax lyrical over a 'beautiful' morning box socials customarily involve dancing ('The Farmer and the Cowman'), and one can sing at a wedding (the song 'Oklahoma'), while comic songs (Ado Annie's 'I Cain't Say No') and love duets ('People Will Say We're in Love') are close enough to convention. But Jud Fry's passionate outburst in 'Lonely Room' is wholly inverisimilar, however 'real' it might seem in emotional terms. Hollywood did not quite know how to respond. *Annie Get Your Gun* transferred well enough to film in 1950 given that it was a 'backstage musical' of sorts (hence 'There's No Business Like Show Business'). So did *Show Boat* (in 1951, as in 1936) and *Kiss Me, Kate* (1953) for similar reasons. Lerner and Loewe's *Brigadoon* (1954), on the other hand, did not, however much it tried to rely on its fantastical plot and exotic location to allow Gene Kelly to sing to, and then dance with, Cyd Charisse in 'The Heather on the Hill.' And even so purportedly faithful a transfer as the film of *Oklahoma!* felt obliged to cut Jud's 'Lonely Room.'[28]

The problems are clear in another of the 1956 film musicals listed by Lee Zhito: *The Court Jester*. This high-budget (eventually, some $4 million) production designed as a vehicle for Danny Kaye, co-starring Glynis Johns, was released by Paramount in VistaVision on 27 January, less than three weeks before *Carousel*. It took the form of a costume musical in the manner of the forthcoming *The Vagabond King*, although its satirical target seems to have been the Disney swashbucklers of the mid-1950s such as *The Sword and the Rose* and *Rob Roy: The Highland Rogue* (1953), in which Johns had appeared. The plot is set in medieval England: Kaye plays the role of Hubert Hawkins—minstrel to the Black Fox (a Robin Hood-type figure)—who infiltrates the court of the wicked King Roderick, usurper of the throne. Hawkins manages to defeat Sir Griswold of MacElwain in a tournament, then the evil Lord Ravenhurst (Basil Rathbone) in a swordfight. His overthrow of King Roderick is aided by a team of midget acrobats, thereby restoring the rightful heir, a baby bearing the purple pimpernel (a birthmark) on its behind. In addition to those acrobats, further novelty was provided by the fast formation marching of the Zouave Drill Team (American Legion, Post no. 29, Jackson, Michigan). All this action, largely done on two mammoth sets constructed on Paramount soundstages (the exterior court-yard and interior hall of a castle), was clearly designed to fill the VistaVision screen. So did some fine panoramic location shots on the coast of the Palos Verdes Peninsula, southwest of Los Angeles.

Visually, *The Court Jester* made better use of VistaVision than, say, *White Christmas*, but the latter's 'let's put on a show' format was more congenial to the presentation of Irving Berlin's songs. Writers Melvin Frank and Norman Panama were involved in the screenplays for both films, but their move also into directing Danny Kaye (first in *Knock on Wood* in 1954) presented them with a different set of musical problems. In the case of *The Court Jester*, Sammy Cahn and Sylvia Fine (Danny Kaye's wife) provided them with eight songs, although in the film's final release, only four were heard complete, with fragments of two others (but all eight were given in full on the 'soundtrack' album issued in 1956). The cuts were no doubt caused, at least in part, by the difficulty of finding diegetic moments in the pseudo-historical context. The problems are solved somewhat by Kaye establishing his character with '(You'll Never) Outfox the Fox,' singing a lullaby to the baby under his protection ('I'll Take You Dreaming'), and performing before King Roderick's court a typical tongue-twisting 'Maladjusted Jester.' But what was seemingly the main song of the film, 'Life Could Not Better Be,' is left to the briefest of reprises right at the end; instead, Kaye introduces it in full in an ingenious title-sequence over the opening credits (with Kaye dressed as a jester, but in a costume not otherwise used in the film), crossing the fourth wall and commenting on the credits themselves.[29] The number finds scant room later on, although its use in the credits does help to define the film as a musical in the first place. One wonders, however, whether *The Court Jester* warrants the term given the limited role of the songs overall. Certainly this is not something that could, or would, have been put on the stage.

## LOCATION SHOOTING

Of course, some straight-to-film musicals made a far better job of the genre, both within the typical constraints but sometimes also beyond them. MGM's *Seven Brides for Seven Brothers* (1954), directed by Stanley Donen, could just as well have been a stage musical in the manner of *Oklahoma!*—as it became in 1978, if none too successfully (the adaptation by Lawrence Kasha and David Landay flopped on Broadway in 1982). The ancestry is clear, and the film's star, Howard Keel, had stepped into the lead roles in the first two R&H musicals on the stage (as Curly and Billy Bigelow). Donen was more in tune than many Hollywood directors with musicals on the silver screen (Vincente Minelli is another case in point): his other directing credits included *On the Town* (1949), *Royal Wedding* (1951), and *Singin' in the Rain* (1952). This sympathy came from his prior experience as a choreographer (in particular, for Gene Kelly), but also because he recognized the fallacy that lay behind cinematic verisimilitude in so far as any musical was concerned. When asked about the opening of *On the Town* shot on the streets of New York, he made his position clear:

> That is not real. That is anything but real, it just happens that the street is real. A musical is like an opera in the sense that it is anything but real. It seems to me that the whole mistake that films made was in trying to make it believable, as if it were happening in reality.[30]

He accepted the essential surrealism of the genre, and in the case of *Singin' in the Rain*, he played with it in gloriously witty ways.

That opening number of *On the Town*, 'New York, New York,' was certainly a cinematic tour de force, with the song (though much of it is instrumental) lip-synched on location shots in the Brooklyn Navy Yard, on the Brooklyn Bridge, then through the sights of Manhattan ending up in Rockefeller Plaza. Most of the rest of film was shot in the MGM backlot and soundstages save for occasional second-unit footage (some used as rear-projected background). This was more the norm given that the conditions for filming could be better controlled and manipulated in the studio, and costs could be kept down. Widescreen formats, however, tended to favour location shooting to the extent that films in CinemaScope and VistaVision often have the air of a travelogue (compare also the Venice scene in *This Is Cinerama*).[31] This is clear also in director Henry King's two films immediately prior to *Carousel* (both for Twentieth Century–Fox and released in 1955): *Untamed* was shot in part in South Africa, and *Love Is a Many-Splendored Thing* in Hong Kong. Stanley Donen said that he had wanted to shoot *Seven Brides for Seven Brothers* on location in Oregon, and that it would have been a better use of money than filming it in two formats (for CinemaScope and normal 35-mm projection); however, for budgetary reasons it was done mostly in the studio, with not much advantage taken of its briefer location shooting (in Sun Valley, Idaho). But as Donen also admitted, 'Seven Brides for Seven Brothers, as far as the studio was concerned, was a B picture and they didn't give a damn about it.'[32]

Rodgers and Hammerstein certainly gave a damn about *Oklahoma!*, and with Fred Zinnemann on board as director, location shooting was clearly part of the plan from the beginning: the cast and crew spent seven weeks (from mid-July 1954) in Arizona and New Mexico. This added significantly to the film's widescreen impact—especially in the Todd-AO version—and also to its air of authenticity. So, too, did the even more unusual choice to situate the bulk of the show's act 1 daytime numbers in this 'real' world outdoors. The contrast with *Seven Brides for Seven Brothers* is striking and presumably was somehow intended: while the latter's famous barn-raising scene was done in the studio, the song-and-dance number 'Kansas City' in *Oklahoma!* was shot at a real railway station (Elgin, Arizona) and also with a moving train.[33] The evening songs in *Oklahoma!* (according to the time span represented in the show; so, most of act 2) had to be done on a soundstage for reasons of lighting, and likewise the dream-ballet. But as long as the sun was shining, here were genuine farmers and cowmen singing their way through life. This was also one reason the film came in way over budget. *Seven Brides* cost $2.54 million, which was fairly typical for larger-scale musicals not at the high end of, say, *There's No Business like Show Business* ($4.34 million). For *Oklahoma!* the figure was $6.8 million.

In fact, Richard Rodgers was somewhat less than enthusiastic over the results:

> Visually, parts of the film were impressive, with some stunning shots of elephant-eye-high corn, the surrey ride, and the

cloud-filled Arizona sky. But the wide-screen process was not always ideal for the more intimate scenes, and I don't think the casting was totally satisfactory. At any rate, from then on—except for *South Pacific*—Oscar and I left moving pictures to moving-picture people and stayed clear of any involvement with subsequent film versions of our musicals.[34]

Nevertheless, he and Hammerstein seem to have felt that filming their shows in their real-world locations was the one novelty that the medium could bring to the stage musical. They exploited it even more in their other self-produced film, *South Pacific* (1958). This was shot mostly on the island of Kaua'i (Hawai'i), and with still more open-air numbers. Again, this had an impact on the budget ($5.61 million). But while Zinnemann had no problem with cowboys singing and dancing outdoors, the director of *South Pacific*, Joshua Logan, seems to have been more anxious over American SeaBees and nurses, French plantation owners, and even Tonkinese immigrants doing the same. The obvious paradox was that the excess of verisimilitude in location shooting would only exacerbate the inverisimilitude of music. Logan tried to compensate by using special light filters to create some 'other' world for several of the songs. He ended up regretting it deeply.

## FILMING *CAROUSEL*

Darryl F. Zanuck at Twentieth Century–Fox would not have wanted to pay $5.61 million or $6.8 million for any film musical, even one with the R&H cachet: he still went overboard for *Carousel* ($3.38 million) and *The King and I* ($4.45 million), but nowhere near to that degree. He cut corners in other ways, too. For *Carousel*, he assigned an in-house director, Henry King, whose prior experience of musicals was limited to *Alexander's*

*Ragtime Band* (1938): he was better known for epic adventures and romantic dramas. The in-house director for *The King and I*, Walter Lang, at least had a stronger track record in the genre (and he had directed the R&H *State Fair*). Zanuck did, however, allow King to go on location as *Carousel* went through production in the second half of 1955: *The King and I*, on the other hand, was done in the studio for reasons of cost, even if Lang and others might have preferred it otherwise.[35]

The named producer of *Carousel* was Henry Ephron, who also wrote the screenplay with his wife, Phoebe. Ephron wanted to try his hand at production, he said, because of the success of his working with Fred Astaire and Leslie Caron on *Daddy Long Legs* (1955).[36] That had mostly been shot in the studio, but *Carousel* needed a different approach, both because of the precedent created by *Oklahoma!* and given that the film was to be a showcase for Twentieth Century–Fox's new response to VistaVision and Todd-AO: CinemaScope 55. It was given a very large advertising budget; the premiere was anticipated by Zanuck's introducing special showings of a demonstration reel of CinemaScope 55 with extracts from *Carousel* and *The King and I*; and the broader marketing played strongly on the still sharper widescreen panoramas than standard CinemaScope, as well as the higher-quality sound (see Figure 5.1).[37] Zanuck also made the connection when appearing directly in a trailer for the film: 'Just as Rodgers and Hammerstein represent the very last word in musical perfection, we feel that *Carousel*, in the new CinemaScope 55, represents the very last word in viewing pleasure.'[38] One problem, however, was that *Carousel* was in general a more intimate musical than that format would suggest. Another was that the setting for the show, Maine, was not as visually enticing as the wide-open spaces of the American Southwest, and less exotic than any island in the Pacific. Nor did it help that much of the action of *Carousel*, and large portions of the music, take place from dusk into evening: Julie

THIS IS A COMPOSITE PHOTOGRAPH DEMONSTRATING THE GREATER EFFICIENCY OF 55mm PHOTOGRAPHY. IT IS ACKNOWLEDGED THAT 55mm IS DEEPER, RICHER, CLEARER AND CARRIES FOUR TIMES MORE PHOTOGRAPHIC INFORMATION.

❶ The images are radiantly bright and sharp and there is a greater feeling of audience participation than anything seen so far! ❷ The backgrounds are as clearly in focus as the foregrounds! ❸ The illusion of depth is greater than anything seen so far! ❹ No distortion – every seat becomes a perfect seat!

FIGURE 5.1 Advertising spread for Carousel (1956): This tended to appear in local newspapers around the time of the opening of the film of Carousel in a given location, as in the Iola Register (Kansas), 26 April 1956 (p. 6), and the Sunday Standard (Singapore) on the 29th (p. 9). The image accentuates the curve of the screen, probably to prompt a more favorable comparison with Cinerama; it also emphasizes the six-channel sound, with the five separate speakers in front (a sixth was positioned within the auditorium for sound-effects). However, few regional cinemas would have had the facilities to show Carousel in this manner.

SOURCE: www.widescreenmuseum.com/widescreen/wingcs6.htm

Jordan and Carrie Pipperidge go to the carousel after work, the opening of act 2 on the island comes at the end of a day devoted to 'A Real Nice Clambake,' and so on. Widescreen vistas are fine in daylight, but there is not much point to them at night.

Furthermore, Maine is hardly thematic to *Carousel* in the way that the soon-to-be-a-state Oklahoma Territory is to

Rodgers and Hammerstein's first show. The source-play, Ferenc Molnár's *Liliom*, is set in the outskirts of Budapest, and while Rodgers and Hammerstein were clear on the need to transplant the action from Hungary to the United States, they could have picked almost anywhere one might find a carnival carousel (they initially thought of Louisiana). Only two songs in the stage *Carousel* have direct references to any setting on the New England coast, and one of them, a rather implausible paean to whaling ('Blow High, Blow Low'), was dropped from the film anyway. The other, 'June Is Bustin' Out All Over,' certainly has brief mentions of Penobscot and Augusta but it would otherwise work for any coastal fishing community that suffered harsh weather in March and had access to clams.

Henry King initially suggested shooting *Carousel* in northern California, but Henry Ephron insisted on Maine: thus 115 actors, dancers, and crew travelled to Boothbay Harbor in mid-August 1955, staying there until early October.[39] At that point, the lead roles were assigned to Shirley Jones (Julie Jordan) and Frank Sinatra (Billy Bigelow). Jones had been discovered by Rodgers and Hammerstein; in a pattern typical for them they used her in stage versions of *South Pacific* and *Me and Juliet* prior to pushing her for the role of Laurey in the film of *Oklahoma!* Sinatra was, of course, a much bigger star, fresh from creating another character of dubious morals, Nathan Detroit, in the soon-to-be-released MGM film of *Guys and Dolls* (rumour has it that Sinatra's costar there, Marlon Brando, was also considered for the role of Billy Bigelow).[40] Presumably this was the studio's idea, but if so, it turned out to be a bad one: Sinatra walked out right as filming started, purportedly because he was unwilling to shoot each scene twice for just a single fee—in CinemaScope and Todd-AO he initially thought, but he was confused, and doubly so when the studio claimed that the CinemaScope 35 and 55 cameras would run simultaneously (though they did not). A million-dollar lawsuit ensued that was later resolved when Sinatra agreed to play in the film of Cole Porter's *Can-Can* (1960).[41] Meanwhile, Gordon MacRae, who had been Curly to Shirley Jones's Laurey in *Oklahoma!*, was brought in as a last-minute replacement, although he later said that he had been campaigning for the role and had even done it on stage as preparation.[42] MacRae probably took a gentler view of the character than Sinatra would have done. But it may have helped render the difficult subject of *Carousel* more palatable by reuniting the couple so happily married at the end of *Oklahoma!*, even though their fates were now quite different.

The early location shooting went well enough, and the citizens of Boothbay Harbor were delighted to watch the filming of the musical numbers that Henry King had elected to shoot there to take whatever widescreen advantage he could of the daylight scenery. 'June Is Bustin' Out All Over' had already been a big production number in the stage show, choreographed by Agnes de Mille; the choreography for the film was done instead by Rod Alexander, and 'June' was done on an even grander scale on the deck and roof of Cousin Nettie's seaside spa—one of the energetic highlights of the film if clearly modelled on the acrobatic barn dance in *Seven Brides for Seven Brothers* (choreographed by Michael Kidd).[43] Somewhat more oddly—but again for widescreen advantage—'When the Children Are Asleep' was shifted from its original position. In the stage version, it comes in the middle of act 1 as a scene for just Enoch Snow and Carrie Pipperidge; the film put it between acts 1 and 2 as Enoch and Carrie sail across to the island for the clambake in the company of a silent Julie and Billy, whose presence makes for an awkward duet, although the sailboats look well enough save for a wholly improbable transition at the end from the midday sun to a gloomy dusk.

There was some confusion, however, about where to shoot the other outdoor numbers. The final Graduation Scene (including the choral reprise of 'You'll Never Walk Alone'), set in the daytime, was done elsewhere in Maine, although Howard Thompson reported in the *New York Times* (on 11 September) that it would be shot in the studio. He also said that 'Mister Snow' and 'If I Loved You'—both nighttime numbers—would be situated 'on the lawn of the Lincoln Home for aged folks' (which still exists, in Newcastle, Maine, on the bank of the Damariscotta River). Henry Ephron certainly intended an outdoor location for them and said that 'Mister Snow' was shot there, albeit with some issues caused by the wind. But while the prior dialogue (between Julie, Carrie, Mrs Mullin, and Billy) does indeed take place outdoors, 'Mister Snow' through the 'Bench scene' seems to have been done on a soundstage (if with the backgrounds perhaps spliced in), maybe again because of lighting issues.[44] Thompson further noted that the first appearance of 'You'll Never Walk Alone' (at Billy's death) would be done on the pier (in Boothbay Harbor, presumably). which may only be partly true given that there appears to be some splicing going on here, too. He was correct, however, that 'A Real Nice Clambake' would be done in 'sunny California' (by which he meant a soundstage) because of the 'intricacies of nighttime photography.'[45]

The weather may have affected matters—Henry Ephron said that luck ran out and 'it began to rain and rain and rain'[46]—although one strange decision had already been made, it seems: Howard Thompson reported that Billy Bigelow's big act 1 number, 'Soliloquy,' would be shot 'on a West Coast beach.' This was indeed the case as Gordon MacRae and the crew went to Point Dume State Preserve, near Malibu, California. Perhaps the filmmakers were worried about finding a spot in Maine where Billy could plausibly muse on the future without interruption. In the stage version of *Carousel*, the number is set on the deck of Nettie's spa. Billy has just heard from Julie that she is expecting a baby; he relays the news to Jigger Craigin and Mrs Mullin, who leave him alone to contemplate the prospect of being a father to a son ('My boy, Bill!') or, he suddenly realizes, perhaps a daughter ('My little girl'). This eight-minute sequence is one of the more remarkable musical moments in *Carousel*, and also perhaps its most operatic in terms of its scale and structure; it does not need crashing Pacific waves to make it any more so. Those waves cause further distraction later in the film as (fifteen years on, according to the time span of the plot) Billy's daughter, Louise, begins her act 2 'Ballet' there, watched by a now-invisible Billy allowed back on earth for a day to do a good deed. The parallel location is predictable enough, although it creates a very awkward transition (by way of a spinning cartwheel that has suddenly appeared on the beach) to the soundstage set for the ballet itself, returning (the cartwheel again) to the 'real' beach for its conclusion.[47] In the case of both Billy (after 'Soliloquy') and Louise (after her 'Ballet'), it is unclear how they get from the Pacific surf to the calmer shores of the Atlantic for their next scenes, should anyone care enough to ask the question (some reviewers did).

That strange choice of location might just be excused as clumsiness in the search for widescreen visual effect. Other troublesome alterations to the stage version of *Carousel*, however, rested in the hands of screenwriters Phoebe and Henry Ephron. The latter claimed that 'the screenplay wasn't difficult and we made as many changes in the dialogue as one dared in a classic.'[48] But those changes were quite significant. Actors Gordon MacRae and Shirley Jones may have made a fine couple in the film of *Oklahoma!*, but they play very different characters in *Carousel*. Billy Bigelow is feckless, maladjusted, and prone to violence: more of a Jud Fry than a Curly McClain. Julie Jordan is a victim of domestic violence and seems to accept its inevitability (in the song 'What's the Use of Wond'rin'?'). The other characters are not particularly sympathetic: for example, even the stage versions of Carrie Pipperidge and Enoch Snow are insufferably priggish, in part because of changes made to the roles in the course of drafting the libretto.[49] And certainly there is no comic relief in the manner of Will Parker and Ali Hakim in *Oklahoma!* The Ephrons seem to have had some difficulty in dealing with the consequences.

One can explain some of those 'problems' of *Carousel* by the date of its creation, towards the end of World War II, and therefore of the social issues with which it sought to engage (including traumatized veterans and penniless war widows). Molnár's play, *Liliom: The Life and Death of a Scoundrel* (Budapest, 1909), also had much to answer for, however. Its eponymous antihero (Billy in *Carousel*) dies by his own hand, is judged in a courtroom 'in the beyond' and sentenced to sixteen years in the 'crimson fire,' and then gains the opportunity to spend one day back on earth to perform some kindly act for his daughter, which he fails to do. The outcome is ambiguous, although Molnár quite strongly suggests that Liliom does not, in the end, gain redemption: he is a 'scoundrel' through and through.

When the play was done in New York—as it was quite frequently in the 1920s and 1930s—it became the fashion to speculate on the nature and outcome of Liliom's fate, often with a more positive spin. This was also the case in the endings added to the three films made of the play in 1921, 1930, and (in French) in 1934.[50] The stage version of *Carousel* followed the trend: Hammerstein dropped the notion of judgment and the 'crimson fire'—his Starkeeper is a rather kindly figure—and he negotiated what he called the 'tunnel' of the last portion of the play by adding the final Graduation Scene, in which Billy's brief words of encouragement to Louise and then Julie seem to be sufficient to make amends. Turning him into a more sympathetic character was inevitable, not least because his eloquent music was bound to make him so anyway. But the film version went even further, not least by rewriting the opening of the show to make it clear that something good could come of Billy in the first place.

Molnár's *Liliom* had gained its fairground prologue in the German translation of the play done in Berlin in 1912 and Vienna in 1913: this was the text followed (with some further revisions) in the English-language version premiered by the Theatre Guild in 1921.[51] Rodgers and Hammerstein followed suit in their stage musical, dispensing with the traditional overture to start straight in with the action at curtain up (over the 'Carousel Waltz'). This left the makers of the film in something of a bind. Film musicals had already started to play with reinventing the typical opening-credits sequence (we have seen the case of *The Court Jester*), or even attempting to dispose of it altogether. For *Carousel*, the Ephrons came up with new pre- and post-credits sequences. The first has Billy polishing stars 'up there'; the Heavenly Friend tells him that 'things ain't going so good for your kinfolk down on earth'; Billy asks whom to see to get permission to exercise his right to go back for a day (the Friend says he should address the Starkeeper); and Billy says that he will 'think about it.' He throws out a star which triggers the opening credits (on a blue screen with stars in the background), done over an abridged version of the 'Carousel Waltz' with a feeble fanfare ending presumably requested by Alfred Newman (the conductor and music supervisor). The scene returns 'up there' as Billy enters the office of the Starkeeper, who notes that Billy has already declined his right of return but invites him to tell his story anyway. As Billy recalls his life as a carousel barker, the image pans down to the fairground (on a studio set), the 'Carousel Waltz' starts up again, and the scene plays out more or less as in the stage version.

Creating a separate 'overture' (over the credits) out of the 'Carousel Waltz' solved a problem for the film, although not in ways Rodgers and Hammerstein had wanted for the stage. Newman's (one assumes) idea of adding musical underscoring to the pre-credits sequence with sounds akin to an orchestra tuning up solved another—quite neatly, in fact—given that this is what one would hear in a theatre prior to any formal music. The pre- and post-credits sequences taken together, however, quite fundamentally changed the nature of *Carousel*, turning its main action (up to Billy's death) into a flashback narrative 'told' by Billy to the Starkeeper. Thus, his later scene 'up there' brings us back to the present, as does Billy's final day on earth. The reason for this revised opening suggested at the time was to prevent audiences from thinking that the death of Billy marked the end of the story, but it is not a particularly strong argument.[52] However, there was a triple benefit to this strategy. First, placing the opening on a set that looks overtly (nay, exaggeratedly) stage-like makes the filmic qualities of the main action all the more striking. Second, the fact that Billy tells his own story warts and all prompts the audience to take a more sympathetic view of things from his perspective. Third, it allows the film to enter a musical world that for all its wide-screen realism is, in essence, a flashback fantasy, and therefore more plausible in terms of its use of the medium.

This was a trick of a kind that had been used in *The Wizard of Oz* (1939), moving from a sepia-toned Kansas to an 'over the rainbow' Land of Oz that was both colourful (literally) and musical. In the case of *Carousel* it sought to allow for the show's far greater use of music—and in a more 'operatic' style—than in the case of *Oklahoma!* However, it was not sufficient: large cuts were still made to the score in terms of individual num-bers ('Blow High, Blow Low,' 'The Highest Judge of All,' and 'Geraniums in the Winder' disappeared completely) and of sig-nificant parts of its various musical 'sequences' that Rodgers and Hammerstein used to move from dialogue into song. This may have been because of concerns over length: 'Blow High, Blow Low' and one of the musical sequences (Carrie's 'You're a Queer One, Julie Jordan') may have been filmed and then cut during editing (they are included in the soundtrack album), perhaps as a result of the decision not to produce a roadshow version of the film.[53] But regardless, even in this safer narrative world, music still posed problems for film, and the screen treatment of *Carousel* did serious damage to the complex musical fabric that Rodgers and Hammerstein had woven for the stage.

Many reviews of the film of *Carousel* were favourable enough, praising the cinematography and the acting, singing, and dancing. According to Edwin Schallert in the *Los Angeles Times* on 17 February 1956 ('*Carousel* Ranks with Best Films'):

> *Carousel* belongs with the very best in screen achievements, because it is amazingly beautiful scenically, singularly rich in romantic appeal and surprisingly philosophical. Moreover it follows the authentic pattern of its originals, the stage play *Liliom* by Ferenc Molnar, and the Rodgers and Hammerstein footlight presentation.

But Schallert's last point was an exaggeration, to say the least, and the film was not the expected success at the box office: the roadshow *Oklahoma!* soon went higher up the rankings, while the more exotic, and more upbeat, *The King and I* dominated the summer and fared much better with audiences and in the award listings.[54] One negative review of *Carousel* by the distinguished dance critic Arlene Croce also picked up on a number of issues that will now have a familiar ring. After complaining about the tendency of film studios to allocate musicals to directors unfamiliar with the genre, and more inclined to favour story content over other parameters, she raised a number of other objections:

> In *Carousel*, CinemaScope 55 presents to the span of the eye New England beaches, churchyards and sunsets, all very pretty and very real, into which the surrealistic de Mille ballet and

the interstellar rovings of Billy Bigelow intrude like perverse thoughts in a cathedral. For here again, the American cinema runs aground on the darkling plain of fantasy, and the failure of *Carousel* is the dual failure to realize an adequate film form for music drama and for fantasy.[55]

Croce considered the film of *Carousel* to represent 'a crisis of form'; my aim here has been to provide some context in which to understand that crisis in terms of how the show became trapped by way of conflicting aesthetic, technological, and economic demands, some of its own making and some the studio's. But most will agree with her: whatever was gained in translating *Carousel* from stage to screen could not compensate for what was lost.

## NOTES

1. This essay expands significantly on the brief discussion of the film version of *Carousel* in Tim Carter, *Rodgers and Hammerstein's 'Carousel'* (New York: Oxford University Press, 2017), which covers in greater depth the original show's creation, content, and reception. I am grateful to Gina Bombola for her comments on a draft of this chapter. Production information for the shows and films discussed here (dates, performance statistics, budgets, box office receipts, and the like) are taken somewhat indiscriminately from the standard sources such as www.afi.com, www.ibdb.com, www.imdb.com, www.playbill.com, www.tcm.com, and even some relevant entries on Wikipedia. I have made no effort to verify or corroborate them by way of in-depth archival investigation; while this might seem a case of scholarly negligence, it is also a practical inevitability, albeit one with obvious methodological consequences. I refer to newspaper articles by way of their author (where indicated), main headline, and date: page references are less useful given that they could vary from edition to edition. However, articles on entertainments tended to

come in the same location in each issue save where they were front-page news. Quotations are lightly edited (for example, to put show or film titles in italic), but I retain the original spellings and punctuation, even if they lead to inconsistency.
Richard Rodgers, *Musical Stages: An Autobiography*, 2nd ed. (Cambridge, MA: Da Capo, 2002), 243.

2. The exception to the cycle (on odd-numbered years) Is *Flower Drum Song*, premiered on 1 December 1958. For 1957, R&H wrote the television version of *Cinderella*, and they had also explored (somewhat diffidently, it seems) the idea of a musical version of Howard Lindsay and Russel Crouse's 1939 play *Life with Father*; for the latter, see '*Life with Father* Pends as Rodgers & Hammerstein's Next Broadway Musical,' *Variety*, 25 July 1956. However, Rodgers was also suffering from illness and depression.

3. '70,000,000 view R&H Cavalcade,' *Variety*, 31 March 1954.

4. For Rodgers and Hammerstein and George Bernard Shaw's *Pygmalion*, the source-play for *My Fair Lady*, see Tim Carter, '*Oklahoma!*': *The Making of An American Musical* (New Haven, CT: Yale University Press, 2007), 243.

5. Compare also the details of out-of-town productions in 'R&H Legits' Summer Meal Ticket; Pull $234,600 Gross Total for Week,' *Variety*, 27 July 1955. The summer 1955 season at the Muny in St. Louis included *Carousel*, *Allegro*, *South Pacific*, and *The King and I*; see REFO:PERD'St. Loo Muny Sked,' *Variety*, 16 March 1955.

6. For a useful overview of these and other issues, see Julie Hubbert, *Celluloid Symphonies: Text and Contexts in Film Music History* (Berkeley: University of California Press, 2011), part 3.

7. Given in Carter, *Oklahoma!*, 225.

8. Joshua Logan, *Movie Stars, Real People, and Me* (New York: Delacorte, 1976), 125.

9. Carter, *Oklahoma!*, 233 (monitoring), 235 (Shelley Winters as Ado Annie), 242 (fire).

10. Carter, *Oklahoma!*, 243–244 (negotiations); Sam Zolotow, 'Producing Team Faces Busy Year,' *New York Times*, 10 August 1953; '*Oklahoma!* Film Set: Stage Success Will Be Made in Todd's Wide-Screen Process,' *New York Times*, 17 August 1953. For the subsequent negotiations over the other R&H shows, see also

'R&H Seek Production Rights to All Their Shows: [*South*] *Pacific* Deal Snagged,' *Variety*, 28 September 1955.

11. Both had recently worked on other stage-to-screen adaptations, however: Hornblow produced *Remains to Be Seen* (1953; based on the Broadway comedy by Russel Crouse and Howard Lindsay, with three added songs), and Zinnemann directed *The Member of the Wedding* (1952; Carson McCullers's drama, based on her 1946 novel).

12. Carter, *Oklahoma!*, 244–249.

13. Hayward and Logan already had some informal control over the film rights to James Michener's *Tales of the South Pacific* before R&H took on the project of turning these short stories into a musical (they also coproduced the Broadway show and retained some rights to it); see Jim Lovensheimer, '*South Pacific': Paradise Rewritten* (Oxford: Oxford University Press, 2010), 46.

14. There were also rumours of an intended Todd-AO film of another R&H musical, although this never came to fruition; see Edwin Schallert, '*Me and Juliet* Prospect Good for Todd-AO,' *Los Angeles Times*, 10 July 1954.

15. Philip K. Scheuer, 'New Wide-Screen Process Enters Battle of Scopes,' *Los Angeles Times*, 27 June 1954. The first of those excerpts probably came from *Untamed* (released on 1 March 1955; the Zulu battle sequence was shot on location in South Africa in spring 1954). The second may have been a screen test for Sheree North, who was later (January 1955) chosen to replace Marilyn Monroe opposite Betty Grable in *How to Be Very, Very Popular* (22 July 1955).

16. The first musical in CinemaScope was Warner Bros.' *Lucky Me* (released on 9 April 1954), starring Doris Day, Robert Cummings, and Phil Silvers.

17. Arthur Hornblow Jr, the producer of the film *Oklahoma!*, argued in favour of dropping the opening credits but met strong resistance from the Directors Guild; see Thomas M. Pryor, 'Hollywood Dossier,' *New York Times*, 23 January 1955.

18. The films of *Carousel* (128 minutes) and *The King and I* (133) were shorter. The cut-down *Brigadoon*, however, was typical for a Gene Kelly musical (and most others): compare *On the Town*

(1949; 98 minutes), *Summer Stock* (1950; 109), *An American in Paris* (1951; 113), and *Singin' in the Rain* (1952; 103).

19. 'Carousel Will Finish in 4X-55M C'Scope,' *Variety*, 21 September 1955.

20. '20th Foregoes Roadshowing of 55m: On Balance, Prefers Fast Playoff of *Carousel* in Short Market,' *Variety*, 16 November 1955; 'Time & Squawks Make "King" 35m,' *Variety*, 29 February 1956.

21. Richard L. Coe's 'New *Carousel* a Jim-Dandy,' *Washington Post*, 22 February 1956—reviewing the film being shown at the Capitol Theatre (Washington, DC)—noted that the roadshow *Oklahoma!* would open in Baltimore on 'Monday night,' which it did (on 27 February).

22. Subsequent stanzas expand the jargon still further (Cinerama, VistaVision, Superscope, Todd-AO, Cinecolor, Warnercolor, Pathécolor, Eastmancolor, Kodacolor . . .).

23. However, it was generally acknowledged that American film musicals did not always do well in non-English-speaking markets because of the problems of vernacular references and of dubbing. As *Variety* reported ('20th's Full Sync on *Carousel* in German,' 3 October 1956), the latter issue was addressed in Twentieth Century-Fox's unusual decision on dubbing *Carousel* into German also to redo the songs as well, with the African American baritone Lawrence Winter (at that time on tour in West Germany) singing Billy, and 'Senta Schoener' (*recte* Sonja Schöner) as Julie.

24. Both Gerald Mast, *Can't Help Singin': The American Musical on Stage and Screen* (Woodstock, NY: Overlook Press, 1987) and Thomas S. Hischak, *Through the Screen Door: What Happened to the Broadway Musical When It Went to Hollywood* (Lanham, MD: Scarecrow Press, 2004)cover some of the broader aesthetic issues, but fewer of the structural ones considered in the present essay.

25. Carter, *Oklahoma!*, 50–58.

26. Compare the case of Pamela Britton, who was Ado Annie in the 'national' company (then playing in Chicago) but left for Hollywood; Carter, *Oklahoma!*, 237. She played the unnamed 'Girl from Brooklyn' opposite Frank Sinatra in *Anchors Aweigh*

(1945) but did not have success in films and soon returned to the stage.

27. Both Hall and Smith were African American, although Rodgers and Hammerstein tended to cast Hall as somehow Asian, both in *South Pacific* and (as Madam Liang) in *Flower Drum Song*.

28. As it did Ali Hakim's 'It's a Scandal, It's a Outrage'; compare Carter, *Oklahoma!*, 246.

29. This was a trick adopted by Bob Hope and Bing Crosby in some of their earlier *Road to . . .* films also from Paramount.

30. From an interview with Donen in 1977, given in Hubbert, *Celluloid Symphonies*, 278.

31. There were also often tax-based reasons to go abroad on location; see the discussion of so-called runaway productions in the 1950s in Hubbert, *Celluloid Symphonies*, 187.

32. Hubbert, *Celluloid Symphonies*, 280.

33. The parallels with *Seven Brides for Seven Brothers* also probably help explain the decision to move one act 1 'outdoor' number in *Oklahoma!* to an interior set. 'Many a New Day,' for Laurey and her female companions, is done indoors, turning it (somewhat problematically) into a women-in-underwear number in the manner of 'June Bride' in the earlier film.

34. Rodgers, *Musical Stages*, 285. The remaining two films of R&H musicals, *Flower Drum Song* (1961) and *Sound of Music* (1965), were done after Hammerstein's death.

35. So Hannah Lewis suggested in her paper 'From Stage to Screen: The Film Musicals of Screenwriter Ernest Lehman' presented at the conference *Music and the Moving Image XII*, New York University, 26–28 May 2017.

36. Henry Ephron discusses *Carousel* in his autobiography, *We Thought We Could Do Anything: The Life of Screenwriters Phoebe and Heny Ephron* (New York: Norton, 1977), 141–174. I have drawn on this for some of the information given below, although like most such casual memoirs, not everything Ephron says can be verified, and in some cases he clearly misremembered things.

37. For the demonstration reel, see Thomas M. Pryor, 'New Film Process Is Shown by Fox,' *New York Times*, 16 November 1955; Edwin Schallert, 'CinemaScope 55 Hailed at Initial Showing

Here,' *Los Angeles Times*, 24 January 1956. 'Big Spark-Up of 20th's *Carousel*,' *Variety*, 18 January 1956, notes an initial adver-tising budget of $1.2 million before the release—including buy-time on the CBS radio network—which was then predicted to reach $2 million with continued publicity.

38. www.tcm.com/mediaroom/video/600658/Carousel-Original-Trailer-.html.

39. Howard Thompson, 'Riding a Cinema *Carousel* Way Down East,' *New York Times*, 11 September 1955; Fred Hift, 'Native Actors See Double in Down East *Carousel* Shooting in Maine,' *Variety*, 14 September 1955. Hift noted that the CinemaScope 55 cameras were noisy, creating severe difficulties for sound re-cording on location. There are various other newspaper reports on the shooting, such as Marjory Adams, 'Movies' New Singing Team Likes Making Pictures in Maine,' *Boston Daily Globe*, 18 September 1955; 'From Fish to Films in Maine: *Carousel* on Location There,' *New York Herald Tribune*, 9 October 1955. Adams notes that Claramae Turner, who played Nettie Fowler, needed to 'rush back' to the West Coast to play Amneris in the San Francisco Opera's production of *Aida*; in fact, she had al-ready done so for the opening night on 15 September, though she had a substitute for the second performance on the 22nd (see archive.sfopera.com). The original stage Nettie Fowler was also played by an opera contralto, Christine Johnson; see Carter, *Rodgers and Hammerstein's 'Carousel,'* 43.

40. For Brando, see Hedda Hopper, 'Gordon MacRae: He Just Had to Play 'Curly'!,' *Chicago Tribune*, 31 July 1955. But this kind of gossip ran rife, often without foundation. Nor is it clear how much one can trust Henry Ephron's claim (*We Thought We Could Do Anything*, 146) that agents for Doris Day and Judy Garland approached him for them to take the role of Julie Jordan, al-though Shirley Jones also says that she had heard rumours about Garland; see her *Shirley Jones: A Memoir*, with Wendy Leigh (New York: Gallery, 2013), 77.

41. 'Sinatra Quits Film Site,' *New York Times*, 25 August 1955 (CinemaScope and Todd-AO); 'Sinatra Sued for Million for Balking over Film,' *Los Angeles Times*, 30 August 1955; 'Zanuck Praises New Fox 55mm Process Rushes,' *Independent Film*

*Journal* 36, no. 4 (3 September 1955): 6 (simultaneous filming but 35 mm now dropped). Among the various other rumours concerning Sinatra's abrupt departure, there was widespread suspicion that he had manufactured an excuse so that he could take a more profitable engagement in Las Vegas instead. Shirley Jones, however, claimed that the pressure on him to leave *Carousel* had come from his then wife, Ava Gardner; see *Shirley Jones: A Memoir*, 84–85. Henry Ephron identified a number of problems with Sinatra (including the singer's anxieties over the music) in *We Thought We Could Do Anything*, 149–150, 154–160. He also noted (158) that the idea of replacing him with Gene Kelly had been vetoed by Richard Rodgers given that his voice was not suited to 'Soliloquy.'

42. MacRae's campaigning (and his performance in a stage production in Dallas, Texas) is reported in Celestine Sibley, 'Hollywood Adds New Glitter to *Carousel*,' *Atlanta Constitution*, 4 March 1956. He did a two-week run in *Carousel* in Dallas starting on 18 July 1955; see 'The Drama Desk,' *Pittsburgh Post-Gazette*, 9 June 1955.

43. De Mille retained some credit for 'Louise's Ballet' in the film version of *Carousel*, but she was very bitter about otherwise being supplanted by Rod Alexander; see Kara Anne Gardner, *Agnes de Mille: Telling Stories in Broadway Dance* (New York: Oxford University Press, 2016), 109–112.

44. Such splicing may have been one of the 'special photographic effects' attributed to Ray Kellogg in the opening credits for the film.

45. Thompson, 'Riding a Cinema *Carousel* Way Down East.' Ephron noted that in Sinatra's absence 'we took the "If I Loved You" location and used it for "Mr Snow," the song between Julie and Carrie. There was a wind that kept blowing their hairdos around, but [Henry] King decided that that made it look real'; *We Thought We Could Do Anything*, 157–158. For 'A Real Nice Clambake' being shot in Hollywood, see 'New England Clambake Staged for *Carousel*,' *New York Herald Tribune*, 16 October 1955.

46. Ephron, *We Thought We Could Do Anything*, 164. However, Ephron says that 'we were getting past the middle of August and it was cold,' which does not square with the chronology. Howard

Thompson noted in his 11 September report that 'the shifting daylight and the weather' had caused some juggling of the schedule early on. Metereological records for Augusta, Maine (the closest available for Boothbay Harbor, albeit inland) report that it rained quite heavily (0.2 inches or more) on 19 and 23 August, and 12, 24, 28, and 30 September, but there were plenty of clear days in between; see the climate database at w2.weather. gov/climate/xmacis.php?wfo=gyx. In September, the daily temperatures tended to be in the 60s (Fahrenheit) or higher. However, such data do not provide evidence of other factors that might have influenced shooting, such as cloud cover.

47. Henry Ephron said that he also wanted to film the ballet on the actual beach but that it would have been too difficult and expensive to roll the sand smooth for each take; *We Thought We Could Do Anything*, 168.

48. Ephron, *We Thought We Could Do Anything*, 145.

49. For example, Hammerstein first planned for Carrie to have a rival suitor, Dwight, creating a triangle in the manner of Ado Annie, Will Parker, and Ali Hakim in *Oklahoma!*; see Carter, *Rodgers and Hammerstein's 'Carousel,'* 40.

50. They are discussed in Carter, *Rodgers and Hammerstein's 'Carousel,'* 84–86.

51. The English translation was credited to Benjamin F. Glazer, although in fact most of it was done (from the German) by Lorenz Hart; see Carter, *Rodgers and Hammerstein's 'Carousel,'* 10.

52. Henry Ephron is noted as making this argument in 'New England Clambake Staged for *Carousel*,' *New York Herald Tribune*, 16 October 1955, where he also credits the idea for the flashback treatment to Darryl F. Zanuck. Bosley Crowther made a similar point about Billy's death in his review of the film, 'Screen: *Carousel* Is Worthy of Stage Original,' *New York Times*, 17 February 1956. He also found some of the settings for the songs odd (including the 'heavy surf pounding' behind Billy Bigelow in 'Soliloquy'), although in general his review was highly favourable.

53. This must have happened late: these two numbers are in fact noted as present in Fred Hift's review of the film in *Variety*, 22 February 1956; Hift in turn must have been relying at least in part on a press release.

54. *Carousel* was nominated for awards by the Directors Guild and Writers Guild (but did not win); *The King and I* was nominated for nine Academy Awards and won five, including Best Actor (Yul Brynner). *Around the World in Eighty Days* won the Oscar for Best Motion Picture, although *The King and I* gained the Golden Globe Award as the Best Motion Picture: Comedy or Musical. The review of *The King and I* in *Variety* (4 July 1956) deemed it 'Blockbuster of the year. One of the all-time greats among musicals. Sure to wow all classes and nations. Socko in all departments: story, performance, production, score.'
55. Arlene Croce, 'Film Musicals: A Crisis of Form,' *Film Culture* 2, no. 2 (issue no. 8; 1956): 25–26, at p. 25.

# 6

# Carol Burnett and the Ends of Variety

## Parody, Nostalgia, and Analysis of the American Musical

ROBYNN J. STILWELL

■□■

THE TELEVISION VARIETY SHOW WAS the last gasp of the vaudeville ticket. It was also arguably the most distinctive genre of television for the first thirty to forty years of the medium. The first huge American television star was made in a variety show: Milton Berle, host of NBC's *Texaco Star Theatre* (1948–55). *The Ed Sullivan Show* (1948–71) reigned for years as a place to be seen and heard for entertainers. Popular culture mostly remembers the singers (Elvis, the Beatles, maybe even Frank Sinatra, Rosemary Clooney, or Bobby Darin); but many variety shows also staged scenes from current Broadway shows, or at least hosted the singers to perform the show's hits, scattered among comedy segments, ballet and jazz dance, classical performance, and the occasional novelty act.

In 1957, initially on *The Tonight Show* and then in prime time on *The Ed Sullivan Show*, a young cabaret singer and comedienne named Carol Burnett made her first big splash by singing 'I Made a Fool of Myself over John Foster Dulles.' After starring on Broadway in the fairy-tale parody musical *Once upon a Mattress* (1959), for which she was nominated for a Tony Award, she became a regular on *The Garry Moore Show*, garnering an Emmy in her last year, 1962. It would be another five years before Burnett would get her own show, although by the time *The Carol Burnett Show* premiered, a generational shift in the television—and wider entertainment—industry was under way.

When *The Carol Burnett Show* premiered in 1967, there were eleven other variety shows on American network television in primetime:[1]

The Ed Sullivan Show (1948–71)
The Red Skelton Hour (1951–71)
The Lawrence Welk Show (1955–82)
The Andy Williams Show (1962–69)
The Hollywood Palace (1964–70)
The Dean Martin Show (1965–74)
The Jackie Gleason Show (1966–70)
The Pat Boone Show (1967–68)
The Jerry Lewis Show (1967–69)
The Smothers Brothers Comedy Hour (1967–70)
Rowan & Martin's Laugh-In (1967–73)
The Carol Burnett Show (1967–78)

By the time *The Carol Burnett Show* left the air in 1978, the only other variety show was the youth-oriented *Donny & Marie Show*, which would end in the next year. Some shows, like *The Lawrence Welk Show* (originally ABC) and *Hee Haw* (originally CBS) had moved into syndication, along with the still-running, Dolly-less *Porter Wagoner Show* and *The Muppet Show* (1976–79), modelled even more literally on the theatrical roots of vaudeville while also operating as a backstage musical.

*Saturday Night Live* had debuted in 1975, and the cable television revolution was on the horizon, but times were changing even at the beginning of *The Carol Burnett Show*'s run. A look at the preceding list reveals that many of the variety shows ended in the next few years, most of them by 1971, particularly those fronted by performers from an earlier generation. In the 1966–67 season, the year before the Burnett show premiered, ABC had made a big push to relaunch a Milton Berle variety show, but the gamble failed; the medium's first star did not reach new audiences. Both of the more youth-oriented shows that debuted in 1967, *Rowan and Martin's Laugh-In* (the format of which explicitly recalled vaudeville and burlesque) and especially *The Smothers Brothers Comedy Hour* often ran afoul of censors in an era of changing mores and a generationally charged political atmosphere.[2]

The success of *The Carol Burnett Show* is certainly down to the musical, comedic, and acting talents of its star,[3] and to the chemistry among her regular players: Harvey Korman, Lyle Waggoner, Vicki Lawrence, and Tim Conway. But the show also negotiated this generational shift through a combination of contemporary reference that was nonpolitical and a nostalgia that was warm but witty. The comedy style of the show relied heavily on parody of other media forms: the annual spoofs of the most memorable television commercials and the soap opera 'As the Stomach Turns' were recurring skits, and in later seasons, the family situation comedy was reworked into the surprisingly trenchant, sometimes genuinely melancholic 'Family' sketches. The show was also an opportunity for Burnett to do what she had always wanted to do—be in the classic movies she had adored growing up. Burnett and her younger sister, Chrissie, lived with their grandmother in Hollywood from a young age because of their parents' alcoholism.[4] Going to the movies was a way of escaping a life of some deprivation. As a child, Carol Burnett wanted to be Betty

Grable. As an adult, Carol Burnett got to *be* Grable. And Joan Crawford, Vivien Leigh, Shirley Temple, Judy Garland, and so many others (including a version of herself and her sister Chris, then played by Vicki Lawrence,[5] in a recurring sketch about modern life taking unexpected turns). The parodies were sharp, particularly about music and performance, but never mean; there was affection as well as substantial knowingness: Joan Crawford reportedly loved 'Mildred Fierce,' though was a little more ambivalent about 'Torchy Song.' 'Went with the Wind' has widely been considered one of the greatest moments of American television, garnering one of the longest and most sustained studio-audience laughs in history when 'Starlett' appears at the top of the 'Terra' staircase wearing a dress made out of the curtains, with the still-attached curtain rod balanced across her shoulders. To the astonished exclamation of appreciation from 'Brat Butler,' she responds, 'I saw it in the window, and I just couldn't resist it.' The parody itself has become a classic.

The hour-long show's format by the 1970s had become semistandardized. The 'bump up the lights' sequence, during which Burnett answered questions from the audience, opened the show, and a series of shorter comedy sketches and musical numbers featured in the first half. The second half was more likely to feature extended, two-act parodies of films. While most of the film parodies were of individual films like 'The Little Foxies' or 'Rancid Harvest,' some were tributes to various eras or studios, such as one of the best-remembered skits, a tribute to the 1930s Universal monster cycle (the gypsy fortune teller has two sons, a rock star and a werewolf, and on a full moon, she can't tell them apart).

Musicals were a good proportion of the full-length parodies, almost all written by Artie Malvin and/or the team of Ken and Mitzie Welch.[6] Some were direct parodies of individual films ('When My Baby Laughs at Me,' 'Beach Blanket

Boo-Boo'). 'Babes in Barns' is primarily a parody of *Babes in Arms*, but incorporates elements from other Mickey Rooney/ Judy Garland films, and 'High Hat' is a synthesis of the Astaire-Rogers RKO cycle. Other sketches compile the works of individual composers (Irving Berlin, George Gershwin, Johnny Mercer, Frank Loesser, for instance) and write original musicals around them, not unlike the musicals of MGM's Freed Unit in the early 1950s (*An American in Paris, Singin' in the Rain*, and *The Band Wagon* all follow the same format).

These sketches engage with the concept of adaptation in at least two, intersecting ways: the materials (book, songs, design, choreographic style), and medium. We talk, rightly, about film and theatre as divergent media with their own specificity; television, for a variety of historical and disciplinary reasons, has much less definition as a specific medium—arguably, this is not surprising, because television is less a specific medium than a window through which we can see adaptations of other, older media, like film, theatre, and even radio.[7] Television shares some traits with theatre (liveness, temporal immediacy, and usually a stage-bound set, either in a theatrical or soundstage setting); it also shares traits with cinema (the ability to record and edit, the framing eye of the camera and its ability for motion, the notional access to location changes). But television also has shortcomings that neither of the older media do: in the context of the United States, the commercial demand for advertising breaks, roughly every fifteen minutes; fewer technological and financial resources for sets, costumes, and writers, composers, and choreographers; and less time for rehearsal and potentially less time for the final product. Thus, a television adaptation is conceptually equidistant from both television and film, and arguably a smaller leap from one or the other than from theatre to film or vice versa. These limitations have historically tended to outweigh any advantages, such as the ability to reach millions at the same instant.

A variety show will have even tighter constraints than a full, free-standing television production, particularly in terms of time. The sets are built on a proscenium stage and performed live before a studio audience, shot on videotape for later editing.[8] Although most of *The Carol Burnett Show* extended parodies were of films, some of those films were themselves adaptations of theatrical productions, like 'Hold Me, Hamlet.' Others are based on vague generic parameters like 'Italian cinema'—'La Caperucita Roja' is based on Mexican folk theatre. Another fairy-tale adaptation, 'Cinderella Gets It On,' bears the impressions not just of theatrical rock musicals but also of popular musical performance on contemporary television and the then-current Blaxploitation cycle of films. These various modes of presentation (film, Broadway, folk theatre, vaudeville, rock musicals, variety shows, rock music shows) are in constant flux, flow, and conversation throughout these parody adaptations. But each is surprisingly precise and consistent in its parodic palette, including musical style, acting and musical performance, set and costume design, narrative structure, and even camera work.

## ON PARODY AS ADAPTATION

On the one hand, it seems obvious—in order to function as a parody, a text must contain a structural and/or stylistic replication of the work being parodied. It is thus a sort of adaptation. But it is worth taking a moment before diving into the analyses of the three Carol Burnett 'musicals' to more precisely define the terms 'adaptation' and 'parody' and what forms they may take.

Not surprisingly, one of the most critical theorists of parody, Linda Hutcheon, has also become a theorist of adaptation. Following a line of argument that we also find in Robert Stam's influential 'Beyond Fidelity' essay,[9] Hutcheon considers adaptation (whether parodic or not) a process of engagement with an original text, not merely a transcription or even a translation. As Paul Edwards summarizes in his review of Hutcheon's *A Theory of Adaptation*,

The distinctiveness of the new artistic product is its invocation, rather than suppression or erasure, of its source: 'To deal with adaptations as adaptations is to think of them as . . . inherently "palimpsestuous" works, haunted at all times by their adapted texts.' . . . An interpretive and critical activity must precede the creative activity of adaptation. For this reason, Hutcheon invites us to view adaptation as a process as well as a product or formal entity; the process entails questions of an adapter's motive and intention.[10]

This conceptualization recognizes a significant overlap in adaptation and parody. It also permits, if not requires, a view of parody as a form of analysis.

Hutcheon's early work on parody had emerged in the mid-1980s, a few years after the end of *The Carol Burnett Show*, and although she is dealing primarily with what might be termed 'high art' in an earlier era, what she has to say about parody resonates quite strongly with the ethos of *The Carol Burnett Show*. In response to other postmodernist theorists like Frederic Jameson, Hutcheon takes exception to the concept of 'blank parody,' insisting on both an engagement with history and a range of affective response:

What I mean by 'parody' here is not the ridiculing imitation of the standard theories and definitions that are rooted in eighteenth-century theories of wit. The collective weight of parodic practice suggests a redefinition of *parody as repetition with critical distance that allows ironic signaling of difference at the very heart of similarity*.

In historiographic metafiction, in film, in painting, in music, and in architecture, this parody paradoxically enacts both change and cultural continuity: the Greek prefix para can mean both 'counter' or 'against' AND 'near' or 'beside.' Jameson argues that in postmodernism 'parody finds itself without a vocation,' replaced by pastiche, which he (bound by a definition of parody as ridiculing imitation) sees as more neutral or blank parody. But the looking to both the aesthetic and historical past in postmodernist architecture is anything but what Jameson describes as pastiche, that is, 'the random cannibalization of all the styles of the past, the play of random stylistic allusion.' There is absolutely nothing random or 'without principle' in the parodic recall and re-examination of the past by architects like Charles Moore or Ricardo Bofill. *To include irony and play is never necessarily to exclude seriousness and purpose in postmodernist art. To misunderstand this is to misunderstand the nature of much contemporary aesthetic production*—even if it does make for neater theorizing.[11] [Emphasis mine]

Hutcheon thus 'de-flattens' both history and specificity, a flattening one often finds in postmodern theory, as in Jameson's 'blank'-ing.

The past as referent is not bracketed or effaced, as Jameson would like to believe: it is incorporated and modified, given new and different life and meaning.[12]

The concern with history will almost necessarily bring up the idea of nostalgia, a concept Hutcheon herself had resisted in a couple of decades of theorizing:

I confess to suffering from an utter lack of nostalgia. But clearly there was also an intellectual issue at stake, since many had repeatedly insisted on the power of postmodern nostalgia.[13] . . .

In other words, despite very strong reservations (based in part on personality limitations), I do know that I should never underestimate the power of nostalgia, especially its visceral physicality and emotional impact. But that power comes in part from its structural doubling-up of two different times, an inadequate present and an idealized past. But this is where I must return to that other obsession of mine—irony—for irony too is doubled: two meanings, the 'said' and the 'unsaid,' rub together to create irony—and it too packs considerable punch. People do not usually get upset about metaphor or synecdoche, but they certainly do get worked up about irony.[14]

So Hutcheon proposes that nostalgia and irony have much in common, structurally, including that they are incomplete, or perhaps better, inert, without an audience:

> Irony is not something in an object that you either 'get' or fail to 'get': irony 'happens' for you (or, better, you make it 'happen') when two meanings, one said and the other unsaid, come together, usually with a certain critical edge. Likewise, nostalgia is not something you 'perceive' in an object; it is what you 'feel' when two different temporal moments, past and present, come together for you and, often, carry considerable emotional weight. In both cases, it is the element of response—of active participation, both intellectual and affective—that makes for the power.[15]

What is powerful in this configuration is not just that it recognizes the work of the audience, no longer the passive receptor of an authorial product. The audience activates connections that an author (individual or corporate/collaborative, in the case of any form of film or television) lays into a work, and a good amount of the response one has to the work is the product of one's own intellectual *and emotional* participation. This recognition of the *emotional* aspect is important in Hutcheon's work; most postmodern theorists have proposed a kind of 'postmodern cool,' inherent in the detachment of

Jameson's 'blank parody.' And yet the affect of the play can be anything from sentimental nostalgia to exhilaration; the emotional joy—a kind of mental runner's high—that comes from intellectual processes is often disregarded, to the point that there is no specific name for it, although I think most of us recognize it.

This interplay between nostalgia, parody, and analysis is a key element of the musical sketches produced by *The Carol Burnett Show*. Yes, they are funny; but they are often funny because of the way in which they *know* how the models work, what the key points of pressure are in the structure and tone that the writers and performers can prod for humour, or a humorous but still highly aware nostalgia. They replicate the models so well that they can stand alone, working even if one is unfamiliar with the model or if the parodies are largely original works based on old forms. And yet, they are also very specific about those models. They are knowing in a way that invokes nostalgia but rarely, if ever, trade in mere sentimentality, unless they engage sentimentality itself for humour in the framing of the parodies for the television show.

## 'HOLD ME HAMLET'

Of the three parodies addressed here, 'Hold Me, Hamlet'[16] has the most obvious and particular precedent: the Cole Porter musical *Kiss Me, Kate*, first a Broadway production in 1948 and subsequently made into a (3D) film in 1953. *Kiss Me, Kate* is itself an adaptation of the Shakespearean comedy *The Taming of the Shrew*. The Burnett Show parody functions on a number of levels: it is a parody of Shakespeare, but turning one of Shakespeare's bloodiest tragedies into a musical comedy is a more significant transformation than from what is, despite its archaic sexism, a romantic comedy. The parody carries through in the alliterative title, but the sketch eschews the double on-stage/backstage narrative; given the time frame of television production, that would be perhaps the easiest feature of *Kiss Me, Kate* to jettison. However, the sketch is introduced as if it is an episode of *Masterpiece Theater* (PBS 1971–), a strategy that at least gestures towards the doubling while also emphasizing the 'classical' and 'high art' connotations of Shakespeare for modern audiences. It also heightens the comedy by lifting up the sketch in preparation for lowering the tone.

The reliance on knowledge of *Hamlet*, and even its performing traditions, is unusually strong in this sketch: 'Alistair Cookie' (Harvey Korman spoofs the *Masterpiece Theatre* host Alistair Cooke[17]; see ▶ video example 24.1) gives the briefest of synopses about Hamlet's father's death and Hamlet's suspicion of Claudius, who has married Hamlet's mother, Gertrude, but the narrative of the sketch is telescoped to a significant degree, with most of the run-time taken up in song; some dialogue sequences last barely more than an exchange. The music is wholly original, although with a clear nod toward Cole Porter, and a sideways glance at Noël Coward, stylistically. The performers referenced include at minimum Coward, Al Jolson, Rex Harrison, Judy Garland, Sophie Tucker, and Gene Kelly. Unlike some of the musical sketches, which essentially follow the flow of the storyline for structure, 'Hold Me, Hamlet' is structured very much like a 'real' musical would be, with a clearly defined first act, then a second act that is truncated by a simple plot resolution, itself a parody of both the convolutions of a Shakespearean drama and the clearing up of misunderstandings/coincidences common in musical comedy. Just as *Kiss Me, Kate* was Porter's transition from number-oriented musical comedies to more integrated book musicals, the sketch hovers between the two models. The first act plays out the overlapping Freudian triangles between Hamlet, Sr/Gertrude/Hamlet and Gertrude/Hamlet/Ophelia, and the

## Table 6.1

### NUMBER BREAKDOWN OF 'HOLD ME, HAMLET'

| | **ACT 1** | |
|---|---|---|
| Chorus | 'Something Stinks in the State of Denmark, Something Smells in Elsinore' | Burlesque |
| Ghost | 'I Never Had it So Good' | Burlesque |
| Gertrude | 'Don't You Love Your Mama Anymore' | Red-hot mama |
| Hamlet | 'G-E-R-T-R-U-D-E' | Sentimental ballad |
| Ophelia | 'Oh, That This Too, Too Solid Flesh Would Melt' | Torch song |
| Ghost & Chorus | 'I Never Had It So Good' | Burlesque Chorus finale |
| | **ACT 2** | |
| Claudius | 'Nobody Does It Like a Dane' | Patter song |
| Hamlet & Ophelia | 'I Never Had It So Good' | Duet |
| Ensemble | 'All Is Well in the State of Denmark, Nothing's Rotten Anymore' | Ensemble chorus finale |

second act resolves the last little bit of adolescent psychological business with Hamlet before a big ensemble finale (see Table 6.1).

The prologue introduces guest star Carl Reiner as the Ghost of Hamlet's Father. With his pale makeup and his armour accessorized by floating bits of white chiffon to signify his ghostliness, he recalls Lionel Jeffries's dithering King Pellinore in the 1967 film of *Camelot*.

He promptly is joined onstage by 'the changing of the guard,' a chorus of female dancers in skimpy 'armour' costumes with exaggerated feather-boa horsetail helmets (see ▶ video example 24.2). They perform a military drill, ornamented by burlesque hip-grinds and a pole-slide along their lance shafts while they sing 'Something Stinks in the State of Denmark . . . Something Smells in Elsinore.' The march-like style recalls Porter's 'Another Opening, Another Show' from *Kiss Me, Kate*, particularly the opening rhythm on 'Something stinks'—a slight enough resemblance not to be a copy of ''nother op'nin',' but to trigger the original in the audience's knowing ear (see ▶ video example 24.3).

The Ghost punctuates the end of the short chorus with a rim-shot like 'Boo!' and the guards gather around him as he sits on a chair. Two of them sit on his lap as he sings, 'I Never Had It So Good,' a jaunty tune ('Since Gert did me in, I've been living in sin . . .') (see ▶ video example 24.4). His (bad) Cockney accent recalls Alfred Doolittle singing 'Get Me to the Church on Time' from *My Fair Lady* (1964). The guards provide vocal 'wah-wah-wah' responses to his lines, and join him in a chorus line finale from 'We'll hey nonny-nonny 'till I'm weak in the knees' to the end of the chorus when they cluster around him once more. As they leave, the chorus does unison dips and bumps, chanting, 'Meet you at the rampart in half an hour!' With his teasing pinches and tickles, and the squeals and titters from the chorus, the whole number is redolent of burlesque. Both chorus and Ghost exit (see ▶ video example 24.5).

Heralds with long trumpets announce King Claudius (Harvey Korman) and Queen Gertrude (Vicki Lawrence). Claudius dismisses the heralds with a wave of the hand, 'Trumpets, blow!' but as Claudius and Gertrude move to embrace and kiss, plangent modernist strings interrupt, cueing them to look across the stage to see that Hamlet (played by guest star Ken Berry) has taken up a 'thinker's pose' in the chair deserted by the Ghost. He is the typical mid-twentieth-century Hamlet, a handsome youth in plain black tights and doublet.

The extended tonality of the strings and their starkness recall any number of modern stagings of Shakespeare, although perhaps particularly the National Theatre productions that were sometimes themselves shown on PBS.

Whereas the staging has until this point been profoundly theatrical—characters facing front (even when standing in profile), with the only camera work moving slightly from side to side to keep the chorus's movements in shot or to cut in for 'takes' from the Ghost—the dismissal of the heralds and reduction of forces to Claudius, Gertrude, and Hamlet introduce a slight change to the camera work. It becomes more fluid; not cinematic by any means, but cutting between the couple and Hamlet on a diagonal, and relying on closer framing that eliminates the full-body shots of the opening. Although not quite shot-reverse shot alternation, it does have the effect of bringing the camera/audience onstage (see ⏵ video example 24.6).

When they notice Hamlet—apparently cued by the strings, a tactic that pierces any cinematic semblance of a nondiegetic state—Gertrude and Claudius quickly agree that Claudius should leave, and Gertrude shoos him offstage, closing the curtained doorway behind him as the camera cuts to Hamlet. He ruminates, 'To be, or not to be, that is the question,' as Gertrude crosses to him, putting her hands on his shoulder and arm with concern, commenting, 'My son, the brooder!' And beneath her exclamation, 'Oh, Hamlet,' the strings change into the introduction for her song, 'Don't You Love Your Mama Anymore' (see ⏵ video example 24.7).

This song plays up the popularity of twentieth-century stagings of *Hamlet* with deep Freudian interpretations of the relationship between Gertrude and Hamlet. Vicki Lawrence, then twenty-five-years-old, was beginning to find her voice as a comedian, and somewhat ironically, she went from playing Burnett's kid sister to specializing in older women; she often did it without makeup, as her most famous role as 'Mama' in the tragicomic southern 'Family' episodes, with just a wig, some padding, and a particular way of holding her face. As Gertrude, she sings, 'Don't You Love Your Mama Anymore' in the musical style of a red-hot mama à la Sophie Tucker, amplified by blaring horns and a simple, but highly syncopated melodic/speech line. Her vocal style, however, is a parody of opera/operetta dame, with a constantly breaking voice reminiscent of (an exaggerated version of) musical comedienne Anna Russell. Ironically, of course, this is much harder to sing than even a straightforward wavering vibrato, but it adds to the sense of Gertrude's 'age,' as does her physical style, which parodies Queen Elizabeth II in her distinctive ways of moving her hands.

The camera primarily maintains a Madonna-like framing of the mother and son (see Figure 6.1a), but at the end, where Gertrude extends the chorus, 'Don't you love your mama, why don't you love your mama . . . while doing simple sidesteps with jazz hands, the camera moves out to catch her 'big finish' (see ▶ video example 24.8).

After a beat for applause, Hamlet rises to take her hands and guide her into the chair as the camera returns to frame them from the other direction. He sits in her lap, reversing their previous pose (see Figure 6.1b), singing 'G-E-R-T-R-U-D-E' as a parody of the sentimental song 'M-O-T-H-E-R (A word that means the world to me).' The 1915 song by Howard Johnson and Theodore F. Morse had been popularized by vaudeville star Eva Tanguay and recorded in 1950 by country star Eddy Arnold, whose smooth Nashville sound aided significant popular crossover over the next two decades. Hamlet performs the song starting in Gertrude's lap, touching her nose and chin as if in a toddler's body-part-learning game as he spells her name; as he moves down to her chin, towards her cleavage on 'U', she slaps his hand away playfully, but her smile is affectionate and

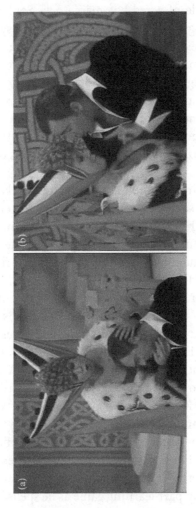

FIGURE 6.1 Gertrude and Hamlet in Madonna and Child pose at the end of Gertrude singing 'Don't You Love Your Mama Anymore'; (b) reversal of position as Hamlet sings 'G-E-R-T-R-U-D-E' and draws attention to her décolletage

familiar, underlining the sexualized reading of their relationship (see ▶ video example 24.9).

As did Gertrude, Hamlet gets up for a few dance moves during the bridge of his song, briefly going down on one knee to lay his head in her lap (see ▶ video example 24.10), then helping lever her up out of the chair with pretended labour for a short tap duet, aided by the pages who come in to handle her train and sweep her upstairs/downstage to watch his little solo that highlights a Jolsonesque 'Mammy' gesture on one knee, towards the camera but away from the theatrically front-facing chorus; Gertrude mediates between the two (see Figure 6.2a). Although evoking Jolson and perhaps Fred Astaire and Ginger Rogers as Gertrude rejoins Hamlet for a brief dance duet, Berry's slim but muscular build, his balletic dance style, and the white collar and cuffs on his stereotypically all-black Hamlet costume recall Gene Kelly in the final ballet from *An American in Paris* (1951). During this dance sequence, the intimate setting has been increasingly 're-theatricalized,' with a front-facing staging. Hamlet even stage-whispers his interjection 'Little Hamlet,' behind a shielding hand, towards the audience at an angle that breaks the fourth wall with the studio audience, but not the camera (see ▶ video example 6.11).

That Gertrude and Hamlet exchange solos at the opening of the act would normally suggest a romantic pairing, and Gertrude is situated between Hamlets Senior and Junior in a symbolic love triangle. The triangles then rotate around Hamlet to introduce Ophelia.

Hamlet melodramatically mopes back to the side of the stage, where he sits at the harpsichord against the splayed wall. As he plays a melancholy introduction, the 'harpsichord' sounds remarkably like a reedy regal organ, and the sound appears to summon Ophelia (Burnett) who sneaks in and covers his eyes, asking, 'Guess who?'

'Mummy!' he cries eagerly, and she shrinks back with a hurt, 'No!' With a disappointed, 'Oh, it's you, Ophelia,' Hamlet turns back to the keyboard (see ⏵ video example 24.12).

Undeterred, Ophelia continues to try to embrace him from behind and launches into the tumbling phrase, 'Oh, that this too too solid flesh would melt into my arms,' with an unexpected, large leap down on 'arms' that plays with Burnett's chesty tenor range. She thus co-opts Hamlet's soliloquy, in which he laments his mother's marriage to Claudius ('Frailty, thy name is woman'), into a lament for Hamlet's self-absorption (see ⏵ video example 24.13).

Ophelia leaves Hamlet's side as he continues to accompany her, and walks to the curve of the harpsichord. From outside the frame, she is handed a corded microphone and with a snap of her fingers, she changes the lighting to a pale pink spotlight. This completes the classic image of a nightclub torch singer, and as she sings, 'I'm in love with the boy in black, but the boy in black is blue,' the 'harpsichord' no longer sounds like a regal, but a piano. The camera focuses in on Ophelia, framing her as if she were on a television variety show (see Figure 6.2b). The music falls into a bluesy strut, and a cutaway shows Ophelia, Hamlet, and the heralds who have arrived, from the other direction, with the pages using their hands to provide the 'wawa' effect on the extra-long trumpets (see Figure 6.2c). But the 'tv show' shot is the predominant mode of framing the number.

The bridge of the song resembles the verse of Porter's 'Night and Day,' with the monotone, syncopated melody over shifting chords; the 'beat beat beat of the tom-tom' replaced by the 'pit pitty pit pitty pitty pat' of Ophelia's heart (see ⏵ video example 24.14). As the intensity builds, the song and the performance slide from generic torch song to a parody of 'The Man Who Got Away' from *A Star Is Born* (1954), with Burnett taking on more and more aspects of Judy Garland's mannered performance,[18] from the hand gestures to the emotional shaking of her

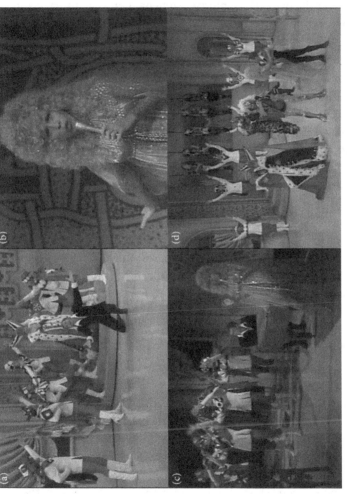

FIGURE 6.2 The different media modes of presentation in 'Hold Me, Hamlet.' (a) A diagonal cinematic angle on Hamlet, while the chorus faces the theatrical front; Gertrude cheats between the two; (b) Ophelia sings as if on a television variety show; (c) the wider shot mimics the set up of a jazz band and torch singer in a nightclub; (d) the entire cast in a square, frontal theatrical mode.

body, to the vocal vibrato and portamento, particularly the deep drop of range before rising in a belt for the finish. Ophelia slides up seductively to sit onto the piano, but it breaks under her weight at the peak of the phrase. Ophelia merely leans back and relaxes, while Hamlet stands to 'direct' the end flourish of the horns like a big band (see ▶ video example 24.15). As Hamlet turns back to the keyboard, Ophelia stretches out to plead, one more time, 'Hold me, Hamlet,' and he merely replies, 'Get thee to a nunnery,' and shoves the harpsichord offstage/offscreen.

The Ghost returns to the stage, with the giggling gaggle of guards, and Hamlet is ecstatic to see his father. He asks if he should avenge his death, and the Ghost brushes it off with a bluff, 'Oh, bug off, my boy, I've never had it so good,' the slightest hint of a reprise before he chases off after his 'bevy of birdies' and Hamlet sinks melodramatically into the chair.[19] 'Oh, woe is me, I have no one to avenge. My father is happy.'

'Then,' says Claudius, with studied eloquence, as he slips through the curtained door. 'Let him rest in peace.' 'Stepdaddy' Claudius suggests that Hamlet should fill his time by giving Ophelia a 'tumble in the hey-nonny-nonny.' Hamlet admits that he doesn't know how, which cues Claudius's surprise (and a string of takes from Korman) and his patter song, 'There's No One Who Can Do It Like a Dane,' which carries numerous echoes of other songs like Porter's 'Let's Do It,' Rodgers and Hammerstein's 'There Is Nothing Like a Dame,' Noël Coward's 'Mad Dogs and Englishmen,' and Alan Jay Lerner and Frederick Loewe's 'The Rain in Spain' and 'A Hymn to Him' from *My Fair Lady*, these latter influences heightened by Korman's performance of Claudius as Rex Harrison[20] (see ▶ video example 24.16).

Encouraged, Hamlet joins in for the end of the song, then Hamlet turns to a reentering Ophelia with, 'The boy in black isn't blue, he's ready for you!' and on the 'wawa' interjections waggles his hips suggestively, prompting Ophelia to respond, 'I never had it so good!' (see ▶ video example 24.17). They recast the opening Ghost + Chorus number into a duet, redistributing some of the lines between them to subtly reshape the lecherous original into a still-sexual but less predatory version. They are framed in a medium close-up two-shot for most of the number, but the camera moves out to frame the entire stage for the finale.

As Claudius and Gertrude reenter, Gertrude comments, 'Well, I always say, "All's well that ends,"' which launches the ensemble into 'All Is Well in the State of Denmark, Nothing's Rotten Anymore,' a reworking of the opening chorus that features now three couples (Claudius and Gertrude, Hamlet and Ophelia, the Ghost and the Captain of the Guards). The theatrical blocking of the number is heightened by Ophelia rhyming 'mellow' in the lyrics with 'Don't forget, next week, *Othello*,' the closest the sketch comes to recognizing internally the onstage/back-stage doubling of the original model *Kiss Me, Kate* (see Figure 6.2d and ▶ video example 6.18).

It also provides a big ensemble for the finale of the Burnett show (as do many of the musicals) (see ▶ video example 6.19). After a commercial break, the short curtain-call ending of the television show always features Burnett singing her signature song, 'I'm So Glad We Had This Time Together' and the cast, still in costume, signing Burnett's autograph book, as the credits roll.

## LA CAPERUCITA ROJA

Fairy tales were a staple of *The Carol Burnett Show* parodies, like 'Snow White: 15 Years Later.' Fairy tales are also a common basis for musicals and for folk theatre, and the three converge in 'La Caperucita Roja,'[21] an adaptation of Little Red Riding Hood as if staged by a Mexican folk theatre troupe. In southern California of the 1970s, this folk art would have been somewhat familiar from at least two contexts. The year of the sketch, 1974, marked the closure of an institution: the folk art festival and cultural centre at Padua Hills, about thirty minutes from Los Angeles, had hosted a dinner theatre based in Mexican folk traditions since the 1930s, performing for audiences largely composed of the Angeleno creative and middle classes.[22] And El Teatro Campesino, a folk theatre troupe founded in 1969 and born from the agricultural workers' rights movement led by César Chavez, was swiftly rising in artistic circles as well as popular awareness.[23] While this referent may be distinctly local to southern California, it is overlaid with cinematic and vaudevillean stereotypes[24] and Burnett's parody of the then-popular variety star Charo (who is Spanish American, not Mexican, although that elision is an exasperatingly common ethnic blurring). Charo's enthusiastic sexuality, tempered by an appealing naïveté (whether genuine or carefully constructed), highlights the subtext of sexual awakening in the story which is likewise bolstered by the burlesque touches to the adaptation.

'La Caperucita Roja' is arguably the most theatrical adaptation of any sort done by *The Carol Burnett Show*. The sketch is introduced by Burnett as if the company were a real theatrical troupe: 'In their first appearance on American television, the world-famous Mexican theatrical troupe, Los Muchachitos and Las Muchachitas de Mexico, with their very spectacular musical version of Little Red Riding Hood, or as they say it, "La Caperucita Roja."' The sketch then opens with an unusual full-stage image, including column-like pillars at the sides of the stage; a red curtain opens to an inner curtain announcing the troupe (see Figure 6.3a), and then those curtains open to reveal dancers accompanying a covered wagon rolling onstage, emphasizing the idea of the show as being put on by a travelling theatrical company, so there is the evocation of a stage-within-a-stage inside the show-within-the-show. We get a rare look at the whole stage at several points during the sketch, including

FIGURE 6.3 The ostentatious theatricality of 'La Caperucita Roja.' (a) The camera frames the entire proscenium, including the side aprons, and a curtain behind the red curtains carries the logo of the 'traveling theatrical troupe' mounting the production; (b) Dancers set up tree flats, and a drop with 'leaves' descends to set the scene in the forest; (c) the Translator mimics Caperucita's gestures as she translates; (d) at the end of the internal play and the sketch, the camera returns to show the entire stage and Carol/Charo/Caperucita tossing tortitas to The Carol Burnett Show audience.

the proscenium arch, the curtains, and the apron to the side in front of the wings. At the end of the sketch, we even see the house; as with 'Hold Me, Hamlet,' the sketch demonstrates a pull-back to the theatrical after a more intimate cinematic/televisual centre of the playlet, but in this case it goes not just to the whole proscenium arch (as at the beginning), but reaches even into the audience, as cookies are tossed into their midst[25] (see Figure 6.3d).

Within the play, Vicki Lawrence—dressed as a flamenco dancer and lisping as if with a Castilian Spanish accent— is the narrator and translator of the internal theatrical play. The Translator is always present on stage in the first act, speaking to the audience, or occasionally on the apron in front of the wings, where she can directly address the audience at home via the camera. One of the traits of the dinner theatre at Padua Hills had been an internal translator for the plays,[26] and the convention is well played for laughs in the sketch.

The Translator begins by introducing the various characters and the actors who will play them as they emerge from the caravan: the brave matador, Don Gorgioso is played by 'the handomest actor in all of Mexico, Lylito Corredo'; the part of the grandmother is played by her own papa, Harvelito Kormano, who comes out in male garb; and the bull is played by 'animal impersonator Carlo Reinero,' who comes on in an outfit similar to Korman's, with a colourful serape over his shoulder and a large ring he places ostentatiously in his nose as he paws the ground. The nose ring will be an object of much humorous 'business' in the play, as the bull replaces the wolf in this telling of the tale. While all of the actors are introduced with humorously (and badly) Hispanicized versions of their real names, 'La Caperucita Roja' is played by 'Charo,' thus Burnett is using an intervening impersonation for her role. As costume designer Bob Mackie noted, Burnett never thought of herself as attractive or sexy, but playing a character like Charo allowed her to play it for laughs. Mackie's costume for 'Charo' as La Caperucita Roja includes very low-rise polka-dotted white trousers with flamenco flounces and a white lace push-up bra with a low décolletage under a hip-length red silk cape, a remarkably revealing outfit for 1970s television. Its daring may be a function similar to Burnett's deflection of sexuality via Charo: if the costume is an exaggeration of a Charo costume, it becomes more parody than 'sexy.'

The Translator kicks off proceedings with, 'Our story starts with a fiesta—what else? At the Fiesta, the girls come to see Don Gorgioso fight the bull. But the boys come for a glimpse of La Caperucita Roja, Little Red Riding Hood, because the boys can't wait to taste Caperucita's tortitas.' The opening musical number 'La Caperucita's Tortitas' is in the style of a son jarocho, and as the Translator informs us from the stage apron, 'Tortitas are small cookies, and Caperucita's tortitas are the sweetest tortitas in town.' The alliteration and allusion creates a not-very-subtle—but also not terribly crass—correlation between Caperucita's tortitas and her breasts.

The Translator's ostentatiously theatrical presence generates a great deal of the comedy in the sketch. She sutures elisions in the story, but in doing so, draws attention to them: after the opening scene, she declares, 'And so a change of scenery is necessary to continue our story.' The caravan is wheeled off to stage left as dancers enter from stage right, carrying flat 'tree' set pieces, and a partial painted backdrop scrolls down from above to fill in the 'leaves' (see Figure 6.3b). The Translator walks over and stands next to a 'tree,' echoing her opening line, 'This is a forest. What else?'

However, the primary source of comedy is in her function as Translator, even though the simple Spanish is generally correct and comprehensible to an American—especially Californian—audience. Her participation is recognized by the characters in the play, and at times regarded as an intrusion or an upstaging.

234 STARS, STUDIOS, AND THE MUSICAL

At the end of the first song, Don Gorgioso the bullfighter comes in to solicit a tortita from Caperucita's basket, and she refuses, as she has throughout the number. She says to the bullfighter, 'Nonononononono, canto . . . porque,' and clears her throat, but as she opens her mouth to sing, the Translator mimics her rhythm precisely with, 'Nonononononono, I sing to you . . . why,' and clears her throat. Burnett as 'Charo,' the actress playing Caperucita, gives her a long look at the intrusion onto her performance, and a medium close-up two-shot isolates the interaction between the two women from the bullfighter, highlighting the interruption, then the frame returns to the three for the number.

In her song about her Abuelita, Caperucita begins singing to Don Gorgioso in a very low register, which is also mimicked by the Translator when she speaks the translation, and when Caperucita mimes 'casita' by drawing a simple house with her finger in the air, the Translator does the same on 'little house' (see Figure 6.3c). On the second stanza, the Translator translates, 'mi Abuelita' as 'same grandmother' while kneeling as Caperucita has, and 'Necessita mi tortita,' becomes an overly clinical 'She requires a cookie.' The next line is broken into two short phraselets, beginning with Caperucita inexplicably singing, 'Or else'—of course, this is not really inexplicable; it is a concept probably too difficult to convey in schoolbook Spanish, but creates another moment of tension as the Translator merely repeats the English phrase and the two exchange a slightly challenging look, with the Translator raising an eyebrow and cocking her head in a 'so what?' gesture. By this time, the two kneeling women are entirely the focus of the number, with Don Gorgioso only represented by the hand to which Caperucita clings, singing emotively, 'Se muere' ['she will pass away'], 'se muere' ['she will pass away,' repeats the Translator, bored, with a slight, rolling, 'get on with it' gesture of her hand], and on the last repetition of 'Se muere,' Caperucita puts her hand over the Translator's mouth and sings directly out to the audience.

A similar by-play features in the introduction of the bull in the forest, who arrives with a flamenco flourish of his arms. The Translator translates his extended cante hondo melisma as 'That is a bull.' He performs another melisma, which she translates as, 'That is a *hungry* bull,' and he burps in the middle of the next melisma, but recovers gracefully, so she walks over to put a familiar hand on his arm and chest, praising him, 'Very nice!' The actor/Bull shrugs slightly, "S all right, I've done better,' in a low voice, not quite a stage whisper. The interjection 'Very nice' (or 'bery nice' in imitation of a Castilian accent) as a compliment from actor to actor, rather than character to character, recurs between Caperucita and the Bull when they execute an extended diminuendo fermata together in their duet, before their cadential last words; and in a later duet, blending his 'Mi estomaco' and her 'Mi abuelita' songs, they turn toward each other on a similar held note. Her nose goes into his mouth, and she says, 'Very nice,' in a nasal voice in the rest before the cadence.

The other main source of comedy, which at times overlaps with the calling out of theatricality, are comedy tropes from vaudeville and burlesque. One could argue that the mixing of Spanish and Mexican, and various regional Mexican styles, is a comic stereotype, although the issue of ethnicity is particularly fraught among Californios,[27] and other common gross stereotypes, such as laziness or jokes about food, are evaded. However, two familiar, more problematic tropes about gender and sexuality are engaged, in the characters of Don Gorgioso and Abuelita.

Don Gorgioso, played by the Rock-Hudson-like Lyle Waggoner, is portrayed as the desirable macho bullfighter (his bright pink and purple outfit is not appreciably more garish than any of Bob Mackie's other 1970s styles). We do not hear his voice until the near the end of the first act, and as a matter of timing to highlight the 'joke,' the Translator actually preempts his line: 'The brave Don Gorgioso asks "Where is the bull?"' and Don Gorgioso stamps his foot petulantly, asking, 'Donde esta el toro!' in a stereotypically sissy accent. He also delivers the words with a distinctly American English accent, which is recalled in the later scene when Caperucita flees the bull.

The other vaudeville stereotype is less pernicious and a favourite character among *The Carol Burnett Show* portrayals. 'Abuelita' is played by Harvelito Kormano, but she is also Harvey Korman in his pneumatic 'Mother Marcus' drag, with an exaggerated comb and mantilla. A Yiddish pantomime dame with an enormous bosom and other rounded attributes, tightly wrapped in an upholstery-like floral dress, Mother Marcus was first introduced as a character in the show's spoof soap opera, 'As the Stomach Turns,' but she became a recurring character for Korman, often (as in both 'La Caperucita Roja' and 'Cinderella Gets It On') as a double portrayal: as Korman playing Mother Marcus playing another character. As Abuelita, Mother Marcus's usual floral housedress is embellished by flamenco ruffles in another floral print altogether, making the double portrayal a visual joke as well. 'Harvelito' has a Castilian lisp, like his 'daughter,' and when he raises his arms, we can also see that what appear to be black tights are just black dress socks, exposing pale skin between sock and skirt ruffle.

Playing into the vaudevillean stereotype of the randy older woman, Abuelita has a suggestive flamenco-style solo, 'My Castanets,' which draws attention to the lightness of Korman's movements in his voluminous padding, but also suggests burlesque when he brings the castanets close to his expansive 'breasts' to click them in accentuating the ends of phrases while shimmying his shoulders. Her song is about loneliness and boredom, so she plays her 'castanets,' further hinting at a euphemism for masturbation.

When the bull has draped Abuelita's mantilla over his horns and taken her place in the bed, he sings to Caperucita, with the lisp, 'I am thick/I have a dithease/I think. . . . I think I am contagiouth/I don't even have the strength to play my cathtanets,' and he makes the castanet gestures near his 'bosom' the way Abuelita did. The burlesque sexuality is played out in the dialogue between Caperucita and the Bull, although her innocence is defused and the tables are turned as she discovers his tail as she goes to sit on his bed. With only a slight roll of her eyes, Caperucita begins a seductive, 'Abuelita what big eyes you have,' punctuating the end of the phrase by touching his tufted tail to his nose teasingly. 'The better to taste and see your tortitas!' The dialogue blunder by Reiner (taste is not appropriate to 'eyes,' although it cuts to the sexual innuendo even more directly) is taken into stride with only a slight grin in reaction by Burnett as Reiner mugs in mock horror to the audience at his mistake. Eventually, Caperucita undrapes the mantilla from one of the Bull's horns and sings, 'Abuelita, how HORNY you are,' and the Bull replies, 'You got it!' Caperucita snatches her basket from his grip and flees through the door. The bedroom set rolls offstage left as Caperucita 'wanders' in the 'forest' and is discovered by the townsfolk/dancers, along with Don Gorgioso.

She encounters Don Gorgioso in the 'forest' and cries, 'El toro es en la casa de mi abuelita!' Don Gorgioso replies, 'No comprendo.' Caperucita sighs heavily and says in a flat American accent, 'The Bull is in the House of my grandmother.'

'The Bull —' asks Don Gorgioso incredulously, and Caperucita responds, 'Si!'

'Is in there?'

'Si.'

'Ha ha,' he laughs theatrically, looking around at the townsfolk before gesturing melodramatically. 'I will kill him.' He takes off his cape and adjusts it as the Bull leaps out balletically, demanding, 'Where are the tortitas?' Don Gorgioso reacts in terror, fleeing offstage.

Caperucita comes forward, addressing the audience directly, 'Matador es pollo, fweh!' The Translator comes in, for the first time in the second act, and translates, 'The bullfighter is chicken, fooey.'

Caperucita then taunts the Bull with her own little cape. After the first pass to stage left, the Bull comments, 'Eh, you're crazy, lady. . . . [D]don't fight ladies,' he protests.

'I'm no lady,' she asserts, and she eventually defeats him. Putting her foot on his back, to pose as if a big game hunter with a trophy, she asks the encircling dancers/townsfolk. 'Should I kill him or let him live?'

'Kill him,' they chant, until Abuelita breaks the ring.

'No!' she protests, with the punctuation of the castanets. 'Let him live.' She pauses, then shimmies her shoulders as she adds, 'With me!' As they embrace, the Translator steps back in to join Caperucita, for a reprise of the Abuelita song, and in the language of the theatrical musical, this finale suggests subversion of musical/romantic comedy narrative resolution. The leading man has fled (and is portrayed as homosexual), leaving only the comic second leads as a couple: The Bull/Abuelita. It would be a stretch to read the other pairing, Caperucita/Translator, in any homoerotic fashion; they are almost antagonists throughout most of the performance, but they are also the two most important characters in the sketch, one the protagonist of the story and one the primary discursive agent.

Although, as noted with 'Hold Me, Hamlet,' it is standard for the 'curtain call' segment of *The Carol Burnett Show* to include the performers in the costumes of the previous segment, this sketch shows unusual theatrical bleed-through: Burnett sings the first two lines of 'I'm So Glad We Had This Time Together,' in literal and rhythmically awkward Spanish, translated by Lawrence, and then the entire company sings the signature farewell song. As the music plays out the credit sequence, the autograph book signing is accompanied by a further extension of the 'curtain call' of the Mexican troupe: Lawrence takes the basket and tosses more cookies to the audience (see Figure 6.3d), and Burnett plays 'bull' to Waggoner's bullfighter.

## CINDERELLA GETS IT ON

*The Wiz*, an all–African American, urban revisioning of *The Wizard of Oz* debuted to great success, critically and commercially, on Broadway in January 1975. It is the clearest referent for 'Cinderella Gets It On,'[28] but not the only one. American popular culture was gradually and belatedly mainstreaming African American performers and culture. *The Carol Burnett Show*'s CBS network introduced two highly popular sitcoms featuring predominantly African-American casts within a year of each other, *Good Times* (1974–79) and *The Jeffersons* (1975–85).[29] Cinematically, the Blaxploitation cycle was beginning a decline from a peak of production in 1973 and 1974, although it was probably not yet visible (the biggest drop off was between 1974, when about ten films in the genre/cycle were released, and 1975, when it was about five). In music, the early 1970s saw a late burst of creativity from Motown and Stax, and 1975 was the year that an underground musical style called disco, gestated in the black and Latino gay dance subculture, would burst into the mainstream with Van McCoy's hit, 'The Hustle.' The Pointer Sisters, a wildly eclectic singing group of 'preacher's kids'[30] from Oakland, had had their first hit in 1973. They sang gospel, were backup singers for Grace Slick, Boz Scaggs, and other Bay Area rock musicians, recorded the 'Pinball Number Count' segments for *Sesame Street*, and performed in classic blues, rhythm and blues, jazz, and swing styles while being the first African American group to perform at the Grand Ol' Opry and to score a country music Grammy. This was all before their guest-starring stint on *The Carol Burnett Show* in November of 1975 (and long before their greatest success in the early to mid-1980s as a techno-pop group with hits like 'Automatic,' 'Jump (For My Love),' and 'I'm So Excited').

With three guest stars who are primarily known as a group, fitting them into an extended sketch is not necessarily easy, but making three sisters into the stepsisters of Cinderella is easy math, especially since fairy tales were a popular source for several extended sketches. Burnett introduces the segment with reference to earlier adaptations of *Cinderella*, including the opera by Rossini and the television musical by Rodgers and Hammerstein[31] but what follows is primarily a television show—a situation comedy in act 1 and a musical performance/dance show like *Soul Train* in act 2.

The opening of the sketch blurs medium specificity, with a mix of the theatrical—the image is of a Playbill—and the cinematic. Like many fairy-tale films, westerns, and future Disney musicals, the opening of the storybook—in this case, the Playbill—eases us into the mythical world. The voiceover announcer (Waggoner) introduces us to scene 1 'The Pad'— the mother figure (Lawrence, again in a matronly but more sexualized role), and her 'three funky daughters from her first stud.' The Stepmother is filing her nails and the three daughters are painting their toenails, listening to a transistor radio, and playing bongos, respectively, as they sing, 'Life is a super gig,' with the Stepmother chiming in, 'I can dig it, I can dig it' (see Figure 6.4a). The living room set-up has the outwardly skewed dimensions of a typical sit-com set (to present more ouwardly to the studio audience and provide more space in which the cameras may move), although it is unclear how much of the contemporaneous audience would catch the resemblance to Shelley Winters's role as 'Mommy,' the white drug kingpin in the hit Blaxploitation film *Cleopatra Jones* (1973). It may be

FIGURE 6.4 Blaxploitation, Disney, and Soul Train: The Many References of 'Cinderella Gets It On.' (a) Vicki Lawrence and The Pointer Sisters as the 'steps'; (b) Mother Marcus appears as the Fairy Godmother; (c) Elfin John plays the disco; (d) the set of the disco with the contemporary popular music television show Soul Train.

only a knowing wink, even a complete coincidence (I doubt it), as the announcer passes quickly to the introduction of the lead, played by Burnett. 'The Mother also had a stepdaughter who came with the second dude. This chick's name was Cinderella. The Stepmother and the Stepsisters were all cool, with-it chicks, but Cinderella was the flip side. She was square.'

In comparison to the neon-coloured fashions of the Stepmother and Stepsisters, Cinderella is dressed in a floral blouse, a red checked gingham apron, green anklets, and saddle oxfords. She has an unflattering red bob, and her light green jumper is nearly the same shade as the walls, making her almost literally fade into the background. Her vocal delivery resembles Shirley Temple's, making her seem even more juvenile compared to the others, who had 'laid bread' on her to go down to the disco to get tickets for the rock concert that night. She got the four last tickets, and the Stepmother takes the fourth, leaving Cinderella to pout. She, too, had wanted to see 'Elfin John.'

When they leave, she cries and taunts herself as a 'drip' and a 'square,' drawing the shape in the air with her forefingers. Her 'I wish' song is comically literal: 'I wish!' she trills operatically, à la Disney's Snow White. The paradoxically overtrained little girl voice sinks in a long portamento down to a waltz, her precise, slightly English-accented delivery reminiscent of Burnett's longtime friend Julie Andrews, who was both Mary Poppins and the first television musical Cinderella (1957): 'I wish I were foxy, I wish I were slick, I wish I were some kind of superchick, a chick who would blow your mind—Tina Turner and Cher combined.' On the last phrase, her voice deepens bluesily. She sings another stanza, then walks away from the camera, hands behind her back, then turns back to Snow White: she twists to sing, 'I wish . . . and a flute trill and nasal voice echo from off-stage left. She puts her hand to her ear, it repeats, they exchange and finally perform the figure in harmony.

A flash bomb goes off in the doorway, and a vision in baby blue sparkles with fairy wings appears. It is Harvey Korman as Mother Marcus as the Fairy Godmother (see Figure 6.4b).

Cinderella does several takes, 'What are you . . . I mean, who are you?'

'You're expecting maybe Tinklebell?' responds the Fairy Godmother in a thick Yiddish accent. 'But first, let me sit, my wings are killing me.' She's performed three miracles already today: 'What miracles I've wrought! I got a doctor to make a housecall. I got *mein Sohn* to visit me. And I saved NYC from bankrupture.' Korman's delivery does the near-impossible in this sketch: he almost breaks up Burnett, but she makes her laugh into a high-pitched Snow White titter, and Korman pinches her cheek, which seems to be an anticipation of a bit of business from a couple of lines later.

'Could you make me into a hip chick?' asks Cinderella.

'You want me to make you into a Lipschitz?' The Fairy Godmother seems taken aback.

Cinderella titters, and the Fairy Godmother pinches her cheek again, but this time Burnett responds, 'Ooh,' as if her cheek is sore from repeated tweaks.

A burst of klezmer dance music accompanies the Fairy Godmother as she declares, 'You are what you wish!' Two 45-rpm records (Lawrence Welk and Guy Lombardo) and a pumpernickel become a chopper motorcycle with a sidecar. Cinderella is turned into a foxy strawberry blonde in a white jumpsuit with a revealing white wrap top, and the Fairy Godmother warns her to return by the stroke of 12. '12 midnight?' asks Cinderella, and the Fairy Godmother responds, 'Are you *meshugena*? Rock functions don't begin until 12 midnight, you must leave by 12 noon.' And they are off to the disco, with the Fairy Godmother driving 'one of these Japanese motorcycles—a Yarmulke!'

Act 2 takes place at the 'rock concert,' where Tim Conway plays Elfin John in Pinball Wizard platform boots, sequined jumpsuit, exaggerated top hat, and glasses. He plays a piano with his name in rhinestones on the side (see Figure 6.4c).

The plain cyclorama with strips of lights, the orange-tinged studio lights, and broad, empty stage for dancing is strongly reminiscent of the set for the classic American dance show *Soul Train* (1971–2006) (see Figure 6.4d), the perfect setting for the act in which Cinderella makes up a dance that becomes an immediate hit. The 'Schlump' melodically parodies Bill Haley and the Comets' 'Rock around the Clock,' which was experiencing a bump of popularity from serving as the theme song of the then-new and wildly popular 1950s-nostalgia sitcom *Happy Days* (1974–84). 'Schlump around the Clock Tonight' draws the attention of Elfin John and passes the hours until the stroke of 12:00. Cinderella tosses him one of her silver platform shoes as she leaves, which in turns becomes a bit of comedy when he comes to their sitcom living room ('the last pad' in his search for his lost chick) and Cinderella is wearing her green-and-gingham outfit, with one saddle oxford and one silver platform shoe. He is, however, unimpressed by her as a 'square,' and leaves, with a vague, 'Glad you got your shoe back.'

Cinderella is heartbroken, but the Fairy Godmother tells her warmly, 'There's other gefilte fish in the sea.' Cinderella responds with a distinctly Templesque 'But I want him!' (Burnett will sing 'I'm So Glad . . .' with a medley of the different voices she has used in the sketch.) The Fairy Godmother agrees, 'You were meant for each other,' and magics Elfin John back as a dweeby household product salesman for a happily ever after.

This last-minute subversion is striking because even the name 'Cinderella' immediately conjures a rise of class (socially and aesthetically). It is a simple inversion— a common trait of many parodies—but does not simply flip gender or position;

it undermines the essential desire for status in exchange for a more realistic relationship. At the risk of claiming too much, I am reminded of the work of Anna E. Altman on parody in feminist fairy tales. She makes a distinction between parody (inversion) and poesis, even though she recognizes that it is not a stark opposition:

> Poesis, in contrast, looks forward, creates new meaning. The term poesis is not a tidy or commonly recognized antithesis to the term parody. It does not identify a genre, and the two terms are not mutually exclusive. But I need a word to set against 'parody,' to stand for what is not parody. The first meaning of the Greek word poesis is 'a making: a forming, creating,' and in that sense I juxtapose it to the critical nature of parody. Feminist fairy tales that are poesis rather than parody use the form of the fairy tale without commenting on it. Or, at least, commentary is not the main point.[32]

The end of Cinderella is inverted, but it does not ridicule like classic parody; it achieves the goal of the original (an implied marriage) without the trappings of acquisitiveness and social climbing demonstrated by the Stepsisters and the Stepmother, who attempts to suck up to Cinderella when she thinks her stepdaughter will be hooking up with Elfin John. Nor is the skit about nostalgia, as much as it traffics in nostalgia. It does not even poke fun at disco, the excesses of which offer several opportunities. 'Cinderella Gets It On,' like the composite Astaire-Rogers musical 'High Hat' and some of the original musicals that *The Carol Burnett Show* composed from pre-existing songs, approaches poesis. They take the form of the musical, and they often do comment on it, but they are also genuine expressions of the form and the creators' deep love and understanding of it.

## PARODY AS TIME CAPSULE

But there is a rather obvious contradiction here: nostalgia requires the availability of evidence of the past, and it is precisely the electronic and mechanical reproduction of images of the past that plays such an important role in the structuring of the nostalgic imagination today, furnishing it with the possibility of 'compelling vitality.' . . .

[A]s Andreas Huyssen[33] has convincingly argued . . .: 'The more memory we store on data banks, the more the past is sucked into the orbit of the present, ready to be called up on the screen,' making the past simultaneous with the present in a new way.[34]

For a generation, perhaps two, of Americans with only the three major broadcast networks and sometimes PBS, in a time before home video, Carol Burnett's parodies were familiar before the originals were. We learned about old movies 'backwards' through the lens of Burnett—I know I saw 'Mildred Fierce,' 'Rebecky,' 'Rancid Harvest,' and 'The Little Foxies' before I ever saw the sources for the parodies. But the sketches ruined none of my enjoyment; if anything, they heightened my awareness of certain plot points or performances. This effect is not even exclusive to audiences: cast member Vicki Lawrence was eighteen when the show started, and in an era without VHS tape or Turner Classic Movies, she was often unaware of the movies, characters, and actors she was called upon to parody; Korman became her tutor. This collegial and even familial chemistry of the show's performers was part of the appeal: over time, a feature of the show that became an attraction unto itself was Tim Conway attempting to break up Harvey Korman. In later years, they even made a nightclub act of that dynamic.

The parodies worked at numerous levels, as individual texts, genres, and media/venue: another recurrent skit was the adventures of 'Funt & Mundane,' a theatrical supercouple based on Alfred Lunt and Lynn Fontanne, and in one episode their intimate drawing room drama was staged at an outdoor amphitheatre, with the comedy coming from the scale of the large stage and the foibles of outdoor performance, including airplane flyovers and insects. Other aspects cut cross-sections, like Korman's affinity for Colman or Burnett's for Garland carrying through sketches where they might not be obvious insertions. Mother Marcus's various incarnations as Fairy Godmother, Caperucita's Abuelita, and numerous other figures is an obvious case, layered onto her historical mash-up of Yiddish (grand)mother and pantomime dame types.

*The Carol Burnett Show* was a time capsule of sorts. It revived, adapted, and reencapsulated earlier entertainment forms with nostalgia that did not temper its wit. But the parody that evokes nostalgia also becomes something more specific and coherent. Costume designer Bob Mackie has pointed out that there are no Carol drag artists; she is, in essence, already one of them, a chameleon, but also inimitable. Comedian Jerry Lewis compares Burnett to his old partner Dean Martin as a classic entertainer: 'We want them as pure as we can get them.' Burnett is thus arguably a figure of poesis, not parody.

## NOTES

1. This does not count afternoon or late-night talk shows like *The Mike Douglas Show* or *The Tonight Show*, which often featured musical performances. It also does not count syndication: in 1968, the most popular variety show in syndication was *The Porter Wagoner Show* (1960–81), which would launch the career of Dolly Parton (1967–75), much as her three years on *The Garry Moore Show* had launched Burnett.

2. In an October 1968 *New York Times* article, creator George Schlatter commented about the critics' and censors' accusations of 'tastelessness': 'Tasteless? The picture of a Vietcong prisoner

being shot in the head ran in every newspaper in the world, and nobody reviewed *them* for a lack of taste. If that is good taste and a joke about the Pill is bad taste, then I will take our particular brand of bad taste any day. I find every hatchet murder being gone into in great detail, which is not only bad taste but lacking in humour. When we're in bad taste, at least we're funny' (cited in https://www.nytimes.com/2015/09/11/arts/tel evision/remembering-rowan-martins-laugh-in.html, accessed 10 July 2017).

3. Burnett would go on to win Emmy Awards for dramatic roles in *Friendly Fire* (1979) and an episode of *Law & Order: Special Victims Unit* (2009), to add to her four awards for musical, comedy, and variety performances.

4. Throughout the chapter, unless otherwise specified, production and biographical information, as well as interview quotes, comes from the DVD extras of the Time-Life compilation of *The Carol Burnett Show*.

5. Lawrence, in fact, legendarily got the job because people thought she looked like Burnett, and the multiple references to the then-seventeen-year-old Lawrence piqued Burnett's curiosity.

6. The Welches are the parents of Americana alt-folk singer-songwriter Gillian Welch, which hints at a similarity of musical specificity and authenticity, if to completely different repertoires.

7. I explore this argument in more detail in a forthcoming book about television, space, and sound.

8. The show traditionally would run two performances on a Friday night—a show recorded at 9:00 PM as the broadcast version, but also a 6:00 PM version that was essentially a dress rehearsal but recorded for 'safety,' a source of editing materials should anything go wrong with the main performance.

9. Robert Stam, 'Beyond Fidelity: The Dialogics of Adaptation,' James Naremore, *Film Adaptation* (2000): 54–76.

10. Paul Edwards, 'Adaptation: Two Theories,' *Text and Performance Quarterly* 27, no. 4 (2007): 5–6.

11. Linda Hutcheon, 'The Politics of Postmodernism: Parody and History,' *Cultural Critique* 5 (1986): 185–186.

12. Hutcheon, 'The Politics of Postmodernism,' 181.

13. Linda Hutcheon, and Mario J Valdés, 'Irony, Nostalgia, and the Postmodern: A Dialogue,' *Poligrafías*. *Revista de Teoría Literaria y Literatura comparada* 3 (1998): 18.
14. Hutcheon, and Valdés, 'Irony, Nostalgia, and the Postmodern,' 21.
15. Hutcheon, and Valdés, 'Irony, Nostalgia, and the Postmodern, 22.
16. Episode 812; aired 14 December 1974.
17. The Cookie Monster similarly plays 'Alistair Cookie,' on *Sesame Street*, although Korman's portrayal appears to predate that more famous one by several years, http://muppet.wikia.com/wiki/Alis tair_Cookie, accessed 18 July 2017.
18. Berry and Burnett also star as Mickey Rooney and Judy Garland in *Babes in Barns*, and a similar duet draws attention to the 'audio dissolve' that Rick Altman describes as typical of a film musical: diegetic sound, such as the piano, is superimposed onto nondiegetic sound as a transition to a full-blown performance. As Berry as 'Rooney' accompanies Burnett as 'Garland' on the piano, conveniently set up on the verandah, she comments, 'I love it when you play, it sounds like a whole orchestra!' Burnett seems to have a particular affinity for Garland, in part because their voice range and style is not dissimilar, but it seems that the vulnerability in Garland's persona resonates with a similar vulnerability in Burnett's that she used comedy to deflect.
19. Normally, these full-length musicals are divided into acts, with advertising intermissions, but 'Hold Me, Hamlet' clocks in at a brisk 14:25.
20. The song even has a gay 'in-joke' not likely to ping broad audiences (or censors) in 1974, but recognizable by musical theatre aficionados and those keyed into the subculture: Claudius strings out adverbs about how Danes 'do it,' and Hamlet interrupts to echo, 'Daily? Gaily?' Claudius takes a beat and replies, 'Some,' before launching back into the song.
21. Episode 716; aired 19 January 1974.
22. For more details, see Kenneth H. Marcus, 'Mexican Folk Music and Theater in Early Twentieth-Century Southern California: The Ramona Pageant and the Mexican Players,' *Journal of the Society for American Music* 9, no. 1 (2015), and Pauline B. Deuel, 'The Commedia Dell'Arte in a Mexican Folk Theatre,' *Hispania* 47, no. 3 (1964).

23. The first widely known El Teatro Campesino play, *Zoot Suit*, written by founder Luis Valdez, premiered in 1978 and launched the career of Mexican American actor Edward James Olmos. A movie of *Zoot Suit* followed in 1981, with Valdez's treatment of the life of early rock 'n' roll star Ritchie Valens, the hit film *La Bamba*, following in 1987.

24. Pauline Deuel argues that the Mexican Players created an analogue to the *commedia dell'arte* in Renaissance Italy by relying on character stereotypes, which are, of course, often found in fairy tales (Deuel, 'The Commedia Dell'Arte in a Mexican Folk Theatre').

25. This effect is not unlike the typical 'stagebound' Busby Berkeley number, where the surrealistic and expansive nondiegetic space of the number is anchored into a theatrical stage at the beginning and end.

26. See Deuel, 'The Commedia Dell'Arte in a Mexican Folk Theatre.'

27. For more legal and historical details, see Marcus, 'Mexican Folk Music and Theater in Early Twentieth-Century Southern California.'

28. Episode 914, aired 29 November 1975.

29. The NBC show *Julia* (1968–71) featured a black single mother, but most of the other characters were white and the stories were more conventional sit-com stories with less of a political charge.

30. 'PKs,' or 'preacher's kids' are familiar expressions in southern American culture, in particular, and have a certain air about them (Tori Amos and Amy Lee of Evanescence are also PKs).

31. ABC would air an original, all–African American version, known as *Cindy* or *Cinderella in Harlem*, a few years later in 1978.

32. Anna E. Altman, 'Parody and Poesis in Feminist Fairy Tales,' *Canadian Children's Literature/Littérature canadienne pour la jeunesse* 20, no. 1 (2007): 23.

33. Huyssen, *Twilight Memories*, 253.

34. Hutcheon and Valdés, 'Irony, Nostalgia, and the Postmodern: A Dialogue,' 20.

# 7

# Flamboyance, Exuberance, and Schmaltz

## Half a Sixpence *and the Broadway Adaptation in 1960s Hollywood*

AMANDA MCQUEEN

■□■

HISTORIES OF THE HOLLYWOOD MUSICAL often posit a decline of the genre in the 1960s and 1970s, brought about in no small part by big-budget adaptations of Broadway shows. Citing a combination of negative reviews and disappointing financial returns, many film historians and genre scholars have concluded that these adaptations fundamentally 'misread public interest,' pushing the film industry into recession and the musical genre into obsolescence.[1] Such claims may seem especially accurate in the case of Paramount's 1967 roadshow adaptation of *Half a Sixpence*. Set in Edwardian England, *Sixpence* tells of Arthur Kipps (played by Tommy Steele on both stage and screen), a draper's apprentice who unexpectedly inherits, loses, and regains a fortune, learning in the process the value of true love and friendship. The stage musical's obvious moral, romance-centric plot, and stock character types were transferred to the screen mostly intact, leading a number of influential critics, including Roger Ebert of the *Chicago Sun-Times* and Renata Adler of the *New York Times*, to declare that *Sixpence* was 'simpleminded, square, old-fashioned,' and 'lavishly, exuberantly out of touch' with the attitudes of the late 1960s.[2] Audiences perhaps agreed; the film performed poorly at the box office, breaking even only because of a strong showing in the United Kingdom.[3]

Yet although *Half a Sixpence* was hardly the smash success Paramount intended, it was not—as is often suggested—a completely misguided production. Rather, it is a product of its immediate industrial context, its form and content shaped by conditions in Hollywood after the breakup of the studio system. First, *Sixpence* is part of the cycle of blockbuster Broadway adaptations that emerged in the mid-1950s as a risk-reduction strategy. Through lavish spectacle and fidelity to their pre-sold stage properties, these adaptations were designed to boost the film musical's financial and cultural viability in a changing and uncertain marketplace. At the same time, director George Sidney and his artistic team give *Sixpence* a distinctly contemporary visual style, akin to that found in the low-budget, youth-oriented films of the Hollywood Renaissance, such as *Bonnie and Clyde* (1967) and *The Graduate* (1967). This fusion of the established prestige adaptation formula and the burgeoning Renaissance aesthetic resulted in a curious mixture of old-fashioned schmaltz and modern stylistic play, yet the choice to combine them had industrial logic. Far from demonstrating generic decline, then, the adaptation of *Half a Sixpence* evidences how 1960s Hollywood combined different commercial and aesthetic strategies in an effort to reshape the film musical for a new industrial climate and prolong the genre's marketability into the 1970s.

## HALF A SIXPENCE AND THE CYCLE OF PRESTIGE ADAPTATIONS

Though Hollywood has always drawn from Broadway to varying degrees in its production of film musicals, the genre's struggles in the 1950s led the industry to approach stage adaptations in a new way. The dissolution of the major studios' production units, which had reduced overhead and increased efficiency, made the musical—an inherently expensive and complicated genre—particularly susceptible to inflating production costs, with budgets quadrupling by the early 1960s.[4] Musicals were also underperforming at the box office, a problem exacerbated by the growing importance of the international market. As domestic audience attendance declined in the decades following World War II, more of Hollywood's income came from abroad, and producers started giving greater thought to foreign audience tastes.[5] But musicals had long proven unpopular outside of English-speaking countries, and it was estimated that they had an international market potential of only about 60 percent to 65 percent of that expected by films in other genres.[6]

By the late 1950s, then, it was clear that film musicals, as they had been made under the studio system, were no longer viable, leaving Hollywood with two options: abandon the genre or rework it to fit the changing industrial climate. Many believed that the musical was unique to Hollywood and was thus the first line of defense against both television and foreign imports, but since current conditions posed significant challenges for the genre, sustaining it would require a variety of new strategies.[7] One such strategy was the production of large-scale, faithful Broadway adaptations like *Half a Sixpence*.

The impetus for this type of film musical arose from the industry's larger interest in blockbuster filmmaking and its corresponding dependence on pre-sold properties. In an effort to remain competitive against the onslaught of television and other leisure activities in the early 1950s, Hollywood began concentrating on fewer but more expensive films.[8] Designed and marketed as special events, these blockbusters aimed to draw people back to the movies with the promise of a unique entertainment experience. Musicals naturally lent themselves to such prestige treatment, and like other blockbusters of the period, top-tier musicals increasingly featured running times of two-and-a-half to three hours (often including an overture and intermission); technological advancements like color, widescreen, stereo sound, and wide-gauge formats; and lavish production designs, and/or exotic locations. Naturally, executing spectacle on this scale required a budget at least two or three times that of an ordinary film product, which from the mid-1960s to the turn of the decade averaged between $2 and $3 million.[9] Budgets for prestige adaptations generally started around $6 million and could rise as high as $25 million. By the 1960s, most blockbusters were roadshow releases. With higher ticket prices and reserved seating, following the model of live theatre, roadshow films played in top-tier first-run houses, and were aimed at a broad audience.[10]

Yet, while blockbusters could potentially yield enormous profits, greater investment in each individual film also meant that studios had more to lose if an expensive production flopped. To offset this financial risk, filmmakers relied heavily on pre-sold source material, and by the mid-1950s, *Variety* had noted a significant uptick in films based on popular stories, novels, and plays.[11] For the musical, Broadway was the most logical and frequently utilized source of pre-sold properties. A successful stage musical would have a long run on Broadway and then spawn regional and touring companies to further extend its life and popularity. The flourishing of original cast albums in the 1940s and 1950s also helped spread familiarity with these shows beyond New York City, and theatrical hits often found national exposure through popular television programs and radio play.[12] Broadway musicals could thus potentially reach a large sector of the American public, and a substantial investment in a film musical would seem less risky if audiences were already aware of both the story and the songs. It was also hypothesized that adaptations would do better in the troublesome foreign markets. Not only were Broadway musicals thought to have the stronger, more sophisticated narratives international audiences preferred, but they were also routinely exported abroad, where they were restaged with local casts in local languages.[13] The fact that a given Broadway show would be tested in foreign markets prior to the release of a film version could thus seem like extra insurance on a genre that remained one of Hollywood's most challenging exports.

The perceived importance of the pre-sold property to a musical's marketability encouraged producers to adapt Broadway shows to the screen with greater fidelity. In earlier decades, it was not uncommon for an adaptation to cut over half of the show's musical numbers and feature a substantially rewritten plot, but in the 1950s, Hollywood began making fewer changes during the adaptation process.[14] While filmmakers 'opened up' adaptations through location shooting, larger casts, cinematography, and editing, they simultaneously brought to the screen all the identifiable and marketable elements of the stage version. Partially incentivizing this more faithful approach were the rising prices for film rights. Inflating production costs in the theatre industry in the 1950s and 1960s made it difficult for producers to secure financing, and the influx of cash that came from selling to Hollywood could be crucial in repaying the substantial investments required for mounting a new musical.[15] Rights holders for hit plays were thus in a strong position to negotiate for the best deal—usually a lump sum plus a percentage of the film's gross over a certain amount.[16] By the 1960s, the standard purchase price for a stage musical was $1 million, but many sold for significantly more, which likely encouraged studios to retain as much of the original show as possible. After all, why pay more than $1 million for a musical only to cut it to pieces?

Yet fidelity was also a promotional strategy. As director-producer Norman Jewison noted regarding the adaptation of *Fiddler on the Roof* (1971), 'The title [of the stage play] is what we are really selling.'[17] That is, retaining the key elements of the stage original was thought to appeal to those already familiar with the musical through the Broadway version, the original cast album, and/or a touring company, and make them more likely to see the adaptation. Indeed, part of the prestige of these films was their promise of an experience analogous to that of seeing the show on Broadway. At the same time, the new standards of blockbuster filmmaking meant these musicals could be bigger and more spectacular than any theatrical production. In short, prestige adaptations positioned the musical as a special event, a unique entertainment experience that could only be found at the movies.

In the early 1950s, the Hollywood musical was already moving towards more faithful adaptations and greater spectacle, but the back-to-back successes of *Guys and Dolls* (1955) and *Oklahoma!* (1955), which pushed both spectacle and fidelity to greater heights than their immediate predecessors, proved the viability of the prestige adaptation formula. Over the next decade and a half, Hollywood producers continued imitating these two musicals in hopes of replicating their strong box office performances, and a cycle of big-budget, faithful adaptations emerged.[18] The cycle reached its peak in the late 1960s with an increased burst of production following the phenomenal success of *The Sound of Music* (1965). Four adaptations were released annually between 1967 and 1969, leading *New York Times* critic Vincent Canby to refer to prestige musicals as an 'industry-within-an-industry.'[19] *Half a Sixpence* appeared during the peak of the prestige adaptation cycle. Based on the H. G. Wells novel *Kipps: The Story of a Simple Soul* (1905), the musical wraps class critique in a love triangle. After inheriting a surprise fortune, draper's apprentice Arthur Kipps is thrust into high society. He jilts his working-class sweetheart Ann Pornick for the wealthy Helen Walsingham, but the snobbery of the Walsingham set makes Kipps realize it is Ann he loves, and they marry. Shortly thereafter, Helen's brother Hubert swindles Kipps out of his money. Kipps realizes what truly matters in life and is rewarded with another financial windfall, this time the dividends from an investment in his friend Harry Chitterlow's successful play. The musical premiered in London's West End in March 1963. It was voted the best new British musical by the London critics and ran for an impressive 678 performances, closing in October 1964.[20] *Sixpence* transferred to Broadway in April 1965. A few of the songs deemed unsuitable for American audiences were cut, while others were expanded into more lavish production numbers with new choreography by Onna White.[21] Reviews for this iteration were somewhat mixed, but the show thrived on word of mouth, becoming a sleeper hit and receiving nine Tony Award nominations, including Best Musical.[22] The original Broadway cast album from RCA Victor, released in May 1965, eventually averaged about 500 disk sales per stage performance.[23]

*Sixpence* was an ideal property for Paramount to adapt: its family-friendly story made it suitable for the roadshow audience, and although it was popular, it was not a blockbuster smash, which made it inexpensive to acquire. Cost was an issue for the studio, which had been struggling financially throughout the decade. Its box office successes had been few, and its production output had dropped due to internal power struggles and management changes pending the 1966 Gulf + Western takeover.[24] *Sixpence* allowed Paramount to participate in the profitable prestige adaptation cycle without the same degree of risk posed by projects like *Camelot* (Warner Bros.-Seven Arts, 1967) or *Hello, Dolly!* (20th Century Fox, 1969), which were significantly more expensive to both acquire and produce.[25] Paramount secured the rights for *Sixpence* in November 1965 for only $250,000.[26] Production started in September 1966, and though the film ran considerably over budget, it still only cost Paramount a reasonable $6 million.[27]

Even with this modest budget, Paramount planned *Sixpence* as a lavish roadshow musical, in keeping with the norms of the prestige cycle. The film's world premiere in London in December 1967 and its American premieres in New York City and Los Angeles in February 1968 were all high-profile charity banquets.[28] Between February and April, *Sixpence* was scheduled for thirty-one domestic roadshow engagements.[29] Paramount also launched a sizeable publicity campaign, which included a five-week, nineteen-city promotional tour by director George Sidney, book and record tie-ins, novelty sixpence souvenirs, and a promotional featurette.[30]

As with other musicals in the prestige adaptation cycle, part of what made *Sixpence* a special event was its fidelity to its source material. The screenplay, written by Dorothy Kingsley, a longtime collaborator of Sidney's with previous experience transferring Broadway musicals to film, adheres on the whole to Beverley Cross's book, and so the film runs 146 minutes with an intermission. However, in response to critics who found the musical a bit lightweight, five of the song-and-dance numbers were cut and two new ones were substituted: 'The Race Is On' and 'This Is My World.' Prestige adaptations commonly included at least one new song for Academy Award consideration, usually penned by the original theatrical songwriter; *Sixpence*'s new songs were also written by David Heneker, in collaboration with Irwin Kostal, the film's music supervisor and arranger. However, the film made sure to retain those songs from the Broadway show that had been consistently singled out, including its three showstoppers, 'Money to Burn,' 'If the Rain's Got to Fall,' and 'Flash, Bang, Wallop.' Paramount's promotional campaign then emphasized this aspect of fidelity through advertisements that referenced the film's theatrical origins and promised movie audiences that they, too, could 'Hear the Showstoppers.'[31]

Most central to Paramount's fidelity strategy, though, was Tommy Steele as Arthur Kipps. Steele rose to prominence in the mid-1950s as Britain's first rock star, and he had appeared on numerous television programs and in several low-budget musical films aimed at the British youth market, including *The Tommy Steele Story* (1957) and *The Duke Wore Jeans* (1958). Thanks in part to collaborations with songwriters like Lionel Bart, Steele soon became part of Britain's mainstream entertainment industry. *Half a Sixpence*, which firmly cemented his shift from rock 'n' roller to traditional song-and-dance man, was written as a star vehicle for him.[32] Steele accompanied his musical from London to Broadway, and his performance was overwhelmingly praised in both stage iterations, with critics often describing his natural talent and charisma at some length. *Variety*, for instance declared Steele 'an eye-opener,' while a feature in the *New York Times* called him 'a song-and-dance man whose mastery is currently unsurpassed by any other performer in the field.'[33] Some, like *Los Angeles Times* critic Charles Champlin, went so far as to argue that the Broadway show had only been 'saved from a quick death . . . by the broad, brash lightfoot ebullience and engaging easiness of Tommy Steele.'[34] When Steele took a short break from Broadway in August 1965, box office proceeds dropped about $10,000, and when he left the show entirely in the spring of 1966, many critics felt the musical had 'lost some of its charm and vitality. . . . What was an exciting show is just okay now.'[35]

Steele was *Sixpence*'s most noteworthy element, so Paramount's negotiations for the rights naturally included his participation.[36] In their effort to re-create the Broadway experience, prestige adaptations commonly featured some members of the theatrical cast reprising their roles. In addition to Steele, *Sixpence* retained Grover Dale as fellow apprentice Pearce and Marti Webb as the singing voice of Ann, played onscreen by Julia Foster. Webb had originated the role in the West End production, and so her ghosting ensured that the quality and style of the character's musical performance adhered to that of the stage original.[37] Yet when a stage musical was known for a strong lead—such as Robert Morse in *How to Succeed in Business without Really Trying* (1966) or Barbra Streisand in *Funny Girl* (1967)—both the fidelity and the success of the film version were thought to depend on having the original actor recreate his or her star-making role.[38] Given how central Steele's performance was to *Half a Sixpence*'s reputation, the property would likely have been considered less valuable without him.

Paramount thus put Tommy Steele at the centre of the film's promotional campaign. Articles distributed via the film's official press book cover everything from Steele's rise to fame, to his penchant for football, to his forthcoming collection of poetry, and he dominates the film's print advertising.[39] The four primary layouts used for newspaper ads, lobby cards, and posters all depict a collage of scenes from the film, either illustrations or photographic stills, at the centre of which is a larger image of Steele dressed in the white suit from the showstopper number 'If the Rain's Got to Fall,' and flashing his trademark toothy grin. The star also appears in all of the smaller collage scenes, making him the most prominent element in terms of both size and frequency. One layout—featuring a background grid of line-drawings of Steele, on top of which are the central 'Rain's Got to Fall' image and an illustrated collage clustered around a straw boating hat—depicts him thirteen times, leaving no doubt that this is his musical (Figure 7.1). Significantly, Paramount's artwork echoes that used for the Broadway show, which also depicts Steele leaping joyfully in his white suit. Many prestige adaptations signalled fidelity to their source in this way, by imitating the advertising of the stage production.

FIGURE 7.1 Print advertising for Half a Sixpence assures fidelity to the stage show by emphasizing Tommy Steele, the musical's most marketable element. Credit: Paramount Film Service Ltd. Half a Sixpence Paramount Press Book and Merchandising Manual. 1967. Author's personal collection.

Ultimately, Tommy Steele was one of the few aspects of the film to garner widespread praise, and even those who disliked the musical acknowledged his talents. Roger Ebert, for instance, concluded that Steele was 'just the performer for this sort of schmaltz. He is, in fact, a very good song-and-dance man, the only member of his generation who bears comparison with Gene Kelly.'[40] Charles Champlin thought the film was long and wearying, but still declared that 'Tommy Steele is a wonder and he gives a dazzling, perfected performance.'[41] Yet casting Steele was entirely in keeping with the norms of the prestige adaptation cycle. The perceived necessity of maintaining fidelity to the pre-sold property meant recreating the marketable elements of the Broadway original on screen, and in the case of *Half a Sixpence*, the single most marketable element was Tommy Steele.

With fidelity assured through screenplay, songs, and especially casting, Paramount set about expanding *Sixpence* into a blockbuster film. Prestige adaptations sought to create spectacle by transforming their stage properties into something cinematic, offering audiences what theatre and television could not. For *Sixpence*, this meant colour and widescreen—both standard for blockbusters of all genres—and location shooting in England. Filming overseas, or runaway production, had become a trend in blockbuster filmmaking, as it could cut costs, attract audiences through exotic and/or realistic settings, and increase a film's international market potential.[42] In the mid-1960s, the United Kingdom became a popular runaway destination, as filmmakers sought to capitalize on London's status as 'the centre of young, fashionable, pop-music-dominated culture,' and American investment in British filmmaking so accelerated through the latter half of the decade, that by 1967, nearly 80 percent of UK films were made with US money.[43] Under its new Gulf + Western management, Paramount had moved aggressively into overseas production, and *Sixpence* was one of eighteen British features the studio had under way in 1967.[44] With location shooting in Eastbourne, Oxford, Henley on Thames, and Tunbridge Wells, and interiors filmed at Shepperton Studios and Associated British at Elstree, *Sixpence* was the first Hollywood musical to be shot entirely in the United Kingdom.[45]

Filming *Sixpence* in England meant the requisite period detail—from gas lamps, to bathing suits, to vintage cars, carriages, and horse-buses—could be recreated not only at a lower cost but also with greater authenticity than would be possible in Hollywood.[46] The realistic Edwardian costumes and settings then became another of the film's promotional angles. Not only would *Sixpence* provide moviegoers the sheer entertainment of a big, Broadway musical, Paramount promised, but it also offered a 'rare view of some of England's most historic and beautiful backgrounds, all photographed in colors that literally glow.'[47] As was common with runaway productions, journalists were invited to junkets on location, which helped generate publicity focused on the film's uniquely meticulous production design.[48] Writing from Tunbridge Wells, for instance, Sally K. Marks told readers of the *Los Angeles Times* how the period props and set dressings were procured from 'some 150 different collectors and antique shops,' and how a 1902 Harrods store catalogue and an 1890 drapers inventory were used to ensure accurate pricing and terminology for the items in Shalford's Emporium, where Kipps is apprenticed.[49]

Another way that prestige adaptations sought to create cinematic spectacle was with large-scale production numbers. With realistic and often exotic backdrops, enormous sets, and huge musical ensembles, filmmakers sought not only to go beyond what would be possible on the theatrical stage but also to push the musical genre to new blockbuster proportions. For these reasons, *Sixpence*'s three showstopper numbers—'Money to Burn,' 'If the Rain's Got to Fall,' and 'Flash, Bang,

Wallop'—are expansive set pieces, each over seven minutes in length and featuring upwards of two dozen singers and dancers. Several numbers, moreover, are staged outdoors, showcasing quintessentially English locations like the River Thames and the seaside resort at Bournemouth. Shooting song-and-dance numbers on location was then promoted as its own form of spectacle, something that made *Sixpence* a film musical 'with a difference.' Unlike most musicals, one press book article explains, which are 'confined to the soundstage,' *Sixpence* 'is a musical that moves, using natural backgrounds as its settings.'[50]

Finally, cinematography and editing add an additional layer of spectacle to *Sixpence*'s authentic locations and large-scale production numbers. For example, the scenes shot at Blenheim Palace, residence of the Duke of Marlborough and birthplace of Winston Churchill, rely heavily on long-shot scales, high angles, and wide-angle lenses to emphasize the building's size, while tracks, tilts, and cranes highlight the interior's ornate marble, brass fixtures, and painted ceiling murals. In the musical numbers, mobile framing and editing ensure uniquely cinematic views of the choreography, while special effects further distance the film from its theatrical origins. The dream ballet 'This Is My World,' for instance, in which Kipps reflects on the loss of his inheritance, uses dissolves and superimposition to produce ghostly figures who appear and disappear, first celebrating his good fortune and then mocking his aspirations of class mobility. Kipps himself floats suspended in the air, and glides uncannily across the floor. The entire scene is filmed through a haze (likely done with a diffusion filter or perhaps more simply by putting Vaseline on the lens), creating blurred figures and abstractions of light that amplify the otherworldly atmosphere, as can be seen in ▶ video example 25.1 and Figure 7.2.

By the early 1970s, critics increasingly felt that adherence to the stage property and over-sized musical numbers made

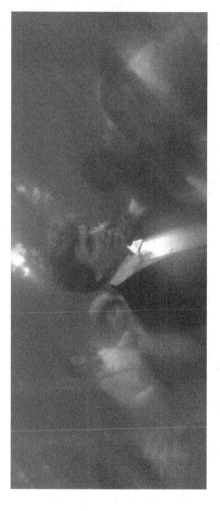

FIGURE 7.2  Cinematic special effects during 'This is My World' help to transform the stage musical into a blockbuster film. Credit: Half a Sixpence. Co-produced and directed by George Sidney. 145 min. Par. 1967. DVD.

prestige adaptations bloated and slow, and indeed by that time the cycle was coming to an end. For producers in the 1960s, however, fidelity and spectacle were well-established risk-reduction strategies, proven to help the musical genre succeed in the new post-studio era by transforming it into a special event. Though *Sixpence* would ultimately not yield blockbuster returns, Paramount's decisions when adapting the musical to the screen were entirely in keeping with industrial norms.

## *HALF A SIXPENCE* AND THE HOLLYWOOD RENAISSANCE AESTHETIC

It was likewise an awareness of current industrial trends that shaped *Half a Sixpence*'s overall visual style. The roadshow adaptation was released the same year as *Bonnie and Clyde* (1967) and *The Graduate* (1967), two films said to have helped usher in the Hollywood Renaissance. Aimed primarily at the reliable youth audience, this group of low-budget films became known for cynical, violent, and sexually explicit content, and for a novel deviation from the classical Hollywood style.[51] Though *Sixpence* obviously differs from the Renaissance films in tone and subject matter, it adopts a similar aesthetic, which gives its nostalgic romance a distinctly late-1960s look.

Of course, new modes of production and developments in technology following the break-up of the studio system had brought about industry-wide shifts in Hollywood film style, including the use of colour, widescreen, and location shooting that began as distinguishing features of the blockbusters.[52] In addition, as David Bordwell explains in *The Way Hollywood Tells It: Story and Style in Modern Movies*, the 1960s also witnessed accelerated editing rates, closer shot scales, greater reliance on wide-angle and telephoto lenses, and more pervasive mobile framing, particularly zooms and hand-held camerawork.[53] These stylistic techniques were not entirely new, but they became more salient in the immediate post-studio period, and they can be found to varying degrees across all of Hollywood's output. Certain films, though, employed these devices more frequently and overtly, and thus were grouped together as evidence of a new American film style, eventually known as the Hollywood Renaissance.[54] Renaissance filmmakers were particularly influenced by a new 'film consciousness,' or a larger awareness of film history and film culture, that arose in the decades following World War II.[55] With the greater circulation of studio film libraries through high-profile reissues and television broadcasts, an influx of foreign imports and a corresponding boom in art house exhibition, the proliferation of domestic and international film festivals, and the establishment of film studies as an academic discipline, cinephiles and the general public alike now had greater access to classical Hollywood cinema and to a variety of alternative filmmaking traditions.[56] In the late 1960s, this heightened film consciousness began to influence mainstream Hollywood, as a new group of filmmakers appropriated stylistic and narrative techniques from European art cinema, cinéma vérité documentaries, experimental films, New York City–based independent filmmaking, old Hollywood films, and even television.[57] In particular, the Renaissance films favoured telephoto lenses, and thus flat, shallow-focus compositions, unusual camera placements, arcing camera movements, zooms, and jarring editing devices like jump cuts, freeze frames, and 'flash cutting'—quick bursts of shots composed of only three to six frames.[58] Many of these films also feature sequences set to nondiegetic pop music, perhaps best represented by the Simon and Garfunkel songs used to convey character subjectivity in *The Graduate*.[59] Overall, the Renaissance films tend to draw attention to their style, creating an aesthetic more typical of art cinema than of average Hollywood fare.[60]

On the whole, the Hollywood musical and the films of the Hollywood Renaissance are viewed as binary opposites, evidence of how old and new, obsolescence and innovation, briefly coexisted—but did not overlap—during a period of industrial transition.[61] Yet while there are certainly musicals that adhere to a more classical style, such as the adaptation of *Hello, Dolly!* (1969), many others were influenced by the same film consciousness that shaped the Renaissance aesthetic. Regarding the adaptation of *Camelot* (1967), for example, director Joshua Logan reportedly stated that he intended to make use of 'all the modern techniques of photography, cutting, sound recording, set decoration and laboratory work that some Italian, English, and French directors have made enormous strides in recently.'[62] Formal experimentation was not uniform across the musical genre, just as it was not uniform across Hollywood filmmaking more broadly, but that experimentation was taking place, including in prestige adaptations like *Half a Sixpence*.[63]

Released the same month as *The Graduate*, *Sixpence* owes much of its affinity with the Renaissance aesthetic to its director's sensibilities. Under contract at MGM through his early career, George Sidney had gravitated towards musicals, eventually directing some of the studio's best-known entries in the genre, including *Anchors Aweigh* (1945), starring Gene Kelly and Frank Sinatra, and *The Harvey Girls* (1946), starring Judy Garland. He worked steadily through the 1950s and 1960s as an independent director-producer, and by mid-decade had one of the industry's strongest box office records.[64] Sidney also had an affinity for Broadway adaptations, having brought *Annie Get Your Gun* (1950), *Show Boat* (1951), *Kiss Me Kate* (1953, in 3D), *Pal Joey* (1957), and *Bye Bye Birdie* (1963) to the screen. For these reasons, Sidney likely seemed the ideal

choice to direct *Half a Sixpence*, and in 1965, he signed a multiple picture distribution deal with Paramount, though only
two films resulted: *The Swinger* (1966), a psychedelic comedy
starring Ann-Margret, and *Sixpence*, which ended up being
his final film.[65]

Yet, although Sidney was undoubtedly an established part
of Hollywood's 'old guard' when he signed onto *Sixpence*, he
was also a director known for an almost formalist approach
to filmmaking, and he reportedly preferred musicals because
they allowed for greater stylistic play.[66] His directorial aesthetic is an eclectic one, drawing influence from 'nearly every
movement, old and new, in film, theater, music, dance and
fine arts,' and often reflexively pushing against contemporary norms with devices like slow and fast motion, still photography, superimpositions, overhead shots, and montage
editing.[67] Crane shots were one of his specialities, leading critic
George Morris to write in *Film Comment* in 1977 that 'What
the track was to Max Ophuls, the crane is to Sidney.'[68] In fact, as
Morris's article indicates, Sidney's aesthetic choices were interesting enough for early proponents of auteur theory, most notably Andrew Sarris, to view him as one of Hollywood's most
significant directors.[69]

Whether directors like Jean-Luc Godard and Michelangelo
Antonioni directly influenced Sidney in the same way they inspired the Renaissance filmmakers is uncertain, but his larger
formalist tendencies are in keeping with the late 1960s vogue
for stylistic experimentation, and *Sixpence* makes frequent use
of the specific techniques associated with the young American
film movement. It is also worth noting that *Sixpence*'s cinematographer was Geoffrey Unsworth, who later shot Stanley
Kubrick's *2001: A Space Odyssey* (1968), while its coeditor was
Frank Santillo, who worked with Sam Peckinpah on *Ride the
High Country* (1962) and *The Battle of Cable Hogue* (1970). Both
Unsworth and Santillo, then, were (or would become) affiliated

with key figures in New Hollywood cinema, and their influence on *Half a Sixpence*'s modern style should not be overlooked.

Though contemporary stylistic techniques—particularly the use of very wide and very long lenses—can be found throughout *Sixpence*, they are particularly pronounced in the musical numbers, perhaps because Sidney, like many film musical directors, viewed song-and-dance sequences as an opportunity for formal play.[70] Many numbers, for instance, feature unconventional compositions that draw attention to the position of the camera. Canted angles are frequently used for emphasis, as in the climax of 'I'm Not Talking to You,' in which Ann's musical scolding of Kipps for having missed their date is punctuated by reaction shots of Kipps's coworkers at noticeably oblique angles. It is also common for objects in the foreground to frame or even obscure the dramatic action. The final chorus of 'Flash, Bang, Wallop,' set in a large pub during Kipps and Ann's wedding reception, features a flurry of such compositions, including a low-angle shot peering up at the dancing guests from behind a curtain in an alcove, and a medium-long shot of Kipps, Ann, and their wedding party partially blocked by a pair of legs dancing on the bar in the centre foreground (Figure 7.3).

Mobile framing is also prevalent in *Sixpence*. Tracking shots, arcs, and Sidney's signature cranes are the most frequent types of camera movement, but the film also makes isolated use of whip pans, evident in 'If the Rain's Got to Fall,' and includes some brief handheld camerawork, most noticeably in 'I'm Not Talking to You,' filmed on the beach at Bournemouth. It is the musical's reliance on zooms, however, that really marks its affinity with the emerging Hollywood style. Sidney was, in fact, an early adopter of zoom lenses, using them sporadically in the 1950s in films like *Pal Joey* (1957). In *Sixpence*, he favours quick zooms, creating noticeable shifts in perspective that tend to function either as musical punctuation, as with the quick

FIGURE 7.3 A wedding guest dancing on the bar in the foreground partially obscures the action and draws attention to the camera position in 'Flash, Bang, Wallop.' Credit: Half a Sixpence. Co-produced and directed by George Sidney. 145 min. Par. 1967. DVD.

push-in on Kipps on the final downbeat of 'Money to Burn,' or as visual rhymes or jokes. A quick zoom in, for instance, simulates Pearce's (Grover Dale) attention to singer Laura Livermore's (Aleta Morrison) ample bosom, while a quick zoom out anticipates the backwards thrust of a starting cannon firing at the regatta.

*Half a Sixpence* employs similarly overt editing techniques. Some of these devices were long-standing favourites of Sidney's, such as using a false match cut to cover a radical change in space.[71] During the romantic duet 'Half a Sixpence,' Kipps and Ann, framed in a long shot, kiss in front of the pavilion on the pier (Figure 7.4a). A match-on-action links this shot to a close-up of the couple (Figure 7.4b), but a zoom out then reveals that Kipps and Ann have magically moved to the other side of the pavilion (Figure 7.4c).

Dramatic shifts in space are also achieved through wipe-by cuts, in which an object passes in front of the camera, disguising the cut to a new shot. In 'The Rain's Got to Fall,' for instance, Kipps, framed in a medium close-up, passes his straw boater hat directly in front of the lens, and when the frame clears, the camera position has changed and three male dancers leap towards the camera in a long shot.

Beyond effecting spatial transformations, however, *Sixpence* also uses editing to break the cinematic illusion, drawing attention to the film's construction. For example, 'Money to Burn,' in which Kipps celebrates using his inheritance to buy a banjo, climaxes with a series of rhythmic, axial jump cuts, each providing a slightly longer view of the ensemble parading across a large theatre stage. Though the cuts are linked by rough matches on action, bits of choreography are omitted with each new framing, making the editing noticeable in a way that classical narrative filmmaking generally considers 'incorrect.' An even more reflexive technique shows a typical day at Shalford's Emporium, with the apprentices and shop

(a)

(b)

(c)

FIGURES 7.4A–C  In 'Half a Sixpence,' a match-on-action from a long shot to a close-up hides a change in space. A zoom out then reveals that Kipps and Ann have impossibly jumped to the other side of the pavilion. Credit: Half a Sixpence. Co-produced and directed by George Sidney. 145 min. Par. 1967. DVD.

girls assisting customers, while Kipps surreptitiously tries to read a letter from Ann and avoid the miserly Mr Shalford. The entire scene comprises a series of still images presented in quick succession, creating the impression of halting, fragmented movement. Of course, this is what cinema is: a rapid series of images that the human eye and brain render as continuous motion. The Emporium scene thus humorously deconstructs the very nature of the filmic medium.

It is in the regatta scene, though, that *Half a Sixpence* most comprehensively employs modern stylistic techniques, and perhaps tellingly, it was this scene that contemporary critics liked best.[72] The race becomes a key narrative turning point when Kipps is asked to row with Hubert Walsingham and thus compete against his fellow apprentices. Should Kipps help Hubert win the race, he will secure both his place in high society and Helen's affections, but in so doing, he will betray his lifelong friends and the devoted Ann. Overall, the sequence alternates between the rowers on the Thames and the spectators on the sidelines, but as it progresses, it increasingly strays from Kipps and his personal drama to feature shots of couples enjoying a small fairground or making out in the tall grass. Nearly every shot in this montage is mobile. Tracking shots follow the boats from the shoreline, or dolly ahead of the Shalford shop girls on their bicycles, as they root for the apprentices. A camera mounted on the spinning carousel creates a dizzying effect, while another mounted near the stern of Kipps's boat is repeatedly splashed with water from his oar (Figure 7.5).

Wide and telephoto lenses are routinely alternated, with zooms and rack focuses shifting attention between planes, as when a zoom out from an extreme long shot of the boats on the river brings into the left foreground a couple kissing behind a tree. As the boats near the finish line, with Kipps and Walsingham pulling ahead to win, the editing pace accelerates. The regatta occupies four-and-a-half minutes of screen time,

FIGURE 7.5 Unusual camera angles contribute to the modern dynamism of the regatta scene. Here, water splashes over a camera mounted alongside the boat. Credit: Half a Sixpence. Co-produced and directed by George Sidney. 145 min. Par. 1967. DVD.

but has 121 shots averaging 1.9 seconds in length, a noticeably quick editing pace for the period.[73] The entire sequence is
dynamic, building the appropriate tension over the outcome
of the race, while also providing comic asides and even brief
moments of pathos, as when a rack focus from Ann to Helen,
accompanied by a fading out of Ann's cries of encouragement
to Kipps, foreshadows that Helen is about to (temporarily) secure Kipps's romantic affection, seen in ▶ video example 25.1.

Significantly, the regatta is accompanied by the song 'The
Race Is On.' Written specifically for the film and performed
by Kipps in voiceover, the song's lyrics provide his stream of
consciousness as he considers what he stands to both gain
and lose should he win the race. As mentioned, Renaissance
films like *The Graduate* helped popularize the use of montage
sequences accompanied by nondiegetic pop songs commenting
on plot or character, and by the early 1970s, many film musicals
were presenting songs through voiceover in explicit imitation.[74] Arthur P. Jacobs, producer of *Goodbye Mr Chips* (1969),
explained to *Variety* that voiceover songs could 'comment on
the action, just like in "The Graduate,"' and he claimed they
would modernize the genre by eliminating its 'oldfashioned'
convention of characters bursting into song to express their
thoughts and feelings.[75] A few earlier musicals, including *It's
Always Fair Weather* (1955) and *Gigi* (1958), use voiceover songs,
and montage sequences in some form can be found throughout
the genre's history. However, musical numbers combining the
two devices become noticeably more frequent after 1967, their
increased use likely motivated not only by the Renaissance
films but also by Richard Lester's Beatles films (*A Hard Day's
Night* [1964] and *Help!* [1965]), which were celebrated for their
fast-cut, proto-music video sequences. Presenting 'The Race Is
On' as a voiceover song laid over a montage thus anticipates
what would soon become an aesthetic trend in the musical
genre, and it can be hypothesized that this scene was designed

to link *Sixpence* with an emerging popular method for joining music and image on screen.

Admittedly, stylistic techniques like jump cuts and zooms create a different overall effect in *Sixpence* than they do in the often cynical Renaissance films precisely because *Sixpence* is markedly different in tone. The rapid, disjunctive editing used to present graphic violence in films like *Bonnie and Clyde* or *The Wild Bunch* (1969) is here used to celebrate buying a banjo or to generate excitement over a boat race. Perhaps it was this unlikely pairing of modern aesthetics and traditional musical comedy that contemporary critics disliked. Most, including Charles Champlin of the *Los Angeles Times*, Archer Winston of the *New York Post*, and Roger Ebert of the *Chicago Sun-Times*, found the film over-directed and busy, privileging style over substance.[76] Renata Adler of the *New York Times* acknowledged that much of the film was beautifully shot, but concluded that Sidney's 'wildly active' direction was likely to interest only those 'in a state that I think is best described as stoned.'[77]

Adler's comment gestures towards a likely motivation for *Sixpence*'s eclectic visual style: to attract the valuable youth audience. If young people—stoned or otherwise—were turning out to see films with novel, art-cinema-derived aesthetics, imparting such an aesthetic to *Sixpence* could give it a much-needed edge over its competition. In fact, the studio pressbook suggests that Paramount did try to market *Sixpence* as a Swinging Sixties film, as an alternate advertising layout features Steele surrounded by the corseted chorus girls from 'Money to Burn' and the tagline 'The Sock It to Me Musical Smash of the Year.'[78] Given the film's disappointing financial returns, it is unlikely that the youth audience attended *Sixpence* in any great number. Nevertheless, the film's overall aesthetic is best understood as an industrially motivated strategy. Aesthetic norms were shifting in Hollywood, and *Sixpence* demonstrates how the musical, no less than any other genre, sought to capitalize on stylistic novelty to capture a specific demographic.

## CONCLUSION

*Half a Sixpence* opened strong, making *Variety*'s list of the top twelve grossing films for both March and April 1968, but consistent underperformance soon caused Paramount to cancel the film's remaining roadshow engagements and put it into general release.[79] *Sixpence* managed to break even thanks to its popularity in the United Kingdom, where Tommy Steele was better known and where the critique of class hierarchies perhaps had greater resonance, but it was hardly the blockbuster success for which Paramount had hoped.[80]

Part of the problem was that *Sixpence* was competing for an increasingly smaller audience against a glut of big-budget roadshow musicals, many of which were adapted from better-known Broadway originals. Indeed, within a few years, the prestige cycle of adaptations would run its course, as all film cycles do.[81] As lavish, faithful productions repeatedly underperformed at the box office, Hollywood responded by reshaping the musical genre once again, this time lowering budgets and focusing on rock musicals aimed more directly at the youth audience.[82] Roadshowing was also no longer the attraction it had been earlier in the decade, and industry insiders began to question whether it was the films or the method of distribution that was causing so many expensive productions to struggle at the box office. Paramount later concluded that roadshowing *Sixpence* had been a mistake, hypothesizing that because of the musical's comparatively small budget, it would have performed better in general release during a major holiday like Easter.[83]

In its odd way, though, *Half a Sixpence* makes industrial sense and helps nuance the common claim that the musical genre in the immediate post-studio period fell into decline simply because it was out of touch with filmmaking trends and audience expectations. On the contrary, *Sixpence* is the way it is precisely because of Paramount's attempts to position the musical in line with multiple contemporary trends. *Sixpence*'s curious mixture of blockbuster spectacle, fidelity to its Broadway source material, and stylistic experimentation evidence Hollywood's long-standing interest in combining filmmaking strategies in the hopes of attracting as wide an audience as possible. For Paramount, wedding the established prestige cycle of adaptations, known to be popular with families, to the youth-oriented aesthetic of the emerging Hollywood Renaissance likely seemed smart, and indeed *Sixpence* was neither the first nor the last musical to try it. *Camelot* (1967), *Finian's Rainbow* (1968), *Sweet Charity* (1969), and *Fiddler on the Roof* (1971) likewise fuse these two production trends. They, like *Half a Sixpence*, demonstrate that the changes the Hollywood musical underwent after the break-up of the studio system were not missteps towards decline, but rather calculated attempts by the film industry to reshape the genre to the needs of a changing marketplace.

## NOTES

1. Matthew Kennedy, *Roadshow! The Fall of Film Musicals in the 1960s* (Oxford: Oxford University Press, 2014), 119. See also, for example, David A. Cook, *Lost Illusions: American Cinema in the Shadow of Watergate and Vietnam, 1970–1979*, History of the American Cinema, vol. 9 (Berkeley: University of California Press, 2000); Thomas Hischak, *Through the Screen Door: What Happened to the Broadway Musical When*

*It Went to Hollywood* (Lanham, MD: Scarecrow Press, 2004); Julie Hubbert, 'The Recession Soundtrack: From Albums to Auteurs, Songs to Serialism (1960–1977)—Introduction,' in *Celluloid Symphonies: Texts and Contexts in Film Music History* (Berkeley: University of California Press, 2011): 289–314; Ethan Mordden, *The Hollywood Musical* (New York: St. Martin's Press, 1981).

2. Roger Ebert, review of *Half a Sixpence*, *Chicago Sun-Times*, 23 May 1968. http://www.rogerebert.com/reviews/half-a-sixpence-1968; Renata Adler, 'Screen: Out of Focus, Out of Touch,' review of *Half a Sixpence*, *New York Times*, 21 February 1968, p. 60.

3. Stuart Byron, 'Roadshow: Glory or Gory?' *Variety*, 5 February 1969, pp. 3, 34.

4. Steven Cohan, 'Introduction: Musicals of the Studio Era,' in *Hollywood Musicals: The Film Reader*, ed. Steven Cohan (London: Routledge, 2002), 13; Peter Lev, *The Fifties: Transforming the Screen, 1950–1959*, History of the American Cinema, vol. 7 (Berkeley: University of California Press, 2003), 219, 222; 'Film Musicals Victimized by Current Inflation,' *Variety*, 22 April 1959, p. 3; 'Ignore Europe, Shoot Tuners,' *Variety*, 7 June 1961, p. 7.

5. Lev, *The Fifties*, 8, 147; Paul Monaco, *The Sixties: 1960–1969*, History of American Cinema, vol. 8 (Berkeley: University of California Press, 2001), 10, 40; 'Films Out of World Touch,' *Variety*, 9 February 1955, p. 23; 'H'wood Figures Foreign Taste Factor in Story,' *Variety*, 10 August 1955, pp. 3, 16.

6. 'Musical Films Hard Sell Abroad,' *Variety*, 30 November 1955, pp. 1, 15; 'Europe Yawns; Tunepix Off,' *Variety*, 26 April 1962, p. 28.

7. 'Video Dead against Screen Musicals, Yet Studios Neglect 'Em - Geo. Stoll,' *Variety*, 15 February 1958, p. 17; 'H'wood's Last Stand: Musicals,' *Variety*, 9 August 1967, p. 22.

8. Lev, *The Fifties*, 107–125.

9. Steve Neale, 'Hollywood Blockbusters: Historical Dimensions,' in *Movie Blockbusters*, ed. Julian Stringer (London: Routledge, 2003), 50; Tino Balio, *United Artists: The Company That Changed the Film Industry*, vol. 2: 1951–1978 (Madison: University of Wisconsin Press, 2009), 132.

10. Neale, 'Hollywood Blockbusters,' 50–51; Balio, *United Artists*, 207–208.

11. Balio, *United Artists*, 125; 'Legit-to-Films Trend Still Hefty; 5 B'way Examples,' *Variety*, 13 July 1955, pp. 3, 22; 'Hit Plays, Novels Priced Sky-High for Hollywood,' *Variety*, 10 August 1955, p. 1.

12. Mark N. Grant, *The Rise and Fall of the Broadway Musical* (Boston: Northeastern University Press, 2004), 4; George Reddick, 'The Evolution of the Original Cast Album,' in *The Oxford Handbook of the American Musical*, ed. Raymond Knapp, Mitchell Morris, and Stacy Wolf (New York: Oxford University Press, 2011), 184–186.

13. Jessica Sternfeld and Elizabeth L. Wollman, 'After the 'Golden Age,' in *The Oxford Handbook of the American Musical*, ed. Raymond Knapp, Mitchell Morris, and Stacy Wolf (New York: Oxford University Press, 2011), 113; 'U.S. Musicals Not Always "Poison,"' *Variety*, 24 October 1956, p. 5; George Marton, '"Bottle It"—Prescription for Marketing Int'l Hits,' *Variety*, 7 January 1959, pp. 13, 54.

14. Thomas Hischak, *Through the Screen Door: What Happened to the Broadway Musical When It Went to Hollywood* (Lanham, MD: Scarecrow Press, 2004), 1–2, 19–20; Raymond Knapp and Mitchell Morris, 'The Filmed Musical,' in *The Oxford Handbook of the American Musical*, ed. Raymond Knapp, Mitchell Morris, and Stacy Wolf (New York: Oxford University Press, 2011), 140.

15. Sternfeld and Wollman, 'After the "Golden Age,"' 112–113; Frank Segers, 'Angels, Angles & Anxiety,' *Variety*, 5 January 1972, pp. 141, 156; Grant, *Rise and Fall*, 306–307.

16. 'Hit Plays, Novels Priced Sky-High for Hollywood,' *Variety*, 10 August 1955, p. 1.

17. Letter from Norman Jewison to Fred Goldberg, Vice President, United Artists, Norman Jewison Collection, box 33, folder 4, Wisconsin Center for Film and Theater Research.

18. Amanda Ann Klein, *American Film Cycles: Reframing Genres, Screening Social Problems, and Defining Subcultures* (Austin: University of Texas Press, 2011), 11.

19. Vincent Canby, '"Fiddler" on a Grand Scale,' *New York Times*, 4 November 1971, p. 52.

20. Rich., 'Shows Abroad: *Half a Sixpence*,' *Variety*, 10 April 1963, p. 60; 'London "Sixpence" Foldo; Due for B'way in March,' *Variety*, 14 October 1964, p. 61; Harold Myers, 'London Crix Pick "Succeed,"' *Variety*, 3 July 1963, pp. 53, 56; Harold Myers, 'What London and Broadway Both Prefer: Boff Musicals,' *Variety*, 6 January 1966, p. 243.

21. 'Writing New Songs for "Half-Sixpence" on B'way,' *Variety*, 4 November 1964, p. 62; Hobe., 'Shows on Broadway: *Half a Sixpence*,' *Variety*, 28 April 1965, p. 62.

22. 'Victor's Quest for New Cast Album Stuff Sparked "Sixpence" B'way Click,' *Variety*, 28 July 1968, pp. 91–92; Jesse Gross, 'Zero, Matthau B'way "Bests,"' *Variety*, 9 June 1965, pp. 1, 62.

23. 'Victor's Quest for New Cast Album Stuff Sparked "Sixpence" B'way Click,' *Variety*, 28 July 1968, pp. 91–92.

24. David A. Cook, *Lost Illusions: American Cinema in the Shadow of Watergate and Vietnam, 1970–1979*, History of the American Cinema, vol. 9 (Berkeley: University of California Press, 2000), 305; 'Paramount Production Pace Despite Its Own "War-Drain" of Resources,' *Variety*, 10 November 1965, pp. 7, 18; 'Par at Americana, G&W at Houston Seeking Merger Approval on Oct. 19; 154-pp Proxy Statement Backgrounds,' *Variety*, 21 September 1966, pp. 3, 17.

25. The film rights for *Camelot* sold for $2 million and the final budget was $15 million. The rights for *Dolly* also sold for $2 million, and the final budget ran up to $25 million (Kennedy, *Roadshow*, 26, 63, 86).

26. 'Chatter: Hollywood,' *Variety*, 11 August 1965, p. 54; '"Half a Sixpence," with Steele, to Par.,' *Variety*, 24 November 1965, p. 4; Kennedy, *Roadshow*, 117.

27. 'Hollywood Production Pulse,' *Variety*, 28 September 1966, p. 22; John Mundy, *The British Musical Film* (Manchester: Manchester University Press, 2007), 212; 'Tunepix: High Risk,' *Variety*, 8 January 1969, p. 15.

28. 'Chatter: London,' *Variety*, 1 November 1967, p. 61; 'New York Sound Track,' *Variety*, 8 November 1967, p. 20; Advertisement, *Variety*, 3 January 1968, pp. 13–16; 'Film Party to Aid Kennedy Games,' *New York Times*, 16 February 1968, p. 25; 'New York Sound Track,' *Variety*, 21 February 1968, p. 26.

29. Advertisement, *Variety*, 3 January 1968, pp. 13–16.
30. 'New York Sound Track,' *Variety*, 7 February 1968, p. 20; Paramount Film Service Ltd, *Half a Sixpence* Paramount Press Book and Merchandising Manual, 1967, 2–3, author's personal collection; 'New York Sound Track,' *Variety*, 28 June 1967, p. 16; 'New York Sound Track,' *Variety*, 6 March 1968, p. 30.
31. *Sixpence* Press Book, 9–12, 14–18.
32. Mundy, *British Musical Film*, 166–176, 213.
33. Hope., 'Shows on Broadway: *Half a Sixpence*,' *Variety*, 28 April 1965, p. 62; Allen Hughes, 'A Most Convincing Dancer,' *New York Times*, 29 August 1965, p. X12.
34. Charles Champlin, 'Movie Review: "Half a Sixpence" Opens at Chinese,' review of *Half a Sixpence, Los Angeles Times*, 23 February 1968, p. C7.
35. Jesse Gross, 'This Is Replacement and Holiday Time for B'way's Show Casts, Too,' *Variety*, 18 August 1965, p. 53; Tomo., 'Legit Followup: *Half a Sixpence* (Broadhurst, N.Y.),' *Variety*, 30 March 1966, p. 86.
36. 'Chatter: Hollywood,' *Variety*, 11 August 1965, p. 54.
37. 'Ask Voice-Doubles Forego Publicity; Did Marni Cost Audrey an Oscar?' *Variety*, 28 February 1968, p.1; Tim Anderson, 'Which Voice Best Becomes the Property? Tie-Ups, Intertexts, and Versioning in the Production of *My Fair Lady*,' *Spectator* 17, no. 2 (Spring/Summer 1997): 76–77.
38. Murf., review of *How to Succeed in Business without Really Trying*, *Variety Film Reviews, 1907–1980*, vol. 11, 1964–1967 (New York: Garland, 1983); Abel., review of *Funny Girl*, *Variety*, 25 September 1968, *Variety Film Reviews, 1907–1980*, vol. 12, 1968–1970 (New York: Garland, 1983).
39. '20 Years of "Sudden" Success,' *Sixpence* Press Book, 7; 'Football Mania Drives Sixpence Crew Crazy,' *Sixpence* Press Book, 6; 'Cockney Poet,' *Sixpence* Press Book, 8.
40. Ebert, review of *Half a Sixpence*.
41. Champlin, review of *Half a Sixpence*.
42. Monaco, *The Sixties*, 11–15.
43. Mundy, *British Musical Film*, 210–211.
44. 'Par O'Seas Hatch by Dozens,' *Variety*, 26 April 1967, pp. 3, 36.
45. ' "Sixpence" Pic Fussy on Turn-of-Century Decor at British Locations,' *Variety*, 28 September 1966, p. 25; 'International

Sound Track: London,' *Variety*, 29 March 1967, p. 29; Robert F. Hawkins, 'Filmusicals' O'Seas Accent,' *Variety*, 3 May 1967, pp. 5, 78.

46. '"Sixpence" Pic Fussy on Turn-of-Century Decor at British Locations,' *Variety*, 28 September 1966, p. 25.

47. 'Living Backgrounds Predominate "Sixpence,"' *Sixpence* Press Book, 6.

48. Balio, *United Artists*, 206–207.

49. Sally K. Marks, '"Half a Sixpence" Worth Every Penny,' *Los Angeles Times*, 10 January 1967, p. D10.

50. 'Living Backgrounds Predominate "Sixpence,"' *Sixpence* Press Book, 6.

51. Monaco, *The Sixties*, 182–186; Mark Harris, *Pictures at a Revolution: Five Movies and the Birth of New Hollywood* (New York: Penguin Press, 2008), 1–4.

52. Monaco, *The Sixties*, 67, 71, 74.

53. David Bordwell, *The Way Hollywood Tells It: Story and Style in Modern Movies* (Berkeley: University of California Press, 2006), 121–144.

54. Bordwell, *Hollywood Tells It*, 146–147, 158; Steve Neale, '"The Last Good Time We Ever Had?": Revising the Hollywood Renaissance,' in *Contemporary American Cinema*, ed. Linda Ruth Williams and Michael Hammond (Maidenhead, Berkshire: McGraw-Hill, 2006), 91.

55. See, for example, Noël Carroll, 'The Future of Allusion: Hollywood in the Seventies (and Beyond),' *October* (Spring 1982): 51–81; John Belton and Lyle Tector, 'The Bionic Eye,' *Film Comment* (September/October 1980): 11–14, 16–17, 79; Jackson Burgess, 'Review of *McCabe and Mrs. Miller*,' *Film Quarterly* 25, no. 2 (Winter 1971–1972): 49–53.

56. Eric Hoyt, *Hollywood Vault: Film Libraries before Home Video* (Berkeley: University of California Press, 2014), 113–119, 176, 180–184, 191; Kristin Thompson and David Bordwell, *Film History: An Introduction*, 3rd ed. (New York: McGraw-Hill, 2010), 327–328, 404; Monaco, *The Sixties*, 44, 54–58; David A. Cook, 'Auteur Cinema and the "Film Generation,"' in *The New American Cinema*, ed. Jon Lewis (Durham, NC: Duke University Press, 1998), 13–14.

57. Neale, 'Last Good Time,' 92; Thompson and Bordwell, *Film History*, 478, 484–486; Cook, 'Auteur Cinema,' 13–14; Hoyt, *Hollywood Vault*, 151, 189, 194.

58. Bordwell, *Hollywood Tells It*, 141–144; Monaco, *The Sixties*, 70, 74–76, 82, 86–87, 70; Thompson and Bordwell, *Film History*, 475–476.

59. Philip Furia and Laurie Patterson, *The Songs of Hollywood* (New York: Oxford University Press, 2010), 236–240; Jeff Smith, *Sounds of Commerce: Marketing Popular Film Music* (New York: Columbia University Press, 1998), 158–160.

60. Bordwell, *Hollywood Tells It*, 120; Monaco, *The Sixties*, 84; Thompson and Bordwell, *Film History*, 478.

61. Neale, 'Last Good Time,' 99–100, 107; Mark Shiel, 'American Cinema, 1965–70,' in *Contemporary American Cinema*, ed. Linda Ruth Williams and Michael Hammond (Maidenhead, Berkshire: McGraw-Hill, 2006), 12–26; Harris, *Pictures at a Revolution*, 3, 421; Kennedy, *Roadshow*, 125.

62. Quoted in Kennedy, *Roadshow*, 31.

63. Bordwell, *Hollywood Tells It*, 158.

64. 'Sidney #1,' *Variety*, 4 January 1967, p. 71.

65. Eric Monder, *George Sidney: A Bio-Bibliography* (Westport, CT: Greenwood Press, 1994), 19, 36–49.

66. Monder, *George Sidney*, 5.

67. Monder, *George Sidney*, 8–16.

68. George Morris, 'George Sidney: A Matter of Taste,' *Film Comment* 13, no. 6 (November–December 1977): 57.

69. Andrew Sarris, 'George Sidney,' in *American Cinema: Directors and Directions, 1929–1968* (New York: Dutton, 1968; Cambridge: DaCapo Press, 1996), 185.

70. Monder, *George Sidney*, 16–17.

71. Monder, *George Sidney*, 19.

72. Champlin, review of *Half a Sixpence*; Otta., review of *Half a Sixpence*, *Variety*, 27 December 1967, p. 6; Adler, review of *Half a Sixpence*.

73. Bordwell, *Hollywood Tells It*, 121.

74. Thompson and Bordwell, *Film History*, 476; Furia and Patterson, *Songs of Hollywood*, 236–237; Smith, *Sounds of Commerce*, 158–160.

75. Stuart Byron, 'Jacobs: "Mr. Chips" Sez Goodbye to Oldfashioned Filmusical Format,' *Variety*, 11 September 1968, p. 21.

76. Monder, *George Sidney*, 234; Ebert, review of *Half a Sixpence*; Champlin, review of *Half a Sixpence*.

77. Adler, review of *Half a Sixpence*.

78. Print Advertisement, *Sixpence* Press Book, 2.

79. 'National Boxoffice Survey,' *Variety*, 28 February 1968, p. 15; 'March's Golden Dozen in U.S.,' *Variety*, 3 April 1968, p. 19; 'Top U.S. April Grossers,' *Variety*, 8 May 1968, p. 11; 'New York Sound Track,' *Variety*, 8 May 1968, p. 32; 'Clutch of Roadshows in Offing; Detail Par's Marketing Plans for Its Youth-Oriented "Romeo & Juliet,"' *Variety*, 14 August 1968, pp. 5, 26.

80. Stuart Byron, 'Roadshow: Glory or Gory?' *Variety*, 5 February 1969, pp. 3, 34; Mundy, *British Musical Film*, 214.

81. Klein, *American Film Cycles*, 35.

82. Hollywood had been producing teen-oriented musicals featuring popular music, including rock 'n' roll, since the mid-1950s. These were mainly low-budget quickies for drive-ins (e.g., American International Pictures' Beach Party series), whereas the rock musicals of the 1970s were generally mid-budget productions, aimed at older teens and young adults (e.g., *A Star is Born* [1976]).

83. Stuart Byron, 'Roadshow: Glory or Gory?' *Variety*, 5 February 1969, pp. 3, 34.

# 8

# The Producers and Hairspray

## The Hazards and Rewards of Recursive Adaptation

### DEAN ADAMS

■□■

BROADWAY MUSICALS HAVE LONG RELIED on adaptation for source material. Relatively few musicals, like *A Chorus Line* or *Book of Mormon*, have been created from scratch; most have great novels (*Les Misérables*, *Phantom of the Opera*), plays (*Green Grow the Lilacs [Oklahoma!]*, *Liliom [Carousel]*), or films (*Billy Elliot*, *Smiles of a Summer Night [A Little Night Music]*) as their source material. While adapting movie scripts into Broadway musicals is nothing new, as Broadway musicals have become more expensive to produce and have had more corporate influence over their financing, producers have taken fewer risks in the selection of material for adaptation. The influence of the Walt Disney Company, with successful musicals appropriate for families based on its film library (*Beauty and the Beast*, *Newsies*, *The Lion King*), has led other producing entities to look at shifting Broadway audience demographics to guide and possibly predict which shows will do well.

Similarly, Hollywood has long depended on Broadway for source material and talent for its musicals. The early years of Hollywood took Broadway shows, stars, and writers and quickly produced cinematic adaptations. The 1936 film version of *Anything Goes*, for example, was released fourteen months after the Broadway opening. In the last four decades, however, only a handful of Broadway musicals have made the transition to film. A string of Hollywood musical bombs of the late 1960s, including *Doctor Doolittle* (1967), *Finian's Rainbow* (1968), *Hello Dolly* (1969), *and Paint Your Wagon* (1969)—each of which lost millions of dollars—set a pattern that made Hollywood producers think twice about producing a big-budget musical.[1] Matthew Kennedy commented on this in *Roadshow: The Fall of Film Musicals in the 1960s*:

> What happened to that once supreme film genre? I have reconciled my childhood memories of the late 1960s musicals with the adult realization that most of them aren't very good. The misjudgments piled up like a freeway collision disaster. Broadway adaptations were often literal and stage bound, as though anything too cinematic would destroy rather than enhance artistic integrity. People who had no business starring in musicals were hired simply because they were movie stars. And genuine talent in front of and behind the camera was not well used, much less nurtured as it was in the Studio Era.[2]

In this century, there were fewer than twenty-five live-action musical films from 2000 to 2015, in part because the genre, like the western, has fallen out of favour. Perhaps contemporary film audiences are used to the hyper-realistic environments that are rendered in even the most outlandish science-fiction worlds and struggle to accept musical theatre's more metaphoric convention of having characters sing their emotional thoughts. Another theory is that since the beginnings of rock and roll (and now hip hop), movie musicals have failed to embrace new musical styles that have greater popular appeal.

Conversely, during the past two decades Broadway has turned much more often to the movies for content. From 2000 to 2015, there were some 185 Broadway musicals produced; forty-nine of these were revivals.[3] The familiarity of hit musicals from the past is one way of encouraging a larger box office advance from an increasingly fickle audience.[4] Of the remaining productions, forty-five were based on Hollywood films—about 30 percent of the total and 40 percent of the nonrevival new musical productions. Since the early 1990s this pattern has accelerated with the advent of Walt Disney stage productions of its animated films: *Beauty and the Beast* (1994), *The Lion King* (1997), *Tarzan* (2006), *The Little Mermaid* (2008), and *Aladdin* (2014).

While many recent Broadway musicals have been derived from nonmusical films (*Big Fish* (2013), *Kinky Boots* (2012), *Bring It On: The Musical* (2011), *Billy Elliot* (2008), *Legally Blonde* (2007), *Big* (1996), few of these works have made it back to the cinema as musicals. Such 'recursive transfers' as *Sweet Charity*, *Silk Stockings*, *A Little Night Music*, *Nine*, and *Little Shop of Horrors* had their roots in cinema, became successful Broadway musicals, and returned to the multiplex in musical form. Nearly all lost money as musical films. Still, in the early 2000s, buoyed by the success of the movie musical version of *Chicago*, both *Hairspray* and *The Producers*, originally based on nonmusical films of the same titles, inspired new Hollywood musical versions even while the original stage versions were still playing on the Great White Way.

A comparison of the film and Broadway incarnations of *Hairspray* and *The Producers* reveals contrasting patterns of content, performance adaptation, casting, length, and audience demographics. The success or failure of each version reflects the changing tastes of the American musical audience in the twenty-first century and the challenges of the musical theatre marketplace. An analysis of the history, artists, and cultures of these films and stage productions reveals the particular risks from recursive transfers. Why was the Hollywood musical adaptation of *Hairspray* so successful while *The Producers* was not? Are there common elements that can predict the success of a Hollywood to Broadway to Hollywood musical journey?

## INITIAL SOURCES

*The Producers* was Mel Brooks's first film in 1968. The story follows the exploits of Max Bialystock and Leo Bloom as they dupe investors into collectively investing more than 100 percent in an intentional flop. The plan backfires when the musical they create, a tribute called *Springtime for Hitler*, becomes a hit and they are unable to pay back investors the earnings on the oversold shares.

Brooks had been a writer for Sid Caesar and others in the Golden Age of Television, and later in the 1970s would create a string of film parodies that were both critical and box office successes, including *Blazing Saddles* and *Young Frankenstein*. The original film of *The Producers*, however, was not universally well received. Renata Adler in the *New York Times* called the film 'shoddy and gross and cruel.'[5] Stanley Kauffmann in the *New Republic* wrote that the film 'bloats into sogginess'[6] and the venerable Pauline Kael called the effort 'amateurishly crude.'[7] Yet over the years, the film has gained in stature and reputation and has nurtured a cult following. The American Film Institute has placed it as number eleven in its 'top one hundred funniest films.'[8]

Brooks won the Academy Award for his screenplay, and Gene Wilder was nominated for best supporting actor. The performances of Wilder and Zero Mostel, both accomplished stage actors, were loud, theatrical, and over the top. This contrasts with the late 1960s' shift in cinematic acting styles in Hollywood films, with *Cool Hand Luke, In the Heat of the Night*, and *The Graduate* all highlighting the method acting style brought to cinematic prominence by Marlon Brando and James Dean a decade earlier. A new Hollywood ratings system also encouraged a more sophisticated variety of films with adult themes. Conversely, in *The Producers*, Brooks, Wilder, and Mostel were reviving a much earlier acting style—the broad vaudeville techniques of the Marx Brothers, Abbott and Costello, and Laurel and Hardy. While *The Producers* was relatively inexpensive to make—somewhat less than $1 million—it made only a small profit on its initial release, earning $1.2 million from a handful of screens. It has subsequently done reasonably well in rentals, DVDs and rereleases, earning shy of $2 million—hardly a flop, but not a runaway success either.[9]

While Mel Brooks worked his way into the mainstream, John Waters would describe himself as a Hollywood outsider. His early films gave birth to an acting company he called 'The Dreamlanders' that were featured in cult films ranging from the outrageous *Pink Flamingos* in the 1970s to the more mainstream *Polyester* and *Hairspray*. The latter was created on a budget of $2 million, a substantial amount for a John Waters film and significantly larger than many of his earlier works— *Pink Flamingos* was reportedly made on a budget of $10,000[10]— but much less than the studio blockbusters of the 1970s and 1980s. The quirky *Beetlejuice*, also released in 1988, had a budget of $15 million.[11]

Like many of Waters's films, *Hairspray* was set in his hometown of Baltimore, in this case in 1963. The film focused on Tracy Turnblad, a plump but engaging young woman who dreams of being on *The Corny Collins Show*, a segregated teen dance programme that devotes one show a month to 'Negro Day.' Waters based the programme on the 'Buddy Deane Show,' the real-life Baltimore dance show that he had danced on in the early sixties.[12] After Tracy dances her way onto the show, her experiences with prejudice in both television and at her school led her to protest the idea of 'separate but equal.' In the original film, her mother Edna is played by Divine, who also plays the bigot Arvin Hodgepile. While *Hairspray* is generally considered one of Waters's most accessible films (and one of the few to receive a PG rating—most range between R and X), it still has many camp moments, such as when the director appears as a crazed psychiatrist zapping Penny with a psychedelic cattle prod.

Commercially, the film did moderately well, earning over $6 million and receiving generally positive reviews. Janet Maslin in the *New York Times* noted that the film was 'bright and bouncy' with 'the actors at their best when they avoid exaggeration and remain weirdly sincere.'[13] While the original *Hairspray* was a comedy, it has serious themes—though delivered in John Waters fashion: 'For me it was always: the outsider wins, and integration prevails. The fat girl stood for gay, black, crippled—all outsiders that society rejects.'[14]

Even though Waters claimed he wasn't trying to create a commercial hit, it had been eight years since he made *Polyester*, and he was looking to do something 'different.' So even though the film is quirky, its dance-show setting and kids as heroes helped build a modest 'family' following beyond the faithful Waters audience. The release also coincided with the beginnings of a robust VHS rental market, and in 1989 *Hairspray* was released on VHS and was available in rental stores, which helped build its following. In fact, producer Margot Lion first got the idea to produce the film as a Broadway musical when she rented a ten-year-old VHS copy of the film.[15]

Both *Hairspray* and *The Producers* were low-budget cult films that were modestly successful but then became Broadway musical hits. Using cult films as source material is no guarantee for Broadway success: for every successful *Little Shop of Horrors*, there is a box office failure like *Cry-Baby*. Cult films provide musical creators with key ingredients: larger-than-life characters with big emotional moments and plots that can be condensed into a two-act musical form. Successful cult films also have a devoted fan base that help introduce the work to a mainstream audience. The adaptation process to create twenty-first-century Broadway musical adaptations and then recursive Hollywood musical versions illustrates the many commercial and aesthetic choices that must be made to find an audience for each version. The creators of these musical stage shows and films took markedly different paths.

## STRUCTURE AND ADAPTATION IN *THE PRODUCERS*

Mel Brooks, encouraged by such titans as Jerry Herman and David Geffen,[16] began writing a musical version of *The Producers* in 1998, thirty years after the film had premiered. The musical numbers 'Springtime for Hitler' and 'Prisoners of Love' were kept largely intact, and Brooks created seventeen new musical numbers that would adapt the storytelling into the standard two-act musical theatre form. The timeframe was changed from the original film's contemporary 1968 setting to 1959, putting the show squarely during the Broadway's musical 'Golden Age.' Many of the jokes in the lyrics pay homage to Broadway's great stars and hits. The now-anachronistic 1968 character of Lorenzo St Dubois (LSD), the hippie who plays Hitler in the play-within-a-play, is eliminated and the 'playwright' Franz is cast as Hitler.

The shift in period reflects the shift of tone as well. The darker comedy of the original 1968 film is replaced by a much brighter atmosphere and visual style. The small, cramped quarters of Bialystock's office in the 1968 film is replaced with a grander, more elegant space. Meehan and Brooks also write more adult jokes for the libretto in the 2001 stage version; for example, the sexual game Max and his little old lady play in the 1968 film is 'The Innocent Little Milkmaid and the Naughty Stable Boy.' Onstage in 2001, it's 'The Virgin Milkmaid and the Well-Hung Stable Boy.'

The opening number in both musicals creates the world of the play and answers the traditional question, 'What is this play about?'[17] The *Producers* film and stage musical versions begin in 1959 on Shubert Alley with Max Bialystock presenting another (spoof) flop, 'Funny Boy.' The 'Opening Night' number segues into the 'The King of Broadway' solo where Bialystock declares that 'I will be on top again, hey!' Max's 'The King of Broadway' lament was filmed, but not used in the final version of the 2005 movie adaptation. Stroman explained that 'The King of Broadway' was removed because 'I felt we needed to get to the line where the whole plot begins as soon as possible.'[18] This, along with the cutting of the late-in-act 2 'Where Did We Go Right,' demonstrated that the movie musical version would start faster and end sooner than the Broadway version. These 'bookend' cuts, however, were the only substantial changes to the book and score from the Broadway musical version. The act 1, scene 2 exposition scene is virtually identical to the original film, and it is the longest nonmusical section of the Broadway version. This serves to introduce the lead male characters, their quirks and charm, and to clarify the conceit of the plot: that producing a bomb can be more profitable than a hit show, provided it's oversold to investors and closes quickly.

Since stage musicals traditionally generally require two-act structures, the Broadway 'Springtime in Hitler' showstopper/climax must occur as late as possible in the second act to minimize the falling action. The build of the first act focuses on bringing the creators of the sure-fire flop together and raising the money from the 'little old lady' investors. Stroman's Broadway act 1 musical finale is an ingenious dancing chorus of old women and their walkers, with Max collecting checks from them as they line up and collapse on each other in a domino fashion. Meehan and Brooks honor the traditional musical theatre structure in the Broadway version while parodying it for the final act 1 tableau (this moment is cut in the film):

> ROGER, CARMEN, and THE TEAM now suddenly appear in spotlight and join ULA, FRANZ, and MAX and LEO in simultaneously singing four separate parts in a manner similar to the quintet at the end of Act One in *West Side Story*.[19]

Act 2 opens with Ula's redecoration of the office in all white, an opportunity to 'clean up' the mess from act 1 as well as provide an appropriate environment for Leo and Ula to flirt like teenagers and dance like Fred Astaire and Ginger Rogers. This provides the beginning of the split between Max and Leo that becomes the true tension of the second act. *Springtime for Hitler* is auditioned and prepared, and finally the show-within-a-show is presented in act 2, scene 4. The inevitable 'success' of the show creates the comic climax but does not resolve the plot. The 1968 source film takes only fourteen minutes to tie up loose ends: the reading of the reviews, Franz's attempted shooting of Leo and Max followed by his attempted suicide, Max's instructions to 'kill the actors,' the attempt to blow up the theatre, the courtroom scene, and the 'Prisoners of Love' finale—and there is even time for Ula's bikini dance.

Mercifully, the musical versions cut both Ula's bikini dance and the attempt to blow up the theatre, and replaced them instead with Ula and Leo's decision to escape to Rio after Max is arrested. The musical versions also double the amount of time to the conclusion (about twenty-eight minutes) and provide Max with an eleven o'clock number in the holding cell where he can sing 'Betrayed,' recounting all of the events of the show in rapid-fire fashion, while reemphasizing the betrayal of his (business) partner. The love triangle is resolved after Leo returns and is sentenced to prison with Max where they can create the show 'Prisoners of Love' in anticipation of their inevitable opening at the Shubert Theatre after they are released. The final image is of Max and Leo walking into the sunset together, their 'bromance' preserved since Ula exited with the 'Prisoners of Love' chorus.

Susan Stroman restaged her original work for film, and many of the original creative team (including costume designer William Ivey Long) reprised their Broadway visual contributions for film. Stroman chose Old Hollywood head-to-toe framing of musical numbers, including a Busby Berkeley over-the-head shot for 'Springtime for Hitler,' reprising the framing from the original 1968 film (see ▶ video example 26.1). While the film 'opened up' to feature New York City landmarks, most visual moments, such as the old ladies with walkers and the water fountain fanfare, were exact replicas of the Broadway adaptation. There were techniques reminiscent of classic Hollywood musicals, yet there were few self-referential textual moments that were based in cinema; instead, the inside jokes and visual puns remained Broadway-centric.

Mel Brooks's writing often features male duos, with one experienced tyrant and one weak or neurotic man, working together to overcome some major obstacle to triumph against society—even if that means committing a crime. This pattern emerges in *Twelve Chairs, The Producers, Blazing Saddles, and Young Frankenstein*. Women in this world are unapologetic stereotypes, either sex objects or grotesque older women. Ula in the original film is nothing more than an object of desire as she flirts with both Max and Leo by dancing seductively to 1960s funk music, and later strips down to nothing more than a bikini. Her two-dimensional type is replaced by a (slightly) more developed character in the musical versions by giving Ula more motivation (to be in the show) and more interaction with the two men (Max leers while Leo learns to flirt). Eventually, Leo marries Ula and they run off to Rio, but Leo's conscience for his 'business partner' brings him to the courtroom to try to save Max. While the 'blond bombshell' type evolved to a more complete character in the musical versions, the gay characters did not. Stuart Kaminsky points out that Brooks's frequent use of outrageous and flamboyant gay stereotypes distracts the audience from any suspicion that male leads have any sexual tension between them:

> It is interesting that Brooks always tries to distance himself from the homosexual implications of his central theme [characters] by including scenes in which overtly homosexual characters are ridiculed. It is particularly striking that these characters are, in *The Producers*, *Blazing Saddles*, and *The Twelve Chairs*, stage or film directors.[20]

While Brooks claims to be an equal opportunity offender, the black and Jewish characters in his films are often more generously written, and they often prevail over the absurd circumstances. In the Broadway musical version of *The Producers*, the Black Man Accountant opens the 'unhappy' section of 'I Want to Be a Producer' by singing in 'Old Man River'–style:

OH, I DEBTS ALL DE MORNIN'
*AN' I CREDITS ALL DE EB'NIN*
UNTIL DEM LEDGERS BE RIGHTTTT . . .[21]

In the 2005 movie version, this introduction was cut, even though the Black Accountant is seated in the same place in the movie as he was on Broadway. While Broadway audiences would appreciate the *Show Boat* reference and parody, the effect might be lost on (or misinterpreted by) the 2005 movie audience.

However, there was no toning down the gay stereotypes between the 1968 film, the Broadway adaptation, and the 2005 film. The characters Roger de Bris and Carmen Ghia, played in the musical adaptations by Gary Beach and Roger Bart, are flamboyant gay characters who reach the pinnacle of absurdity in the musical number 'Keep It Gay' that includes the anachronistic appearance of The Village People's sailor, cop, biker, and Indian characters in the final dance. Even though Broadway has long been associated with gay men who are its principal artists, creators, and performers, shows as recent as *Book of Mormon* (Elder McKinley), *Something Rotten* (Brother Jeremiah), and *Spamalot* (Lancelot) continue the tradition of broad comedy that *The Producers* showcases at the expense of the gay characters in the show. Responding to this kind of humour, Nathan Lane said, 'There are people who can't wait to be offended. Then they wonder why they are not invited to more parties. Who has time for that? Mel's take on homosexuals is that we're these flamboyant extraterrestrials.'[22] Brooks reflected in 2014 on shifting audience attitudes and how Hollywood plays it much safer:

> The prejudices or whatever, the restrictions, should have thoroughly diluted by now, and here we are—it's amazing. We're playing it safe. I don't think the individual person is playing it safe, but I think the organizations—let's call them television networks or studios—they're playing it safe. They don't want to get sued. They don't want to lose the Latino endorsement or the black endorsement or the Jewish endorsement.[23]

Brooks doesn't include the 'LGBT endorsement' in his list, but another film released in the same year as *The Producers* in 2005, *Brokeback Mountain*, showed that audiences might be ready for a more serious embodiment of gay characters: it grossed over $177 million worldwide on a budget of $14 million.[24]

## STRUCTURE AND ADAPTATION IN *HAIRSPRAY*

While Mel Brooks supervised every word and lyric in *The Producers*, John Waters declined the option to write the book for *Hairspray* when producer Margo Lion approached him in the spring of 1999: 'What I realized was that the play had to become something different from the movie for it to work. It had to cross over into something else. I think I would have been crazy to do that [write the book] . . . and I think the writers did a great job. I was in the middle of writing a movie.'[25]

The Broadway *Hairspray* shares one of *The Producers'* book authors, Thomas Meehan, who, with Mark O'Donnell, refashioned the original film into a two-act musical. Songwriters Marc Shaiman and Scott Wittman created a score of twenty-one musical numbers that replaced the original movie's dance tracks. The score pays homage to early sixties rhythm-and-blues and pop music but also infuses it with a big Broadway sound. Its transition to the Broadway stage as a musical in 2003 cleverly toned down some of the more subversive parts of the original film while highlighting the politics of race, gender, and sexuality in a nonconfrontational musical theatre idiom.

New Line Cinema, which holds the rights to the original film, became interested in developing the Broadway show into a musical film soon after the show won eight Tony Awards, including Best Musical.[26] Craig Zadan and Neil Meron, the successful producers of the Oscar-winning *Chicago*, were hired to supervise the production. Their experience in producing screen versions of Broadway shows includes the live television broadcasts of *The Sound of Music* and *The Wiz Live!* They also supervised the 2016 television adaptation of *Hairspray Live! Hairspray*'s original book authors Thomas Meeham and Mark O'Donnell wrote the first screenplay draft, but they were replaced for the 2007 film version by Leslie Dixon,[27] a screenwriter with extensive experience in family comedies (*Overboard, Mrs Doubtfire*). Her script remained faithful to the plot of the Broadway show but removed much of the campiness.

Hiring Dixon was the first of many decisions to select Hollywood professionals instead of the original Broadway creative team to supervise the making of the film. Production began in late 2004, about the same time as *The Producers*. Adam Shankman, a director/choreographer with roots in music videos, was hired to stage the new version, and he met with John Waters early in the process. Waters gave him the same advice on adaptation that he had given the Broadway team, 'Don't do what I did, don't do what the play did. You've gotta do your own thing.'[28]

While the 1968 version of *The Producers* contained two original songs by Mel Brooks, and both were retained in the musical versions, John Waters's *Hairspray* featured twenty-eight popular songs in its soundtrack, ranging from 'Day-O' to 'The Madison.' For the Broadway musical, these recorded songs were jettisoned and a new score was created by Marc Shaiman and Scott Wittman. The structure for the new *Hairspray*, like *The Producers*, followed traditional conventions of musical theatre construction. Unlike *The Producers*, there were more substantial plot and character changes in the Broadway musical: Velma von Tussle becomes a composite of Amber's Mother, Tammy the Stage Manager, and Arvin Hodgepile (Divine's male alter ego). The race riot that ends act 1 in the musical version ('Big, Blond, and Beautiful') sets up the 'Big Dollhouse' opening for act 2. Tracy escapes from prison rather than getting a governor's pardon. Seaweed frees Penny from her bedroom prison creating the 'Without Love' song opportunity.

The 2007 *Hairspray* musical film opens with a *West Side Story*-like flyover of the city. The opening number, 'Good Morning Baltimore,' reveals everything we need to know about the world surrounding the musical and its protagonist Tracy. In the 2007 film, director Shankman has Tracy arriving at school on top of a garbage truck mirroring the way that Barbra Streisand appears on a New York Harbor tugboat while singing 'Don't Rain on My Parade' in *Funny Girl*. Unlike the musical version of *The Producers*, the visual references point to Golden Age film musicals, not stage productions. Dana Heller, in her comprehensive critical edition *Hairspray*, catalogues a number of similar cinematic reference points, including 'Without Love' which recalls Judy Garland's love note to Clark Gable 'You Made Me Love You.'

The 2007 film musical ending resolves a number of plot moments differently: Little Inez winning, Velma getting fired, and Amber appearing to spark an interest in an African American boy were all crucial and symbolic moments for the new film version. Tracy's 'victory' in this version is winning Link to conclude the heteronormative fantasy that love transcends size, and Little Inez's surprise victory (a surprise even to those who know the Broadway show) concludes the fantasy that soon skin colour won't matter in America.

This adaptive evolution and significant changes in *Hairspray* are in sharp contrast to the adaptations of *The Producers*, which stick closely to the original. Some adaptation theorists state that fidelity is the most important criterion to use in analyzing adaptations (Leitch 2003). Leitch argues, however, that 'Fidelity to its source text—whether it is conceived as success in re-creating specific textual details or the effect of the whole—is a hopelessly fallacious measure of a given adaptation's value because it is unattainable, undesirable, and theoretically possible only in a trivial sense.'[29] Given *Hairspray*'s successes at each stage of significant adaptation and *The Producers*' failure as a faithful reproduction, faithfulness to the source material(s) is not necessary for popular success.

## RUNNING TIMES AND AUDIENCES

The 1965 musical film adaptation of *The Sound of Music* was the capstone of many successful Rodgers and Hammerstein movie adaptations of their Broadway hits, and its record-setting box office became a hopeful benchmark for musical films that followed. While the R&H adaptations might cut the occasional musical number (e.g., 'Lonely Room' in *Oklahoma!*), the plot and song structure would remain essentially intact. This meant that the film adaptations might run as long as the Broadway original. Television, the rise of the multiplex, and audience habits would change this model over the course of several decades to shorter, tighter film adaptations of Broadway shows.

The running time for the 2001 Broadway *The Producers* was typical for live musicals of the last two decades, about two hours, thirty-five minutes not including intermission. An analysis of the twenty-five top-grossing Broadway musicals of all time (a list that includes both *The Producers* and *Hairspray*)[30] reveals that the average running time of a Broadway musical is two hours and thirty minutes, not including intermission. The running time for the 1968 *The Producers* film was eighty-eight minutes, a relatively short time, but not atypical of the period or what a new filmmaker would be able to convince a studio to finance. The 2005 musical film version, however, clocks in at 134 minutes, a substantial length relative to other movie musicals: of the top ten highest-grossing movie musicals since 1975, the average running time was 115 minutes,[31] nineteen minutes shorter than *The Producers*. Only the epic *Les Misérables* was longer (160 minutes).

The 2007 *Hairspray* musical film is almost an hour shorter than the Broadway version, about 116 minutes, and is more in line with the typical length of Broadway musical film adaptations in the 2000s. As noted earlier, Dixon and Shankman were encouraged to 'do your own thing,' and the film was structured in a way that some musical numbers were cut ('Mama I'm a Big Girl Now,' 'The Big Dollhouse') and others reduced in length ('It Takes Two'), serving to streamline the music and plot and reduce the running time. Cinematic audiences often have not seen the Broadway original and are more accepting (or ignorant) of the changes Hollywood makes to the source material; at the same time, these audiences apparently do seem to care about the length of the adaptation.

From 1960 to 1969, nineteen films were produced based on Broadway musicals, with the average running time of 141 minutes. The second-longest film was *The Sound of Music*, the highest-grossing musical of all time despite its running time of 174 minutes.[32] Conversely, there were only nine Broadway musical-to-film transfers in the 2000–9 decade, and the average running time was 125 minutes, sixteen minutes shorter than the average of the 1960s. The three highest-grossing musicals of the decade had the shortest running times: *Mamma Mia!* (109 minutes), *Chicago* (113 minutes), and *Hairspray* (116 minutes). While length alone is not a metric for quality, it is interesting to note that the relationship of running times to box office earnings reversed from the 1960s to the 2000s (Figure 8.1). Musical films *under* 120 minutes in the 2000s were twice as likely to return big box office numbers (average = $229 million net) than those that were longer, whereas musical films *over* 141 minutes in the 1960s were twice as likely to show a substantial profit (average = $54 million net). The roadshow theatrical releases of the 1950s through the early 1970s contributed to this phenomenon by presenting musical films in reserved-seat engagements in major markets like New York City, Los

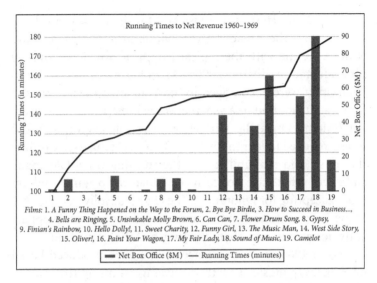

Films: 1. *A Funny Thing Happened on the Way to the Forum,* 2. *Bye Bye Birdie,* 3. *How to Succeed in Business...,* 4. *Bells are Ringing,* 5. *Unsinkable Molly Brown,* 6. *Can Can,* 7. *Flower Drum Song,* 8. *Gypsy,* 9. *Finian's Rainbow,* 10. *Hello Dolly!,* 11. *Sweet Charity,* 12. *Funny Girl,* 13. *The Music Man,* 14. *West Side Story,* 15. *Oliver!,* 16. *Paint Your Wagon,* 17. *My Fair Lady,* 18. *Sound of Music,* 19. *Camelot*

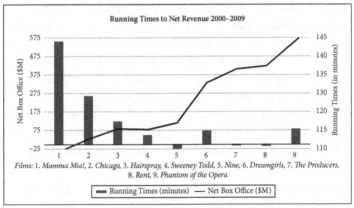

Films: 1. *Mamma Mia!,* 2. *Chicago,* 3. *Hairspray,* 4. *Sweeney Todd,* 5. *Nine,* 6. *Dreamgirls,* 7. *The Producers,* 8. *Rent,* 9. *Phantom of the Opera*

FIGURE 8.1 Comparison of running times to net revenue in Broadway musical films in the 1960s and 2000s.

Angeles, Chicago, and Washington, DC. These tended to be longer films (the original roadshow print of the nonmusical *Gone with the Wind* ran almost four hours), and were shown with an intermission, much like a Broadway show. Because of the long running times, theatres could book only one or two showings a day, limiting their income. For most musical roadshow releases, there was an overture, an entr'acte, and exit music. Musicals that had successful roadshow releases included *Oklahoma!* (1955), *South Pacific* (1958), *My Fair Lady* (1964), *Sound of Music* (1965), *Oliver!* (1968), *Funny Girl* (1968), and *Fiddler on the Roof* (1971).[33] By the time the 1972 film of *Cabaret* was released (124 minutes long), multiplexes were becoming the norm, and shorter running times prevailed. In the new millennium, it would appear that audiences still prefer shorter musical film adaptations.

## CASTING STRATEGIES IN MUSICAL FILM ADAPTATIONS

Replacing the originators of Broadway musical roles in the film adaptations with 'bankable Hollywood stars' is nothing new, and it has led to some interesting casting and miscasting over the years: *West Side Story* (Natalie Wood replacing Carol Lawrence), *My Fair Lady* (Audrey Hepburn replacing Julie Andrews), *The Sound of Music* (Julie Andrews replacing Mary Martin), and *Hello Dolly!* (Barbra Streisand replacing Carol Channing). In each case, Hollywood executives weighed potential 'star buzz' with the creative achievement of the original cast member.

Marketing studies[34] have looked at 'star buzz' as a method for hedging a movie's success. 'Film buzz' refers to the word of mouth that a film receives after it opens while 'star buzz' is more likely to enhance a film's prospects *before* it opens.[35] A star's power can reduce the 'terror of the box office'[36] Arthur De Vany theorizes that only a handful of stars are associated with higher revenue for their films, and most of these are not Broadway stars.[37] As an example, the 2005 film of *Rent* retained much of its original Broadway cast. The Broadway production had a devoted following of 'Rentheads' who would see the show numerous times,[38] and even though this was a very 'New York' show, it also did well on tour in major urban areas. The film, however, was a costly failure, earning only $31 million of its $40 million budget.[39] On the other hand, the *Mamma Mia!* film, despite receiving mixed notices for the casting of nonmusical stars like Meryl Streep and Pierce Brosnan,[40] was a huge success, earning over $600 million on a budget of $52 million.[41] While the tone and content of these two musicals is quite different and can account in part for the commercial potential, the strategy of keeping original Broadway casts for movie adaptations has not paid off in the twenty-first century.

Mel Brooks was responsible for approving the casting of all three versions of *The Producers*.[42] In 2001 he turned to Nathan Lane and Mathew Broderick at the end of the cast album recording session and proclaimed, 'We've got to make this [production] into a film!'[43] By recording the performances and musical numbers much as they had appeared on Broadway, the chemistry between Nathan Lane and Matthew Broderick could be further exploited and preserved. Lane's response to Brooks's idea was, '. . . with Danny DeVito as Max and Ben Stiller as Leo,' to which Brooks's immediate reply was 'No, you guys do it!'[44] With few exceptions, the original Broadway cast reprised their characters in the 2005 film. This idea of 'preservation' of the cast (and production) prevented the recursive film version from becoming a reimagined interpretation. The only exceptions were that Brad Oscar was replaced as Franz Liebkind by Will Ferrell, and Cady Huffman was replaced by Uma Thurman in the film. While Thurman and Ferrell lent a certain amount of Hollywood firepower favoured by the studio, they were not in leading roles. There is no question that Nathan Lane and Matthew Broderick have Broadway star power: their reunion in Broadway's revival of *The Odd Couple* (2005–6) and

*It's Only a Play* (2014–15) helped ensure enormous advance sales. *Playbill* reported that *The Odd Couple* sold $7 million in tickets on its first day of public sales.[45] Their 'star buzz' as a team, however, did not extend into films. This is further illustrated in a comparison of the marketing materials seen in ▶ video example 26.2, where Thurman is front and centre in the film's poster.

Unlike *The Producers*, the casting of the 2007 *Hairspray* followed the Hollywood tradition of replacing original stage cast members with more familiar Hollywood stars. John Travolta, Michelle Pfeiffer, Christopher Walken, Zac Efron, and Amanda Bynes were cast in featured roles. The latter two were chosen because of their teen appeal: Efron had recently appeared in Disney's highly successful *High School Musical* and Bynes had a large television and film teen base. Consistent over all three versions of *Hairspray*, an unknown actress, in this case Nikki Blonsky, was 'introduced' into the lead role of Tracy. This emphasizes the 'outsider' quality that she represents and reinforces her innocence.

Queen Latifah, who had been nominated as Best Supporting Actress in the 2002 *Chicago* film production, was cast as Motormouth Mabel. Latifah, a Grammy-winning hip-hop artist who is as adept with traditional pop vocals as she is with rap, helped reinforce the feminist message of the film and reach a broader music audience. Her rap and hip-hop work in the 1990s had caught the notice of critics and scholars alike, and Robin Roberts in the *African American Review* had praised Latifah's 'Ladies First' video: 'This dramatic and powerful rendering of an African American feminist message through a rap music video shows that even so unpropitious a setting as music videos or rap can be turned to feminist ends.'[46]

Consistent in the three *Hairspray* versions is the casting of Tracy Turnblad's mother Edna by a male actor. In John

Waters's original, Divine maintained the 'Dreamlanders' tradition of playing both a male and a female character in the same film, characters that represent the polar opposite of the other. His portrayal of Edna in drag is both campy and honest; 'she satirizes the myth of femininity, in particular the symbolic representation of motherhood marked by its repression of desire.'[47] *Hairspray* is a study of contrasts in its three mothers: the maternal Edna, the affectionate and open-minded yet outspoken Motormouth Mabel, and the cold and uncompromising Velma. The *New York Times* review noted, 'There's something touchingly humble about Mr Fierstein's performance, as there was about Divine's in the movie.'[48] Fierstein's Edna shared many of *Gypsy*'s Mama Rose's qualities: she was loving to Tracy, but she was a physical force to reckon with later in the story. Fierstein's gravelly voice and powerful stage presence provided a similar kind of gender double meaning to his/her relationship to her husband as well as to Tracy. Like Divine's performance, the interpretation could challenge heteronormative assumptions without offending the tourists:

> *Hairspray*'s now a tourist-friendly show; its second tour is out now, selling out in places like Tulsa, and all these places. So obviously, it took a little name recognition to get it out there, but it does great business. It does great business in New York for mainly kids and families—mothers and families, what you would probably call "red state folks," I guess.[49]

John Travolta was a surprise casting choice in the 2007 musical film since many had expected another gay man to play Edna as this casting offered the queer illusion of a happy marriage of two men. Waters stated in 2004, 'It encourages men to be married and have a functional marriage. [Same-sex marriage] isn't actually a part of the plot. [In the story] it's a marriage between a woman and a man, but everybody knows that [the woman] is a man. All of those things are really exciting if you can make them appeal to a whole family.'[50]

The casting of John Travolta, however, was more reminiscent of the casting of Robin Williams in *Mrs Doubtfire*: his latex-enhanced face is soft, and his performance is studied. While charming, Travolta misses all of the queer power of the previous two interpretations. His masculinity is buried in an elaborate fat suit and makeup, and he speaks in a tempered feminine voice. This is the most 'family-friendly' of the three interpretations because it doesn't challenge the heteronormative status quo (see ▶ video example 26.3). Director Adam Shankman said he cast Travolta in part because he is a musical film icon, having appeared in *Grease*, one of the most commercially successful Hollywood musicals, and *Saturday Night Fever*, a nonmusical film that nonetheless showcased Travolta's skill as a dancer. Shankman has stated that he saw Travolta as Edna as a dancing Hippo from *Fantasia*, one who could 'dance on clouds.'[51] The commercial considerations are clear: Travolta's star power is ranked by 'The Numbers' at 37th place, while Harvey Fierstein's ranks at 1,383.[52]

'Star buzz' as a casting strategy paid off in the movie adaptation of *Hairspray* but not in *The Producers*. Even though Harvey Fierstein's Broadway Edna received rave notices equal to those of Lane and Broderick, the casting of John Travolta created 'buzz' about the film along with an ensemble cast of movie, music industry, and television stars. Uma Thurman is draped provocatively across the desk in the posters for the 2005 version of *The Producers*, but she and Will Ferrell ('The Numbers' = #86) were in secondary roles, and Nathan Lane (#737) and Matthew Broderick (#543), while veterans of both stage and screen, did not create the same 'buzz' that they did on Broadway.

## CONCLUSION: FINDING AN AUDIENCE FOR STAGE-TO-SCREEN ADAPTATIONS

Beyond the aesthetic, structural, and cultural differences among the two Broadway shows and four films, the success or failure of each of the productions can also be attributed to the target audience demographics. The original film of *The Producers* was made in 1968, a year when substantial changes were happening culturally and socially in the United States, reflected in the habits of ticket buyers. The Motion Picture Association of American had just introduced a rating system,[53] and more sophisticated films were being aimed at younger audiences. Forty-eight percent of the moviegoing audience that year were between sixteen and twenty-four years old.[54] The top-grossing films of that year were *2001: A Space Odyssey* (gross: $56 million), the musical *Funny Girl* with Barbra Streisand ($52 million), and Disney's *The Love Bug* ($51 million).

*The Producers* film of 1968 was aimed at an older demographic, one that would remember and had enjoyed the Sid Caesar–style television comedies of the fifties. Neil Simon, who was also part of the *Show of Shows* team, had his play *The Odd Couple* transformed into a film in 1968 to great acclaim and box office: it was the fourth highest-grossing film of the year ($44 million). Both films feature male leads of opposite types, but *The Producers* is about two men and a swindle, while *The Odd Couple* focuses on two men trying to reset their lives after divorce. *The Odd Couple* also had the advantage of being based on a hit Broadway play that gave it name recognition at the box office.

Since the early 2000s, tourists have purchased 66 percent of all Broadway tickets, and their average age is 42.5. Fifty- to sixty-year-olds comprise the largest single group of theatregoers. The older audience would have had a memory of the Mel Brooks movies of the 1960s and 1970s as well as knowledge of the Golden Age of musicals from the 1940s through the early 1960s. This nostalgia would have driven the audiences to see the Broadway adaptation of *The Producers* supervised by Mel Brooks that recycled the same plot and characters as the original film while sending up the traditions of musical theatre.

These ticker buyers, older and affluent, helped drive up demand for the show and inspired the producers to introduce 'premium seating' with fifty prime seats at each performance at a cost of $480 each.[55] While the well-heeled older patrons who could afford tickets made the Broadway show an expensive commodity, this over-fifty demographic accounted for only 21 percent of the moviegoing audience in 2008 (Figure 8.2). While reviewers pointed to the 2005 musical film's lack of success because it was too much of a 'faithful' rendition of the Broadway hit rather than a unique cinematic adaptation, there is no evidence that there was a substantial target audience for this kind of film in the first place. A big-screen musical cannot be successfully marketed to only 21 percent of the potential marketplace.

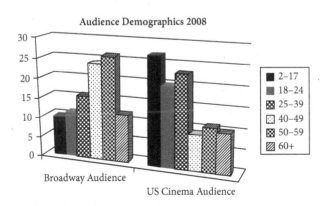

FIGURE 8.2 Audience Demographics of Broadway and Cinema Audiences - 2008.

The Broadway show's success also seemed to rely on the leading characters' chemistry. Jesse McKinley wrote in the *New York Times* in November 2003 that attendance at the Broadway *Producers* had dropped precipitately after Nathan Lane and Matthew Broderick had left the show. When Broderick and Lane returned for a four-month encore in early 2004, tickets were sold out for their entire engagement. Then sales fell again.[56] The audience that supported the show was also considered:

> One theory, especially prevalent among insiders, is that, with its low-brow Mel Brooks humor and winking high-brow references, 'The Producers' is designed to appeal to show-biz savvy literates. And that demographic, the thinking goes, is growing smaller by the day.
>
> 'I'm going to be blunt,' said Rocco Landesman, the President of Jujamcyn Theaters, which owns the St. James. 'The show is good, the audiences are bad. It never occurred to me that this show was pitched too high for a Broadway audience.' With today's Broadway audience largely made of out-of-towners and tourists, he said, 'two-thirds of the show sails entirely over the heads of the audience.' And the fewer people who get the jokes, the fewer people who tell their friends to go.[57]

Sociologist Herbert Gans in his 1974 book *Popular Culture and High Culture* theorizes: 'Broadway musicals used to be written for the upper-middle public, but today this is only occasionally the case, although its younger members are probably the major consumers of folk music and melodic rock.'[58] Conversely, he reasons that film musicals are for the lower-middle class as '[they] remain loyal to American films, although they may only go to see big musicals and other spectaculars.'[59] While the broad humour of the original version of *The Producers* might appeal to a divergent audience, the Broadway and movie-musical references in the 2005 film version might also 'sail over the heads of the audience,' particularly the 'lower-middle class' movie audience outside of New York City. That same audience might also recognize that *Hairspray* celebrates the lower-middle class underdogs while *The Producers* abuses them.

*Hairspray* was a breakout success for John Waters in 1987 and was part of a movement of outrageous cult films of the 1970s and 1980s. Like the 1968 movie of *The Producers* (and *Little Shop of Horrors*), it was a low-budget film. *Hairspray*, however relied on camp, nostalgia, and a quirky sense of humour. It found a niche audience in the larger, under-thirty demographic. The Broadway production of the *Hairspray* musical had the nostalgic fifties-style popular songs and nostalgia from the pre-Beatles 1960s to appeal to the older audience while it thematically focused on the youthful hopes and dreams of the teenage characters for the younger audience. This was the *Grease* for the new millennium: it could feature contemporary pop stars while (unlike *Grease*) offering retrospective social commentary. The adaptation of the musical film in 2007 kept the heart and spirit of the original production, but was squarely aimed at the younger demographic:

> The secret of the new film . . . is best summed up in a word: 'Reinvention,' says producer Craig Zadan, who, with Neil Meron, guided 2002's 'Chicago' to six Oscars. 'The movie musicals that have failed [in the past] simply filmed the Broadway show they were based on. We don't do that,' Zadan says. 'You honor the show, but then you say, "Well *this* is great, but *that* won't work." You reinvent it for people who don't know the show.'[60]

The current crop of planned Hollywood musicals—*The Book of Mormon, Spring Awakening, Avenue Q,* and

*Wicked*—are all aimed at this younger demographic. The recent film adaptation of *Into the Woods* highlights one of Stephen Sondheim's most commercial works, and while it pulls from classic fairy tales, it is a contemporary piece. Following in the footsteps of *Hairspray*, the recent film adaptation demonstrates that using stars (Johnny Depp and Meryl Streep), targeting a family audience by editing out potentially salacious content, and staying relatively short (124 minutes) can be a successful formula. The anticipated film production of *Gypsy* with Barbra Streisand, which would presumably attract an older audience, has been put on hold twice since 2012. Screenwriter Richard LaGravenese has stated, 'The difficult problem [with *Gypsy*] is making it cinematic,'[61] but whether it could reach a younger audience and earn back its $50 million budget on a film with an aging star must certainly be a concern.

Even though 40 percent of Broadway musicals since 2000 have been based on film sources, the Hollywood musical films planned or in production in 2017 are either original works or adaptations of plays and books and not originally based on a film. Of the most recent Broadway musicals based on films— *Once, Bullets over Broadway, Rocky, Ghost, Kinky Boots, Bring It On: The Musical, Legally Blonde: The Musical, Carrie: The Musical*—none is currently slated for recursive musical film adaptations.

The Walt Disney Company, however, has seen the commercial potential in its film library and has created a new kind of recursive adaptation of at least two of its animated films that have had Broadway success: *Beauty and the Beast* (2017) and *The Lion King* (2019). By creating live-action-with-computer-generated-imagery films based on the Broadway and Hollywood hits, a new breed of film-to-stage-to-film adaptations featuring contemporary stars, target demographics, and shorter running times emerges.

*Hairspray*'s success and *The Producers*' movie musical failure have cemented a new exemplar of recursive adaptation that promises to be a turning point in future Hollywood musicals.

## NOTES

1. According to TheNumbers.com, *Hello Dolly!* (domestic gross: $33.2 million; budget $25 million) and *Paint Your Wagon* (domestic gross $31.68 million; budget $20 million) were both in the 'highest grossing' lists of their years, but the expensive budgets (plus marketing and distribution costs) meant that their backers lost money.
2. Matthew Kennedy, *Roadshow! The Fall of Film Musicals in the 1960s* (New York: Oxford University Press, 2015), 6.
3. I counted these shows using Playbill.com databases, and I am indebted to Ken Davenport's theproducersperspective.com work noted below to confirm my counts.
4. I've used Broadway.com and Playbill.com databases for my count. I also recommend producer Howard Sherman's 'Do Revivals Inhibit New Broadway Musicals?' (http://www.hesher man.com/2012/07/10/do-revivals-inhibit-new-broadway-music als/ and Ken Davenport's 'Does a Revival's Success Depend on the Success of the Original?' (https://www.theproducerspers pective.com/my_weblog/2015/11/50-years-of-broadway-musi cal-source-material-a-by-the-numbers-infographic.html for analysis on revivals and the statistical advantage they have over new shows.
5. Renata Adler, 'The Producers,' *New York Times*, 9 March 1968, p. A38.
6. Stanley Kauffmann, 'The Producers,' *New Republic* 158, no. 15 (April 1968): 24.
7. Pauline Kael, *Going Steady* (Boston: Atlantic Monthly Press, 1970), 66.
8. American Film Institute, 'AFI's 100 Years . . . 100 Laughs,' http://www.afi.com/100Years/laughs.aspx, accessed 30 June 2016.

9. Damon Wise, 'The Making of The Producers,' *Guardian*, 15 August 2008, https://www.theguardian.com/film/2008/aug/16/ comedy.theproducers, accessed 12 February 17.

10. 'Box Office: *Polyester*,' Internet Movie Database, http://www. imdb.com/title/tt0069089/, accessed 12 February 2017.

11. 'Box Office: *Beetlejuice*,' Internet Movie Database, http://www. imdb.com/title/tt0094721/, accessed 12 February 2017.

12. Jessica Goldstein, 'On Hairspray's 25th Anniversary "Buddy Deane" Committee Looks Back,' *Washington Post*, 18 January 2013, https://www.washingtonpost.com/entertainment/tv/on-hairsprays-25th-anniversary-buddydeane-committee-looks-back/2013/01/17/a45a1cc2-5c23-11e2-88d0-c4cf65c3ad15_story. html?utm:term=.8516f36a010e, accessed 12 February 2017.

13. Janet Maslin, 'Film: "Hairspray" Comedy from John Waters,' *New York Times*, 28 February 1988, p. C17.

14. J. Wynn Rousuck, 'A Conversation with John Waters and Margo Lion,' in Marc Shaiman, Thomas Meehan, Scott Wittman and Mark O'Donnell, *Hairspray: The Roots* (New York: Faber and Faber, 2003), 12.

15. Rousuck, 'A Conversation with John Waters and Margo Lion,' 8.

16. Mel Brooks and Tom Mehan, *The Producers: The Book, Lyrics, and Story behind the Biggest Hit in Broadway History! How We Did It* (New York: Roundtable Press, 2001), 19.

17. Jerome Robbins popularized the opening number 'rules' in his influence in the creation of 'Comedy Tonight' as a show doctor on *A Funny Thing Happened on the Way to the Forum* and the creation of 'Tradition' for *Fiddler on the Roof*. See Altman and Kaufman, *The Making of a Musical: Fiddler on the Roof* (New York: Crown, 1971).

18. Michael Buckley, 'Stage to Screens: "The Producers" Film—Chatting with Stroman and Beach,' *Playbill.com*, 20 November 2005, http://www.playbill.com/article/stage-to-screens-the-producers-film-chatting-with-stroman-and-beach-com-129302, accessed 15 January 2017.

19. Brooks and Meehan, *The Producers*, 154.

20. Stuart M. Kaminsky, 'Mel Brooks—Director,' http://www.filmre ference.com/Directors-Be-Bu/Brooks-Mel.html, accessed 1 February 2017.

21. Brooks and Meehan, *The Producers*, 97.
22. 'Nathan Lane: Hollywood, Homophobia and Mel Brooks,' *Independent*, 17 December 2005, http://www.independent. co.uk/arts-entertainment/films/features/nathan-lane-hollyw ood-homophobia-and-mel-brooks-519486.html, accessed 2 February 2017.
23. Jeff Labrecque, 'Blazing Saddles at 40: A Conversation with Mel Brooks,' *Entertainment*, 1 May 2014, http://ew.com/arti cle/2014/05/01/blazing-saddles-mel-brooks/, accessed 15 January 2017.
24. 'Box Office: *Brokeback* Mountain,' Internet Movie Database, http://www.imdb.com/title/tt0388795/business?ref_=tt_dt_bus, accessed 5 February 2017.
25. Marc Shaiman, Thomas Meehan, Scott Wittman and Mark O'Donnell, *Hairspray: The Roots*, 7.
26. Dana Heller, *Hairspray* (New York: Wiley-Blackwell, 2011), 122.
27. Heller, *Hairspray*, 123.
28. Adam Shankman, 'Putting New Moves on *Hairspray*,' interview with Terry Gross, *Fresh Air*, National Public Radio, 19 July 2007, http://www.npr.org/templates/story/story.php?storyId=12093 815, accessed 15 December 2016.
29. Thomas Leitch, 'Twelve Fallacies in Contemporary Adaptation Theory,' *Criticism* 45, no. 2 (Spring 2003): 161.
30. I have used the Internet Broadway Database (IBDb.com) and the original *Playbills* to calculate running times.
31. I used Box Office Mojo to calculate gross income and the Internet Movie Database to look up running times.
32. The longest is *Camelot*, which at 179 minutes is still substantially shorter than the original Broadway show that ran well over three hours.
33. Matthew Kennedy theorizes in *Roadshow! The Fall of Film Musicals in the 1960s* that Hollywood tried too hard to replicate the success of *Sound of Music* and ended up with failures like *Camelot*.
34. A. S. Ravid, 'Information, Blockbusters, and Stars: A Study of the Film Industry,' *Journal of Business* 72, no. 4 (October 1999): 463–492.
35. Ekaterina Karniouchina, 'Impact of Star and Movie Buzz on Motion Picture Distribution and Box Office Revenue,'

*International Journal of Research in Marketing* 28, no. 1 (2011): 62–74.

36. Arthur De Vray, *Hollywood Economics: How Extreme Uncertainty Shapes the Film Industry* (New York: Routledge, 2004), 242–268.

37. De Vany, *Hollywood Economics*, 92.

38. Kay Hymowitz, 'Among the "Rentheads," ' *Wall Street Journal*, 13 June 2008, p. W.11.

39. Boxoffice mojo.com, http://www.boxofficemojo.com/movies/?id=rent.htm, accessed 17 February 2017.

40. In his *New York Times* review (18 July 2008, p. E1) of the film, A. O. Scott stated, 'It is safe to say that Ms. Streep gives the worst performance of her career.'

41. Boxofficemojo.com. http://www.boxofficemojo.com/movies/?id=mammamia.htm, accessed 17 February 2017.

42. Brooks and Meehan, *The Producers*, 35.

43. Mel Brooks, *Recording the Producers: A Musical Romp with Mel Brooks* (Masterworks Broadway, DVD), 1:22:33.

44. Brooks, *Recording the Producers*, 1:22:45.

45. Robert Simonson. '*Odd Couple* Sells $7 Million in Tickets in First Day of Sales,' *Playbill.com*, 7 June 2005, http://www.playbill.com/article/odd-couple-sells-7-million-in-tickets-in-first-day-of-sales-com-126359, accessed 4 February 2017.

46. Robin Roberts. ' "Ladies First": Queen Latifah's Afrocentric Feminist Video,' *African American Review* 28, no. 2 (Summer 1994): 257.

47. Angela Stukator, ' "It's Not Over . . .": Comedy and Body Politics,' in *Bodies Out of Bounds: Fatness and Transgression* (Berkeley: University of California Press, 2001), 209.

48. Ben Brantley, 'Theatre Review: Through Hot Pink Glasses, a World That's Nice,' *New York Times*, 16 August 2002, p. E1.

49. 'Interview: Adam Epstein; Producer of *Hairspray, Wedding Singer*,' *Broadway Bullet*, posted 19 June 2007, http://www.broadwaybullet.com/?p=147.

50. Chris Davis, 'The Man Who Hated Musicals,' *Memphis Flyer*, 17 December 2004, http://www.memphisflyer.com/memphis/the-man-who-hated-musicals/Content?oid=1115686, accessed 10 January 2017.

51. Shankman, 'Putting New Moves on *Hairspray*.'

52. http://www.the-numbers.com/people/. This aggregator calculates star power based on average box office and number of films.

53. The original Motion Picture Association ratings system was introduced in November 1968 as a replacement for the 1930s Motion Picture Production Code in order to provide greater flexibility to filmmakers who wanted to make more sophisticated films while (voluntarily) restricting the age groups that could gain admission. The first ratings included M (Mature: parental discretion advised) and R (Restricted: persons under sixteen admitted only with a parent or guardian).

54. A 1968 Yankelovich and Associates survey that had been commissioned by the Motion Picture Association of America (MPAA) concluded that 'being young and single is the overriding demographic for being a frequent and enthusiastic movie-goer.'

55. Jesse McKinley, 'For the Asking, a $480 Seat,' New York Times, 26 October 2001, p. A1.

56. According to the Internet Broadway Database, attendance fell beginning March 2002 after Lane and Broderick left, dropping to a low of 61 percent the week of 7 September 2003. Attendance jumped back to 100 percent from January to April 2004 when they returned. Sales steadily declined afterwards until the show closed in 2007.

57. Jesse McKinley, 'The Case of the Incredible Shrinking Blockbuster,' New York Times, 2 November 2003, p. AR1.

58. Herbert J. Gans, Popular Culture and High Culture: An Analysis and Evaluation of Taste (New York: Basic Books, 1970), 83.

59. Gans, Popular Culture, 86.

60. Brantley Bardin, 'The Mane Event,' New York Daily News, 15 July 2007, http://www.nydailynews.com/entertainment/tv-movies/mane-event-article-1.267872, accessed 10 February 2017.

61. Robert Viagas and Michael Gioia, 'Barbara Streisand Gypsy Film Script Loses Backer/Distributor,' Playbill.com, 3 August 2016), http://www.playbill.com/article/barbra-streisand-gypsy-film-script-loses-backer-distributor, accessed 4 February 2017.

# 9

# Rescoring *Anything Goes* in 1930s Hollywood

ALLISON ROBBINS

■ □ ■

ON 24 JANUARY 1936, PARAMOUNT released *Anything Goes*, a musical starring Bing Crosby and Ethel Merman. Based on the Broadway show of the same name, it met with frustration from Richard Watts Jr, a *New York Herald Tribune* film critic familiar with the stage version:

[T]he cinema edition of 'Anything Goes' is, despite its attractive pictorial background, a dull and commonplace musical comedy, with several good songs and a great mass of ineffective comedy and romance. Since on the stage it was one of the outstanding musical shows of recent seasons, I think that I may not be altogether wrong in blaming its decline on the failure of the picture to follow the original edition more carefully.[1]

Watts's main complaint was the film's purging of Cole Porter's 'distinguished and exhilarating' music; gone were 'All through the Night,' 'Blow, Gabriel, Blow,' and other songs.

Watts's critique of *Anything Goes* mirrors many accounts of Broadway-to-Hollywood musical adaptations, which are typically judged by their fidelity to a cherished songwriter's original score. Most damning is when the studios replace the music of a Broadway giant with tunes by Hollywood songwriters. 'In Hollywood nothing is sacred, especially a New York songwriter,' Thomas Hischak grumbles; 'Irving Berlin, the Gershwins, Jerome Kern, and all the great songwriters saw their Broadway scores skewered beyond recognition.'[2] Why Hollywood producers altered Broadway's music in the 1930s is rather straightforward. In order to avoid expensive synchronization licences and to profit from sheet music and record sales, the film industry had made a substantial investment in music publishing companies in the late 1920s. Newly written songs by Hollywood songwriters were then copyrighted to in-house publishing firms, and the studios subsequently made money from songs plugged in their films. There was thus financial incentive to drop an old score and add a new one when a studio bought and adapted a stage property.

That said, the studios' financial motivations were intertwined with an aesthetic division within the songwriting community itself, and in many ways, the Hollywood and Tin Pan Alley mergers finalized rather than initiated Broadway's separation from a popular music industry focused primarily on stand-alone, hit songs. Below, I detail how this economic, aesthetic, and cultural context shaped Paramount's film adaptation of *Anything Goes*. At the studio, the musical confronted a production environment in which interpolations were common, song sales mattered more than wit, and risqué content was frowned upon, a combination that proved deadly for Porter's score. I detail the cuts and revisions to his music as well as the songs that the studio added after music department head Nathaniel Finston assigned Leo Robin, Richard Whiting, and other songwriters to the film. The resulting adaptation epitomizes Hollywood's commercial approach to making musicals, much as the stage version reflects Broadway's increasing disinterest in songs that appealed to as broad an audience as possible. Hollywood's devotion to and Broadway's divorce from hit songwriting makes faithful film adaptations unlikely, I argue, especially when 'fidelity' is defined by allegiance to Broadway's canonized songwriters rather than the commercial goals of Hollywood's tunesmiths.

## PARAMOUNT, MUSIC PUBLISHING, AND STUDIO SONGWRITERS

In the summer of 1928, seven years before Paramount would begin production on *Anything Goes*, the studio offered to buy the song catalogues of Harms and Robbins Music, then the two largest music publishing companies in the United States.[3] The studio's bid, the first of its kind in Hollywood, ultimately failed, but in August of the same year, the studio struck a more modest deal with Harms, in which Paramount and the publishing firm together created Famous Music Corp. The first songs entered into the Famous catalogue were theme songs associated with moving pictures; Paramount and Harms agreed to split evenly any royalties earned from sheet music sales and licencing fees.[4] In 1929, however, Warner Bros. purchased Harms and its associated firms, including Famous Music Corp., which complicated Paramount's original deal with the publishing company. Paramount reacted by purchasing 80 percent of the stock of Spier & Coslow, Inc., a small independent publishing company headed by Larry Spier and Sam Coslow.[5]

This purchase and other labyrinthine deals between the studios and publishing houses affected how individual songwriters like Spier and Coslow obtained contracts in Hollywood. At first, lyricists and composers who went west following the Tin Pan Alley mergers moved from studio to studio, in part because songwriter contracts in the film industry were only six- or twelve-month agreements. But following the Warner Bros.-Harms deal, many songwriters saw their agreements revised, and in the early 1930s, each studio contracted a more or less stable group of songwriters as studio music departments were established and associated publishing houses stabilized. At Paramount, Nathaniel Finston hired Coslow (who received a five-year contract with the studio when it acquired his publishing firm), Leo Robin, Richard Whiting, Gus Kahn, Fred Ahlert, Roy Turk, and Walter Donaldson.[6] Cole Porter was not a member of this cohort; in the 1920s Harms published his songs, and after 1935 he worked with Max Dreyfus's Chappell, Inc., a publishing house that remained independent from the Hollywood studios.[7]

The film and music industry mergers affected not only which studios hired which songwriters but also the songs they produced for Hollywood films. For starters, different studios had access to different existing catalogues—Warner Bros., for example, could use the music of George Cohan, Victor Herbert, and Sigmund Romberg free of charge after a deal with Witmark.[8] The main goal of Hollywood's acquisition of publishers, however, was to control copyright of new songs plugged in their pictures. In adaptations of stage works, this focus resulted in shredded Broadway scores, as studio songwriters replaced existing songs with their own. It also affected the kinds of songs they added. Though the stage and screen shared the same popular song conventions, there were nonetheless important stylistic differences between Broadway and Hollywood songs.[9] The film industry, with its close ties to music publishers, continued to rely on Tin Pan Alley's approach to songwriting, while Broadway songwriters, especially those who worked on book musicals, deliberately moved away from a broadly popular aesthetic. 'In effect,' Philip Furia and Laurie Patterson note, 'writing songs for Hollywood was less like writing for a Broadway musical and more like working on Tin Pan Alley.'[10]

Broadway's stylistic separation from Tin Pan Alley was apparent as early as the 1910s, when some publishers claimed that stage hits were more of a gamble. A song that went over on the stage could potentially sell sheet music and earn profit for a publisher, but it was not what Edward M. Wickes, author of *Writing the Popular Song* (1916), referred to as a 'natural hit' that 'could be made popular by any up-to-date publisher.'[11] 'In saying that a stage song does not sell,' Wickes explains, 'I mean that the average stage song is like a hundred-to-one-shot in a horse race. There is always a slim chance for either to win out, but few like to bank on the chance.'[12] Notably, what made a stage song risky was not its structure, which Wickes describes as similar to a 'straight comic song,' with 'short verses, extra choruses, and obvious puns in the lines preceding the repetition of the title at the end of the chorus.' There was, however, a difference in the overall quality, in that in 'the majority of cases the stage song is a cleverly written piece of work, containing some very good lines.'[13]

In the 1920s and 1930s, the clever quality of stage songs, also referred to as production songs, became more pronounced. In *The Art of Song Writing* (1928), Al Dubin explains that though production songs and hit songs encompass the same genres— ballads, novelty songs, comedy songs, dance songs, semi-classic songs, and patriotic songs—production songs 'have a style that is somewhat different from the average popular song which can be noted only by studying them carefully.'[14] Abner Silver and Robert Bruce's *How to Write and Sell a Song Hit* (1939) offers more detail on this stylistic difference. Production songs, they argue, were distinguished by qualities that conveyed professionalism, artistry, and complexity. They altered the standard 32-bar form and used the ABAC song form more often than the average AABA hit, because that pattern 'has the advantage of enabling the writer to give an unusual 'punch' ending to the song.'[15] The lyrics were often 'more outstanding than the tune' and contain 'tricky and clever rhyming schemes'—Silver and Bruce cite Cole Porter's 'You're the Top' as an example, as well as the songs by Richard Rodgers, Lorenz Hart, and Irving Berlin.[16] Finally, production songs required 'a trained singer to give the melody full justice.'[17] 'The amateur should steer away from attempting to write this type of song,' Silver and Bruce write. 'It is obvious that the producer of a musical show or a musical picture would insist upon having recognized professional writers work on the musical score.'[18]

The shift towards sophistication on the stage has been observed by scholars of the musical and is typically attributed to changes in stage productions. In the 1910s, up-and-coming songwriters usually interpolated songs into existing shows, but by 1920, Geoffrey Block notes, 'Berlin, Kern, and Gershwin had also composed Broadway scores of their own.'[19] Most of these scores were associated with a story, requiring songs that were 'conceived or revised for specific characters in specific situations.'[20] Narrative complexity thus led to musical complexity, Block argues, as songwriters supported character and plot development. Similarly, Phil Furia argues that the 'self-contained songs and sketches' of 1920s and 1930s revues encouraged attention to 'particularized character or situation,' which led to 'wit and sophistication' in lyrics and music.[21] Like Block, he suggests that the format of stage productions—in this case revues rather than book shows—created a shift in musical and lyrical style.

Writing in 1930, Tin Pan Alley chronicler Isaac Goldberg had a different interpretation. He attributed the increasing sophistication of Broadway lyrics not to book shows or witty revues but to the aesthetic goals of 'modern' songwriters like Porter, Hart, Ira Gershwin, Howard Dietz, Paul James, and Dorothy Fields. These men and women belonged to what Goldberg called an 'undiscriminating cult of sophistication,' and with their 'sometimes distressingly self-conscious' lyrics, they hoped to restore 'the words to something like the importance that they had in the flourishing period of our higher class musical show.' Their efforts, Goldberg writes, 'may yet help to improve dialogue, and so lead to plot and to a more organic conception of what we loosely call comic opera.'[22] But there were consequences in striving for a highbrow art. 'So doing,' Goldberg warns, 'they endanger their popularity, as truly good words always endanger a song in Tin Pan Alley. They make, as truly good music makes, for smaller and better audiences. This may be art, after a fashion, but as business it is no fashion at all. Wherever we find a pronounced quality in words or music we may be sure that we have begun the ascent from Tin Pan Alley.'[23] Here, Goldberg identifies the divide that would define Hollywood and Broadway throughout the 1930s: the wit and sophistication of Broadway was rarely at home in the blatantly commercial setting of Hollywood's Tin Pan Alley.

A desire to write highbrow songs likely had special significance for Broadway songwriters who were Jewish, as their ethnic identity remained closely associated with commercial entertainment. As Andrea Most notes, the most successful Broadway songwriters were the 'Ivy League-educated, 'uptown' Jews,'[24] and for them, achieving a sophisticated aesthetic on Broadway paralleled their rise in sociocultural status. Most writes, 'As they achieved success, they moved from urban Jewish neighborhoods to exclusive (and often restricted) addresses in Manhattan, Long Island, Connecticut, and rural Pennsylvania. During the Depression and war years, they largely distanced themselves from Jewish organizational and religious life.'[25] This distancing from some aspects of Jewish experience included, it seems, an aesthetic distance from Tin Pan Alley, where many first-generation Jews got their start in show business. Dorothy Fields, Jerome Kern, and Richard Rodgers likely sought the labels they earned in one of Louis Sobol's 'Voice of Broadway' columns: Fields was called 'most sophisticated,' Kern, 'most erudite,' and Rodgers, 'most elite.'[26]

Not all Jewish Americans felt the need or desire to separate themselves from Tin Pan Alley, and for those who continued to work in 'lowbrow' entertainment outlets like Hollywood, the upward mobility of Fields, Kern, and Rodgers was as much a break from Jewish identity as it was a source of inspiration. Rodgers's initial meeting with Jack Warner underscores that the Jewish producers in Hollywood were well aware and somewhat wary of songwriters' aspirations. Upon welcoming him and Lorenz Hart to Hollywood in the 1930s, Rodgers remembers that Warner greeted them 'in the thickest Yiddish accent I've ever heard. "I dun't van't none of your highbrow sunk-making," he warned us as his smile quickly vanished.'[27] It was a joke, but one with a bite. Kurt Weill experienced a similar reprimand in 1937 from producer Walter Wanger, who told Weill his music was not 'popular enough' for his picture. When Weill told Wanger that he could write 'as popular songs' as Ralph Erwin and Robert Stoltz 'but better,' Wanger replied, 'To hell with better, I don't want better.'[28] Broadway retained clear highbrow associations for songwriters who were not Jewish as well. Al Dubin's daughter Patricia McGuire remembers Dubin saying that he too could have written 'nothing but sophisticated lyrics' like Porter if he 'had been a millionaire's son.' 'Cole Porter didn't have to please Warner Brothers,' Dubin complained; 'I have to write lyrics that the general public will buy; songs that have commercial appeal; that make money. If I could have written whatever I wanted, whenever I wanted, I might have been a lot better lyric writer.'[29]

By the early 1930s, songwriters who worked on opposite sides of the highbrow-lowbrow divide started having a difficult time working together. The collaboration between Richard Whiting and Oscar Hammerstein on the book show *Free for All* (1931) is a case in point. Whiting had established himself as a Tin Pan Alley songwriter in the 1910s and 1920s and had been on staff at Paramount since 1929 writing hits for Maurice

Chevalier, and Hammerstein had recently collaborated with Kern on several book shows in the 1920s. Whiting claimed Hammerstein was difficult to work with, however, because he did not write lyrics that 'meant something in every line.' Robert Russell Bennett clarifies,

[Whiting] probably meant that every line of a pop lyric has to make its own point. 'Beyond the Blue Horizon' means all it will ever mean as long as it lives. 'Yes, Sir, That's My Baby' and you go and cash your ticket. 'Ain't She Sweet!' That's all you need to know or ever will know. In Oscar's theater you have time to develop your story: 'Fish gotta swim and birds gotta fly. I gotta love one man till I die. Can't help lovin' that man of mine.'[30]

Hammerstein was, in other words, the modern lyricist described by Isaac Goldberg. 'Can't Help Lovin' That Man' has a catch like any other Tin Pan Alley hit, but it resonates because of the allusions to inevitability that build to the hook: fish swim, birds fly, I love. Whiting, by contrast, preferred lyrics that did not need an elaborate buildup.

The film studios, with their associated publishing firms, were happy to exploit the rift in the songwriting community, as most Hollywood songwriters wanted hits as badly as the studios that hired them. Sam Coslow describes what Hollywood meant to him:

By means of the film, the song was pounded into the ears and brains of millions of people—literally captive audiences. With radio, you could keep on talking, reading, playing cards, or doing any number of things that might take your attention away from the music. But in a movie house, you had no choice but to listen—and we made damn sure that [a song] was reprised vocally a few times in the film, and scored orchestrally at the hint of any love scene. It was far and away the most effective form of songplugging the public had ever been exposed to, and the

> Hollywood music crowd capitalized on it to the hilt. . . . Instant hits—the songwriter's Utopia![31]

Broadway songwriters interested in book musicals found Hollywood anything but a utopia. 'He never told me in so many words, but Jerry Kern must have been miserable in Hollywood, and I know Oscar Hammerstein was,' Richard Rodgers writes in his autobiography. 'The people who succeeded in moving pictures—and I'm talking primarily about lyricists and composers—were those who did not have an extended background in the theatre.'[32]

Rodgers speaks from his own experience. He and Hart had contributed songs to Paramount's 1932 film *Love Me Tonight*, a musical that remains beloved by critics for a score that blurs the boundary between spoken and sung dialogue in order to give 'the entire film a firmer musical structure,' in Rodgers's words.[33] The film was less impressive, however, from a commercial perspective. Paramount's music department head Nathaniel Finston received stats on song sales from *Love Me Tonight* along with other musicals produced at the studio between 1929 and 1933. 'Isn't It Romantic?', the top song from *Love Me Tonight*, sold fewer than 40,000 copies (see Table 9.1). Only one film produced in the same five-year period, the lackluster *Paramount on Parade*, had a less impressive return. By contrast, *The Big Broadcast*, a musical starring Bing Crosby and released the same year as *Love Me Tonight*, sold over 200,000 copies of Leo Robin and Ralph Rainger's song 'Please.'[34] *Love Me Tonight* may have been a critical darling, but the bottom line was that Rodgers and Hart did not produce a mega-hit for the studio. That Paramount turned to musicals featuring Bing Crosby singing hit songs made financial sense.

This quantitative focus on song sales also points to how Hollywood songwriters were assigned to films. Department heads like Finston took a songwriter's artistic strengths into

Table 9.1

# TOP-SELLING SONGS IN PARAMOUNT MUSICALS, 1929–1933

| Production | Year | Song title | Composer | Lyricist | No. Copies sold |
|---|---|---|---|---|---|
| Innocents of Paris | 1929 | 'Louise' | Whiting | Robin | 385,058 |
| Sweetie | 1929 | 'My Sweeter Than Sweet' | Whiting | Marion, Jr. | 175,315 |
| Love Parade | 1929 | 'Dream Lover' | Schertzinger | Grey | 70,146 |
| The Big Pond | 1930 | 'You Brought a New King of Love to Me' | Fain, Kahal & Norman | Norman | 275,750 |
| Honey | 1930 | 'Sing You Sinners' | Harling | Coslow | 110,229 |
| Paramount on Parade | 1930 | 'Sweeping the Clouds Away' | Coslow | Coslow | 36,221 |
| Monte Carlo | 1930 | 'Beyond the Blue Horizon' | Harling & Whiting | Robin | 80,957 |
| Playboy of Paris | 1930 | 'My Ideal' | Whiting & Chase | Robin | 64,309 |
| The Big Broadcast | 1932 | 'Please' | Rainger | Robin | 216,035 |
| One Hour With You | 1932 | 'One Hour With You' | Whiting | Robin | 75,100 |
| Love Me Tonight | 1932 | 'Isn't It Romantic?' | Rodgers | Hart | 37,266 |
| Hello, Everybody | 1933 | 'Moon Song' | Coslow | Coslow | 117,084 |

account when delegating production assignments, but the biggest factor was a songwriter's capacity to write a top-selling tune. Those writers who made a studio the most money were rewarded with more films and higher salaries in hopes of replicating past successes. In 1934, only one Paramount film, the Bing Crosby vehicle *She Loves Me Not*, boasted especially strong song sales: collectively, the four songs featured in the film—'Straight from the Shoulder, Right from the Heart,' 'I'm Hummin', I'm Whistlin', I'm Singin',' 'Put a Little Rhythm in Everything You Do,' and 'Love in Bloom'—sold more than 350,000 copies.[35] The two songwriting teams who worked on that picture, Robin and Rainger and Mack Gordon and Harry Revel, were already at the top of the studio's payroll and had received several production assignments (see Table 9.2).[36] When

## Table 9.2

### SONGWRITER SALARIES AT PARAMOUNT, 1934

| Songwriter | Total Salary Earned | No. Productions Assigned |
| --- | --- | --- |
| Mack Gordon | 44,300.00 | 12 |
| Ralph Rainger | 30,800.00 | 16 |
| Leo Robin | 25,783.32 | 14 |
| Harry Revel | 24,200.00 | 12 |
| Arthur Johnston | 21,000.00 | 11 |
| Sam Coslow | 19,525.00 | 14 |
| Lorenz Hart | 7,500.00 | 1 |
| Richard Rodgers | 7,500.00 | 1 |
| Ray Noble | 7,500.00 | 3 |
| Richard Whiting | 6,750.00 | 3 |
| Sam Fain | 2,250.00 | 1 |
| Irving Kahal | 2,250.00 | 1 |
| Ann Ronnell | 1,500.00 | 1 |

Paramount purchased the rights to *Anything Goes* in January of 1935, the studio saw no reason to disrupt this system. Producers informed Finston that 'it may be necessary to select songs written by our writers for Bing Crosby'[37] rather than hire Cole Porter to write new songs, as they had planned to do. Robin and Richard Whiting, who had written songs for the crooner in several other films, were assigned to *Anything Goes* on 9 August 1935;[38] they worked with Frederick Hollander to create three new songs, while Hoagy Carmichael and Edward Heyman sold the studio one more.[39] Paramount clearly hoped to put more song hits in the mouth of their best songplugger.

## *ANYTHING GOES* FROM STAGE TO SCREEN

For Paramount, the prospect of an *Anything Goes* film adaptation had undeniable commercial appeal: with more than 400 performances on Broadway, the stage show was a financial and critical success. Brooks Atkinson writing for the *New York Times* called it 'a thundering good musical show' and 'hilarious and dynamic entertainment.'[40] The *Los Angeles Times* critic was equally effusive: '"Anything Goes" is one of those pat successes, the kind that a first-night audience senses immediately, the kind that producers dream of in their more optimistic vagaries.'[41] The actual producer in this case was Vinton Freedley, an experienced Broadway veteran who with Alexander Aarons had overseen the popular Gershwin musical comedies of the 1920s. In *Anything Goes*, he had a Cole Porter score and a dynamite cast that included Ethel Merman, William Gaxton, and Victor Moore.

The show's status as a hit belies the fact that it was, as Geoffrey Block writes, 'hastily, perhaps even frantically, put together.'[42] The book was not finished when rehearsals began on 8 October 1934. Freedley had received two drafts from Guy Bolton and P. G. Wodehouse; these scripts, whose working titles included *Crazy Week* and *Hard to Get*, told a story that included a bomb threat on an ocean liner. An oft-told anecdote claims that the tragic, real-life sinking off the coast of New Jersey of the *SS Morro Castle* led Freedley to demand revisions. Bolton and Wodehouse biographer Lee Davis convincingly argues, however, that Freedley's hope for a Hollywood adaptation—before the Broadway show even had been staged—led him to seek changes.[43] Like several other Broadway shows in the early 1930s, the first Bolton-Wodehouse draft of *Anything Goes* was a Hollywood satire: it featured an ex-Hollywood scenario writer as one of the main characters, and Bolton and Wodehouse, drawing from their own experiences in the studios, peppered the book with digs at and jokes about the film industry.[44] Freedley, according to Bolton, objected.[45] Bolton and Wodehouse's second draft removed the Hollywood treatment, kept the ocean liner catastrophe, and was once again turned down by Freedley, this time because it was, as Davis writes, 'a hopeless mess.'[46] Howard Lindsay and Russel Crouse completed the third re-write, which kept only the basic outline of the first two drafts.[47]

The completed Lindsay-Crouse book for *Anything Goes* takes place on the SS *American* as it travels from New York to London. The two main characters are Reno Sweeney (Merman), an evangelist turned entertainer, and Billy Crocker (Gaxton), who despite his affection for Reno, deflects her advances. Before the ship departs, Billy travels to the dock to see Reno, who is booked to perform onboard; he stows away on the ship once he realizes that Hope Harcourt (Bettina Hall) is one of the ship's passengers. Hope, an American heiress, is engaged to Sir Evelyn Oakleigh (Leslie Barrie), a British nobleman who seems more interested in studying American slang than in interacting with his fiancée. In order to stay on the boat, Billy accepts the help of Moonface Martin

(Moore), a gangster who is travelling undercover as a priest. Unbeknownst to Billy, Moonface gives him the ticket and passport of another gangster who never made it onboard, Snake Eyes Johnson, the FBI's Public Enemy Number One. Billy, mistaken for Snake Eyes, must prove his innocence in order to win Hope. By show's end, Billy pairs romantically with Hope and Reno with Sir Evelyn.

Freedley negotiated with Paramount less than two months after the show's opening on 21 November 1934, unsurprising given that he had asked for a studio-friendly book. According to a *Variety* report, Freedley received 'eighty-five thousand dollars, plus 10 per cent of gross, once rentals passed the one-million-dollar mark.'[48] The *Hartford Courant* called the deal 'the major theatrical buy of the season' and reported that 'W.C. Fields will re-create the part played by Victor Moore; Bing Crosby will assume the role played by William Gaxton and Queenie Smith is up for the Ethel Merman part. Cole Porter's music, including 'You're the Top,' is part of the purchase, with Porter contracted to write three new numbers for the screen presentation.'[49] Of these proposed production details, only one, Bing Crosby's role, would come true.

Production on the film version of *Anything Goes* began in the late summer of 1935. Directed by Lewis Milestone, it used a shooting script by Walter DeLeon, Sidney Salkow, John C. Moffitt, and Francis Martin that Thomas Hischak describes as 'pretty much an abridged version of the stage libretto.'[50] Some of the stage show's original dialogue is included more or less verbatim, like the pun-filled conversation between Moonface and high society matron Mrs Wentworth. Most cuts were an effort to please the Hays Office, Hollywood's self-imposed censorship office that in 1934 gained new power under Joseph Breen. His office requested, for example, that the show's memorable phrase 'hot pants' be removed, as well as comedic situations deemed questionable.[51] All of the characters transferred more or less intact, with only a few minor changes. Hope is no longer an American debutante, for example, but rather 'an English heiress on the run,'[52] and Sir Evelyn is her handler, charged with bringing her home to marry a man whom she does not love. The relationships between characters remain the same: Reno is still sweet on Billy yet ends up with Sir Evelyn, and Billy wins over Hope by the time the credits roll.

The film adaptation had an almost entirely new cast. British-born actress and singer Ida Lupino won the role of Hope, perhaps explaining why the character's nationality switched from American to British, and comedic actor Charles Ruggles took the role of Moonface. Crosby was cast as Billy and received top billing above Merman, who reprised her role as Reno. The studio's marketing of the film focused on him, often at the expense of her: studio press releases, according to Caryl Flinn, 'maintained that Ethel had an unrequited crush on Crosby and other nonsense,'[53] depicting Merman as yet another woman swooning over the crooner's charms rather than as an established star in her own right. Clearly, the studio was tapping into Crosby's celebrity persona that it cemented in his feature films leading up to *Anything Goes*, especially *She Loves Me Not* (1934), *Here Is My Heart* (1934), and *Mississippi* (1935). All of these films depict Crosby as a good-natured singer (or songwriter, in the case of *She Loves Me Not*), who wins over the girl with a sincere and well-timed croon.[54] With a cost of $1.1 million, *Anything Goes* was reportedly Paramount's most expensive Crosby production up to that point,[55] and as such, it is best understood as one in a series of Bing Crosby films as much as an adaptation of the stage show.

Indeed, if the stage production revolved around Merman, the film version of *Anything Goes* orbits around Crosby (see Table 9.3).[56] The film cuts five Porter songs that do not feature Crosby's character Billy, including the ensemble numbers 'Bon Voyage' (act 1, scene 2), 'Where Are the Men?' (act 1, scene 4),

Table 9.3

## SONG ORDER IN STAGE AND FILM VERSIONS OF *ANYTHING GOES*

| Stage: *Anything Goes* (1934) | Film: *Anything Goes* (1936) |
|---|---|
| **Act I** | |
| Scene 1: 'I Get a Kick Out of You' (Reno) | 'Anything Goes' (Reno) |
| Scene 2: 'Bon Voyage' (Boys/Girls) | 'I Get a Kick Out of You' (Reno) |
| 'All through the Night' (Billy/ Hope/Sailors) | 'Sailor's Chantey' (Four Sailors) |
| Scene 3: 'Sailor's Chantey' (Four Sailors) | 'Sailor Beware' (Billy) |
| Scene 4: 'Where Are the Men?' (1st & 2nd Girls/Girls' Chorus) | Reprise: 'Sailor's Chantey' (Billy/Four Sailors) |
| 'You're the Top' (Reno/Billy) | 'Moon Burn' (Billy) |
| Scene 5: Reprise: 'Sailor's Chantey' (Four Sailors) | 'My Heart and I' (Billy) |
| Scene 6: 'Anything Goes' (Reno/ Four Sailors) | 'You're the Top' (Reno/Billy) |
| Reprise: 'You're the Top' (Reno) | Reprise: 'You're the Top' (Reno/Billy/Moonface) |
| | 'Shanghai-De-Ho' (Reno/Billy/ Chorus) |
| **Act II** | |
| Scene 1: 'Public Enemy Number One' (Four Sailors/Passengers) | |
| 'Blow, Gabriel, Blow' (Reno/ Company) | |
| Scene 2: 'Be Like the Bluebird' (Moonface) | |
| Reprise: 'All through the Night' (Hope/Billy) | |
| Reprise: 'I Get a Kick Out of You' | |
| Scene 3: 'The Gypsy in Me' (Hope) | |
| Reprise: 'Anything Goes' (All) | |

and 'Public Enemy Number One' (act 2, scene 1), as well as the solos for Moonface and Hope, 'Be Like the Bluebird' (act 2, scene 2) and 'The Gypsy in Me' (act 2, scene 3). One Porter song, 'Sailor's Chantey,' was revised to include Crosby's character in its reprise. Three of the new songs—'Sailor, Beware,' 'Moon Burn,' and 'My Heart and I'—were added specifically for Crosby's crooning persona; these were the songs that the studio hoped had hit potential, and they also served to replace Billy and Hope's duet 'All through the Night,' reportedly cut for censorship reasons discussed below. The remainder of the film's score gives Merman a chance to perform the stage show's most popular songs, including 'Anything Goes,' 'I Get a Kick Out of You,' and 'You're the Top.' All of these Porter songs were revised, however, and Crosby figures prominently in the latter. The new finale number, 'Shanghai-De-Ho,' features both Merman and Crosby.

The revisions to the Porter songs retained in the film were mostly the result of demands from the Hays Office, which was not receptive to Porter's risqué lyrics. Richard Watts Jr, whose review opens this chapter, points out the most noticeable lyric change: in 'I Get a Kick Out of You,' he complains, 'the timorous manufacturers refuse to allow Miss Merman to sing anything about cocaine, and make her use the radio's bowdlerized substitute about "that perfume from Spain." '[57] It was Breen and his employees who deemed the sniff of cocaine problematic.[58] There were similar revisions to 'Sailor's Chantey.' The film retains that song's first verse and refrain, changing the word 'hell' to 'heck,' but the reprise of the song drops the adulterous second verse, in which a sailor 'hankerin' for the dames' is encouraged to seek out 'certain passengers' wives.' In its place, a newly written verse has the sailors complain of being out at sea.[59] If minor tweaks saved 'I Get a Kick Out of You' and 'Sailor's Chantey,' the title song 'Anything Goes' was beyond help: the Hays Office worried that even naming the film *Anything Goes* 'might be objected to' given the 'flavour' of the title song's lyrics.[60] Paramount producers tried their best to make the song work and hired the poet and lyricist Brian Hooker to revise the song. But as Gary Giddins notes, 'despite three rewrites and submissions,' 'Anything Goes' never receives a full performance in the film; Merman sings only the first phrase during the opening credits.[61] The censors also had problems with 'All through the Night' and Reno's 'Blow, Gabriel, Blow.' The first was deemed too suggestive in its description of love and 'ecstasy,' and the latter, they worried, might be interpreted as a burlesque of religion.[62] The film version discards both. Given Paramount's dedication to Crosby and its own songwriters, producers might have done so anyway.[63]

Indeed, the Hays Office cannot claim all of the changes made by the studio. Breen did not target 'You're the Top,' for example, and yet the studio made significant lyrical revisions to the song. Here, the changes suggest that the studio perceived Porter's trademark sophistication as a problem. In the film, Merman and Crosby's performance retains the initial verse of the song but deletes the majority of the eight original choruses. In their place are four mostly new refrains contributed by Porter's second cousin lyricist Ted Fetter.[64] Fetter drops most of the European references in Porter's lyrics. Gone are the Colosseum, the Louvre, Strauss, Shakespeare, the Mona Lisa, and Camembert, and added are references to St. Louis pitcher Dizzy Dean, Niagara Falls, Boston beans, and Paramount star Mae West. One new pop culture reference seems especially crafted for Crosby: Merman sings, 'You're Paul Whiteman's tummy,' to which Crosby responds, 'Oh, you should see him!' (Crosby, who in 1926 signed with the Rhythm Boys in Whiteman's band, *had* seen Whiteman's tummy.) The film version of 'You're the Top' does include some of the Porter's original highbrow references—Botticelli, Keats, and Shelley still get a shout out—but overall, Fetter aims at a middlebrow

American demographic, not at Porter's typical New York audience, which Miles Krueger has described as a 'constricted group of *cognoscenti*, who went to the same night spots, read the same newspaper columns, and spent weekends at the same estates.'[65]

The added choruses of 'You're the Top' also tap into another popular culture phenomenon—that of writing new lyrics for Porter's song. As promotion for the stage production, Freedley had set up songwriting competitions in which fans could submit additional refrains to Porter's hit songs, the prizes being free tickets to the show.[66] This fan activity apparently went far beyond Freedley's initial contests. Ten months after the show premiered, *New York Times* critic Brooks Atkinson describes how 'You're the Top' in particular was subject to creative extrapolations: 'Now that Mr. Porter has set the pattern of it,' he writes, 'every one enjoys composing additional verses for private consumption—satiric, humorous or ribald, as the case may be.'[67] Merman and Crosby's screen performance of 'You're the Top' participates in this game, as can be seen in ▶ video example 27.1. Merman opens the first refrain by singing that Crosby is 'the Swanee River,' a line from Porter's act 1 reprise of the song. She then adds new lyrics about a V8 flivver, the walls of China, and Santa Claus. Crosby exclaims, 'Make more!' after she finishes her new refrain, and she appeases him. There is no embarrassment in rewriting Porter's song, because, after all, audience members were doing it too.

Nor was Paramount apologetic about adding new songs to the film. In a way, Crosby needed new songs, given that most of Porter's score had been handcrafted for the original Broadway cast. As Porter told Merman biographer Peter Martin, 'I really tailor-made [my songs] for her because I know her range so well.'[68] He particularly appreciated Merman's nuanced rhythmic delivery and her diction, qualities that suited the syncopation and fast-paced lyrics of 'You're the Top,' 'Anything

Goes,' and 'Blow, Gabriel, Blow.' Crosby had an excellent sense of rhythm too, as proved by his jazz-inflected scatting in the 'Dinah' number from *The Big Broadcast* (1932). But he was not known for delivering a tumble of lyrics in quick succession; his crooning style was laid back and more suited to songs that left space for his trademark Irish mordent. With this crooning style in mind, 'All through the Night' was not a great fit for Crosby either. Porter wrote the song especially for the original Billy, William Gaxton, who needed a song with a limited range.[69] As I suggest below, the new song 'My Heart and I' suits Crosby much better than Porter's song.[70]

If Crosby needed songs that fit his singing style, he also needed more to sing than Porter's score offered his character Billy. Three of the film's new songs—'Sailor Beware' by Leo Robin and Richard Whiting, 'Moon Burn' by Edward Heyman and Hoagy Carmichael, and 'My Heart and I' by Robin and Frederick Hollander—fit the bill. Collectively, these songs depict Billy's slow but sure wooing of Hope, creating a familiar crooning narrative that is present in nearly every Crosby film of the early to mid-1930s. The numbers also effectively plug the studio's newly copyrighted music: no other star performance interrupts the succession of Crosby songs in the middle portion of the film's total running time.

For the first Crosby song, 'Sailor Beware,' Robin and Whiting's title is suspiciously similar to Porter's 'Buddie, Beware,' a song that was originally sung in act 2 of the stage production before it was replaced by a reprise of 'I Get a Kick Out of You.'[71] In the stage show, the song was Reno's warning to men that she would be an expensive wife, one who requires first-row seats at a show and wine with dinner. Robin and Whiting's rewrite of the song is now a warning from Billy to the sailors, as can be heard in ⏵ video example 27.2. He describes the 'Oriental' and 'Continental' girls who live in the East and the West; the musical arrangement, in which drums bang out a 'primitive' rhythm, suggests that while these women may be appealing, they are also dangerous. The best women for the sailors are at home, and as Crosby reminds them that 'some bonnie lies over the ocean,' the melody quotes the familiar tune 'My Bonnie Lies over the Ocean.' In using this musical quotation, Robin and Whiting construct a catchy song that already feels familiar to listeners.

Though directed at the ship's sailors, 'Sailor Beware' is the first song in which Hope hears Billy's voice. He sings outside of her cabin, perched from a crow's nest as he addresses the men on deck; she lies asleep her in cabin, dressed in a revealing nightgown and resting her head on a ruffled pillow (see ⊙ video example 27.3). The camera cuts to a close-up of her just after Billy sings the 'My Bonnie' reference, indicating visually that she is Billy's bonnie. As his voice spills into her room, she opens her eyes, cocks her head slightly as she listens, and cracks a knowing smile, entranced by the man outside her window. This sequence parallels earlier Crosby numbers like 'With Every Breath I Take' in *Here Is My Heart* (1934) and the reprise of 'Soon' in *Mississippi* (1935), which show Crosby's voice, not his physical body, cracking the veneer of feminine propriety and awakening a woman's sexuality. Paramount was playing with Crosby's identity as a crooner who seduced women via the radio and recordings.

After a female character falls in love with Crosby's voice, she then has to experience his charms in person. Crosby films are thus filled with romantic serenades in which he sits close to a woman and pleads his case. *Anything Goes* is no exception, with Billy singing directly to Hope in both 'Moon Burn' and in 'My Heart and I.' The first number gets him close but not quite close enough. Hope sees Billy from her cabin as he paints the ship's porthole windows while perched on a suspended platform over the sea. She peers out of her window, and at the sight of her, he impulsively pulls the platform up to her level and launches into 'Moon Burn' (see ⏵ video example 27.4), a song that details how he will be burned by the moonlight as she embraces and kisses him that evening. As Billy leans into her cabin through the window, Hope powders her nose, checks herself in the mirror, and dons a hat, enjoying his attention. She does not reply whether she will join him under the moon, but she is clearly open to his advances. In 'My Heart and I,' Billy completes his seduction of Hope in the privacy of a lifeboat. The song has all the trademarks of a crooning ballad: it is performed at a slower tempo than the previous two numbers, and it features an octave drop in the A phrase, which allows Crosby to slide seductively into sustained notes that showcase his lower register. Initially, the song is filmed in a two-shot; Hope and Billy sit next to each other as Billy leans into her. But for a repeat of the song, the camera moves to a close-up of Hope's face as she gazes into the distance, immersed in his voice. She turns to him when he kisses her, marking the end of the number, the shot, and the scene itself, as seen in ⏵ video example 27.5. After three Crosby songs, Hope has fallen for Billy.

Each of these new Crosby songs features an easy-to-sing melody, generalized lyrics, and an oft-repeated hook, but Robin and Hollander's 'My Heart and I' was designed to be the film's bestseller. In addition to Crosby's onscreen performance, it is also referenced in dialogue throughout the film, arranged as underscoring, and used as the film's closing musical tag. Superficially, 'My Heart and I' shares many characteristics with Porter's cut song, 'All through the Night.' The lyrics of both relate to the relationship of Billy and Hope, and they share an AABA form in which the second and third A phrases differ slightly from the first. The songs' similarities prove less important, however, than their differences, which demonstrate what separates a Hollywood hit from a sophisticated Broadway song.

Leo Robin wrote pop lyrics in which the meaning was clear and to the point. Certainly, the conceit of 'My Heart and I' is apparent in the song's opening phrase: Billy sings that he has conferred with his heart about his feelings for Hope and then professes his love to her. Robin's rhymes (*charms-arms*, *start-heart*, and *true-you*) are predictable, but nonetheless, the song is a bit coy. His heart, defined as a separate entity, gives Billy a team member of sorts; he never has to sing the vulnerable phrase, 'I love you,' and instead can couch his feelings with the phrase, 'We're so in love with you.' By contrast, Porter's song is more suggestive in its depiction of love and reveals the significance of the phrase 'all through the night' only at the end of the chorus. At first, the song appears to describe an intimate meeting between Billy and Hope that lasts all night. Porter incorporates several internal rhymes (*night-delight*, *night-height*, *above-love*) before making an especially creative rhyme at end of the first two A phrases (*me* with *ecstasy*). Only in the last A phrase does Porter clarify that Billy and Hope's meeting is imagined rather than real, lasting all through the night because it occurs in a dream. As Raymond Knapp writes, the song is ultimately 'about being apart,' even though it purports to describe the most intimate of encounters.[72]

The melodies of 'My Heart and I' and 'All through the Night' suit their respective lyrics. 'My Heart and I' is easy to sing. The opening phrase spans the range of an octave and contains only diatonic pitches, which rest comfortably within a standard progression that moves from I to ii7 to V. This harmonic predictability helps the amateur singer to stay in tune. 'All through the Night,' written for the limited range of Gaxton, was also supposed to be easy to sing, but like Porter's witty lyrics, presents its own difficulties. As Knapp observes, the tune consists of 'an obsessively descending chromatic scale' that often maintains 'an aching major-seventh or minor-ninth dissonance with the bass as it falls.' The result, Knapp notes, is that one loses 'the reality of the home key along the way,'[73] and only at the end of the first phrase, when the melody finally breaks away from the descending half steps and leaps upward to the fifth scale degree, does a clear sense of harmonic stability return. The chromatic melody and harmony make sense from a lyrical and narrative perspective, as they convey the disorientation of desire that Billy and Hope feel. But from a commercial perspective, the song is not easy to hum.

Moreover, the hook of 'My Heart and I' is far more memorable than the hook of 'All through the Night.' Robin repeats the song's title at the beginning of every A phrase, and each time, Hollander pairs 'my heart and I' with the same melodic shape: an ascending third for 'my heart,' and then an octave lower, an ascending second for 'and I.' The octave displacement creates a lovely call-and-response effect, as if the heart calls out first and is answered by the head; it also makes the hook stand out from the rather mundane stepwise melody that fills the rest of each A phrase. Compare that hook construction with the A phrases of 'All through the Night.' Porter uses the title lyrics at the beginning of the first and second A phrases, but rather than highlight them melodically, he essentially buries the hook's lyrics in the sinking chromatic melody. The half-step descent that sets 'all through the night' is similar to the half-step descent of the following lyrics 'I delight' and 'in your love.' The A phrase, as a result, does not offer a tuneful motive that is easily detached from its context. Nor does Porter offer his listeners many repetitions of the hook. In the last A phrase, the final iteration of the song's title is set to a short melodic turn that ends on the upper tonic, the highest pitch in the song. Knapp argues that this final melodic cadence 'completes an ascending registral shaping across the "A" phrases' that peaks at the end of the chorus.[74] But as satisfying as that registral shaping might be, changing the hook's contour in its final appearance diminishes the song's ability to plug itself.

Like 'My Heart and I,' the other songs added to Paramount's *Anything Goes* were designed to get in the ears of the audience. Even so, producers did not leave their appeal to chance, and in Sam Coslow's words, they 'made damn sure' to repeat and reprise the songs whenever possible. The choruses of 'Moon Burn' and 'My Heart and I' are each repeated in their initial performances, giving listeners the chance to hear the lyrics twice. The latter song's repeat even gets narrative reinforcement from Hope: 'Could we hear it again,' she implores, "My Heart and I'?' The song that gets the most repetitions is 'Sailor Beware.' Crosby sings the chorus twice, and male and female vocal choruses join him for two more repeats. The quadruple plugging of this song seemed to work on Richard Watts Jr, the *New York Herald Tribune* critic who was otherwise unimpressed by Paramount's treatment of Porter's score. Watts conceded, 'It should be reported on the picture's behalf, though, that there is a good new song called "Sailor, Beware." '[75] Even a Porter fan, it seems, was susceptible to the plugging of Hollywood.

## ON FIDELITY

In his comments on Paramount's changes to Porter's score, Watts argues he is justified in criticizing the film for not following the stage version more clearly. Fidelity here, as in other critiques of Hollywood adaptations of stage musicals, is defined as faithfulness to the original score. It is worth asking, however, if Broadway itself abides by the same standards that it expects from Hollywood. Stage musicals are, after all, in a constant state of revision during rehearsals, try-outs, initial Broadway runs, and subsequent revivals. Criticizing Paramount's *Anything Goes* for not being faithful to Porter's original score is less persuasive when one considers that in the second half of the twentieth century, Broadway and the West End were not particularly faithful to the 1934 stage production, either.

The revivals of *Anything Goes* were shaped by the Rodgers and Hammerstein model that developed in the 1940s and

1950s. These postwar musicals typically feature serious plots borrowed from existing plays and novels; characters who have clear psychological motivations; and so-called integrated scores, in which songs relate to the plots and characters at hand. *Anything Goes* does not fit this model at all. Its plot is satiric, comedic, and haphazard; its characters don disguises and make wisecracks as much as they express their true feelings; and most of the songs, though tied to the story, were crafted for the performers as much as the characters. In an attempt to fix these issues, Block notes, 'producers and directors for the past thirty years' have continually revised the book and interpolated additional songs.[76]

Some of the problems perceived in the 1934 book are relatively easy fixes. Most Broadway revivals update the dialogue to remove the 1930s topical humour as well as the racially insensitive treatment of the show's two Chinese characters. Deficiencies in the show's characters and plot take more work. The relationship between Reno and Sir Evelyn is especially vexing. In the original production, Sir Evelyn is depicted as effeminate and does not sing, while Reno is boisterous and has the major hits of the show. That they end up together does not abide by modern expectations of musical comedies.[77] To make the relationship more persuasive, the 1962 revival gives Evelyn a risqué duet with Reno ('Let's Misbehave,' originally written for Porter's 1928 show *Paris*), and the 1987 revival gives him his own solo ('The Gypsy in Me,' a song sung by Hope in the 1934 production). The 1987 revival treats the other main characters 'more seriously' as well: Timothy Crouse, who worked with John Weidman on the revised book, explained, 'If there is one emotional ingredient we've added, it's passion for the characters,'[78] and director Jerry Zaks described Reno, Billy, Hope, and Sir Evelyn as 'people dealing with the ramifications of trying to fall in love,' citing the show's working title *Hard to Get* as support for his interpretation. 'Even though so many improbable things go on,' Zaks noted, 'we strove to ground everything in a recognizable reality.'[79]

Is the 1936 film version more or less faithful than these stage revivals? Paramount's *Anything Goes* retains much of the 1934 production's humour, even with the changes requested by the Hays Office, so in terms of the book, it is far more faithful than the stage revivals. But the sticking point for the film adaptation remains Porter's music: it contains less of it, while the stage revivals add more of it. The 1962 revival of *Anything Goes*, Block points out, 'incorporated no less than six songs out of a total of fourteen from *other* Porter shows,'[80] though no mention of these additions is made in Lewis Funke's *Times* review of the show. Reporting on the 1987 revival, *Times* critic Stephen Holden writes that it is 'quite a different creature from the 1934 romp' but does not judge it more harshly as a result. Frank Rich's review of the same show calls its interpolation of Porter songs as 'keeping with contemporary practice.'[81] The 1936 film version's interpolations are completely typical of 1930s Hollywood practice, and yet its status as a faithful adaptation remains in question. At issue, of course, are the authors of the new music: Leo Robin, Richard Whiting, and Frederick Hollander are not Cole Porter.

In discussions of fidelity, the focus on the original songwriter and his music relates to the canonization of Broadway songwriters, the very men and women who throughout the 1930s strove to differentiate their music from what they perceived as the lowbrow commercialism of the film studios. In this light, the call for fidelity to a stage score moves beyond a simple desire to see a beloved Broadway production represented accurately onscreen and entangles itself with the aesthetic ideology of highbrow art. Such a belief may suggest a moral high ground in which the art of the stage trumps the money of the screen, but it also downplays the fact that Broadway songwriters used the rhetoric of art for their own

348 | STARS, STUDIOS, AND THE MUSICAL

promotional and commercial agendas. The ascent from Tin Pan Alley that began in the 1930s was deliberate, and it continued into the 1940s when the notion of 'integration' became attached to Rodgers and Hammerstein's *Oklahoma!* Integration, as James O'Leary has demonstrated, was 'never simply a formal principle to begin with. It was a performative act of cultural positioning.'[82] In invoking it, he argues, Rodgers and Hammerstein were able 'to situate the show in an expansive cultural field that included not only middlebrow Broadway but also highbrow art.'[83] The call for faithful Hollywood adaptations of beloved stage scores relies on a similar cultural positioning, in which Broadway aficionados separate themselves from the mainstream, popular aesthetics of Hollywood.

There are, of course, contradictions in this cultural positioning. Broadway songwriters and producers have always had significant commercial interests in the success of their shows, because they, like Hollywood songwriters, want to make money from their efforts. The commercial success of Broadway, moreover, remains closely tied to Hollywood. In the case of *Anything Goes*, these ties are clear in Vinton Freedley's careful guidance of the show's book, in which he rejected a Hollywood satire in hopes of developing a product that could be sold to the film industry down the road. And as Paramount's resulting adaptation of *Anything Goes* demonstrates, anything does not actually go in Hollywood: the industry has its own standards, different from those of the stage, which it follows consistently and methodically. Broadway and Hollywood both desire hits, and to hedge bets, each relies on the conventions and stylistic elements associated with their chosen platform, whether the stage or the screen. In this light, Paramount's *Anything Goes* is entirely faithful, not to Cole Porter, but to its star Bing Crosby and to the studio's hit songwriters.

# NOTES

1. Richard Watts Jr, '"Anything Goes"—Paramount,' *New York Herald Tribune*, 6 February 1936.
2. Thomas Hischak, *Through the Screen Door: What Happened to the Broadway Musical When It Went to Hollywood* (Lanham, MD: Scarecrow Press, 2004), 3.
3. For an excellent history of the Hollywood and Tin Pan Alley mergers, see the second chapter of Katherine Spring's *Saying It with Songs: Popular Music and the Coming of Sound to Hollywood Cinema* (New York: Oxford University Press, 2013).
4. Spring, *Saying It with Songs*, 54–55.
5. Spring, *Saying It with Songs*, 59–60.
6. Spring, *Saying It with Songs*, 61–63. In addition to a salary, Coslow was also offered 'a handsome weekly drawing account against royalties.' Coslow, *Cocktails for Two: The Many Lives of Giant Songwriter Sam Coslow* (New Rochelle, NY: Arlington House, 1977), 96.
7. Robert Kimball, ed., *The Complete Lyrics of Cole Porter* (New York: Vintage Books, 1984), 475.
8. Douglas Gomery, *The Hollywood Studio System* (New York: St. Martin's Press, 1986), 109.
9. Other scholars have argued that in terms of formal conventions, there are no notable differences between Broadway and Hollywood songs. Spring writes that 'the popular song form that was characteristic of the 1920s Tin Pan Alley and Broadway productions continued to dominate the output of songwriters who were writing for both stage and film.' Spring, *Saying It with Songs*, 61. Charles Hamm makes a similar argument, writing that there is 'no way to tell, from listening to a song by Irving Berlin or any of his contemporaries, whether it was written for vaudeville, musical comedy, the movies, or simply composed for radio play and possibly recording.' Hamm, *Yesterdays, Popular Song in America* (New York: W.W. Norton, 1979), 339. My point is that though formal conventions stayed more or less the same, there is a stylistic difference between songs composed by those songwriters who worked primarily in Hollywood and those songwriters who worked primarily in New York.

10. Philip Furia and Laurie Patterson, *The Songs of Hollywood* (New York: Oxford University Press, 2010), 10.

11. Edward M. Wickes, *Writing the Popular Song* (Springfield, MA: Home Correspondence School, 1916), 113. Daniel Goldmark, in his survey of fifty songwriting manuals published between 1899 and the late 1930s, argues that these guides offer a clear picture of how the industry wanted outsiders to see their work. See REFO:JARTGoldmark, '"Making Songs Pay": Tin Pan Alley's Formula for Success,' *Musical Quarterly* 98, no. 1–2 (Spring–Summer 2015): 3–28. For a thorough account of the rise of Tin Pan Alley, see David Suisman, *Selling Sounds: The Commercial Revolution in American Music* (Cambridge, MA: Harvard University Press, 2009).

12. Wickes, *Writing the Popular Song*, 34.

13. Wickes, *Writing the Popular Song*, 34–35.

14. Al Dubin, *The Art of Song Writing* (New York: Majestic Music Company, 1928), 9–10. Dubin wrote this book very quickly to earn extra cash, which may explain his brief description of production songs. See Patricia Dubin McGuire, *Lullaby of Broadway, Life and Times of Al Dubin* (Secaucus, NJ: Citadel Press, 1983), 94–95.

15. Abner Silver and Robert Bruce, *How to Write and Sell a Song Hit* (New York: Prentice Hall, 1939), 54–55.

16. Silver and Bruce, *How to Write and Sell a Song Hit*, 9–10, 27.

17. Silver and Bruce, *How to Write and Sell a Song Hit*, 66–67.

18. Silver and Bruce, *How to Write and Sell a Song Hit*, 66–67.

19. Block, 'The Melody (and the Words) Linger On: American Musical Comedies of the 1920s and 1930s,' in *The Cambridge Companion to the Musical*, ed. William A. Everett and Paul R. Laird (New York: Cambridge University Press, 2008), 109.

20. Block, 'The Melody (and the Words) Linger On,' 116.

21. Philip Furia, 'Sinatra on Broadway,' in *Frank Sinatra and Popular Culture*, ed. Leonard Mustazza (Westport, CT: Praeger, 1998), 163, 165.

22. Isaac Goldberg, *Tin Pan Alley, a Chronicle of the American Popular Music Racket* (New York: John Day, 1930), 231. For more information on Goldberg, see Ryan Banagale, 'Isaac

Goldberg: Assessing Agency in American Music Biography,' *American Music Review* 34, no. 2 (Spring 2010): 8–9, 15.

23. Goldberg, *Tin Pan Alley*, 232.

24. Andrea Most, *Making Americans: Jews and the Broadway Musical* (Cambridge, MA: Harvard University Press, 2004), 8.

25. Most, *Making Americans*, 27.

26. Quoted in Charlotte Greenspan, *Pick Yourself Up: Dorothy Fields and the American Musical* (New York: Oxford University Press, 2010), 70. Greenspan cites an undated clipping in the Dorothy Fields scrapbook held at the Museum of the City of New York.

27. Richard Rodgers, *Musical Stages, an Autobiography* (New York: Random House, 1975), 138.

28. Kurt Weill, *Speak Low (When You Speak of Love): The Letters of Kurt Weill and Lotte Lenya*, ed. and trans. Lys Symonette and Kim H. Kowalke (Berkeley: University of California Press, 1996), 220.

29. McGuire, *Lullaby of Broadway*, 147.

30. Russell Bennett, *The Broadway Sound, the Autobiography and Selected Essays of Robert Russell Bennett*, ed. George J. Ferencz (Rochester, NY: University of Rochester Press, 1999), 125–126.

31. Coslow, *Cocktails for Two*, 98.

32. Rodgers, *Musical Stages*, 166.

33. Rodgers, *Musical Stages*, 156.

34. The information for Table 9.1 is compiled from a Paramount Interoffice Memo, dated 9 May 1933, in the Nathaniel Finston Papers, American Heritage Center, University of Wyoming, box 1, folder 10–1 Exhibits, Estimates & Costs—Paramount.

35. 'Song Writers Assignments and Costs (From January 1st, 1929 to December 1, 1934),' box 1, Nathaniel Finston Papers, AHC. The 1934 films that had the next highest songs sales were *We're Not Dressing* (more than 230,000 song sales), which was also a Bing Crosby film, and *Murder at the Vanities* (more than 150,000 song sales).

36. Data in Table 9.2 come from 'Song Writers Total Earnings and Number of Assignments (From January 1st, 1929, to January 1st, 1935),' box 1, Nathaniel Finston Papers, AHC.

37. Inter-office communication with subject, 'Producers' Tentative Plans for Musical Productions,' 23 August 1935, box 1, Nathaniel Finston Papers, AHC.
38. Inter-office communication with subject, 'Producers' Tentative Plans for Musical Productions.'
39. Gary Giddins notes that 'Moonburn' was Carmichael's 'first movie sale.' Giddins, *Bing Crosby: A Pocketful of Dreams, the Early Years, 1903–1940* (Boston: Little, Brown, 2001), 392.
40. Brooks Atkinson, 'The Play: "Anything Goes" as Long as Victor Moore, Ethel Merman and William Gaxton Are Present,' *New York Times*, 22 November 1934.
41. '"Anything Goes" Scores Real Success on Broadway,' *Los Angeles Times*, 28 November 1934.
42. Geoffrey Block, *Enchanted Evenings: The Broadway Musical from* Show Boat *to* Sondheim (New York: Oxford University Press, 1997), 44. My summary of the show's production history draws from Block's account as well as the description Caryl Flinn offers in *Brass Diva: The Life and Legends of Ethel Merman* (Berkeley: University of California Press, 2007), 66–73.
43. Other sources support Davis's account of the rewrites, as Block describes in *Enchanted Evenings*, 43–44. Porter biographer George Eells writes that Freedley had always thought the Bolton-Wodehouse book was tasteless and used the *Morro* disaster as an excuse to seek another rewrite. Eells, *The Life that Late He Led: A Biography of Cole Porter* (New York: G.P. Putnam's Sons, 1967), 110–111.
44. Examples of stage plays and musicals that had satirized Hollywood include George Kaufman and Moss Hart's *Once in a Lifetime* (1930), Richard Rodgers and Lorenz Hart's *America's Sweetheart* (1931), and Sam and Bella Spivack's, *Boy Meets Girl* (1935). Charlotte Greenspan briefly discusses these shows in *Pick Yourself Up: Dorothy Fields and the American Musical* (New York: Oxford University Press, 2010), 80–82, 120–126.
45. Quoted in Lee Davis, *Bolton and Wodehouse and Kern: The Men Who Made Musical Comedy* (New York: James H. Heineman, 1993), 331.
46. Davis, *Bolton and Wodehouse and Kern*, 332.
47. Davis, *Bolton and Wodehouse and Kern*, 334–336.

48. Quoted in Flinn, *Brass Diva*, 74. Gary Giddins gives a conflicting report of the deal, writing that the movie rights cost $100,000. Giddins, *Bing Crosby*, 391.
49. 'Paramount Studios Win "Anything Goes,"' *Hartford Courant*, 20 January 1935.
50. Hischak, *Through the Screen Door*, 28.
51. One scene was cut, for example, because 'it could be construed . . . that a woman passenger was asking directions to the ladies' room.' Giddins, *Bing Crosby*, 392.
52. Hischak, *Through the Screen Door*, 29.
53. Flinn, *Brass Diva*, 75.
54. Crosby's film shorts, in which he usually plays some version of himself, established his masculine crooning persona in the early 1930s. Allison McCracken details these shorts and some of his other films from the early 1930s in *Real Men Don't Sing: Crooning in American Culture* (Durham, NC: Duke University Press, 2015), 288–303.
55. Giddins, *Bing Crosby*, 391.
56. This outline of the 1934 stage version is adapted from Geoffrey Block's breakdown of the show in *Enchanted Evenings*, 325.
57. Watts, '"Anything Goes"—Paramount.'
58. The letter describing this objection is noted by Giddins, *Bing Crosby*, 392. Giddins cites a letter Joseph Breen sent to Paramount executive John Hammell, 9 September 1935, MPAA Production Code Administration Files, Academy of Motion Picture Arts and Sciences (AMPAS).
59. To my knowledge, there is no archival evidence that the Hays Office requested these changes. I observed these changes when comparing the film performances of 'Sailor's Chantey' with Porter's original lyrics for the show, available in Kimball, *The Complete Lyrics of Cole Porter*, 166–176.
60. Quoted in Flinn, *Brass Diva*, 74. Flinn cites a letter signed K. L., 29 July 1936, MPAA Production Code Administration Files, AMPAS.
61. Giddins, *Bing Crosby*, 392. The objection to 'Anything Goes' is from a letter from Joseph Breen to Paramount executive John Hammell, 9 September 1935, MPAA Production Code Administration Files, AMPAS.

62. Flinn, *Brass Diva*, 75, and Giddins, *Bing Crosby*, 392. Flinn cites a letter from Vincent Hart to Joseph Breen, 10 January 1935, MPAA Production Code Administration Files, AMPAS.

63. Notably, Paramount did not follow all of the censors' suggestions. The Hays Office had flagged Robin and Hollander's 'Shanghai-De-Ho' because of the 'plainly vulgar meaning' in the lyrics, 'Soon the chows and Pekinese will stay away from cherry trees.' The line remains in the film, however, sung cheekily by Merman. Giddins, *Bing Crosby*, 392. Giddins cites a letter from Joseph Breen to Paramount executive John Hammell, 9 September 1935, MPAA Production Code Administration Files, AMPAS.

64. Flinn, *Brass Diva*, 75. Ted Fetter's role in the rewrite to 'You're the Top' is also discussed in William McBride, *Cole Porter, a Biography* (New York: Vintage Books, 1998).

65. Quoted in Block, *Enchanted Evenings*, 50.

66. Flinn, *Brass Diva*, 72.

67. Brooks Atkinson, 'Catching Up on Song: Ethel Merman, Cole Porter, and a Couple of Tunes from "Anything Goes,"' *New York Times*, 15 September 1935.

68. Quoted in Flinn, *Brass Diva*, 69.

69. Initially, Gaxton was supposed to sing Porter's 'Easy to Love' for the act 1 love duet, but that song was deemed too difficult for him. Porter composed 'All through the Night,' as a replacement. Block, *Enchanted Evenings*, 45. Porter's 'Easy to Love' was later sung by Jimmy Stewart in the Eleanor Powell musical *Born to Dance* (1936).

70. Ethan Mordden argues that 'All through the Night' 'would have sounded great on Bing Crosby,' but Crosby's glacial performance of the song in the 1956 film adaption of *Anything Goes* is not particularly engaging. Mordden, *When Broadway Went to Hollywood* (New York: Oxford University Press, 2016), 122.

71. Block, *Enchanted Evenings*, 325.

72. Raymond Knapp, *The American Musical and the Formation of National Identity* (Princeton, NJ: Princeton University Press, 2005), 93.

73. Knapp, *The American Musical and the Formation of National Identity*, 93.

74. Knapp, *The American Musical and the Formation of National Identity*, 94.
75. Watts, ' "Anything Goes"—Paramount.'
76. Block, *Enchanted Evenings*, 45.
77. Knapp posits that Porter suggests a 'semi-closeted homosexual dimension' throughout the songs of *Anything Goes*, a subtext that 'goes a long way toward explaining why Sir Evelyn himself gets no song to sing, which he would surely have gotten if we were meant to believe that, in the end, he truly "gets the girl" in the conventional sense.' Knapp, *The American Musical and the Formation of National Identity*, 89–90.
78. 'Son Helping to Update Crouse's "Anything Goes," ' *New York Times*, 25 August 1987. Also quoted in Block, *Enchanted Evenings*, 50.
79. Stephen Holden, 'A Glimpse of Olden Days, Via Cole Porter,' *New York Times*, 18 October 1987. Also quoted in Block, *Enchanted Evenings*, 50.
80. Block, *Enchanted Evenings*, 47.
81. Lewis Funke, 'Theatre: "Anything Goes," Revival of Musical Opens at Orpheum,' *New York Times*, 16 May 1962; Frank Rich, 'The Stage: "Anything Goes," ' *New York Times*, 20 October 1987; and Stephen Holden, 'A Glimpse of Olden Days, Via Cole Porter.'
82. O'Leary, '*Oklahoma!*, "Lousy Publicity," and the Politics of Formal Integration in the American Musical Theater,' *Journal of Musicology* 31, no. 1 (Winter 2014): 180.
83. O'Leary, '*Oklahoma!*, "Lousy Publicity," ' 144.

# SELECT BIBLIOGRAPHY

Acevedo-Muñoz, Ernesto R. West Side Story *as Cinema: The Making and Impact of an American Masterpiece*. Lawrence: University Press of Kansas, 2013.

Altman, Rick, ed. *Genre: The Musical*. London: Routledge and Kegan Paul, 1981.

Altman, Rick. *The Hollywood Musical*, 2nd ed. Bloomington: Indiana University Press, 1993.

Andrew, Dudley. *Concepts in Film Theory*. Oxford: Oxford University Press, 1984.

Ansen, David. 'Madonna Tangos with Evita.' Newsweek, 15 December 1996.

Astaire, Fred. *Steps in Time*. New York: Harper, 1959.

Aylesworth, Thomas G. *Broadway to Hollywood: Musicals from Stage to Screen*. Twickenham, UK: Hamlyn, 1985.

Banfield, Stephen. *Jerome Kern*. New Haven, CT: Yale University Press, 2006.

Barrios, Richard. *A Song in the Dark: The Birth of the Musical Film*. New York: Oxford University Press, 1995.

Birkett, Danielle, and Dominic McHugh. *Adapting The Wizard of Oz: Musical Versions from Baum to MGM and Beyond*. New York: Oxford University Press, 2018.

Block, Geoffrey. *Enchanted Evenings*, 2nd ed. New York: Oxford University Press, 2009.

Block, Geoffrey. *Richard Rodgers*. New Haven, CT: Yale University Press, 2002.

Bordwell, David. *The Way Hollywood Tells It: Story and Style in Modern Movies*. Berkeley: University of California Press, 2006.

Bordman, Gerald. *American Musical Theatre: A Chronicle*, 3rd ed. New York: Oxford University Press, 2000.

Bordman, Gerald. *Jerome Kern: His Life and Music*. New York: Oxford University Press, 1980.

Bradley, Edwin M. *The First Hollywood Musicals: A Critical Filmography of 171 Features, 1927 through 1932*. Jefferson, NC: McFarland, 1996.

Brantley, Ben. *Broadway Musicals*. New York: Abrams, 2012.

Brown, Peter H. 'Desperately Seeking Evita.' Washington Post, 5 March 1989.

Burton, Jack. *The Blue Book of Hollywood Musicals*. Watkins Glen, NY: Century House, 1953.

Cantu, Maya. *American Cinderellas on the Broadway Musical Stage: Imagining the Working Girl from* Irene *to* Gypsy. Basingstoke, UK: Palgrave Macmillan, 2015.

Cartmell, Deborah, and Imelda Whelehan. *Screen Adaptation: Impure Cinema*. Basingstoke, UK: Palgrave Macmillan, 2010.

Casper, Joseph Andrew. *Stanley Donen*. Metuchen, NJ: Scarecrow Press, 1983.

Ciccone, Madonna. 'The Madonna Diaries. Vanity Fair, November 1996.

Citron, Stephen. Sondheim and Lloyd-Webber: The New Musical. New York: Oxford University Press, 2001.

Cohan, George M. *Twenty Years on Broadway and the Years It Took to Get There: The True Story of a Trouper's Life from the Cradle to the 'Closed Shop.'* New York: Harper and Brothers, 1925.

Cohan, Steven, ed. *Hollywood Musicals: The Film Reader*. London: Routledge, 2002.

Cohan, Steven, ed. *The Sound of Musicals*. London: BFI, 2010.

Croce, Arlene *The Fred Astaire and Ginger Rogers Book*. New York: Vintage Books, 1972.

Davis, Lorrie, with Rachel Gallagher. *Letting Down My Hair; Two Years with the Love Rock Tribe—from Dawning to Downing of Aquarius*. New York: A. Fields Books, 1973.

Decker, Todd. *Music Makes Me: Fred Astaire and Jazz*. Berkeley: University of California Press, 2011.

de Giere, Carol. *Defying Gravity: The Creative Career of Stephen Schwartz from* Godspell *to* Wicked. New York: Applause and Cinema Books, 2008.

de Giere, Carol. *The Godspell Experience: Inside a Transformative Musical*. Bethel, CT: Scene 1 Publishing, 2014.

De Mille, Agnes. *Dance to the Piper*. Introduction by J. Acocella. New York: New York Review Books, 2015 [1952].

Delamater, Jerome. *Dance in the Hollywood Musical*. Ann Arbor: UMI Research Press, 1981.

Doherty, Thomas. *Hollywood's Censor: Joseph I. Breen and the Production Code Administration*. New York: Columbia University Press, 2007.

Donnelly, K. J., and Elizabeth Carroll, eds., *Contemporary Musical Film*. Edinburgh: Edinburgh University Press, 2017.

Dyer, Richard. *Only Entertainment*, 2nd ed. London: Routledge, 2002.

Easton, Carol. *No Intermissions: The Life of Agnes De Mille*. New York: Da Capo Press, 2000.

Eddie Mannix Ledger. Los Angeles, Margaret Herrick Library, Center for Motion Picture Study.

Editors of *Consumer Guide* with Phillip J. Kaplan. *The Best, Worst and Most Unusual: Hollywood Musicals*. New York: Beekman House, 1983.

Edwards, Paul. 'Adaptation: Two Theories.' *Text and Performance Quarterly* 27, no. 4 (2007): 369–377.

Eller, Claudia. 'Crying's Over, "Evita" Finds Backers.' Los Angeles Times, 11 December 1993.

Elliott, Kamilla. *Rethinking the Novel/Film Debate*. Cambridge: Cambridge University Press, 2003.

Evans, Peter William. *Top Hat*. London: Wiley, 2010.

Everett, William A., and Paul R. Laird, eds. *The Cambridge Companion to the Musical*, 3rd. ed. New York: Cambridge University Press, 2017.

Everett, William A. *Sigmund Romberg*. New Haven, CT: Yale University Press, 2007.

Fehr, Richard, and Frederick G. Vogel. *Lullabies of Hollywood: Movie Music and the Movie Musical, 1915–1992*. Jefferson, NC: McFarland, 1993.

Feuer, Jane. *The Hollywood Musical*, 2nd ed. Basingstoke: Macmillan, 1993.

Fisher, James. *Historical Dictionary of American Theater: Beginnings*. Lanham, MD: Rowman and Littlefield, 2015.

Fordin, Hugh. *M-G-M's Greatest Musicals: The Arthur Freed Unit*. New York: Da Capo Press, 1996 [1975].

Forman, Miloš, with Jan Novak. *Turnaround: A Memoir*. Villard/ Random House, 1993.

Forrest, Jennifer, and Leonard R. Koos, eds. *Dead Ringers: The Remake in Theory and Practice*. New York: State University of New York Press, 2002.

Forte, Allen. *The American Popular Ballad of the Golden Era 1924– 1950*. Princeton, NJ: Princeton University Press, 1995.

Franceschina, John. *Hermes Pan: The Man Who Danced with Fred Astaire*. New York: Oxford University Press, 2012.

Furia, Philip, and Laurie Patterson. *The Songs of Hollywood*. New York: Oxford University Press, 2010.

Gardner, Kara A. *Agnes De Mille: Telling Stories in Broadway Dance*. New York: Oxford University Press, 2016.

Ganz, Andrew. 'In Upcoming Revival of Evita, Che Will Be the "Everyman," Not Che Guevara.' February 2012. Playbill.com.

Gänzl, Kurt. *Ganzl's Book of the Broadway Musical*. New York: Schirmer Books, 1995.

Geraghty, Christine. *Now a Major Motion Picture: Film Adaptations of Literature and Drama*. Lanham, MD: Rowman and Littlefield, 2008.

Giddins, Gary. *Bing Crosby: A Pocketful of Dreams, the Early Years, 1903–1940*. Boston: Little, Brown, 2001.

Gilbert, James. *Men in the Middle: Searching for Masculinity in the 1950s*. Chicago: University of Chicago Press, 2005.

Gontier, David F. Jr, and Timothy L. O'Brien. The Films of Alan Parker, 1976–2003. Jefferson, NC: McFarlandgr ingoinbuenosaires.com.

Gorbman, Claudia. *Unheard Melodies: Narrative Film Music.* Bloomington: Indiana University Press, 1987.

Goldmark, Daniel. 'Adapting *The Jazz Singer* from Short Story to Screen: A Musical Profile.' *Journal of the American Musicological Society* 70, no. 3 (Fall 2017): 767–817.

Grant, Mark N. *The Rise and Fall of the Broadway Musical.* Boston: Northeastern University Press, 2004.

Gray, Susan. *Writers on Directors.* New York: Watson-Guptil, 1999.

Green, Stanley. *The World of Musical Comedy.* New York: Ziff-Davis, 1960.

Grode, Eric. *Hair: The Story of the Show that Defined a Generation.* Foreword by James Rado. Philadelphia: Running Press, 2010.

Hall, Sheldon. 'Tall Revenue Features: The Genealogy of the Modern Blockbuster.' In *Genre and Contemporary Hollywood*, edited by Steve Neale, 11–26. London: BFI, 2002.

Harris, Mark. *Pictures at a Revolution: Five Movies and the Birth of New Hollywood.* New York: Penguin Press, 2008.

Harvey, Stephen. *Directed by Vincente Minnelli.* Foreword by L. Minnelli. New York: Museum of Modern Art/Harper and Row, 1989.

Hemming, Roy. *The Melody Lingers On: The Great Songwriters and Their Movie Musicals.* New York: Newmarket, 1986.

Hirschhorn, Clive. *Gene Kelly: A Biography.* London: W. H. Allen, 1974.

Hischak, Thomas. *Broadway Plays and Musicals: Descriptions and Essential Facts of More Than 14,000 Shows through 2007.* Jefferson, NC: McFarland, 2009.

Hischak, Thomas S. *The Oxford Companion to the American Musical: Theatre, Film, and Television.* Oxford: Oxford University Press, 2008.

Hischak, Thomas S. *Through the Screen Door: What Happened to the Broadway Musical When It Went to Hollywood.* Lanham, MD: Scarecrow Press, 2004.

Hirschhorn, Clive. *Gene Kelly: A Biography.* Foreword by F. Sinatra. London: W. H. Allen, 1974.

Horn, Barbara Lee. *The Age of Hair: Evolution and Impact of Broadway's First Rock Musical.* New York: Greenwood Press, 1991.

Hubbert, Julie. '"Whatever Happened to Great Movie Music?" Cinéma Vérité and Hollywood Film Music of the Early 1970s.' *American Music* 21, no. 2 (2003): 180–213.

Hubbert, Julie, ed. *Celluloid Symphonies: Texts and Contexts in Film Music History.* Berkeley: University of California Press, 2011.

Hutcheon, Linda. 'The Politics of Postmodernism: Parody and History.' *Cultural Critique* 5 (1986): 179–207.

Hutcheon, Linda. *A Theory of Adaptation*, 2nd ed. New York: Routledge, 2013.

Hutcheon, Linda, and Mario J. Valdés. 'Irony, Nostalgia, and the Postmodern: A Dialogue.' *Poligrafías. Revista de Teoría Literaria y Literatura comparada* 3 (1998–2000): 18–41.

Jewell, Richard B. 'RKO Grosses, 1929–1951: The C. J. Tevlin Ledger.' *Historic Journal of Film, Radio and Television* 14 (1994): 37–49.

Jones, John Bush. *Our Musicals, Ourselves: A Social History of the American Musical Theatre.* Lebanon, NH: Brandeis University Press, 2003.

Kantor, Michael, and Lawrence Maslon. Broadway: The American Musical. New York: Bulfinch Press, 2004.

Kennedy, Matthew. *Roadshow! The Fall of Film Musicals in the 1960s.* New York: Oxford University Press, 2014.

Kessler, Kelly. *Destabilizing the Hollywood Musical: Music, Masculinity and Mayhem.* New York: Palgrave Macmillan, 2010.

Kimball, Robert, ed. *The Complete Lyrics of Cole Porter.* New York: Vintage Books, 1984.

King, Geoff. *New Hollywood Cinema: An Introduction.* New York: Columbia University Press, 2002.

Kirle, Bruce. *Unfinished Show Business: Broadway Musicals as Works-in-Process.* Carbondale: Southern Illinois University Press, 2005.

Klein, Amanda Ann. *American Film Cycles: Reframing Genres, Screening Social Problems, and Defining Subcultures.* Austin: University of Texas Press, 2011.

Knapp, Raymond. *The American Musical and the Formation of National Identity.* Princeton, NJ: Princeton University Press, 2005.

Knapp, Raymond. *The American Musical and the Performance of Personal Identity.* Princeton, NJ: Princeton University Press, 2006.

Knapp, Raymond, Mitchell Morris, and Stacy Wolf, eds. *The Oxford Handbook of the American Musical*. New York: Oxford University Press, 2011.

Kogan, Rick. 'The Original "Grease" Was Born in Chicago.' Chicago Tribune, 29 January 2016.

Kracauer, Siegfried. *Theory of Film: The Redemption of Physical Reality*. New York: Oxford University Press, 1960.

Laird, Paul R. *The Musical Theater of Stephen Schwartz*. Lanham, MD: Rowman and Littlefield, 2014.

Lawson-Peebles, Robert, ed. *Approaches to the American Musical*. Exeter, UK: University of Exeter Press, 1996.

Leitch, Thomas. 'Twelve Fallacies in Contemporary Adaptation Theory,' *Criticism* 45, no. 2 (Spring 2003): 150–153.

Lerner, Alan J. *The Street Where I Live: The Story of My Fair Lady, Gigi and Camelot*. London: Hodder and Stoughton, 1978.

Leve, James. *American Musical Theater*. New York: Oxford University Press, 2016.

Levy, Emanuel. *Vincente Minnelli: Hollywood's Dark Dreamer*. New York: St Martin's Press, 2009.

Long, Robert E. *Broadway, The Golden Years: Jerome Robbins and the Great Choreographer-Directors, 1940 to the Present*. New York: Continuum, 2001.

Lovensheimer, Jim. *South Pacific: Paradise Rewritten*. New York: Oxford University Press, 2010.

Magee, Jeffrey. *Irving Berlin's American Musical Theatre*. New York: Oxford University Press, 2012.

Mast, Gerald. *Can't Help Singin': The American Musical on Stage and Screen*. Woodstock, NY: Overlook, 1987.

McArthur, Colin. *Brigadoon, Braveheart and the Scots: Distortions of Scotland in Hollywood*. New York: I. B. Tauris, 2003.

McClary, Susan. *Feminine Endings: Music, Gender, and Sexuality*. Minneapolis: University of Minnesota Press, 1991.

McElhaney, Joe. *The Death of Classical Cinema: Hitchcock, Lang, Minnelli*. Albany: State University of New York Press, 2006.

McElhaney, Joe, ed. *Vincente Minnelli: The Art of Entertainment*. Detroit, MI: Wayne State University Press, 2009.

McHugh, Dominic. *Loverly: The Life and Times of My Fair Lady*. New York: Oxford University Press, 2012.

McHugh, Dominic, ed. *Alan Jay Lerner: A Lyricist's Letters*. New York: Oxford University Press, 2014.

McLean, Adrienne. *Being Rita Hayworth: Labor, Identity, and Hollywood Stardom*. New Brunswick: Rutgers University Press, 2004.

McMillin, Scott. *The Musical as Drama*. Princeton, NJ: Princeton University Press, 2006.

McNally, Karen. *When Frankie Went to Hollywood: Frank Sinatra and American Male Identity*. Urbana: University of Illinois Press, 2008.

Mera, Miguel. 'Invention/Re-invention.' *Music Sound and the Moving Image* 3, no. 1 (Spring 2009): 1–20.

Miller, Scott. 'Inside Evita." 2010. New Line Theatre.org.

Miller, Scott. *Rebels with Applause: Broadway's Groundbreaking Musicals*. Portsmouth, NH: Heinemann, 2001.

Minnelli, Vincente, with H. Arce. Foreword by A. J. Lerner. *Vincente Minnelli: I Remember It Well*. Hollywood, CA: Samuel French, 1990 [1974].

Mordden, Ethan. *The Hollywood Musical*. New York: St Martin's Press, 1981.

Mordden, Ethan. *When Broadway Went to Hollywood*. New York: Oxford University Press, 2016.

Morris, Mitchell. 'Cabaret, America's Weimar, and the Mythologies of the Gay Subject.' *American Music* 22 (2004): 145–157.

Most, Andrea. *Making Americans: Jews and the Broadway Musical*. Cambridge, MA: Harvard University Press, 2004.

Mueller, John. *Astaire Dancing: The Musical Films*. New York: Wings, 1985.

Mundy, John. *Popular Music on Screen: From Hollywood Musical to Music Video*. Manchester: Manchester University Press, 1999.

Naremore, James, ed. *Film Adaptation*. London: Athlone Press, 2000.

Neale, Steve. *Genre and Hollywood*. London: Routledge, 2000.

Nollen, Scott Allen. *Abbott and Costello on the Home Front: A Critical Study of the Wartime Films*. Jefferson, NC: McFarland, 2009.

Norton, Richard C. *A Chronology of American Musical Theater*, vol. 2. New York: Oxford University Press, 2002.

O'Brien, Daniel. *The Frank Sinatra Film Guide*. London: Batsford, 1998.

O'Brien, Lucy. *Madonna: Like an Icon*. New York: Bantam Press, 2008.

Oja, Carol J. *Bernstein Meets Broadway: Collaborative Art in a Time of War.* Oxford: Oxford University Press, 2014.

O'Leary, James. *'Oklahoma!*, 'Lousy Publicity,' and the Politics of Formal Integration in the American Musical Theater.' *Journal of Musicology* 31, no. 1 (Winter 2014): 139–182.

Parker, Alan. 'EVITA – Alan Parker – Director, Writer, Producer Official Website.' Web.

Patinkin, Sheldon. *'No Legs, No Jokes, No Chance': A History of the American Musical Theater.* Evanston: Northeastern University Press, 2008.

Pomerance, Murray. *The Eyes Have It: Cinema and the Reality Effect.* New Brunswick, NJ: Rutgers University Press, 2013.

Richards, Stanley, ed. *Great Rock Musicals.* New York: Stein and Day, 1979.

Rodosthenous, George. *Twenty-First Century Musicals: From Stage to Screen.* New York: Routledge, 2017.

Rodgers, Richard. *Musical Stages: An Autobiography.* New York: Da Capo Press, 1995.

Rogers, Ginger. *Ginger: My Story.* New York: HarperCollins, 1991.

Sanders, Julie. *Adaptation and Appropriation.* New York: Routledge, 2006.

Schreger, Charles. 'The Second Coming of Sound,' *Film Comment* 14, no. 5 (September/October 1978): 34–37.

Sennett, Ted. *Hollywood Musicals.* New York: Harry N. Abrams, 1981.

Sheward, David. New York review: Evita. 5 April 2012. Backstage. com.

Shmoop Editorial Team. 'Culture in the Reagan Era.' Shmoop. Web.

Sinyard, Neil. *Filming Literature: The Art of Screen Adaptation.* London: Croom Helm, 1986.

Slater, Thomas J. *Milos Forman: A Bio-Bibliography.* New York: Greenwood Press, 1987.

Smith, Helen. *There's a Place for Us: The Musical Theatre Works of Leonard Bernstein.* Farnham, UK: Ashgate Press, 2011.

Smith, Jeff. *Sounds of Commerce: Marketing Popular Film Music.* New York: Columbia University Press, 1998.

Spring, Katherine. *Saying It with Songs: Popular Music and the Coming of Sound to Hollywood Cinema.* New York: Oxford University Press, 2013.

Stam, Robert. 'Beyond Fidelity: The Dialogics of Adaptation.' In *Film Adaptation*, edited by James Naremore, 54–76. London: Athlone Press, 2000.

Stam, Robert. *Literature through Film: Realism, Magic, and the Art of Adaptation*. Malden, MA: Blackwell, 2005.

Stam, Robert, and Alessandra Raengo, eds. *Literature and Film: A Guide to the Theory and Practice of Adaptation*. Malden, MA: Blackwell, 2003.

Starr, Larry. *Gershwin*. New Haven, CT: Yale University Press, 2010.

Stempel, Larry. *Showtime: A History of the Broadway Musical Theater*. New York: W.W. Norton, 2010.

Sternfeld, Jessica. *The Megamusical*. Bloomington: Indiana University Press, 2006.

Stubblebine, Donald J. *Broadway Sheet Music: A Comprehensive Listing, 1918–1937*. Jefferson, NC: McFarland, 1996.

Studlar, Gaylyn. *Precocious Charms: Stars Performing Girlhood in Classical Hollywood Cinema*. Berkeley: University of California Press, 2013.

Swain, Joseph. *The Broadway Musical: A Critical and Musical Survey*. Lanham, MD: Scarecrow Press, 2002.

Symonds, Dominic. *We'll Have Manhattan*. New York: Oxford University Press, 2015.

Symonds, Dominic, and Millie Taylor, eds. *Gestures of Musical Theater: The Performativity of Song and Dance*. New York: Oxford University Press, 2014.

Taraborelli, J. Rando. *Madonna: An Intimate Biography*. New York: Simon and Schuster, 2002.

Taylor, John R., and A. Jackson. *The Hollywood Musical*. London: Secker and Warburg, 1971.

Tharp, Twyla. *Push Comes to Shove*. New York: Bantam, 1992.

Thelen, Lawrence. *The Show Makers: Great Directors of the American Musical Theatre*. New York: Routledge, 2000.

Thomas, Bob. *Astaire: The Man, the Dancer*. New York: St Martin's, 1984.

Thomas, Tony. *The Films of Gene Kelly: Song and Dance Man*. Foreword by F. Astaire. New York: Carol, 1991.

Traubner, Richard. *Operetta: A Theatrical History*, rev. ed. New York: Routledge, 2003.

Turk, Edward Baron. *Hollywood Diva*. Berkeley: University of California Press, 1998.

Whitfield, Sarah, ed. *Rethinking Musical Theatre*. Palgrave, 2019.

Wilder, Alec. *American Popular Song: The Great Innovators, 1900–1950*. New York: Oxford University Press, 1972.

Wilk, Max. *They're Playing Our Song*. New York: Zoetrope, 1986.

Winer, Deborah Grace. *On the Sunny Side of the Street: The Life and Lyrics of Dorothy Fields*. New York: Schirmer, 1997.

Wolf, Stacy. *Changed for Good: A Feminist History of the Broadway Musical*. New York: Oxford University Press, 2011.

Wolf, Stacy. *A Problem Like Maria: Gender and Sexuality in the American Musical*. Ann Arbor: University of Michigan Press, 2002.

Woller, Megan. ' "Happ'ly-Ever-Aftering": Changing Social and Industry Conventions in Hollywood Musical Adaptations, 1960–75.' PhD diss., University of Illinois Urbana-Champaign, 2014.

Woller, Megan. 'The Lusty Court of *Camelot* (1967): Exploring Sexuality in the Hollywood Adaptation.' *Music and the Moving Image* 8, no. 1 (Spring 2015): 3–18.

Wollman, Elizabeth L. *Hard Times: The Adult Musical in 1970s New York City*. New York: Oxford University Press, 2013.

Wollman, Elizabeth L. *The Theater Will Rock: A History of the Rock Musical, from Hair to Hedwig*. Ann Arbor: University of Michigan Press, 2006.

Wood, Michael. *America in the Movies: Or, 'Santa Maria, It Had Slipped My Mind.'* New York: Columbia University Press, 1989.

Wood, Robin. *Hollywood from Vietnam to Reagan . . . and Beyond*. New York: Columbia University Press, 2003.

Yudkoff, Alan. *Gene Kelly: A Life of Dance and Dreams*. New York: Back Stage Books, 1999.

Ziegfeld, Richard, and Paulette Ziegfeld. *The Ziegfeld Touch: The Life and Times of Florenz Ziegfeld, Jr.* New York: Harry N. Abrams, 1993.

Zadan, Craig. *Sondheim and Co.*, 2nd ed. New York: Harper and Row, 1986.

# INDEX

*For the benefit of digital users, indexed terms that span two pages (e.g., 52–53) may, on occasion, appear on only one of those pages.*

Tables and figures are indicated by *t* and *f* following the page number